The Emergence
of the
Speech Capacity

The Emergence
of the
Speech Capacity

D. Kimbrough Oller
University of Maine

Psychology Press
Taylor & Francis Group

New York   London

KH

First published by

Lawrence Erlbaum Associates, Inc., Publishers
10 Industrial Avenue
Mahwah, NJ 07430

This edition published 2012 by Psychology Press

Psychology Press
Taylor & Francis Group
711 Third Avenue
New York, NY 10017

Psychology Press
Taylor & Francis Group
27 Church Road
Hove, East Sussex BN3 2FA

Cover design by the author's son, Laban D. Eilers

Library of Congress Cataloging-in-Publication Data

Oller, D. Kimbrough.
The emergence of the speech capacity / by D. Kimbrough Oller
    p. cm.
    Includes bibliographical references and index.
ISBN 0-8058-2628-9 (cloth : alk. paper) —
    ISBN 0-8058-2629-7 (pbk : alk. paper)
1. Language acquisition. 2. Oral communication. 3. Animal
    communication. 4. Primates. 5. Language and languages.
    —Origin. I. Title.
P118.O43 2000
401'.93—dc21
                                                    99-052021
                                                       CIP

7/30/15

Contents

Chapter 6: The Grounding of Vocal and Gestural Development in Biology and Experience: Physical Foundations for Speech and Sign Language — 112

Chapter 7: Canalization Results: The Stability of Protophone Development in a Variety of Contexts — 122

Preface

THE MAGIC OF BABYTALK

My three children have grown up and gone on to live on their own, but the memories of the first moment that I saw each one of them stay with me. In these first encounters they were instantaneously engaging. Children connect with people by vocalization, gesture, and facial expression from the beginning of life.

Beth, my eldest, was 36 months old the first time I saw her, eating Cheerios, a fact I recall because she told me so, as she asked my name, along with a variety of details of my private life, while insisting on informing me extensively regarding the virtues of her little sister who could not yet walk, talk, or eat Cheerios, but was fun to play with anyway, or so I was informed. "Beff," as she called herself, was some chatterbox, but in fact, so are most healthy children by age 3. It is their nature to talk, and it is our nature to be enthralled.

Even at much younger ages, the gift of communication is deeply human, and its active pursuit by infants is undeniable. A few minutes into my first conversation with Beth, Rebecca, my future wife, brought the baby sister, Jenna, 6 months of age, into the room where she was seated on a blanket. She smiled at me immediately and maintained her balance well, looking at me repeatedly, grinning intermittently, swinging a rattle, and engaging me about as well as her sister had, but without a single word. Yet she did speak, after a fashion, with those burbly baby sounds that characterize the middle of the first year of life.

It was not long thereafter that I became Beth and Jenna's father. A few years later, I was present at the birth of their brother, Laban, and here I had the opportunity for the first time to observe that active communication between parent and infant can begin from the first moment of life. I remember plainly how his eyes fixed on me when he was handed to me in the delivery room, how his gaze followed, tracking my finger as I tested his well-being. After all the months we had prepared for his arrival, seeing him for the first time was captivating. His voice was also like a magnet, as he cried, not bitterly, but as if he were frightened, perhaps chilled in the moments after coming into the world. It was a sound entirely familiar to those of us who spend much of our professional lives attending to babies, but crying was unique that day.

There was no language in what passed between Laban and me the day he was born, not in the normal sense of the term *language*, and yet essential bases of living were conveyed. If I have one regret in life, it may be that I was not present the days my daughters were born.

It is important to me now, in laying out this work on the development of communication in infancy, to focus on the intuitive marvel of the process by which humans come to transmit so much to each other, both in information and in feeling. Familiarity is said to breed contempt according to Aesop's maxim, but it does not seem to work that way with babies. Analysis of how they act, especially how they sound, has occupied a great portion of my time for three decades of professional activity, but the depth of my personal reaction to children has not been dulled. Over a period now approaching 30 years, I have had the pleasure of conducting four longitudinal studies focusing on scores of families and their babies along with cross-sectional studies involving hundreds of others at the University of Washington and the University of Miami. Similar work is now being continued at the University of Maine.

I study the way we react to babies and the way they present themselves to us in part because these interchanges represent such critical features of our humanity. The events of communicative development in the first year of life are, in many ways, recognized and understood by human beings without any formal experience or instruction. Babies cry, and we react intuitively. Babies goo, and we smile, speaking in a special register that seems to be made precisely for talking to infants. Babies utter reduplicated babbling sounds, and we recognize those sounds as being nearly speech. The naturalness of these capabilities is comforting and fulfilling in ways that few aspects of life can be.

THE INTERPRETATION OF OUR VOCAL HERITAGE

To understand how it is that humans are so inclined and so able to connect emotionally with infants and how they can comprehend so much from what infants do, it is necessary to take stock of the natural gifts infants bring to communication. Systematic research is useful to unravel such riddles. The interpretive framework of *infraphonology* was formulated to provide a system of guidance. In light of the interpretive framework, the patterns of development seem clear, contrary to the midcentury belief that infant vocalizations were random vocal meanderings. Infant sounds now seem much like an embryological form of speech, differentiating, elaborating, and systematically growing toward a mature form. The pattern of vocal development is robust in the face of social deprivation and premature birth. At the same time, deaf babies show unmistakable delays in vocal growth, delays that seem more plausible in the light of the new framework.

The longitudinal studies of vocal development and the formulation of an infraphonological approach in the context of those studies have yielded a bountiful product to present in this book, but recently, something more has begun to take shape, as I have begun to ponder broader issues that are implied in vocal development, the issues of origins and evolution. Perhaps it is a phenomenon of age, the sort of thing that makes people study genealogy when they inevitably encounter their own mortality. More than ever I am interested in who we are and who our ancestors were. I have come to suspect that in the alluring baby sounds of the first 6 months of life there lie heretofore unnoticed clues to the origins of the human capacity for speech.

ACKNOWLEDGMENTS

Research described is this volume has been supported for many years by multiple sources. Of special importance in recent years have been grants from the National Institutes of Health (R01-DC00484, R01-NS26121, R01-HD30762, 5R01-DC01932, awarded to D. K. Oller), and significant philanthropic support from Austin and Martha Weeks and Jerome and Rita Cohen.

I greatly appreciate the comments and suggestions on this volume from Charles Snowdon, John Locke, and Marc Bornstein. My gratitude also goes out to the many students and colleagues who have played crucial roles in providing inspiration to these efforts. A short list of key collaborators that deserve my thanks would include William Doyle, Leslie Wieman, Bruce Smith, William Gavin, Dale Bull, Carmen Benito-García, Kathleen Vergara, Roberta Turner, Michael Lynch, Michelle Steffens, Devorah Basinger, Vanessa Lewedag, Barbara Pearson, Alan Cobo-Lewis, Lynn Weissler Miskiel, Peter Mundy, Daniel Messinger, Marygrace Yale, Christine Fullmer Delgado, A. Rebecca Neal, Heidi Kern Schwartz, Edward Miskiel, and Rafael Delgado. There is one more name to mention, that of my primary colleague and wife of 25 years, Rebecca Eilers, to whom I hereby dedicate this volume. Her name is cited many times in the following pages, but citations are inadequate to account for the contributions she has made to the endeavor represented here.

1

Interpretation of Communication Systems: The Role of Infrastructural Modeling

BABBLING AS A STEP TOWARD LANGUAGE

The descendants of Noah, flourishing in the bounty of the plains of Shinar, grew proud according to the Genesis account. They showed such hubris as to build an enormous tower intended to elevate humankind to the level of heaven. As punishment for this arrogance, God struck the people down, the story tells, making it impossible for them to understand each other's speech. Amidst the confusion that resulted, the tower could not be finished, and the plain came to be called Babel (Genesis 11:9) to reflect the disorder that resulted from the sudden appearance of many different languages among the ancient people of the earth. The narrative includes an ancient assumption about the nature of human understanding: Intelligible language is implied to be at the very heart of it, and without comprehensible language we are seen to be condemned to chaos.

English inherited a word that resembles the name Babel to designate the speech-like sounds of infancy. *Babble* does not consist of words or sentences, and in this sense, it presents an unintelligibility and chaos similar to that caused by the many languages that confounded the builders of the tower. Even if babbling does not communicate linguistic meanings, however, it includes syllables and other word-like sounds. One can hardly deny the intuitive impression that it is deeply significant as an indicator of the emergent mind. Babbling communicates a great deal about who human infants are. When they babble, they seem to reach toward the goal of talking and aspire to that level of human understanding that only language seems able to provide.

The intuitive impression of parents that babbling is related to speech (Locke, 1993; Papoušek, 1994) is supported by the fact that no other mammal is heard producing sounds that are so much like talking. Even the great apes, our nearest relatives, show "no instinctive desire to babble in babyhood" (Langer, 1942, p. 116), and to the extent that apes vocalize, the results bear only a distant resemblance to the sounds of speech. Within the entire order of the primates there is little precedent for the speech-like babbling found in human infants. According to Marler (1977), "primate young are not known to 'babble'" (p. 64). However, it has recently been discovered that at least one species of new world monkey, the pygmy marmoset (*Cebuella pygmaea*), produces babbling-like sequences of sounds in the early weeks of life (Elowson, Snowdon, & Lazaro-Perea, 1998; Snowdon, Elowson, & Rousch, 1997). The discovery modifies the understanding of babbling in general, but even so, the infant babbling sounds of the pygmy marmoset scarcely resemble the sounds of speech. Instead they bear an acoustic resemblance to the species-specific sounds of adult pygmy marmosets. As far as can be told, only the human produces babbling sounds that truly resemble speech.

As might be expected, given the perceived resemblance, normal infant babbling provides one of the important indications that human communicative development is on track. Recent empirical studies show that babies who start producing well-formed syllabic babbling relatively late in the first year tend to start talking relatively late in the second year (Oller, Eilers, Urbano, & Cobo-Lewis, 1997; Stoel-Gammon, 1989). Also, infants who produce a relatively impoverished inventory of vocalizations in the first year tend to show anomalies in speech development at later points (Jensen, Boggild-Andersen, Schmidt, Ankerhus, & Hansen, 1988; Lyytinen, Poikkeus, Leiwo, & Ahonen, 1996; Menyuk, Liebergott, & Schultz, 1986; Yoder, Warren, & McCathren, 1998). Perhaps most important, infants that do not show normal development of speech-like babbling are at risk for certain disorders, especially deafness (Eilers & Oller, 1994; Kent, Osberger, Netsell, & Hustedde, 1987; Oller, Eilers, Bull, & Carney, 1985; Stoel-Gammon & Otomo, 1986; Vinter, 1987). Even intelligence in later life appears to be predicted by babbling patterns (Cameron, Livson, & Bayley, 1967).

Given that babbling manifests a growing capacity of the infant to produce sounds that resemble speech, and given that well-formed sounds resembling those of babbling are required for the production of meaningful words, it might seem there should be no reason to raise any empirical question about the importance of babbling as a precursor to talking. Yet the question was raised quite earnestly in the middle of the 20th century when a sharp discontinuity was posited to occur between the sounds of babbling and the sounds of early speech (Jakobson, 1939/1971a, 1941). This theoretical position discouraged the intuitive assumption that babbling is a foundation for speech. The theory was hard to dispute empirically because it was not clear how best to describe the sounds of infancy nor how to compare them with the sounds of speech. It took several decades for the community of scholars to settle on a descriptive approach capable of revealing unequivocally the sense in which the sounds of infancy systematically manifest the emergence of a capacity for speech.

The problem that had to be solved can be viewed as one of methodology and theoretical foundations. The seemingly most natural way to go about describing infant sounds can be confusing and misleading because that seemingly natural method includes the assumption that all babbling sounds can be categorized phonetically exactly as speech is categorized. In spite of the resemblance between babbling and speech, this method proves to distort the nature of babbling, making it impossible to track the development of baby sounds as they increasingly approximate the sounds of language across the first year of life. This inappropriate style of description—distorting baby sounds to force them into the categories of adult speech—contributed fundamentally to the midcentury turmoil of thought about vocal development. The resolution to that turmoil has produced a greatly enriched understanding of babbling and of the speech capacity that it heralds.

ALPHABETICAL TRANSCRIPTION OF BABBLING AND OTHER SOUNDS

When babies babble, it is tempting routinely to portray their sounds in terms of the same units of description that are used to characterize mature speech. Sometimes the method seems to work well, especially if the baby has reached the second half-year of life and babbles a special way characteristic of that age, producing well-formed syllables such as "mama" or "dada." By that age, the sounds produced by infants resemble speech to a remarkable extent. Yet the great bulk of the sounds that babies emit in the first months of life are quite different from well-formed "mamas" and "dadas." These early sounds of babies seem much more remote from speech as it occurs in adults, or even in toddlers who speak one word at a time.

If one gives in to temptation when the very young infant produces the articulated sounds of the so-called gooing period, for example, and taking the cue suggested by the name of the period, one alphabetically portrays the baby as having said "goo," one runs the risk of egregiously mischaracterizing the sounds. Even among baby sounds that are of the technical gooing variety, the great majority cannot be accurately portrayed in an alphabetical transcription as any of the possibilities one might propose: "goo," "googoo," "oogoo," "uhguh," and so forth.

One way to prove the point is to show that the transcriptions thus proposed are unlikely to pass a phonetician/reader test. If a skilled phonetician, not having heard the infant, is presented with transcriptions of the baby's sounds and is asked to read them aloud, the renditions produced by the phonetician will accurately reflect what is written in phonetic symbology, [gu], [gugu],

[ugu], [ʌgʌ], and so forth, but in the great majority of cases the pronunciations will differ quite noticeably from the infant sounds on which the transcriptions were based. A person who listens to the tape recording of the infant is likely to conclude that the phonetician's reading is not based on the baby sounds. Appropriately transcribed syllables produced by adult speakers of a mature language, on the other hand, do typically pass the phonetician/reader test, even if the syllables are produced by speakers of languages unfamiliar to the phonetician. When they are read back by a skilled phonetician, a native listener of the language can recognize the sounds as the syllables produced by the native speaker.

Yet transcriptions in the International Phonetic Alphabet (IPA) fundamentally fail to characterize the sounds of very young infants (Lynip, 1951), as evidenced by the fact that they usually cannot pass the same test. Phonetician readings of transcriptions based on infant sounds resemble those sounds only indirectly. Infant utterances do not correspond to the precise individual consonants and vowels specified in transcriptions, and consequently there is usually no way to find an appropriate transcription for them within the IPA. Often there seem to be a number of possible transcriptions for an individual infant utterance, based on individual auditory impressions of different phoneticians, but none of them is likely to pass the reader test.

Although modifications can be made to create a transcriptional system specific to very young infant sounds, the required modifications are far from trivial. To achieve the goal of adaptation for infant sounds, the intentions of the IPA have to be thoroughly revamped and reconstructed from the ground up. The resulting system cannot have the sort of syllabic and segmental character that is found in the IPA. The new system for very young infants must be composed of more global categories in terms of which baby vocalizations are actually structured,[1] rather than being composed of the neatly segmented consonants and vowels of the IPA.

The IPA is designed to transcribe well-formed syllabic or segmental units of natural languages. Well-formed (or *canonical*) syllables can serve as minimal rhythmic units in words and sentences, whereas other sounds, even if they are produced by the human vocal system, are not well-suited to serve as speech, and in general cannot (because of their inherent acoustic structure) count as segments or syllables of words or sentences. Ultimately, here lies the flaw in transcribing baby sounds in the IPA. The great majority of the vocalizations in the first half-year of life, both gooing sounds and a variety of other

---

[1]The categories of a more appropriately designed system are given global names that are not intended to indicate particular consonant or vowel articulations. The new system takes stock of the fact that each category (goos, squeals, raspberries, growls, and so forth) can vary considerably from one utterance to another, and that the individual utterances rarely show the sort of crisp structuring that would be required to fit the dimensions of consonants and vowels.

categories of baby sounds, are not pronounced in such a way that they could serve as the syllables of words or sentences.[2]

The basis for objecting to the alphabetical portrayal of baby sounds from the first months of life runs deeper than mere concern over accuracy of transcriptional depiction. In using categories of a mature linguistic system to transcribe infant sounds that do not in fact fit the categories of the mature linguistic system, one drops the opportunity to discern the emergence of basic properties of the speech system in the primitive vocalizations of infancy. The budding features of speech found in gooing and other baby sounds are not yet fully integrated to yield mature, human phonology. Nonetheless the sounds babies produce in gooing and in other categories of vocalization are full of interest, as they help reveal the enigmatic backdrop to the remarkable human aptitude for talking.

Just as we may mischaracterize infant sounds by transcribing them alphabetically, so when we depict a rooster's crowing as "cockadoodledoo," we run the risk of fumbling an opportunity and confounding ourselves with false analogy. The same rooster is supposed to say "kikiriki" in Spanish, and the difference between the two alphabetic renditions of crowing provides a clear indication that neither one is apt. Roosters do not learn to speak Spanish, and "cockadoodledoo" does not pass the phonetician/reader test.

People with a gift for mimicry are able to produce more veridical renditions of rooster crowing, renditions that depart radically from the speech-based, phonetic characterizations of "cockadoodledoo" or "kikiriki." Some ornithological field workers are good enough at producing the songs of certain birds that they find themselves subjected to territorial attacks by the members of the species they imitate. Of course the sounds that inspire such attacks are never characterizable in terms of alphabetical sequences of phonetic transcription. It appears that no alphabetical transcription can pass the bird's equivalent of the phonetician/reader test.

Choosing to describe the sounds of other species by shoe-horning[3] their vocal communications into the categories of mature human speech compromises our rich perceptions and squanders the occasion to identify profound relations between speech and the vocal communication systems of other species.

---

[2]Occasionally well-formed syllables are produced in the first months of life by normal infants. These sporadic productions appear to be accidental because they occur only rarely amidst much greater numbers of ill-formed utterances. In contrast, the well-formed syllables of the later stages of infancy do not appear to be accidental, but instead show signs of intentionality; babies produce them repetitively, imitatively, and in playful social interaction. The term *intentionality* is addressed in chapter 12, which introduces a framework for interpretation of the extent of intentionality of infant vocal acts.

[3]The writings of Gould (1989) inspired this usage. He used the term *shoe-horning* to describe the manner in which many of the mysterious fossils of the Cambrian explosion were first misassigned to familiar, modern groups of animals, before it was determined that they represented previously undescribed groups, 15 to 20 new phyla, and 20 to 30 new kinds of arthropods.

INFRASTRUCTURAL DESCRIPTION IN THE SCIENCES

Good mimicry is, of course, insufficient by itself to lay the groundwork for insightful comparisons of differing vocal systems, although it may furnish a useful starting point. Eventually, a more intellectually revealing approach must be supplied. The primary theoretical claim I propose in this volume is that to understand the complex structure and flexibility of language, and to account for its origins and its development, it is important to draw a distinction between operational units and infrastructure. In accord with the distinction, alphabetical transcription of infant sounds (or nonhuman sounds) constitutes an operational-level description that is usually inappropriate. To clarify and illuminate infant vocal development and to provide a basis for interspecies comparisons and fruitful evolutionary speculation, a system of interpretation that incorporates an infrastructural level is required.

An approach distinguishing infrastructure and operational units is relatively new in the investigation of infant vocalizations, although it has played a critical role in many of the important results of modern work in infant vocal development. On the other hand, a distinction of this sort is commonplace in modern linguistic theory (although the term *infrastructure*, as far as I know, has not been used in linguistics in quite the way it will be used here)[4] and has played a critical role in many of the sciences for a century or more.

Consider chemistry, for example (chapter 5 presents additional examples of the relation between infrastructures and operational levels in other sciences). We recognize operational categories of chemistry in substances such as water, air, stone, soil, and so on. Operational categories within any domain of potential science are the superficial, commonsense categories of function in terms of which we relate to the domain. For chemistry, the operational categories are physical materials and substances humans have dealt with day to day for hundreds of thousands of years, categories in terms of which primary decisions about life are made even by modern humans. There is much about the ways we relate to these operational categories that is systematic. We know that if one adds soil to water, the result is mud. On the other hand, stone plus water does not change either substance very much. The water in a rocky stream is good to drink, whereas mud is another matter, so to speak.

The systematic relations among these operational categories are useful to recognize, and they are empirically verifiable. The combination of soil and water yields mud, and both the soil and water can be extracted from mud by squeezing and filtering: The process of combination is thus reversible. Such systematic, reversible relations among operational-level categories are the material of a primitive sort of chemical science.

---

[4]For example, generative linguistics (Chomsky, 1957, 1967, 1981) has had an infrastructural flavor from its inception. A primary goal of Universal Grammar (UG) is to characterize the ways that language units can be formed. The theory of UG outlines an infrastructure that specifies limits on the nature and form of linguistic units that can occur in natural languages.

Yet in spite of the ease with which we recognize such systematic relations among substances, if we think only in terms of operational-level categories, we achieve no insight into their ultimate origins nor into the profound relations among them. Such an understanding requires an infrastructural model that characterizes the relations among operational-level substances in a deeper way (see Fig. 1.1).

The chemical infrastructural model posits hidden units, atomic elements, and molecules. Atoms combine according to physical principles specified in the infrastructural model, and when the whole theoretical structure of principles and elements is in place, it is possible to specify the composition of all operational-level substances, and to predict the ways in which substances will combine or change in form under varying circumstances of temperature or pressure. The infrastructural model posits unseen particles, properties of particles, and processes of interaction, and in so doing provides a basis for deep understanding and prediction. The relations between first-order units (elementary particles) and lowest order or operational units are provided within the infrastructural model in terms of laws of combination; elements at each order of complexity (from particles to atoms to molecules of varying complexity) are described in terms of physical parameters of measurement such as mass, form, charge, viscosity, and so on.

Operational categories
(lowest-order functional units:
air, water, stone, etc.)

Infrastructural model (atomic theory, thermodynamics, etc.):
(specifies first-order units [elementary particles], and properties
of function and interaction for both first-order and lower-order units)

Prime parameters
(includes dimensions of description for units:
mass, form, charge, viscosity, elasticity, color, number, etc.)

FIG. 1.1.   Example of a familiar infrastructural system: Chemistry.

Chemistry has been understood to provide a characterization of relations between an infrastructural model, physical parameters, and operational substances since at least the beginning of the 19th century with the work of Dalton. The power of the model, in this general form, is not now questionable in educated company. Perhaps what is surprising is that it took many generations for the infrastructural approach to be developed appropriately and to be accepted generally. The popular attempt of antiquity to characterize all substances in terms of operational-level categories such as earth, air, fire, and water seduced early theorists from the classical Greeks onward into speculations that hindered understanding and created resistance against more fundamental modeling (Lindsay, 1970; Multhauf, 1967).

A basic flaw in the ancient approaches to chemistry was that they depended on the assumption that all operational-level substances were composed of other operational-level substances. In a sense, this was a shoe-horning error, not unlike the phonetic transcription of infant gooing, squealing, or raspberries. Substances were described and explained as other substances, even though the conceptualization required contorting the characteristics of one substance to fit those of another. For example, the numerous minerals that were recognized in ancient times were deemed by some ancient thinkers to constitute varying forms of water under the influence of fire. All sorts of operational-level categories, including living things, such as birds or flowers, were accounted for similarly in terms of the presumed basic operational-level categories of earth, air, fire, and water (see Lindsay, 1970). There was no satisfactory empirical basis for the presumed transformations posited to account for the composition of all things in terms of a small set of common operational categories, but the shoe-horning description maintained its forceful role in ancient thought probably because it held the appeal of familiarity and tangibility. All the units of description, the elements, were operational, entirely accessible to the minds of theorists and the public alike.

An infrastructural approach, by contrast, encourages a kind of modeling in which the deep units and processes in terms of which operational categories are composed may be hidden, abstract, and fundamentally different from the operational units. The price of hidden units and processes is unfamiliarity and a consequent challenge to habits and expectations. The benefits, however, of positing hidden units and processes can be extraordinary, because a well-formulated infrastructural model represents the reality of the system it portrays, characterizing its operational units in terms of the components and processes that truly underlie them.

It is my contention that the same kind of descriptive temptation that limited the insights of theoretical chemistry for centuries has long stifled our ability to characterize relations among communicative systems, whether developing or mature, human or nonhuman. The temptation has been particularly strong in the study of infant vocalizations, where the attraction of operational-level alphabetical transcription has often deflected attention away from the recognition of the genuine categories of infant sounds and the infrastructural principles of speech that are systematically implemented in the infant vocal categories.

AN INFRASTRUCTURAL MODEL
FOR HUMAN PHONOLOGY

Before approaching the infrastructural alternative in infant vocalizations, consider a traditional operational-level phonetic description in detail. Table 1.1 offers examples of transcriptions that might be provided for infant vocalizations across four 2-month periods of age for normal infants. These examples presented in the IPA constitute a synthesis of the kinds of results that have been reported in numerous studies of baby sounds going back as far as the 18th century and extending to very recent time (for discussion and citations, see chap. 2). Both consonants and vowels are depicted for each 2-month period, and some of the particular syllables, according to the transcriptions, occur at every age.

On the whole, these depictions of infant sounds are misleading because they imply well-formedness of syllables produced by the infants at every period, when in fact well-formedness would not occur for the great majority of sounds until the fourth age. Transcriptions such as those in the table shoehorn infant sounds into mature, familiar categories that may appeal to our day-to-day awareness of language, but they confound understanding just as surely as did the ancient characterization of all chemical substances in terms of the categories of earth, air, water, and fire.

One way to illustrate the confounding nature of the transcriptions is to ask a phonetician to read the transcriptions in Table 1.1 aloud; the resulting pronun-

TABLE 1.1

Example Results From Operational-Level Description of Infant Vocalizations at Four Ages.

Ages in Months	Tokens of Various Sound Types Selected Randomly From Transcripts
0–1	ə, hə, ʌ, œ, β, əʔə, əhə, u, uə, hɪ, əɪ, βʊ, ʌwu, m̩, …
2–3	əʔə, ɪ, gu, ugu, œ, gə, ə, hə, ɣ̩, ʊ, m̩, gʌ, ʁ, ʊɤʊ, ɤʊ, βʊ, əgə, ɤʊ, œg, guə, β, ʁə, …
4–5	ə, œ, ɪ, β, hə, m̩, i, e, bʌ, əbʌ, ʙ̩, ʙœ, əʔə, əhə, ʙu, uə, hɪ, əɪ, βʊ, gʌ, ʊɤʊ, ɤʊ, əgə, ju̯, dæ, …
6–7	ə, hə, əhə, dɪdæ, i, e, bʌ, əbʌ, ʙ̩, ʙœ, əʔə, dæ, ɪdæ, ʌwʌ, β, o, u, ju̯ja, baba, m̩, pəbʌ, …

ciations will be notably different from the great majority of infant productions at least for the first three age ranges specified in the table. By the fourth age range, the productions of the infant and the readings of the phonetician will match much better.[5] The fact that infant productions advance markedly from the first age to the fourth is partially revealed by the results of the phonetician/ reader test, but it is obscured by the transcriptions themselves, which seem to show perfectly well-formed utterances at all four ages. The operational-level description afforded by transcription offers a poor basis for insight into the fundamental nature of the progression that occurs across the ages.

Every time one shoe-horns infant sounds into operational syllabic or segmental categories, one presumes that the infant sounds are already well-formed. This approach begs the question of when and how canonical speech-like sound production is achieved and obscures any advancement from primitive sounds to fully canonical ones because every sound is treated as if it already possesses the features that occur in the mature system.

A fragment of results from an infrastructural alternative to the traditional approach is outlined in Table 1.2. I have suggested the name *infraphonology* for the realm of study assessing the infrastructure of human speech sounds (Oller, 1989; Oller & Lynch, 1992). Through infraphonological description, we furnish a general basis for understanding the sounds of mature speech and interpreting infant sounds in relation to universal principles of well-formedness of mature sounds (see chap. 4).

Phonetic transcription is held in abeyance in the infraphonological approach (it is not used until the fourth stage, and even then it is applied with caution), and instead infant utterances that appear to be precursors to speech are categorized more globally, avoiding shoe-horning. Each individual operational-level category is given a general designation (quasivowel, goo, marginal babble, etc) to indicate particular features that typify the category, and these global designations prove to be useful even in the fourth stage. All the utterance types that appear to be precursors to speech, from quasivowels to canonical babbling, are referred to jointly as *protophones* (see chap. 3). To understand the nature of the infant vocal achievements that protophones demonstrate, an infrastructural model is needed. The model highlights the principles of speech systems that are mastered with each protophone type. The infraphonologically inspired interpretation of protophones specifies the extent of well-formedness of each category by characterizing each in terms of adherence to principles that phonological sequences in human languages must obey (chaps. 4 and 5).

---

[5]Even at the fourth age range, segmental phonetic transcription yields a precarious interpretation of infant sounds. Although phoneticians may be able to hear well-formed consonants and vowels in the infant utterances at the fourth age, it appears that segmental transcription imputes more structure to the utterances than they actually possess (MacNeilage & Davis, 1990). The shift in apparent transcribability that occurs at the fourth age is not, then, absolute. However, improvement in transcribability is notable from any of the first three ages to the fourth in terms of how likely it is that any individual utterance will pass the phonetician/reader test.

TABLE 1.2

Infraphonological Interpretation of Infant Vocalizations at Four Ages

Ages in Months	Global Protophone Categories Mastered	Principles of Syllable Well-Formedness Mastered
0–1	Quasivowels	Normal phonation
2–3	Gooing	Articulation
4–5	Marginal babbling, full vowels	Full resonance
6–7	Canonical babbling	Rapid formant transition

The quasivowel sounds that occur during the first 2-month period in Table 1.2 meet an infraphonological *phonation* principle that is required by well-formed or canonical syllables of mature speech. In keeping with the principle, the vocal cord vibration that occurs in quasivowels is of the normal phonation variety, the kind of phonation that occurs in speech (but not in crying, shrieking, sneezing, etc.). Similarly, the gooing sounds that are mastered during the second 2-month period meet an *articulation* principle. Canonical syllables require articulation or movement of the supraglottal vocal tract, opening or closing of the tract through movement of the lips or tongue. In gooing, the articulation principle is incorporated because the tongue moves discernibly during normal phonation, yielding a primitive (although still not fully well-formed) consonant-like sound (Zlatin, 1975a).[6] Consequently, two key principles (phonation and articulation) are under the infant's command in the second period in gooing, whereas only one of the principles is commanded in the first period. Across the four ages, the principles of canonical syllable formation are systematically accumulated, as indicated in the figure, until at the last age, infants produce well-formed syllables that abide by four key principles.

All canonical syllables, the prime rhythmic units of phonological systems in natural languages, must abide by these four infraphonological principles. Infant canonical syllables of the fourth age pass the phonetician/reader test relatively well. Canonical babbling can be transcribed phonetically and then can be read aloud by phoneticians with substantial accuracy; the readings recognizably correspond to the baby productions. Baby sounds at this point are

---

[6]Zlatin (1975b) provided phonetically sophisticated characterizations of primitive consonant-like sounds in gooing. In an intriguing analysis, she noted that infants produced "variations on a theme," composed of normal phonation during which tongue movement occurred extremely variably from utterance to utterance. The transcribability of the utterances was distinctly limited by this instability of tongue gestures, but still gooing seemed to represent a realm in which infants could systematically explore movements of the tongue that would eventually be required for consonant production.

sufficiently well-formed to serve as exemplars of potential words in natural languages. Through its reference to principles of well-formedness, the infraphonological interpretation provides a clarifying perspective on how infant sounds across the four ages reveal progressive approximation to the mature speech system (for further discussion of this point, see chap. 4).

LEVELS IN AN INFRAPHONOLOGICAL SCHEME

The theoretical approach implied in the infraphonological model is parallel to the infrastructural systems of other sciences. An infraphonological system, one of two major divisions in an infrastructural model of human language, as depicted in Fig. 1.2, includes structures that specify (or generate) the indefinitely large class of possible well-formed operational-level sounds (including segments, syllables, phonological phrases, etc.) that can occur in natural languages. The principles of infraphonology are formulated with reference to acoustic and articulatory parameters, and they specify how canonical or fully well-formed operational units are constructed in terms of those parameters. The principles indicate the limits on how acoustic features (durations, frequencies, amplitudes, and resonance characteristics) can be implemented in speech-like sounds and on how articulation and phonation must be performed to meet the requirements of well-formedness. Sounds violating the principles can easily be produced by the human vocal tract, but when they are

Operational categories
(examples of functional units: particular phonological features,
segments, syllables, phonological phrases, etc.)

Infraphonology
(specifies principles generating the entire class of potential well-formed operational units
and specifies properties of utilization and function of such units)

Prime parameters
(dimensions of description for units:
amplitude, duration, frequency, resonance, etc.)

FIG. 1.2.   Infraphonological modeling.

produced, normal listeners recognize that the sounds are not speech. These nonspeech sounds may be recognized as some kind of fixed signal (crying, laughing, shrieking, etc.), some kind of vegetative sound (coughing, sneezing, hiccoughing, etc.), or some other kind of vocalization (perhaps an imitation of infant protophones or animal sounds).

The principles themselves in an infraphonological approach are primary points of reference in interpretation. In this newly designed search for understanding of the development of the speech capacity, operational-level questions, such as whether or not a newborn infant did or did not produce a [b], are avoided. Instead, at each point in time, the question is more fundamental. We seek to determine the extent to which infant sounds reveal command of the principles of well-formed speech sound construction. Further, we encourage description of the operational categories of infant sounds on their own terms with no shoe-horning. Infant sounds are called protophones in general and are given individual infant-appropriate operational-level titles, but they are not forced into the frames of mature alphabetical categories where they do not fit.

One might ask why we do not simply describe sounds of very young infants acoustically (and/or articulatorily), as such an approach would possess the key advantage of avoiding phonetic transcription and consequent shoe-horning. In this alternative proposal (suggested by Lynip, 1951), every sound would be described physically, in terms that are adaptable to any vocalization.

To answer the question it is useful to refer to Fig. 1.2 again. Acoustic and articulatory description are clearly important, but purely acoustic or articulatory description is no more revealing than a purely transcriptional approach. The latter focuses description at the top or operational level in the diagram. The former merely moves description to the bottom, or prime-parameter level of the diagram, without ensuring any sort of principle-based insight. A shift to prime-parameter description supplies no improvement in interpretation because acoustic or articulatory measurements do not in and of themselves provide information about the degree to which sounds approximate speech. Without theoretical guidance, there is no limit to the number of prime-parameter measurements (of duration, frequency, amplitude, etc.) that can be made for any vocalization, and no way to tell which measurements are pertinent to speech.

The infraphonological principles provide the critical guidance needed to focus attention on the features of acoustics and articulation that are particularly relevant in speech. The infraphonological model involves all three levels of the diagram and specifies the interrelations among the levels; it utilizes acoustic and articulatory parameters in defining the limits on operational-level units. This is a basic feature of the infrastructural approach. Instead of focusing attention exclusively at one level of potential characterization (operational or prime), it provides a systematic, theoretically rich basis for maintaining perspective on the relation between operational and prime physical levels.

KEY ACHIEVEMENTS
IN INFRAPHONOLOGICAL MODELING

Until fairly recently, the sounds of infancy were viewed as deeply bewildering in their complexity. Baby sounds were prominently referred to as random or wild and were often assumed to be unrelated to speech (Jakobson, 1941; Mowrer, 1952). This misleading view (see chaps. 2 and 3) held sway partly because operational-level description had produced only confusing, miscategorized data. One result of the confusion was that there was no useful stage model of infant vocal development prior to the last quarter of the 20th century. Phonologically relevant stages could not be discerned in the context of purely operational-level description. The putative data in Table 1.1, where the same kinds of phonetically transcribed sounds appear to occur at all points in time, provide a glimpse of the perplexity prior theorists must have experienced in the attempt to address infant vocal development in the context of purely operational-level description.

On the other hand, stages of infant vocal development practically jump out at us in the course of longitudinal study focused on intuitively based categorization of protophones informed by awareness of the fundamental nature of phonological units. Much of the recent wave of work in vocal development launched in the mid-1970s began with just such intuitively based categorization (see chap. 3). The common-parlance names for protophones (gooing, raspberries, squealing, growling, babbling, etc.) were adopted and elaborated to include terms such as *quasivowel, full vowel, marginal babbling,* and so on. The decision to use global, intuitively based categorization was made in part because the philosophical inadequacy of shoe-horning had become obvious to researchers by the 1970s, but the choice was supported by the additional intuitive expectation that the pattern of occurrence of protophone categories might make some sort of deep phonological sense.

Through direct longitudinal study avoiding the shoe-horning error, it was quickly discovered that in the first few months of life there are systematic stages of vocal development, each one typified by particular protophones. In Table 1.3, which presents only a minor modification of Table 1.2, we see the four stages that are now recognized in an international consensus from recent research in vocal development (see chap. 3).[7] The ages represented in the four stages of Table 1.3 overlap, reflecting the empirical fact that the stages of development to not appear in accordance with a strict, uniform timetable across individual infants. The characterization of stages works well, but not perfectly. Its advantage is that it specifies an order of events and a logic to explain the order.

---

[7]The consensus is informal. Different investigators use somewhat different terminology and sometimes include more detailed breakdowns, such that one stage from the figure might be characterized as two substages. However, the general nature of stages is not in contention.

TABLE 1.3

Stages of Infant Vocal Development as Seen Through Infraphonological Interpretation

Names of Stages	Onset Ages in Months	Protophones Mastered	Infraphonological Principles Mastered
Phonation	0–2	Quasivowels	Normal phonation
Primitive Articulation	1–4	Gooing	Articulation
Expansion	3–8	Marginal babbling, full vowels, raspberries, squealing	Full resonance
Canonical	5–10	Canonical babbling	Rapid formant transition

Practically as soon as the stages came into focus, the primary protophones were seen to adhere to particular principles of speech sound well-formedness in mature languages. It became possible to notice the progression in well-formedness of protophones, and to observe that the apparent phonetic content of late babbling is closely related to that of early meaningful speech, whereas the earlier protophones are systematically more distant from speech (chap. 3).

The recognition of stages in vocal development represented a new understanding in itself, and it also provided a basis for the identification of abnormalities in vocal development. Investigators soon found that vocal development was delayed in infants who were congenitally deaf. The onset of one of the key protophone stages was severely retarded. This delay had been hidden in prior operational-level phonological descriptions; in fact it had been widely believed that deaf and hearing infants produced the same kinds of vocal sounds throughout the first year of life. In the context of the infraphonological model, the delay in deaf babies came into such clear focus that it would be impossible ever again to miss it. The groups of profoundly deaf and normally hearing infants proved to be utterly distinct in the onset of the most conspicuous protophone category, canonical babbling. Deaf infants were found often to be delayed in the onset of canonical babbling by more than a year (see chap. 4).

THE IMPORTANCE OF DISTINGUISHING THE PRODUCER FROM THE RECEIVER

The infrastructural approach is applicable to both the producer and the receiver of communications. The approach does not imply, however, that both the producer and the receiver command the same infrastructural properties and principles. There are often important differences. Adults, for example, command a rich linguistic infrastructure, whereas infants command only a fragment of it. Yet adults can listen to infant vocalizations and perceptually impose aspects of their own system on infants' productions. Adults can in some cases perceive infant productions as if the infant productions were structured more richly than they are.

The shoe-horning of precanonical protophones into categories of alphabetical transcription provides the most obvious example of the ability and tendency of adult listeners to perceive infant productions in a way that is inconsistent with the infrastructural organization of the infant producer. There are more subtle but equally important examples. Even when infants produce syllables that meet all the requirements of the canonical syllable definition, phonetic transcription can still be misleading, depending on how it is utilized. The adult listener or transcriber hears infant canonical syllables in such a way that they seem perfectly transcribable in alphabetical terms, with consonants and vowels of the IPA. Yet the infant producer may not command the distinction between consonants and vowels fully; in fact the infant may have virtually no awareness of it. As far as the infant mind is concerned, syllables may constitute unanalyzed wholes that happen to meet certain requirements allowing adult listeners to interpret the syllables analytically.[8]

There are good reasons to believe that at the onset of the canonical stage, and for many months thereafter, infants do not command a segmental system of consonants and vowels, but only a system incorporating unanalyzed syllables. Empirical evidence to back up this idea has been presented in various forms, notably by MacNeilage & Davis (see Bernhardt, 1992; MacNeilage & Davis, 1990; Vihman, 1992; and for a review see Vihman, 1996). One of the kinds of evidence is that babies in the early stages of canonical syllable control (even after the onset of meaningful words) produce syllables that do not show the permutations that they would show if segmentally organized (MacNeilage & Davis, 1990). For example, infants tend to produce some syllables that sound like [ba], more or less, and some syllables that sound like [dɪ], more or less. What infants tend not to do is produce syllables that sound like [bɪ] or [da].[9] The value of having segments in a phonological system is dependent on the Recombinability[10]

---

[8]The remarkable ability of infants to discriminate auditorily among minimally paired adult syllables (e.g., [ba] vs. [da]) in laboratory experiments (Eilers, Morse, Gavin, & Oller, 1981; Eimas, Siqueland, Jusczyk, & Vigorito, 1971) does not contradict this claim. Discrimination might be accomplished by reference to features that, from the infant's perspective, apply to syllables as wholes.

[9]MacNeilage and Davis (1990) provided a good mechanical reason for the particular associations of consonant-like elements with vowel-like elements. The [d] articulation positions the tongue near a point for the [ɪ]-vowel. So if a [d]-like tongue articulation occurs, an [ɪ]-like vowel articulation is the most natural follower. If a labial articulation occurs, the tongue does not need to move from a low position that seems naturally to accompany lip and jaw movements, and as a result, the vowel following [b] tends to be one that is low, either [a] or something like it.

of segments from one position to another. Recombinability makes it possible for a small number of consonants and vowels to generate a much larger number of syllables; 25 different consonant-vowel (CV) syllables can be generated by recombining five consonants and five vowels. Without Recombinability, the five consonants might each be bound to one of the five vowels, yielding only five syllables. Further, in the absence of Recombinability there is no necessary basis for assuming that the producer of such a five-syllable system commands a segmental (consonant and vowel) analysis at all. If Recombinability does not occur, then we might as well think of a [ba]-like syllable as an unanalyzed syllable that has a labial characteristic of articulation and a [dɪ]-like syllable as an unanalyzed syllable that has a lingual characteristic of articulation. Perhaps a different symbol system is called for. Single symbols for each syllable type could be proposed because the [b] versus [a] distinction as well as the [d] versus [ɪ] distinction implied in the IPA transcriptions appear to be artifacts of adult perception, at least from the perspective of the system of distinctions that the child commands.

Infants do not show a general command of Recombinability in early syllable production, and consequently they cannot be assumed to possess the distinction between consonants and vowels; that is why transcription of infant sounds, even transcription of canonical syllables, must be interpreted with caution. From an adult receiver's perspective, it may be possible to hear an infant production as containing transcribable segments. The sounds thus transcribed can even pass the phonetician/reader test. However, from the infant's perspective the segments may not yet really be there.

The danger of operational-level description, then, in infant and child speech appears in at least two forms. On the one hand, operational-level segmental description of precanonical sounds is fundamentally misleading for both the child, who does not intend to produce segments, and the adult perceiver, who does not recognize transcribed sequences as representing infant utterances when the phonetician/reader test is conducted. On the other hand, operational-level segmental transcription of canonical sounds may seem perfectly appropriate from the adult listener's perspective even though the child still does not necessarily intend to produce segments.

Whereas transcription is applicable to different extents at different points in development, infraphonological interpretation is appropriate at all points in development, from the perspective of both the adult listener and the child producer. During the precanonical stages, infraphonology elucidates progress by showing step-by-step accumulation of well-formedness principles. During postcanonical stages, including those of meaningful speech, infraphonology

---

[10]The term *Recombinability* is capitalized to indicate that it represents an infrastructural "property" of potential communication systems. Throughout the book, property names are capitalized. The properties model is summarized in chapter 12.

provides a framework for the interpretation of the accumulation of principles related to Segmentation and other properties of advanced signal systems.

NEW DIRECTIONS: THE POTENTIAL ROLE OF INFRASTRUCTURAL MODELING IN COMPARATIVE ETHOLOGY

The benefits of the shift from traditional operational-level phonological descriptions to infraphonological ones may extend beyond those that have been seen up to the time of this writing. One potential area of growth concerns comparative vocal ethology. A model of description for communicative actions that begins with infrastructural principles may have the power to uncover secrets of the relations that obtain among vocal systems of differing species. Instead of being confined to either operational-level comparison or undirected physical (especially acoustic) parameter comparison, it may be possible to characterize vocal similarities and differences in terms of the kinds of properties and principles of well-formedness and unit construction that each species presents. In this sort of descriptive comparison, the deep nature of phylogenetic relations may become more apparent, because the measures of similarity can be less anthropocentric and more biologically general than in operational-level comparisons. Sounds of each species, human or nonhuman, can be characterized independently at first in terms of a species-specific operational system and in terms of physical (acoustic or articulatory) vocal dimensions that are species general, but are manipulated differently by different species in their varying communication systems. Later, comparisons between the systems can be made at an infrastructural level.

As suggested in Fig. 1.3, comparisons among species in this infrastructural approach are not made directly at operational levels nor at physical-parameter levels, but instead at the level of infrastructural principles and properties of systems; no arrows connect the operational levels of the three systems. The arrows indicate that all the types of vocal systems represented in the figure (speech, human fixed vocal signals, and nonhuman primate signals) are related to a particular infrastructural system. Units in every system can be described in terms of a common set of physical parameters, and the differences and similarities among systems can be elucidated at the infrastructural level by comparisons across systems.

Some of the most useful comparisons of human and nonhuman primate systems may prove to be found at the infrastructural levels of maximally similar system components; humans possess a fixed vocal system (consisting of cries, laughs, moans, etc.) that has many of the same features as the vocal systems of other primates. Figure 1.3 suggests comparisons between fixed vocal systems, and in chapter 14, a preliminary proposal about infrastructural similarities between human and nonhuman primate fixed vocal systems is detailed. Thus, whereas physical descriptions across species have a common

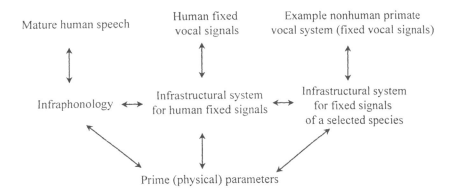

FIG. 1.3. Preliminary sketch of infrastructurally-based comparisons among vocal communication systems across species.

basis in acoustic and articulatory measurements in the infrastructural comparative approach, the connective power of an infrastructural model goes further than invoking a common set of physical parameters. The model appeals to species-independent infrastructural properties and principles of potential temporally based communication systems, of which speech and other vocal systems are all representatives (chaps. 12 and 14).

As in the description of human infant vocalizations, the distinction between producer and receiver is critically important in the description of nonhuman communication systems. The intentions of the animal producer of a communicative act may not match those of the receiver. Current work on vocal communication in nonhuman species (e.g., see review of the primary issues in Owings & Morton, 1998) emphasizes the fact that the producer and receiver may not have the same goals. The producer may benefit from deceiving the receiver, and the receiver may benefit from foiling the producer's potential deception. The acts of production and reception may involve varying degrees of intentionality on both sides, and species may show more elaborate abilities or more rapid development in reception than in production (see Seyfarth & Cheney, 1997; Snowdon et al., 1997). The key point is that the activities on the two sides may be extremely different, and the infrastructural descriptions that will be needed to take account of the abilities underlying them in such cases will also differ.

INFRASTRUCTURAL MODELS OF BOTH SIGNALS AND COMMUNICATIVE VALUES

The infraphonological model depicted in Fig. 1.2 focuses on the transmission units, the *signals* of languages. To address all the features of language, the infrastructural approach must go beyond the realm of sound itself, beyond signals, to include the usage of sounds as well. Usage implies a lot. When Shakespeare commented on the unchanging aroma of a rose by whatever name it might be given, he emphasized the critical distinction between *signal* and *value*. The concept of a rose and all that it entails is always to be distinguished from the name or other symbol that may refer to the concept. Shakespeare recognized that in communicative acts, there is always a distinction to be drawn between the content (value) of the communication and the action (signal) that transmits it.

Humans use communication to transmit a wide variety of values including motives, illocutionary forces, implications, metaphors, and literal semantic content. The uses of communicative signals are addressed in the second major division of a full infrastructural model of language. This second division of the infrastructural approach is informed by the fields of semiotics (Peirce, 1934; Sebeok, 1968), pragmatics of communication, (Austin, 1962; Morris, 1938), and design features of communication systems (Hockett, 1977). The infrastructural principles and properties that apply to signals are referred to as infraphonological and those that apply to functions or values of vocal actions are referred to as *infrasemiotic*. Just as the infraphonological model specifies principles and properties of signaling units in potential natural languages, the infrasemiotic model (see Fig. 1.4) specifies principles and properties in the formation of communicative values.[11] These principles and properties constitute dimensions along which communicative values can be elaborated.

Any description of language that would fail to treat functions of language in social interaction would be incomplete. Any attempt to address comparative ethology or evolution of behavior must likewise encompass functions of acts, because in the dog-eat-dog history of species, functional significance determines survivability.[12] The existence of vocal communication systems in other species is motivated especially by social and regulatory functions (see Dawkins & Krebs, 1978; Owings & Morton, 1998), and it is seen as crucial to maintain a distinction between the usage of vocalizations and their signaling forms (see recent discussion in Seyfarth & Cheney, 1997). In the perspective of deep time, functionality of communication systems must determine the survivability of communicative features, just as functionality of the system as a

---

[11]Clearly, the formation of well-formed units, such as sentences or phonotactically well-formed syllable sequences, is specified in two related levels. At the first level, the infrastructural system specifies the principles that languages can choose from in delimiting a class of units. At the second level, each individual language implements a subset of those principles within its particular grammar to delimit the set of sentences and syllable sequences that can occur in that particular language.

[12]Still, some vocal communication systems can be manipulated independent of their social functions, a fact that has been emphasized regarding human speech (see, e.g., Chomsky, 1966). We can speak utter nonsense, and we can toy with our vocal capabilities. Consider the wondrous but unintelligible version of Russian spoken by Sid Caesar. Also, beware the Jabberwocky and the slithy whatchamacallits. Yet however apparent these linguistic nonsense capabilities may be, the existence of speech is motivated in the long run by its regulatory, social, and informational functions.

Operational categories
(includes functional units of value: particular lexical meanings,
syntactic functions, semantic paradigmatic relationships, illocutionary forces, etc.)

Infrasemiotics
(specifies principles generating the entire class of potential well-formed operational
units of value and specifies properties of utilization and function of such units)

Prime parameters
(includes dimensions of description for raw material of units:
cognitive categories, social interactive functions, etc.)

FIG. 1.4.   Infrasemiotic modeling.

whole must play a role in survivability of the species. The choice of the term
value to represent all sorts of functions (including referential meanings, regulatory functions, etc.) that communication can serve is thus intended to encourage the interpretation that growth of a language-like system is guided by
its role in an evolutionary scheme of barter where the fittest communicative
traders survive.

PROPERTIES AND PRINCIPLES

I have referred here to both principles and properties of communicative infrastructure. These are among the hidden units, the underlying structures that
specify the nature and composition of the familiar operational-level units of
any system. In the theory of communicative infrastructure, *properties* are the
fundamental realms in which a communicative system (whether human, animal, or extraterrestrial) may evolve; infrastructural *principles* specify
implementation of properties (when and if the properties are incorporated
into a system).

At a general level, the posited properties considered here (especially in chap. 12) are intended to represent a fixed storehouse from which communicative systems are able to choose as they evolve. As each property is incorporated into a system, it is implemented through principles that can vary somewhat from system to system. Thus vocal communicative systems can be said to vary in terms of whether or not they include particular properties or in terms of the extent to which or the ways in which each of the properties is implemented through a selected set of principles.

To make the terms clearer, let us to proceed to examples outlined in Fig. 1.5. As noted with regard to infraphonology, principles can refer to rules that specify or generate the class of phonological units that languages can possess. The rules of canonical syllable formation discussed previously in conjunction with the vocal development stage model constitute one set of such principles. The infrastructural property that canonical syllable principles implement is called *Syllabification.* Syllabification requires a specific set of principles defining a class of minimal rhythmic units for any communicative system. To develop a powerful communication system, it is necessary to define minimal rhythmic units of the system efficiently; otherwise development of a more complex rhythmic system or a subsyllabic segmental system would be impeded. Thus the principles of Syllabification selected within a system can be crucial to the potential success of the system as a communicative vehicle. One reason we, as speakers of natural languages, can pronounce or understand sentences quickly is that the syllables of sentences in human languages are all well-defined temporally; syllables are required by infraphonological principles to fit within a limited range of durations both for formant transitions and for syllables as a whole. This range limitation, imposing a requirement of rapid transitions and rapid syllables, provides a frame around which the production and reception of speech are structured. The speed of communication would be hampered if syllables were allowed to be longer than the upper limit of the range, not only because it would take longer to say things, but because listeners would not have such a clear idea about where to focus their auditory attention; they would not know what temporal window to look through during the perception of speech.

So any rich communicative system is pressed to develop the property of Syllabification in order to attain efficiency of production and reception. The property can be implemented at varying degrees of complexity and efficiency through selection of particular principles to implement the property. Thus, the principles of implementation of Syllabification can differ across systems. Human language, for example, requires that syllables have rapid transitions between key internal elements of the syllable (consonants and vowels), and at a more detailed level of implementation, that these transitions take the form of rapid spectral changes. For example, when we say [da], we produce a quick gesture that the ear records and the brain recognizes in part because it tracks the rapid change in spectral transitional information that corresponds to the rapid movement of the tongue and jaw in producing the syllable. Another species that might develop a powerful system of communication could conceivably select a principle of transition based on a different acoustic feature. Instead of spectral changes, the transitions could be carried by rapid sweeps of fundamental frequency, for example. A less powerful communicative system might require no rapid transition principle at all. Many sorts of differences among species in how they might implement principles are, thus, logically possible.

Another property of human vocal communication also presented in Fig. 1.5 is termed *Designation*. Any powerful communicative system must be capable of designating things in the world so that attention to those things (or their conceptions) can be mentally shared. For example, a baby at 12 months of age points and vocalizes, designating an object in the vicinity. Listeners tend to look toward the object and share an understanding with the infant that both parties to the interaction are thinking about or noticing the object. This sort of joint attention act is often not motivated by an infant's desire to obtain an object. It constitutes instead an act of mental contact between the infant and the receiving individual, an act built on pointing, alternating gaze, and accompanying vocalization (Butterworth, 1996).

In the infrastructural model, Designation is a property of possible communicative systems; infrastructural principles of Designation specify possible means of implementing designative acts. In primitive acts, humans designate by vocalizing while alternating gaze or while pointing to objects with fingers, chins, sticks, and so on. The combination of pointing or gaze with vocalization provides a basis for the receiver to understand that the sender of a communication is making reference to an object. In addition, particular vocalizations can be reserved for the designation of particular categories of conditions, entities, or events. In such cases of category-specific association the use of a particular vocalization can be the sole means of Designation, and can thus constitute a primitive word.

A nonhuman Designation system could incorporate somewhat different principles of Designation, or could implement only a subset of the human principles. For example, the system might include no use of alternating gaze, or might focus more heavily on shared attention through shared touching of objects. A topic of particular interest is whether or not Designation occurs at all in some (presumably intelligent) species.

Figure 1.5 presents a schematic regarding 4 of the 18 properties considered in chapter 12 along with corresponding principles for each. Segmentation, discussed earlier, is another infraphonological property addressed in chapter 12. One of the fundamental goals of this volume is to explore the possibility that the infrastructural properties proposed may provide a particularly useful perspective from which to consider comparative ethology of communication as well as evolution of language and language-like systems.

Example properties	Example principles of human speech
Syllabification (infraphonological) ↑ Recombinability (infraphonological)	Normal phonation, articulation, full resonance, rapid transition, ... Repetition, alternation, embedding, ...

| Designation (infrasemiotic) ↑ Propositionality (infrasemiotic) | Vocal coordination with pointing, category-specific vocal association, ... Word-order constraints, inflection, ... |

FIG. 1.5.   Principles and properties in the infrastructures of communicative systems.

A HIERARCHY OF INFRASTRUCTURAL PROPERTIES

A culminating point in this work is built on the idea that the infrastructural system of natural languages, including both infraphonological and infrasemiotic components, is naturally organized hierarchically.[13] Some properties logically presuppose others, and evolving communicative systems can adopt the more basic properties without adopting the more advanced ones. On the other hand, command of the advanced ones requires that the more basic ones be in place. This arrangement may establish a basis for useful evolutionary speculations.

The property of Recombinability, for example, exemplified in Fig. 1.5, cannot occur in the absence of Syllabification in an evolving communication system. A system must possess minimal rhythmic units to be able to recombine them through principles such as repetition, alternation from one unit to another, embedding, and so forth. If Syllabification is not sufficiently well defined, there will be limits on the ways Recombinability can be implemented. For example, in a system where durations of minimal rhythmic units are allowed to vary without restriction (because Syllabification is not richly defined), a recombination of units could not easily fit into a general rhythmic frame needed to facilitate pronunciation and understanding. According to this reasoning, solid command of Recombinability requires solid command

---

[13]This may be the most significant way that the present system differs from that of Hockett (Hockett & Altmann, 1968; see chap. 12).

of Syllabification. Logically speaking, the requirement does not work in the opposite direction. Syllabification does not presuppose Recombinability. The unidirectional relation is indicated by the arrow in the figure.

Similarly, the infrasemiotic property of Propositionality presupposes Designation, but not the reverse. A proposition inherently contains at least two terms, a topic and a comment. One cannot construct a comment about a topic unless one can refer to that topic. Designation is the property required to specify topics within any interaction. Communicative systems cannot, then, introduce the property of Propositionality until Designation is (at least to some degree) already in place. In fact Propositionality presupposes several infrastructural properties of which Designation is just one.

In proposing this hierarchical system of properties, the goal is partly to offer a solid frame, a common ground for comparison among species. The success of the model hinges in part on the claim that the posited properties are constant across deep time and that they represent hidden units and relations underlying all possible vocal communication systems. The hypothesis is that if the properties are correctly formulated, they will represent the unchanging possibilities that confront every potential species that evolves toward a complex vocal communication system.

If the reasoning is correct, these properties and their naturally logical relations also provide a model of natural possible staging points in vocal communication evolution, points at which relative stasis of evolution might occur. The possibility that a communicative system could incorporate only a subset of the more basic properties from the infrastructural hierarchy is suggested by the nature of communication in babies. Modern human infants communicate in ways that include only a subset of the properties posited here, and at the earliest stages, the properties that are commanded are predictably the more basic ones from the hierarchy. Even though infants do not use the whole adult system, they do communicate in important ways. As they grow, they communicate more effectively, incorporating additional more advanced properties and elaborating the control of principles associated with each one. At each successive stage, the improved communication capability of the infant provides an existence proof. It proves there can exist intermediate stages of communicative capability between those seen in non-human primates and mature human language. There can exist various levels of simplified languages, if you will, possessing only basic properties of mature human language, to varying extents.

Following this reasoning further, the evolving communication systems of ancestral hominids may also have successively incorporated subsets of the properties hierarchy. At each stage of evolution they may have been able to communicate in ways that surpassed the capabilities of any other primates of the time and of their ancestors. The hierarchy of properties, then, provides a model of natural evolutionary staging points. By taking stock of data from the natural laboratory of vocal development in human infants, we obtain empirical information verifying that some of the presumed logically possible evolutionary stages do in fact occur.

HOW THIS EFFORT DIFFERS FROM PRIOR CHARACTERIZATIONS OF LINGUISTIC EVOLUTION

There have been a great many efforts to discern the evolutionary origins of language dating to even before the mid-1700s, when Johann Gottfried Herder won the first prize in a famous essay competition on "glottogenesis" at the Berlin Academy of Science. Most of the efforts have fallen on infertile ground, but there have been a number of recent, more intriguing efforts. The most successful ones, in my opinion, have had a distinctly infrastructural flavor. In particular, Bickerton (1981, 1990) has written of *protolanguage* in human ancestors, putting flesh on the idea that primitive hominid communication may have been important, even if it lacked all the features of modern language. The work focuses on possible evolution of properties of language, especially in the syntactic domain.

Bickerton's efforts have concentrated on how linguistic syntax expanded out of presumably primitive abilities to combine words or word-like units in ways analogous to syntactic patterns of pidgin languages (languages of trade that typically consist of very small vocabularies and very simple rules of combination for sentences). The changes in linguistic capability from such primitive syntax to more complex language may have taken place relatively recently, in terms of the deep time of evolution. It has been suggested that the shift occurred around the time of the Upper Paleolithic era (perhaps 35,000 years ago) when humans painted realistic characterizations of animals and left hints of visual symbolism on cave walls (Binford, 1981; White, 1989).

The present work focuses on evolutionary changes that may have taken place much earlier. Some of the changes may have taken place millions of years ago. This work contrasts with that of Bickerton and others in that the infrastructural principles and properties to be considered here represent more primitive features of possible linguistic systems than those considered in Bickerton's work. For example, Bickerton approached the question of linguistic evolution starting from a point at which communication in modern words already existed, whereas my speculations start from a point long before words existed.

Even with this difference in mind, I deem the two approaches largely compatible. They are both infrastructural in intent. Their examples have merely been drawn from different points in time in the possible evolution of communicative systems.

Much of the uniqueness of the approach here owes to the fact that it is founded in empirical study of infant development in the first months of life. The reasoning is guided by the fact that each stage of infant vocal development corresponds to a point where crucial features of the infrastructure for a speech capability are added. It would be logically possible, based on the vocal capabilities available at each of these points (and assuming the existence of certain additional mental and social capabilities), to develop a primitive communication system that would be more elaborate than any system that is known to be available in monkeys or apes.[14] With each successive stage of such evolution, the communication system that could be formed would be superior in power and presumable survival value to that of each prior stage. In various stages of our hominid ancestry, communicative systems may have emerged in a sequence of steps suggested by (although not fully specified by) the stages of infant vocal development in the first year or life, each step providing communicative tools that made emerging humanity more able to survive in a changing world (chap. 13).

The claim is not that the ontogeny of speech recapitulates its phylogeny, but that both phylogeny and ontogeny are governed by a common set of infrastructural possibilities. Phylogeny may not proceed precisely as ontogeny does, but similarities of the progression in both cases should be understandable in the light of the natural logic detailed in the infrastructural model. As a result, there should be interesting similarities between evolution and development, with the latter providing certain empirical tests of plausibility for the former. The infrastructural model provides interpretive guidance in both cases.

What we have seen in the past 20 years of growth in systematic knowledge about infant vocalizations has rendered a spark of inspiration. There is, I think, something extraordinary about human development, both ontogenetically and phylogenetically, something that is augured by the protophone stages of the first months of infancy. As we approach the bubbling, gurgling infant landscape, we need to put on our infrastructural lenses and earphone filters as we step forward into the colorful, buzzing garden where the ability to talk is growing.

PLAN OF THE BOOK

This volume presents a nine-part thesis:

1. Vocal development cannot be well understood if it is founded on traditional descriptive approaches that shoe-horn infant sounds into mature operational speech categories through phonetic transcription (chap. 2).

---

[14]Limits on our knowledge of nonhuman primates limits the generality of this claim. I have no stake in proving the uniqueness or superiority of human communication. The goal here is to outline *a framework for comparison* that might offer a new direction for development of understanding. As new information is gathered about nonhuman primates, adjustments will obviously need to be made in the details of how humans and nonhumans are similar and different with regard to each infrastructural property and associated principles.

2. The traditional approach needs to be replaced by an infrastructural one. As seen through an infraphonological framework, human infants go through clear stages of vocal development during the first few months, each stage typified by particular protophones (chap. 3).

3. Viewed this way, the sequence of vocal achievements of the first year is neatly organized by infraphonological theory and follows a logic that suggests a naturally connected pattern leading from primitive vocal capabilities to richly structured abilities that are exploited in talking (chaps. 4 and 5).

4. The logical growth of vocalizations as elucidated by infraphonological theory is deeply embedded in our biological makeup, and key stages of development are robust, resisting interference from such factors as environmental deprivation or premature birth; as a result, important practical applications to disorders of communication can be derived (chaps. 6–8).

5. Not only the physical quality of protophones, but also the nature of their usage shows infants progressively building a vocal tool of remarkable flexibility and power starting from the first months of life (chaps. 9 and 10).

6. The usage of protophones can be best understood in the context of a general theory of the potential functions of communication (a theory of value) that helps lay further groundwork for cross-species comparisons and fruitful evolutionary speculations (chap. 11).

7. Humans manifest the critical elements of their vocal capability at a surprisingly early point in development; in fact the initial aspects of the vocal divergence from other primates can be seen in the first months of life. The comparison of human and nonhuman primate vocal systems is most fruitfully seen within the context of a general infrastructural account of fundamental properties in potential vocal communication systems. This account must specify aspects of sounds (an infraphonological matter) and also aspects of usage and value (an infrasemiotic matter; chap. 12).

8. In the context of this broad infrastructural account, the sequence of development in the human infant may provide revealing clues regarding the steps that our hominid ancestors took in their journey toward spoken language. It seems likely that for millions of years before the eruption of full-fledged syntax (which may have occurred at around the time of the Upper Paleolithic era), the hominid line had been accumulating progressively powerful vocal communication capabilities (chap. 13).

9. Infrastructural modeling of fixed signal systems in humans and nonhuman primates can provide enhanced comparative insights. In the context of such comparison, notable similarities emerge, highlighting the sense in which human communication capabilities and those of other animals may be built in accord with species-universal infrastructural possibilities (chap. 14).

2

Myths About Babbling
and the Tradition of Transcription

INTUITIONS ABOUT BABBLING
AND THE ACADEMIC PENDULUM

In both empirical outcome and theoretical background, academic understanding of infant vocalizations has been fundamentally enhanced since the
mid-1970s. The long historical trail to this new perspective included two
switchbacks. Scholars began two centuries ago by assuming that babbling was
a key precursor to speech. In the middle of the 20th century the long-held
view was reversed in the minds of most scholars; it came to be believed (especially in the research areas of linguistics and child language) that there was no
important relation between infant sounds and the early sounds of talking.
The recent turn in favor of the original view is based on formulations and discoveries that have occurred during the last quarter of the 20th century. The
outcomes of the recent work are sufficiently solid that it would appear the importance of babbling as a precursor to the speech capacity is now permanently
established. The task of this chapter is to recount early landmarks of the
winding path that has led to the present vantage point from which infant development of speech can be understood, and to highlight the sense in which
the instability of historical positions can be attributed to the inherently confusing description of infant vocalizations in terms of operational-level categories of mature speech.

Before proceeding with the tour of this academic history, it is important to
note that the swing between contrasting views in the literature in infant vocalizations had no major impact on public thought, at least not in the modern
United States. I base this observation on experience with hundreds of families
from all walks of life, as well as hundreds of clinicians including pediatricians,
nurses, speech pathologists, and audiologists. The great majority of them
seem to have been uninfluenced by the academic pendulum of vocal develop-

ment theory, and have instead taken a homegrown, intuitive approach to understanding baby sounds. They seem consistently to adhere to the assumption that the pageant of infant development must proceed according to a stable script wherein every manifestation of development has a crucial role. In this view, the sounds of the first months are seen, unquestionably, as important indicators of development. The parents we have met through research generally assume further, without any prompting from laboratory staff, that abnormality in the emergence of babbling should be taken as a danger signal; and clinicians who work with child speech have typically viewed normal babbling as a marker of well-being (Gesell & Amatrudo, 1941).

In their enthusiasm about the importance of infant sounds, parents and clinicians have often tended to analogize babbling to speech, drawing parallels in the most direct way possible. To characterize the sounds, they pronounce them, imitating with the accents of their native language, adapting the baby sounds to their own mature phonology. An English-speaking parent or pediatrician might characterize a 2- or 3-month-old baby as saying "goo," "oogoo," or "huh," depictions that are consistent with alphabetical operational-level descriptions discussed in chapter 1 (Table 1.1).

The tendency to characterize sounds of babies in terms of native language sounds of adults appears to be adopted without hesitation, even though parents and clinicians recognize that their own imitations do not replicate precisely the sounds produced by infants in the first months of life. The tendency to present an alphabetically styled rendition seems perfectly natural, and was shared by generations of scholars, but it embodies a stricture of thought and description, an entanglement that misdirected the study of infant vocal development for nearly two centuries.

THE BEGINNING OF SYSTEMATIC RESEARCH IN VOCAL DEVELOPMENT: DIETRICH TIEDEMANN

Originating at the end of the 18th century, the earliest published research on infant vocalizations incorporated the parent and clinician's approach to description, characterizing the sounds of babies unhesitatingly in terms of mature native language sounds of the authors. Flowering fully in the 19th century, during the Victorian period, and continuing into the 20th century, the literature also accepted by assumption the idea that babbling plays a key role in speech development.

During this first period, daily attention to nature was not just a scientist's activity. In the Victorian age, naturalism was a fad (Barber, 1980) and amateur observations of birds, flowers, and butterflies were among the Western world's most popular parlor talk. Many individuals established collections of botanical or insect specimens to be pored over after dinner. It was in this social context that the study of infant babbling took off with individual parents' diary-based observations of their own children.

The research has been brought forward from its primary beginnings in Germany by Bar-Adon and Leopold (1971), who compiled English translations of selected portions of the early literature. Starting from ground zero, with no scientific literature to guide the foray, the earliest observations show insight that may be consistent with the timeless intuitive knowledge of parents about their infants. Dietrich Tiedemann was a philosopher from Marburg, who, at around the time of the American Revolution, in the very earliest period of this naturalist fervor, kept a diary on the development of language in his son Friedrich (who would go on to become a famous anatomist). Here we taste early recorded notations on babbling:

> After all manner of exercise in the production of tones, and after the acquisition of some skill in using the speech organs variously, he commenced on the 14th of March [at five months of age], to articulate consciously and to repeat sounds. His mother said to him the syllable "ma"; he gazed attentively at her mouth, and attempted to imitate the syllable. Furthermore, it was observed that when he heard a word easy of pronunciation, his lips would move as he softly repeated it to himself. (Tiedemann, 1787/1971, p. 14)

Tiedemann's assumption that babbling and speech are related is reflected in his reference to "speech organs," and to the notion that the infant "consciously" pursues "syllables" and even "words." The assumption conforms to an intuitive view held by many parents. However Tiedemann noticed one feature of his baby's actions that appears to have eluded most observers until quite recently. Although the phenomenon of silent mouthing of speech-like sounds referred to in the passage has been informally noted in our laboratory and others, it remained largely unstudied in systematic research until the work of Meier, McGarvin, Zakia, and Willerman (1997).

The suggestion that Friedrich could imitate and repeat syllables or words at 5 months of age may seem overly bold in light of modern efforts. The study of imitation in infancy proves to be both theoretically and methodologically difficult. The best current evidence suggests that syllables are not truly imitated by infants so young, although documentation for imitation of certain intonation patterns appears solid (see e.g., Kessen, Levine, & Wendrich, 1979).

If indeed the infant Friedrich did produce well-formed "ma" syllables at this age, then the passage constitutes, to my knowledge, the earliest recorded account of the onset of canonical babbling, one of the most important indicators of normal development in the first year of life. The age suggested in the passage is consistent with modern reports. Calculating from Friedrich's birthdate, he was 25 weeks old, easily within a single standard deviation of the mean for onset of canonical babbling in normally developing infants ($M = 26.4$ weeks, $SD = 4.69$) as reported in a recent longitudinal compilation (Eilers, Oller, et al., 1993). Current research indicates that parents virtually always recognize the onset of canonical babbling (Oller, Basinger, & Eilers,

1996), even if they do not have unambiguous ways to refer to it, and they typically react to it by attempting to impose interpretations that may guide the infant toward understanding of words, presumably because canonical babbling sounds so much like speech (Papoušek, 1994). The interpretations parents give to babbling usually take account of the lack of "meaningfulness" in the baby sounds; parents generally presume that infants so young do not have knowledge of the conventional references of words. Yet they often assume canonical babbling must come from speech. Hence it is interpreted to be imitative, as it apparently was by Tiedemann.

Thoroughly modern issues were raised in this two-century-old commentary. Tiedemann's (1787/1971) summary includes an intriguing early description of a phenomenon that is one of the hottest topics in current child development research, joint attention:

> Visible signs of reflection and of the ability to differentiate appeared on May 13th [at 6 months of age]. Whenever he met with anything novel or strange he would point his finger at it to call other people's attention to it, and employed the sound "ha! ha!" That the pointing as well as the exclamation was addressed to others is apparent from the fact that he was satisfied as soon as people signified that they also had taken note. One may gather from this how deep in human nature lies the desire to reveal themselves to others, and to feel their participation in anything that strikes our interest. (p. 14)

It is widely believed nowadays that sharing of attention toward objects is a critical precursor to language learning (see, e.g., Mundy, Kasari, & Sigman, 1992; Tomasello & Farrar, 1986). If a child is capable of recognizing that someone else is looking at an object, and realizes that both persons are focused on the same object, then the child has taken a key step toward being capable of understanding that a name might be given to that object. Without the ability to share attention to objects, it is hard to imagine how a motivation to label (that is, to learn nouns), or an understanding of the nature of labeling could be achieved. The communicative property of Designation (see chap. 12) specifies the dimension along which shared attention is developed. Tiedemann sensed the importance of Designation and described the vocal and gestural actions that implement it.

Parental description of infant actions is a primary form of information in child development research, whether from a systematic diarist such as Tiedemann or from a parent participant in university research programs. Descriptions produced by parents prove useful in part because they reflect the ecologically most significant interpretations of infant actions. As infants grow, adults adapt the pattern of their parenting to fit the capabilities of the baby at the time. This intuitive parenting (Papoušek & Papoušek, 1987) includes changes in what parents assume about babies' speech readiness based on growth in babbling (Papoušek, 1994). Therefore the assumption that babbling and speech are related may be deeply embedded in our psyches, and may tend to be reflected almost by force of nature in the opinions of parents.

HISTORICAL ROOTS OF THE SHOE-HORNING APPROACH TO DESCRIPTION IN BABBLING

Tiedemann understood that babbling and speech were related, but he characterized that relation by describing the sounds babies produced exclusively in terms of alphabetical-level mature speech sounds, exemplified in the quoted passage by the syllable "ma." This was not just Tiedemann's approach. As far as I can tell, from the earliest systematic observations on infant sounds, a primary aspect of the descriptive method always included alphabetical transcriptions that forced the primary objects of study, the utterances of babies, into the operational-level categories of mature linguistic phonologies. The pattern is seen clearly in early descriptions of vocalizations of the first months of infancy by Sigismund, whose original work of 1856 was summarized later by Preyer. According to Preyer (1889), Sigismund had found

> as the first articulate sounds made by a child from Thüringen, *ma, ba, bu, appa, ange, anne, brrr, arrr:* these were made about the middle of the first three months. Sigismund is of the opinion that this first lisping, or babbling consists in the production of syllables with only two sounds, of which the consonant is most often the first; that the first consonants distinctly pronounced are the labials. (p. 17)

It is important to take special note of the fact that Sigismund's focus in the transcribed utterances was on sounds of the first quarter of the first year of life, a period during which infant vocalizations typically show great divergence from the patterns of well-formed speech.

The transcriptional approach to description of infant sounds was general throughout the 19th century. Frederick Tracy, the Canadian psychologist who had studied with Wundt in Germany where most of the original work on infant vocal development had been done, transmitted the history of that work to the North American audience in a broad summary from his book, *The Psychology of Childhood*, at the beginning of the 20th century:

> The vowels usually precede the consonants; and of the vowels, *a* with its various shadings is generally the first to appear. In one case the following series was developed: *e-a-u.* In another, the sound of *a-a*, as an expression of joy was heard in the tenth week.
> Long before the sixth month, the primitive vowels are combined with one another ... and with consonants. ... In a great many cases, the first consonants to make their appearance are the labials, *b-p-m*, and these are almost always initial at first, and not final. The easy consonant *m* combined in this way with the easy vowel *a*, yields the familiar combination *ma*, which by spontaneous reduplication, becomes *mama.* (Tracy, 1909/1971, p. 33)

In this early literature, the emphasis on the relation of babbling and speech is unequivocal, and as authors sought a way to portray that relation, the transcriptional temptation appears to have been irresistible. Protophones, the precursor sounds to speech in infancy, were represented in alphabetical terms with little or no hesitation. In the prewar era, Lewis (1936) provided an extensive review of literature from both Europe and the United States focused entirely on, as the title suggested, "Infant speech." The work presented data from the first month of infant life in alphabetical terms. Even sounds that the author attributed specifically to such functions as crying and feeding were unambiguously treated in terms of well-formed phonetic categories: "There can be little doubt ... [concerning] the origin of the nasals *m, n, ...* they are expressive of hunger; that is, they are the audible manifestation of the mouth movements which are bound up with that state" (Lewis, 1936, p. 35).

There was no notable change in this descriptive attitude by the middle of the century. In Europe, Antoine Grégoire, the Belgian Professor of Classical Languages at Liège, and one of the most influential investigators of the time, provided extensive and detailed descriptions of sounds from his two sons in strictly alphabetical terms:

> At the age of 2½ months the two children produced the groups *ere, re, erere,* repeated to the point of boredom, in an exercise of babbling which lasted several minutes in the case of the older. The *r* survived in such groups until the 14th month in the younger and a little longer in the older, along with the synonymous groups *ram ram.* Now the *r* heard in the beginning stage was precisely the untrilled pharyngeal *r* used in French of the environment. (Grégoire, 1948/1971, p. 93)

The description almost certainly refers to gooing, one of the earliest protophone categories. Gooing typically cannot be appropriately characterized with alphabetical or phonetic transcription. Such characterization is deeply misleading, because it presumes syllabic well-formedness that most gooing utterances simply do not possess. In a footnote, Grégoire (1948/1971) took the alphabetical description even further, into a portrayal of trills, including the most unfavorite protophone for most mothers, the raspberry: "Later on trilled uvular *r* was added and even trilled labial *r* (in the cluster *br*)" (p. 93).

Raspberries, like gooing, fail to abide by certain infraphonological principles, and their transcription consequently conveys fundamentally false implications. The phonetic descriptions of these writings on vocal development communicated a broad commitment to treating the sounds of infancy in much the same way that linguistic field workers might describe the mature sounds of a newfound language. In field work, transcription is an essential step toward phonemic analysis. However, in the early years of observational research in infant vocalization, transcription led up a blind alley because it presumed well-formedness where none was to be found, and in the absence of fitting procedures, the study of babbling was vulnerable to fundamental misapperceptions.

THE MYTHS OF MIDCENTURY

By the era around World War II the failure in empirical portrayal of infant sounds had left the field open to a reversal of interpretation regarding infant vocalizations. It became academically fashionable to discount the previously long-standing belief in an important relation between babbling and speech. This empirical opinion had emerged consistent with a newly formulated general theory of language development. However, during the postwar era there was little or no empirical research supporting the posited discontinuity. The theory probably took hold because existing evidence was hard to interpret and easy to misinterpret, given that it was based on alphabetical transcription. Moreover, most of the activity in research that arose in the decades after the war, with the flowering of the influence of generative grammar, was focused in other areas of child language.

Even into the early 1970s there was no field of infant vocalizations to match the flurry of activity that was found in child syntax (Brown & Bellugi, 1964), semantics (Bloom, 1970; Clark, 1973; Gathercole, 1982), and phonology (Edwards, 1971; Ferguson, 1973; Ingram, 1974). At that time phonological studies of development were focused almost exclusively on early meaningful speech (Edwards, 1971; Ferguson, 1973; Ferguson & Farwell, 1975; Greenlee, 1974; Leonard, 1971b) to the near exclusion of babbling. Many in the 1960s and 1970s seem to have assumed that there was no point in pursuing infant vocal development because they had been given to believe that babbling and speech were unrelated.

Since that time, infant vocalizations has become a subspecialty within child language and infancy research, an effort reflected in the work of a substantial number of investigators in North America, Europe, and Japan. This growth has been fostered by a burgeoning consensus that there is much to be gained by scrutinizing the possible precursors to mature intellect and communicative abilities in infant vocal and gestural action. Yet, outside the expanding young field, the primary beliefs about infant sounds that originated in the middle of the century have persisted, and child development textbooks still asserted some of the myths regarding infant vocal development in the 1980s and 1990s (Clarke-Stewart, Perlmutter, & Friedman, 1988; Krantz, 1994; Zigler & Stevenson, 1993).

Consider four fictions that arose during or shortly after the World War II era.

1. *The universal phonetic myth*: Infants produce all the sounds of all the world's languages, with ease.

2. *The discontinuity of babbling and speech myth*: There is no phonetic relation between babbling and speech.
3. *The random babbling myth*: Baby babbling sounds are produced at random, wildly.
4. *The deaf babbling myth*: Deaf and hearing infants produce the same types of sounds, and only differ in that deaf infants cease to babble toward the end of the first year of life.

If someone at the beginning of the modern era of work in child language had chosen deliberately to confound future students of infant vocalizations, they could scarcely have furnished disinformation more effective than that embodied in these four claims. Research was both discouraged and muddled by them. The story of how they came to exist is both theoretically and methodologically instructive and the falsehoods inherent in the claims can be shown to depend, in large measure, on the misallocation of infant sounds to categories to which they do not pertain, the operational-level categories of mature speech segments.

THE LEGACY OF JAKOBSON

The first three myths appear to have originated with Roman Jakobson, perhaps the most well-known of all the Prague school linguists. He had lectured all over Europe, speaking with a flair that had made him a celebrity, and with a force of personality that is far from forgotten since his passing. His foreign accent did not deter him. "I speak Russian, in seven languages," he is rumored to have said. His influence was deeply felt on both sides of the Atlantic, and toward the end of his life, he crossed over from Europe to North America and held faculty positions at Columbia and Harvard. During that era he collaborated with the most eminent of phonologists, including Morris Halle, and with the father of the field of speech acoustics, Gunnar Fant.

Jakobson (1941) authored an influential work (one of the most cited writings in the history of linguistics) on the relations among meaningful speech errors in normal children and adult aphasics, errors that he determined to be predictable based on sounds found universally in natural languages. He emphasized the existence of laws of *irreversible solidarity*. An example of the laws can be seen in the fact that children learning languages with fricative consonants such as [s] or [z], often substitute stop consonants such as [t] or [d]. The word "zip" in English might thus be pronounced "dip" by a 2-year-old. There can be said to be a relation of irreversible solidarity between stops and fricatives, stops always being in the position of favor. Similarly, in keeping with generally applicable laws of irreversible solidarity, the world's languages show the same preference for stops over fricatives.

The acquisition of fricatives presupposes the acquisition of stops and in the same way the existence of the former implies that of the latter in the phonemic systems of the world. There is no language without stops, but on the other hand there are some languages in Oceania, Africa, and South America which lack fricatives, completely; examples in the Old World are Kara-Kalpak and Tamil, both of which lack independent fricative phonemes.

When there is a relation of irreversible solidarity between two phonemic units, the secondary unit cannot appear without the primary unit, and the primary unit cannot be eliminated without the secondary unit. This order prevails in the existing phonemic system and governs all its changes. The same order determines language-learning, as we have ... seen in a nascent system. (Jakobson, 1939/ 1971a, pp. 77–78)

Empirical studies have generally confirmed that, indeed, the universally occurring segments of natural languages are favored heavily by young children when they begin to speak, and that linguistically rare sounds are essentially absent when children (at around 2 years of age) produce the words of the language they are learning (see review in Locke, 1983).

Jakobson's interpretation brought into relief the tendencies of children all over the world to utilize a common set of universal syllables in early speech. Prior to his work, there had been numerous accounts of phonological development, but observations had been individual, and appeared to be both language specific and confusing in their diversity. Leopold (1939, 1947), author himself of one of the key works in child language development, described Jakobson's contribution to the study of early speech development: "Jakobson's theory of child language can be said to have brought order into the bewildering array of facts accumulated by observation, which seemed to lack a common denominator until his broad principles were applied to them" (cited in Bar-Adon & Leopold, 1971, p. 75). He characterized Jakobson as "the scholar who cut the Gordian knot" in the study of speech development (Leopold, 1971b, p. 135), and added that "the linguistic study of children's language learning will have to build henceforth on Jakobson" (p. 139).

Jakobson's stature owes in no small measure to his having clarified the relation between early speech and phonological universals, highlighting the generality of linguistic lawfulness. This contribution has stood the test of time, and it provided an enduring point of connection between child language and historical linguistics. Studies by such 19th-century scholars as Franz Bopp, August Schleicher, and Jacob Grimm (of fairy-tale fame) had made it clear that languages constantly change at a variety of levels of structure; the existence of phonological universals had been interpreted by Jakobson to suggest there must be deep forces that keep certain kinds of structures in place regardless of circumstances. The phonological laws that bind things together, in the Jakobsonian view, operated broadly across both ontogeny of speech in individuals and historical development of languages across generations.

JAKOBSON ON BABBLING

In scientific revolutions, and Jakobson was clearly a major contributor to one, new insights in one realm are sometimes accompanied by new limitations of vision in another. As Jakobson created a potent new conception of universality in phonological laws, he provided organization to the otherwise great complexity of early speech, but simultaneously he apparently overshot the mark in deriving implications of his model regarding babbling. His views on vocalization in the prelinguistic infant appear to have been developed deductively, in keeping with a general conception that had restricted the field of vision too severely. When a theory has such power, one runs the risk that "the comfortably familiar becomes a prison of thought" (Gould, 1989, p. 27).

Consistent with his theoretical model, and based on selected empirical information from the transcription-based literature in infant vocal development, Jakobson asserted that the sounds of babbling did not fit the same pattern as early meaningful speech and phonological universals. Myths 1 through 3 manifest the contentions he formulated about babbling, and all of them revolve around the central thesis that the universal lawfulness of phonology emerged swiftly at the beginning of meaningful speech.

> During the babbling stage (période du babil) the child produces the most varied sounds with ease (for example, clicks and palatalized, rounded, affricated, hissing, uvular consonants, etc.) nearly all of which he eliminates when he proceeds to the stage "of a few words" (to use Oscar Bloch's term), that is to say, when he adopts the first semantic values. It is true that some of the sounds which tend to disappear are unsupported by the example of the speech of the environment, where they do not exist. But there are others that share the same fate although they are present in the speech of the adults, and the child reacquires them only after long efforts. This is often the case with velars, sibilants and liquids. The child used these articulations frequently in babbling. (Jakobson, 1939/1971a, p. 76)

Jakobson's version of the first myth was, then, that infants produce rare sounds of mature languages frequently and "with ease" during babbling. These sounds included, in his contention, some that are documentably absent in certain languages although some of the types mentioned are represented in English—velars such as [k] and [g] (the hard first consonant in "goat" but not the soft one in "gin"), sibilants (a subclass of fricatives including [s] and [z]), as well as liquids such as [l] and the English "r," phonetically written as [ɹ].

The claim that babbling included these nonuniversal sounds (although the same sounds are shunned by children in early meaningful speech) was soon advanced by other writers, citing Jakobson. In keeping with the confidence in Jakobson's portrayal, Velten (1943/1971) contended that not only could U.S. infants produce rare sounds from English, but also from other unfamiliar languages:

> In a multitude of books on infant language it has been established that the acquisition of language properly speaking is preceded by a period, called ... [the] babbling stage, during which the speech organs are developed and incessantly exercised. Even the most outlandish sounds, i.e., speech sounds which the child has certainly never heard, may be produced and perfectly articulated during this time. An American child may produce velar spirants, voiceless nasals, retroflex sibilants, etc. During the early stages a uvular *r* is quite common. (p. 82)

Myth 1 asserted that babbling included outlandishly difficult sounds, produced by infants with no trouble regardless of auditory experience. Jakobson (1941) carried his idea to a radical extreme by contending that at the height of babbling the infant "is capable of producing all conceivable sounds" (p. 21), and "all articulations equally well" (p. 50).

To understand the flaws that underlie the myth, it is important to recall the discussion of shoe-horning categorization in chapter 1. Infants in the first months of life, do not typically produce well-formed segments or syllables of any language. Consequently the claim that infants in the first months of life produce particular speech segments ([l], [k], [r], etc.), rare or not, is misleading. When a precanonical infant produces vocalizations including features that may in some regard sound like rare phonetic units of natural languages, there are usually good reasons not to transcribe the sounds alphabetically at all, because the early infant utterances usually violate well-formedness principles presupposed by transcription. The sounds can be globally categorized, but segmental transcription misses the mark.

Granted, in late babbling (in the canonical stage) well-formed syllables do occur, and these syllables can be transcribed with greater validity. Yet it will be seen (in chap. 3) that in studies where canonical babbling has been transcribed, rare sounds of languages occur extremely infrequently, and many of the possible sounds of languages have never been observed in canonical stage infants to our knowledge. Therefore the universal phonetic myth proves to be misleading for precanonical infants and empirically false for canonical infants.

Myths 2 and 3 are, of course, closely related to Myth 1 in spirit, because all of them are deductively derived from the model of universal phonological laws and the assumption that the universal structure of phonology takes effect with the beginning of meaningful vocal communication. Myth 2 highlights the presumed break between babbling and speech, the discontinuity advocated in the Jakobsonian conception of vocal development. The infant who is viewed as phonetically omnipotent in babbling "loses near all of this ability to produce sounds in passing over from the pre-language stage to the first acquisition of words" (Jakobson, 1941, p. 21). Jakobson (1962/1971b) gave an example of the proclaimed discontinuity:

During the babbling period in the infant's development, many of the uttered syllables consist of a vocalic sound succeeded by a consonantal articulation. The most natural order of sound production is an opening of the mouth followed by its closure. ... As soon as the child moves from his babbling activities to the first acquisition of conventional speech, he at once clings to the model "consonant plus vowel." The sounds assume a phonemic value and thus need to be correctly identified by the listener, and since the best graspable clue in discerning consonants is their transition to the following vowels, the sequence "consonant plus vowel" proves to be the optimal sequence. (p. 215)

The sounds of infants in babbling are thus said to change dramatically at the onset of meaningful speech, in favor of universal patterns (here, the universal CV syllable), patterns for which no such preference (according to Jakobson) is seen before meaningful speech. Grégoire, whose diary descriptions were utilized by Jakobson, adopted the Jakobsonian view in subsequent writings. Referring to his two sons' production of what he had described as a uvular *r* in babbling, Grégoire (1948/1971) said:

Now the *r* heard in the beginning stage was precisely the untrilled pharyngeal *r* used in French of the environment which the children, two years later, had such trouble to produce correctly. Why were the groups *ere* etc., given up and then forgotten completely? ... The children themselves allowed them to disappear. (p. 93)

Grégoire (1948/1971) referred to the French "r" as "pharyngeal," emphasizing that it is articulated at the back of the mouth with the dorsum or the root (not the tip) of the tongue. There is no dispute that this pattern of articulation is rare for consonants in natural languages. Jakobson himself pointed out that sounds articulated at the front of the mouth, [b] and [d], for example, were primary and that back sounds (such as this purported pharyngeal articulation) presupposed front sounds in a relation of irreversible solidarity. Further, the French "r" is a fricative, which as a class is also nonuniversal. Thus back sounds are clearly less common than front sounds in natural languages. According to Grégoire's account, his children both babbled the linguistically rare back "r" of French very commonly, and then gave it up when beginning to speak, deleting it or substituting universal sounds for many months before installing the "r" into the speech repertoire.

In light of modern analyses of infant vocalizations, it seems clear that the "pharyngeal *r*" described by Grégoire (1948/1971) in his infant sons' prelinguistic vocalizations had been a feature of gooing (from the Primitive Articulation stage; chap. 1), and to say that it was "precisely" a sound of mature French is in the best case questionable, and in the typical case almost certainly unsupportable. Gooing sounds are produced with enormous variability and usually lack the well-formed margin–nucleus relations that are found in real, well-formed syllables. Consequently, to say that the sound was "pre-cisely" one of French is to misinform.

Another much-discussed feature of the presumed discontinuity from bab-bling to speech (Myth 2) was embodied in a purported change from a very large repertoire in babbling—one that was said to include all kinds of sounds, even the outlandish ones—to a small repertoire of only universal syllables in early speech. Jakobson (1939/1971a) said that at the beginning of speaking, the "phonetic abundance of babbling (gazoullis) gives way to phonemic re-striction" (p. 76) or "phonemic poverty" (Jakobson, 1941, p. 25). In this view, the simple oppositions of consonants and vowels as seen in universal patterns took over suddenly, as soon as the infant sought to transmit meanings.

The presumed discontinuity was emphasized to such an extent that advocates and reviewers of the Jakobsonian approach came to speak of an empirically un-verified *silent period* that they presupposed must occur between babbling and speech (Carroll, 1960/1971; Velten, 1943/1971). The break was portrayed as nearly absolute, a claim disputed by modern observations (e.g., Elbers & Ton, 1985; Jouanjean-L'Antoëne, 1994; Vihman & Miller, 1988) that show widespread mixing of babbling and early speech in children all over the world.

The idea of randomness in babbling, invoked by Myth 3, became another central focus in keeping with the idea that all kinds of adult phonological ele-ments were producible by the infant vocalizer. Jakobson (1962/1971b) re-ferred to "wild sounds of babbling exercises" (p. 215), and Grégoire (1948/1971) called babbling "unformed, unorganized" (p. 92). Reviewing the Jakobsonian perspective for the *Encyclopedia of Educational Research*, Carroll (1960/1971) said, "The particular sound types uttered by the babbling child have little relevance for later learning, for the types appear in more or less ran-dom sequences which bear little relation to the sequence observed after true language learning starts" (pp. 205–206).

The notion of randomness in babbling has been restated many times (see, e.g., Lenneberg, 1969; Mowrer, 1952; Osgood, 1953). One of the intentions of this technically inaccurate description (no biological behavior is observed to be entirely random, if it is subjected to systematic study) is innocuous. Often the term *random* is used to imply that a behavior observed does not obey a par-ticular kind of constraint. The usage does not imply that the behavior has no structure at all. For example, developmentalists have often wished to focus on the repertoire of playful actions of infants at early stages, actions on which in-fants seem to draw in subsequent stages when new motoric capabilities are manifest. Scientists may refer to these early playful actions as random because they do not display the full structure of the more elaborate fully developed ac-tions. Babbling may be viewed as a playful action, having no linguistic mean-ing, and thus no conventional communicative goal. To call it random in this regard (i.e., in regard to its meaningfulness) does not have to imply that bab-bling has no phonetic regularities. However, Jakobson (1941) encouraged that interpretation by calling babbling "wild" in its phonetic character, by saying infants could produce "all conceivable sounds ... equally well," (p. 21) and by emphasizing (according to his view) the orderliness of early child speech in contrast. Therefore the potentially innocuous meaning of random is clearly not what he had in mind. His contention was to portray babbling as phonetically random and without form.

DISCONTINUITY AND NATIVISM

In Jakobson's linguistics, human vocal communication was notable in part because it emerged in discontinuous leaps, metamorphoses that indicated that universal laws of language were at stake in development. The reasoning takes the following form. With the beginning of meaningful speech, radically new phonological patterns entirely distinct from those of babbling come into play; consequently, it is reasonable to assume that maturation of a special linguistic capacity is responsible. If learning were at stake, surely the change from babbling to speech would be more gradual. The reasoning concludes that there must be deep forces and innate tendencies to account for the crisp, clean lines of phonological patterning.

Jakobson's belief in the ubiquitous influence of phonological laws channeled his expectations in very specific directions with regard to babbling. It encouraged belief in major discontinuity. However, there are other possibilities of interpretation for those of a nativist inclination, possibilities that require no claim of discontinuity. Biology could be seen to play a fundamental role in development of a speech capacity even in the absence of a phonetic discontinuity at the onset of meaningful speech. Interest in the biological foundations of language does not impose a Jakobsonian perspective on babbling *per force*. It could be that the biological foundations of phonological capability are expressed much earlier than Jakobson imagined. Empirical data on phonetic similarities between babbling and early speech (see chap. 3) suggest, indeed, that the underpinnings of the speech capacity are to be found in the first year of life.

The shaky foundations of the empirical evidence Jakobson cited for his position are easy to point out. He had focused on primarily diary-oriented observations of infant sounds, and both the literature he reviewed and his own descriptions adapted baby sounds to mature linguistic categories through phonetic transcription. These categories were central to the developing field of phonological universals, a realm that had been based on mature languages of the world. The adaptations had worked adequately with young child speech (where well-formed syllables are used routinely), but they failed to provide an appropriate basis for categorizing early infant vocalizations.

DEAFNESS AND BABBLING

Myth 4, the one that suggested deaf and hearing infants babbled alike, was born later than the others. It is often attributed to Lenneberg (1967), whose treatise on *The Biological Foundations of Language* attracted considerable attention in the late 1960s and 1970s. It was one of the most important documents inspiring biologically oriented research into language and language ontogeny. Lenneberg's inspiration continues to be felt in contemporary language research.

The primary empirical publication that specifically addressed deaf babbling was by Lenneberg, Rebelsky, and Nichols (1965). The work considered the vocal development of a single deaf infant, whose vocalizations were described along with those of a second deaf infant in the famous book.

> Cooing appeared at about three months, babbling sounds were heard at six months and later, and laughter and sounds of discontent seemed identical with those of the hearing population. ... No precise quantitative measurements of the amount of vocalization could be made on the children after the first three months, but subjectively the hearing children were much more vocal in the presence of others than the deaf. (Lenneberg, 1967, pp. 139–140)

These are the words that apparently generated many subsequent citations (e.g., Clarke-Stewart et al., 1988; Fischer & Lazerson, 1984; Krantz, 1994; Zigler & Stevenson, 1993) to the idea that deaf and hearing infants babble alike in content, and only differ in amount. The idea was not consistent with certain prior studies reporting differences in deaf and hearing infant vocalizations, but these had been based on anecdotal observation (Mykelbust, 1954), or had been published in places that were at the time hard to access for readers in the Western world (Murai, 1961). It has always been difficult to identify deaf infants for study, so there was little literature to contradict Lenneberg's contention, and the deaf babbling myth would become one of the most commonly repeated claims, not just within the field of infant vocalizations, but within the entire field of child development.

Lenneberg (1967) noted the existence of certain early vocalizations, which he referred to with the single term *cooing*. He appeared to include what often is called gooing in this category,[1] but he did not note other protophone groups, most conspicuously canonical babbling. Jakobson had influenced this characterization of infant vocalization, and consistent with that influence, Lenneberg resisted characterizing any of the sounds of infancy, even in the late stages, in terms that would suggest relations with phonetic properties of speech. Only when speech itself would begin would Lenneberg's (1967) characterization turn toward phonetics: "The mass of random sounds begin to be lined up into some fundamental classes that contrast with one another in

---

[1]See his commentary (pp. 276 ff), which describes modulations of the vocal tract shape in face-to-face interactions where the baby engages in what he called cooing. The ages at which this cooing is said to occur suggest that the phenomenon is indeed what is referred to often as gooing in modern stage models of vocal development.

terms of articulatory mechanisms, roughly corresponding to some of the distinctive features described by Jakobson, Fant and Halle" (p. 279).

Lenneberg also maintained an affinity to the Jakobsonian legacy by invoking the notion of randomness in infant sounds and by appealing to the construct of distinctive features that played a central role in Jakobson's laws of irreversible solidarity. However, his theme was out of tune with the legacy in one critical regard, because unlike Jakobson, he clearly did assume that early infant sounds and speech were related. In his view as a physician and a scholar, cooing was a precursor to speech, and both were biologically predetermined. The conclusion from the research conducted under his direction that auditory experience did not play an important role in babbling was used to reinforce his contention that biology, not experience, was the key player in the game of precursors to speech.

Lenneberg's (1967) investigation, based on observations from two deaf infants, failed to take note of the wide variety of infant protophones—just a few categories of sounds were counted. On the other hand, his approach had the advantage of explicitly avoiding phonetic transcriptions of infant utterances in the first months of life:

> Although cooing sounds are "vowel-like," we must guard against describing them in terms of specific speech sounds of English, for example. They are neither acoustically, nor motorically, nor functionally speech sounds ... because the articulating organs move somewhat erratically and discoordinately.

> By about six months the cooing sounds become differentiated into vocalic and consonantal components ... but ... the sound patterns are very different from nonsense words that follow the phonological rules of English. (pp. 277–278)

Still, Lenneberg did not offer a systematic alternative to transcription, no other way to draw the critical analogy between the sounds of infancy and the features of speech. To him baby sounds were erratic and discoordinated until the beginning of speech. He had no coherent theory of the nature of speech to guide his interpretation. His spectrographic comparisons of infant vocalizations and adult speech yield little clarification, because it is hard to know which among the many acoustic features seen in the displays should be attended to—some seem similar, some different from mature speech—and the book provides no principles to indicate what features of infant sounds are important in the spectrograms.

Because Lenneberg avoided phonetic transcription of babbling, he left a void for many who sought to utilize his claim in developing a coherent story about infant development and who expected to be presented with transcriptional data to support it. To fill the perceived empirical gap in Lenneberg's argument, citations to the deaf babbling myth sometimes addressed evidence from another study (Mavilya, 1969) that reported phonetically coded data on babbling from three infants that had been diagnosed as deaf.[2] The study reported that deaf and hearing infants babbled similarly through most of the first year of life,[3] but that vocalizations of deaf infants began to drop out later, with fewer sounds than in hearing infants late in the first year and thereafter. The early similarity of babbling in deaf and hearing infants, as reported in the study, supported Lenneberg's view that early babbling was based on maturation rather than learning. However, in Mavilya's work, infant utterances at all ages were coded in the categories of English phonemics. Although there is no way to be sure, it is possible that the transcriptional approach was responsible for the apparent patterns of development in Mavilya's study. It is now clear from more recent evidence obtained through protophone categorization instead of transcription that deaf infants generally present a very distinct pattern of vocal development from that of hearing infants. Purely adult-based phonetic coding makes it difficult, if not impossible, to recognize the differences (see chap. 4).

The appeal of the deaf babbling myth seems to be attributable to the strong nativist tendencies of much current speculation in linguistics and child language, the same tendencies that seemed to make Jakobson's babbling views popular. The common nativist flavor was maintained through the deaf babbling myth in spite of the differences in content of Jakobson's and Lenneberg's specific claims about when in development the linguistically significant biological events of speech development might occur. Both saw language as a profound human capability, and both presented views easily adapted to the idea that innate principles impose structure on the development of speech.

BABBLING DRIFT AND THE PROBLEM OF SHOE-HORNING

During the same era that the myths predominated, a separate trend of research emerged that seemed to hint at important effects of experience in babbling. The *babbling drift* hypothesis suggested that babbling sounds drift toward sounds of the parent language across the first year of life (Brown, 1959). The literature of the era sometimes suggested that the hypothesis had been well-verified empirically (McCarthy, 1950/1971), although the data were

---

[2]The study did not have access to current methods of hearing evaluation for infants. Consequently, it could be that not all three of the infants evaluated were congenitally profoundly impaired, even though they showed profound impairments later, when they could be evaluated with more certainty. Even with more modern tools of assessment available, it is difficult to obtain unambiguous information about hearing status of infants across time. As a result, progressive hearing loss (where impairments intensify across the first months or years of life) complicates the interpretation of vocal development in deaf infants.

[3]It is possible that some or all the deaf infants studied by Mavilya and Lenneberg were more precocious than most deaf infants. Although most appear to show very sharp dissimilarities of babbling development with regard to hearing infants, some deaf infants with good oral language potential show patterns of vocal development that are much more similar to hearing infants. Consequently it is possible that the apparent differences between outcomes of these studies and those of more recent research are due to mere differences in the particular infants sampled.

actually ambiguous. Even today, the babbling drift hypothesis is being pursued actively, and whether or not it has been verified is somewhat controversial, and may depend on the precise formulation of the hypothesis. It is a tricky matter to determine whether or not babbling changes toward patterns of the ambient language, in part because the drift idea, like the four myths, is typically based on an assumption that implies coding by shoe-horning of infant sound categories into adult ones. To obtain a common metric, all sounds at every age must be categorized in the same way to make comparisons across ages, and the style of common coding that has been chosen has often been that of phonetic transcription (de Boysson-Bardies, Sagart, & Bacri, 1981; de Boysson-Bardies, Sagart, & Durand, 1984). Thus even in the case of the interesting and plausible claim that babbling may change in ways that are specifically affected by special (not universal) properties of the language environment, we find that progress may be limited by the problems of shoe-horning, the ubiquitous temptation and continuing peril of research in infant vocal development.

PHONETIC TRANSCRIPTION AS THE STANDARD TOOL OF BABBLING DESCRIPTION

Little direct empirical work was done with the intention of confirming the myths on infant vocal development. Support came mostly from citations to prior diary studies and relatively casual observations, followed by compounding of the citations in subsequent writings. Many of the diary works that could be cited had involved only one or two children (Grégoire, 1948/1971; Leopold, 1947; Taine, 1877/1971; Tiedemann, 1787/1971; Velten, 1943/1971). But at midcentury, a much bigger cadre of studies was conducted by Irwin and his colleagues (Chen & Irwin, 1946; Irwin, 1947a, 1947b, 1948; Irwin & Curry, 1941). The studies involved extensive recordings and transcriptions of a broad sampling of thousands of utterances from scores of English-learning infants across the first year of life. The utterances were coded in terms of the IPA, the repository of symbols developed by the International Phonetics Association (and updated periodically) to enable standardized phonetic and phonemic transcription of natural languages. Actually, the authors of the various studies directed by Irwin utilized only a fragment of the IPA, which is designed to allow characterizations of hundreds of potential speech elements that can function contrastively in the world's many languages. Irwin and his colleagues utilized only that portion of the IPA that could account for the contrastive or phonemic sounds of English plus a very few additions.

EXCURSUS ON PHONETICS AND PHONEMICS

As it will be useful to distinguish phonetic and phonemic transcriptions hereafter, now is an appropriate point for a brief excursus on terminology and symbology. The roughly alphabetical level of analyses of speech sounds corresponds to *segments* or *phones*. Segments can be considered in two fundamentally different ways. Insofar as they constitute contrastive units (yielding different meanings) within a particular language, they are called *phonemes*, and are symbolized in slashes. Thus the English phonemes /p/ and /b/ yield minimally different words such as "big" versus "pig," "rabid" versus "rapid," and "cab" versus "cap," where in each pair of words, the meaning difference is signaled by the sound contrast. Most analyses of English suggest that there are about 40 phonemes in the language, but there is a wide variety of variations in pronunciation of each of these phonemes based on regional dialect, utterance-to-utterance deviation, and allophonic variation. *Allophones* are conditioned by phonetic context. For example, the /p/ in "pig" is aspirated (has a brief period of voiceless h-like noise after the lips part) whereas the one in "rapid" has no such aspiration. This difference is determined by position; in initial position or before a stressed vowel but not after an /s/, /p/ is aspirated; otherwise it is not. The difference in these two allophones of the /p/ phoneme can be represented in phonetic (as distinct from phonemic) transcriptions that are placed in square brackets. Phonemically "pig" may be written as /pɪg/, but phonetically it is commonly represented as [pʰɪg], with the superscript *h* representing the aspiration. The phonemic /p/ in "rapid," on the other hand, precedes an unstressed vowel and so has no aspiration and is represented [ɹæpɪd]. The IPA offers an inventory of symbols that are adaptable to both phonetic and phonemic transcription of natural languages.

IRWIN'S TRANSCRIPTION-BASED STUDIES

In Irwin's transcriptions, no distinction between phonetic and phonemic characterizations was drawn. The coding was done at an essentially phonemic level, even though phonemes pertain to meaningful speech only, a fact that was noted derisively by linguists in later reviews of Irwin's misapplication of the notion of phoneme to infant sounds (Carroll, 1960/1971). Phonemes are defined as the units that convey distinctions of linguistic meaning. Because early infants command no meanings, they possess no phonemes. However, at this level, the complaint against Irwin is merely one of terminology.

A more important difficulty resides in the fact that the phonemic-level transcription he used ignored sounds of other languages as well as allophonic variants of English phonemes, even though the infants were clearly exposed to all the allophones of each phonemic type, and (as far as anybody knew) might have been capable of producing sounds from other languages as well. The transcriptions did not account for pronunciations of segments from languages other than English (with a very few exceptions), and they further failed to account for child pronunciations that might correspond to the well-known allophonic variants of English phonemic units.

The Irwin transcriptions formed an important base of knowledge about infant vocalizations for decades, and helped to spawn the babbling drift idea (cited in McCarthy, 1950/1971). For example, the data were interpreted to suggest a progressive growth in the number of speech sounds of English produced by English-learning infants across the first year. Even in the first 2 months of life, infant vocalizations were described as /h/s, /g/s, /ɑ/s, /u/s, and so on, and the data were presented in histograms comparing proportion of production of each phoneme from early infancy through adulthood. This categorization was apparently accepted by much of the academic community interested in infancy (although not the linguistics community) for decades after the publication of the results. McCarthy (1950/1971), for example, relied heavily on Irwin's studies in a review that concluded:

> The average child uses about seven different sounds in the first two months and ... this number increases to about twenty-seven by 2.5 years. At first, the sounds are predominantly vowels in a ratio of roughly 2:1. This ratio reverses at the end of the first year when consonant types exceed the vowels. ... Vowels are five times more frequent than consonants in the first two months ... only four vowels occur with appreciable frequency in newborns, the most frequent being æ. (p. 105)

Many had accepted Irwin's approach. Sounds of crying, gooing, squealing, and raspberries were all unified under a common rubric, and it appeared thus that babies were developing phonemes, the contrastive units of their mother tongue, right from the start.

Irwin's results showed no sharp discontinuity between babbling and speech, but this fact did not unseat Jakobsonian theory. The reasons the Jakobsonian views continued to prosper may have had to do in part with separation of fields of inquiry, with parallel trends of thought and publication. The linguistics and child language fields were influenced heavily by Jakobson. The developmental psychology field was more influenced by Irwin. The impact of Irwin's research proved most significant on the issue of babbling drift. The Jakobsonian theory was focused in other realms that were logically related to Irwin's outcomes, but remained academically separate. Still, the two academic trends shared one important methodological feature: Both supported characterization of infant sounds in terms of the operational-level categories of mature speech segments. In both cases this feature was a source of significant confusion.

During the period of my first empirical efforts in infant vocalizations, a colleague interrupted a colloquium I was presenting to question my decision to research the topic. He pointed out that Irwin's studies were available: Why do more data collection? It was a helpful question to address, because the most fundamental problem for progress in the understanding of infant vocal development lay in the very method of data collection.

3

Reversing the Field:
The Recognition of Protophones

AN INITIAL IMPRESSION OF PROBLEMS
WITH THE PHONETIC TRANSCRIPTION OF BABBLING

Irwin's influential approach (see, e.g., Irwin, 1947a, 1947b; Irwin & Curry, 1941), based on transcription of infant sounds primarily in terms of English phonemic categories, was misdirected in various ways. On the one hand, the transcriptional system he used was too biased toward English to yield general conclusions. Babies in the first year of life produce sounds that bear at least some resemblance to rare phonetic units from many languages, not just from English. Grégoire (1948/1971), for example, had noted the occurrence of consonantal uvular trills, the rolled *r* sounds (transcribed in IPA as [ʀ]) found rarely in languages (occasionally in some forms of French, regularly in Lisbon Portuguese), but sometimes seen as isolated productions in early infant vocalizations. An American English-biased transcriptional approach would be unlikely to capture the trilling characteristic of such infant sounds because American English does not include trills of any kind. In this regard, Irwin's approach was weak by virtue of its ethnocentricity, as his transcriptions must have involved assignment of non-English-like sounds to English categories.

Still, the problem with Irwin's approach was much more deep-seated than misallocation of segments from one language to those of another. As noted, the bulk of the utterances of infants younger than 6 months of age are not appropriate for transcription in terms of any of the IPA segmental symbols. Even the uvular trills of Grégoire's infant were most likely embedded in precanonical gooing rather than in well-formed syllables; consequently transcription of the trills as syllabic units was most likely inappropriate (see chap. 2). Irwin had been criticized on this point before on the grounds that "there is no International Phonetic Alphabet for the utterances of a baby" (Lynip, 1951, p. 226). The critiques were isolated, however, and for many years, the

49

transcriptional approach remained the standard method, both in developmental psychology and in linguistics, where Jakobson's approach also supported phonetic transcription of infant sounds.

In the early 1970s three independent groups of researchers in the United States (directed respectively by Betty Stark at Johns Hopkins, Marsha Zlatin-Laufer at Purdue, and by me at the University of Washington) came to reject strict transcription of infant sounds,[1] and replaced it by categorizing infant utterances broadly and intuitively, drawing on descriptions that could be found in nursery conversations and the vocabulary of parenthood. Therefore, instead of entering segmental symbols in transcripts, the investigators began to enter terms such as goo, coo, raspberry, squeal, and so on. The intuitive approach was more satisfying simply because it made no assumptions about well-formedness of the sounds. Babies often produced sounds repetitively, varying the acoustic character of the categories somewhat, but maintaining an identifiability to the broad categories that seemed largely consistent with the nursery terminology. In addition to the terms of the common parlance, a few brand new appellations (quasivowel, marginal babble, etc.) were also invented to account for certain sound types that seemed potentially relevant to speech development, but for which the language seemed to provide no easy terms. The invented terms were used somewhat loosely at first, but eventually they, along with the names drawn from common usage, would be given technical definitions.

At the outset, these categorizations were not taken very seriously. They were formulated largely as a means of setting certain categories aside during the transcription of tape recordings, while investigators focused on the most speech-like, syllable-like utterances of the babies. The categories did not seem easily interpretable phonetically, so they were systematically left out to enhance observation reliability for the remaining sounds and to prevent shoe-horning. However, it was hard to suppress an intuitive reaction that seemed to suggest these untranscribable sounds were themselves important somehow in speech development.

From very early in this empirical work, cries, laughs, burps, coughs, sneezes, and so on were treated as fundamentally different categories from the untranscribable categories that seemed relevant to speech, the protophones. A record of the protophones was kept during review of tape recordings, whereas cries, laughs, and so on were left out entirely, in keeping with the idea that the protophones might constitute specialized precursors to speech, wheraes the others were clearly something distinct. After all, cries, laughs, and so on occur as adult vocalizations, and they are treated as extralinguistic

---

[1] Also in the early 1970s, there emerged European opposition to the strict use of phonetic transcription in infant vocalizations and young child speech. The work was in part inspired by the thinking of the school of prosodic phonology (Firth, 1957) and has been summarized in Waterson (1971, 1987).

in that case. It was decided to assume they could be treated as extraphonological in infancy as well.

STAGES OF DEVELOPMENT IN THE LIGHT
OF PROTOPHONE CATEGORIZATION

The use of protophone categorization revealed aspects of development that had been opaque during the era of shoe-horning studies of baby sounds, and the research soon produced a body of longitudinal data on infant vocalizations that suggested neatly discernible patterns. In the earliest summaries of the data, ordered stages, during each of which particular protophones assumed prominence, became apparent (see chap. 1 for summary and more detailed treatment in chaps. 4 and 5). Comfort sounds (dubbed *quasivowels*) came first, shortly after birth, followed by gooing in the second or third month, then a rapid expansion starting at the fourth or fifth month that included raspberries, many vowel-like sounds, squealing, growling, and near-syllables that acquired the name *marginal babbling,* and then the most conspicuous vocal event of all, at around the sixth or seventh month, the well-formed syllables of what was soon called *canonical babbling* (Oller, 1976, 1980a). By the time canonical babbling was in place in an infant, the inhibitions of investigators about segmental transcription abated, because the sounds of the baby appeared by then to fit appropriately into the categories of the IPA, and it felt comfortable both to categorize the sounds as canonical babbling and to transcribe them phonetically, much as one might transcribe the sounds of a foreign language in linguistic field work.

EMPIRICAL EVALUATION
OF THE CLAIMS OF JAKOBSON

Because transcription in IPA categories seemed sensible for canonical syllables, it was possible to evaluate the Jakobsonian claims in familiar terms without obvious shoe-horning. It was deemed acceptable then to evaluate canonical babbling (but not precanonical sounds) directly in terms of the kinds of IPA segments that could be heard in well-formed syllables to see if they represented all the sounds of the world's languages (testing Myth 1 from chap. 2), to see if they were dramatically different from sounds that occurred in early meaningful speech (testing Myth 2), and to see if they occurred at random (i.e., with roughly equal frequency, testing Myth 3). Such an empirical comparison based on an ongoing longitudinal study of normal development was soon conducted in our laboratories at the University of Washington. The study focused on the canonical utterances of babbling infants at 6 to 8 and 12 to 13 months of age. The data could be compared with well-documented information about sounds occurring in early meaningful speech (and by implication in phonological universals as specified by Jakobson, 1941).

The analysis revealed very much the same patterns in canonical babbling and in early meaningful speech. The results thus directly contradicted Jakobson's central thesis that phonologically universal patterns emerged suddenly with the beginning of speech. It appeared that babbling was, after all, phonetically related to early meaningful speech. In fact, every one of the eight well-documented patterns of child speech error (for evidence of the patterns of early speech see, Albright & Albright, 1956; Dyson, 1988; Edwards, 1971; Ferguson, 1973; Ferguson & Farwell, 1975; Greenlee, 1974; Ingram, 1974; Ingram, Christensen, & Veach, 1980; or see Locke, 1983, for a review) that were evaluated in the study was found to be reflected in highly reliable syllable preferences of babbling. The results from the published study (Oller, Wieman, Doyle, & Ross, 1975) are summarized in Table 3.1.

As seen in Table 3.1, the tendency of children in meaningful speech to reduce consonant clusters (e.g., in trying to say "bring" a 2-year-old might delete a consonant and produce "bing") was matched by a tendency of babbling infants to use consonant clusters rarely; more than 90% of consonant-like elements occurred singly rather than in clusters in babbling. Similarly, final consonant deletion in young meaningful speech (e.g., "ball" pronounced as "ba"), was paralleled by a strong preference for initial consonants over final ones in babbling. Substitution errors of early meaningful speech (e.g., "ring" pronounced as "wing") are unidirectional ("r" is replaced by "w," but not the reverse, so "wing" would not be pronounced as "ring"), and thus manifest a preference of young children for some sound types over others. The very same preferences were seen in all cases in babbling ("w," a glide consonant, was more common than "r," a liquid; "t," a plosive, was more common than "s," a fricative, etc.).

In the context of this investigation, all the Jakobsonian babbling myths were countered. The universal phonetic myth was contradicted by the fact that infant babbling showed an essential absence of many rare sounds of languages such as ejectives, implosives, lingual trills, and lateral clicks, sounds that are well-documented as occurring in certain languages around the world. Even the English "r," in its normal pronunciation with retroflexion of the tongue tip, was absent in almost all the child samples that were examined. Similarly, high front rounded vowels (such as the "u" in French "tu avais voulu") were missing. Many of the sounds of natural languages were entirely absent from the babbling samples, contradicting the predictions of the universal phonetic myth, which asserted that all the sounds of all the world's languages should have been present; in fact few rare sounds of languages occurred at all, a pattern of absence that perfectly paralleled that of early meaningful speech.

Predictions of the discontinuity between babbling and speech myth were inconsistent with indications that canonical babbling was extremely similar to early meaningful speech in terms of phonetic patterns.[2] The similarity was

---

[2]Although similarities between babbling and early speech are very salient, there are empirical indications of some discernible babbling-speech differences for individual children (see, e.g., MacNeiluge, Davis, & Matyear, 1997).

so great that the bulk of the well-documented patterns of speech sound error in young children could be predicted in advance on the basis of apparent phonetic preferences of canonical babbling. The random babbling myth was also contradicted in light of strong preferences seen in babbling for certain sound types over others. The tendencies were highly reliable statistically, refuting the expectation of randomness in phonetic repertoire.

THE INTUITIVE PLAUSIBILITY
OF REDUPLICATED SEQUENCES

A teaching tool to illustrate the nature of commonly occurring babbling syllables is presented in Table 3.2. The two left columns (presented in the English orthography and the IPA, respectively) list plausible, and indeed common, reduplicated sequences of babbling heard in the age range of 8 to 12 months. The two right columns list logically possible reduplicated syllable sequences that essentially never occur.

Students are able to relate confidently to the list represented in Table 3.2 from their own experience and intuition, recognizing the common sequences and finding the others humorously improbable. Infants simply do not produce sounds that are complicated, and rare sounds apparently seem complicated. Instead, infants choose from a near universal inventory of syllables that includes the ones in column 1 (orthographically) and 2 (transcribed phonetically) of the table.

EARLIER EVIDENCE CONTRADICTING
THE JAKOBSONIAN VIEW

The summarized study was far from the first to note significant similarities between the syllables produced in early speech and the syllables of late babbling. Well prior to Jakobson's writings, the resemblance between reduplicated sequences in early words and babbling had been noted (Lewis, 1936; Taine, 1877/1971; Tracy, 1893). Moreover, there were indications contradicting the existence of a silent period between babbling and speech, as had been posited by Jakobson. Instead, babbling and speech had been found to be intermixed during the second half of the first year of life. It had been reported that after infants began to speak meaningfully, they continued babbling off and on for many months, mixing speech and babbled utterances.

Papa was pronounced for more than a fortnight unintentionally and without meaning, as a mere twitter, an easy and amusing articulation. It was later that the association between the word and the image ... was fixed. ... There was an insensible transition from the one state to the other, which is difficult to unravel. The first state still returns at certain times though the second is established; she still

TABLE 3.1

Results From Comparison of Late Babbling and Early Meaningful Speech

Type of Error in Early Meaningful Speech	Examples of Error[a] Orthographic	Examples of Error Phonemic to Phonetic	Similar Tendency Found in the Babbling Study
Consonant cluster reduction	"stuck" → "tuck" "bring" → "bing"	/stʌk/ → [tʌk] /brɪŋ/ → [bɪ̥ŋ]	94% of consonants occurred as singletons
Final consonant deletion	"ball" → "ba" "bath" → "ba" "dig" → "dih"	/bɑl/ → [bɑ] /bæθ/ → [bæ] /dɪg/ → [dɪ]	90% of consonants occurred nonfinally (37% initially, 53% medially)
Initial position deaspiration	"pin" → "bin" "tail" → "dail" "cap" → "gap"	/pɪn/ → [bɪn] /tejl/ → [dejl] /kæp/ → [gæp]	98% of plosives (stops) were produced without aspiration[b]
Final position devoicing	"big" → "bick" "bad" → "bat"	/bɪg/ → [bɪk] /bæd/ → [bæs]	About two thirds of final obstruents[c] were unvoiced
Initial position stopping	"thick" → "tick" "sad" → "tad"	/θɪk/ → [dɪk] /sæd/ → [dæd]	89% of initial obstruents were stops
Final position spirantization	"pat" → "pass" "pit" → "pits"	/pæt/ → [bæt] /pɪt/ → [pɪts]	76% of final obstruents were not stops
Gliding (also called 'liquidation')	"rock" → "wock" "lip" → "wip"	/rɑk/ → [wɑk] /lɪp/ → [wɪp]	83% of semivowels were glides
Fronting of dorsal consonants	"come" → "tum" "girl" → "dirl"	/kʌm/ → [dʌ̃m] /gɚl/ → [dɚl̥]	75% of nonlabial consonants were apical

^aThese examples are intended to represent commonly occurring error types in 2-year-old English-learning children. There is variation child to child that muddies the waters a little regarding the stability of these patterns. Children usually produce some of the errors on the list but not all, and many times the general pattern of errors is present but is not applied in all contexts (i.e., children will make errors with particular words on some occasions but not others). These variations do not, however, obscure the overall patterns of phonological error seen in young children. The examples are presented in an orthographic approximation (in column 2) that is intended to make their interpretation easily accessible to a wide readership. Of course, little children do not always produce English-like segments, so the orthographic renderings do not always reveal the precise pronunciations that would be most common in children (e.g., a 2-year-old's pronunciation of what has been rendered here as "pass" would typically not include the fully grooved alveolar fricative "s" of adult English, but rather a bladed, slit articulation, that more resembles an alveolar fricative that occurs in Mandarin). Similarly, the listed pronunciation "tuck" under cluster reduction, suggests an aspirated initial "t" that would rarely occur in child speech at such an early age. The actual child production would more commonly be voiceless and unaspirated, sounding to the American ear like "d," but in fact lacking prevoicing. The phonemic and phonetic versions of the errors are provided to clarify for the linguistics audience the pronunciations intended by the orthographic renderings. It should also be noted that the examples have been simplified (in both orthographic and phonemic and phonetic versions) to suggest a single error type on each word, whereas actual pronunciations of children often involve multiple error types on any word (e.g., "bring" might show both cluster reduction and final deletion, yielding "bi," [bɪ]).

^bPlosives in English include /p/, /t/, and /k/, which are aspirated before stressed vowels and in word initial position, as well as /b/, /d/, and /g/ (the hard variety as in "go" but not the soft variety as in "gin"), which are never aspirated.

^cObstruents include plosives, fricatives, and affricates. The fricatives include /f/, /s/, /θ/ ('th'), /ʃ/ ('sh'), /v/, /ð/ (the voiceless version of 'th'), /z/, and /ʒ/ (as in the "g" of "beige"). Affricates in English are /tʃ/ ('ch') and /dʒ/ ('j').

sometimes plays with the sound though she understands its meaning. This is easily seen in her later words, for instance in the word *kaka*. To the great displeasure of her mother she still often repeats this ten times in succession, without purpose or meaning, as an interesting vocal gesture and to exercise a new faculty; but she also often says it with a purpose when there is occasion. (Taine, 1877/1971, pp. 22–23).

Although Jakobson's theory of early child speech was greatly admired, there was evident doubt among some of the key figures of child language research of his own era regarding his claims about babbling. Leopold (1953/1971a), who was one of the great supporters of Jakobson's universalist theory of early meaningful speech, reported that reduplicated babbling and early speech had been similar in his research.

Jakobson and others exclude babbling from their analyses. I find striking oppositions, however, which might perhaps be characterized as a sort of experimental prepatterning. The postulated phonemic contrast between fully open vowels and fully closed stops, was also prepatterned in babbling combinations like [baba, dididi], and so was the early structural syllable pattern, consonant-vowel, both of which were carried over without break or relearning into imitative speaking with meaning. (pp. 136–137)

Thus a reading of the diary-based literature in infant vocal development, both before Jakobson and contemporary to him, would have provided much reason for doubt about the discontinuity claim. As the era of modern research in child language began to get off the ground, additional studies began to ap-

TABLE 3.2
Plausible and Implausible Babbling Sequences

Common sequences		Absent sequences	
Orthographic	*Phonetic*	*Orthographic*	*Phonetic*
bababa	[bababa]	skaskaska	[skaskaska]
dadada	[dadada]	aldaldald	[aldaldald]
mamama	[mamama]	rarara (English "r")	[ɹaɹaɹa]
wawawa	[ʋaʋaʋa][a]	shashasha	[ʃaʃaʃa]
yayaya	[jajaja]	plaplapla	[pʰla pʰla pʰla]
nanana	[nanana]	rarara (Spanish trilled "r")	[rarara]

[a]Infants and young children typically do not produce a rounded [w] but a flatter labialized glide [ʋ].

pear, providing further evidence of phonetic similarities between babbling and speech (Cruttenden, 1970; Menyuk, 1968; Murai, 1963; Nakazima, 1962; Vanvik, 1971), all of them antedating our own studies of babbling.

IMPORTANCE OF THE DISTINCTION
BETWEEN CANONICAL AND PRECANONICAL SOUNDS

The most significant factor in reversing the Jakobsonian view of babbling may not have depended on empirical evidence contradicting his theory. The contradictory empirical evidence by the early 1970s was based on the methodology of phonetic transcription, and it was this methodology, applied too generally, that had been the source of much of the confusion about the nature of infant vocalizations for many generations. Even when the transcription-based studies were improved by focusing only on canonical (and thus transcribable) syllables, their impact remained incomplete. They could show that Jakobson had been mistaken in some regards, but the quantitative data based on transcription did not explain why.

A more telling departure from Jakobsonian beliefs that arose during the 1970s resided not in the contradictory data, but in the mere differentiation of canonical babbling[3] from other protophones. On the one hand the differentiation allowed comparison between canonical syllables of babbling and canonical syllables of early meaningful speech, apples and apples. The precanonical oranges were left aside, and because they were, the data seemed cleaner than they would have otherwise.

Another step is needed to explain why the data seemed cleaner. Transcription of precanonical infant sounds such as gooing or raspberries creates inevitable confusion because, although these sounds bear some resemblance to sounds of natural languages, infants do not commonly produce them in well-formed syllables. When infants do produce sounds resembling trills (as in raspberries, sometimes) and back sounds (as in gooing) they usually produce them in isolation, a rare and noncanonical syllabic form, or in marginal syllables that do not meet canonical syllable requirements[4] (see chaps. 4 and 5). Consequently they only partially resemble the sounds that occur in real speech contexts and are easily differentiated auditorily from real speech sounds. Gooing and raspberries are identifiable as categories of infant sound, but if they are transcribed phonetically, the result cannot usually pass the phonetician/reader test (chap. 1). The reason the data of comparison show the similarity of babbling and speech more cleanly when they compare canonical syllables only is that precanonical syllables cannot be appropriately measured

[3]The term *canonical babbling* was not actually used until later publications (e.g., Oller, 1980a). Still the initial schema for the definition was provided. The term used in the 1975 publication was "speech-like" utterances of infants.

[4]Syllabic consonants are specifically excluded from the ranks of canonical syllables because they are rare in languages and because they do not abide by several infraphonological principles. Marginal syllables are excluded because they violate the rapid formant transition principle.

and counted according to the transcriptional metric in the first place. Such description offers no appropriate means of comparing precanonical sounds with early speech, or for that matter, with canonical babbling.

When two very different theoretical styles meet, they often seem to talk past each other. As soon as canonical and precanonical protophones were distinguished, a new theoretical style was implied, although not yet fully laid out. It contrasted with the traditional approach in which all infant sounds were transcribed and no distinction of well-formedness was invoked. From the perspective of people who advocated the traditional approach, the elimination of many seemingly rare speech sounds of babbling from the comparison with early speech (on the grounds that they were noncanonical) seemed to be bound up in circular reasoning. The new approach had found great similarities between babbling and speech, but from the perspective of advocates of the traditional approach, the outcome seemed to depend on eliminating from consideration many babbled sounds (e.g., the ones that occur in raspberries) that tend to be different from early speech.

From the vantage point of the new approach, however, the theoretical circularity appears to be on the other side. The new approach proposes that infant sounds should be treated differentially in accord with the degree to which they meet criteria of well-formedness in speech. The sounds that do meet the criteria are transcribed and can be compared quantitatively with speech sounds of young children, but the ones that do not meet the criteria need to be categorized another way and need to be compared with speech in terms of the extent to which they conform to the principles of well-formedness.

The new thinking rejects the idea that transcription should be applied to all infant sounds equally. The IPA is a system supplying symbols for sounds that occur (or can occur) as contrastive phonetic units in natural languages. Precanonical protophones, along with an indefinitely large class of other possible sounds that occur in nature, do not occur as contrastive phonetic units in natural languages. To transcribe such sounds phonetically is to presume the sounds meet criteria they do not meet. Any empirical question posed through phonetic transcription of such sounds thus seems uninterpretable viewed from the new perspective. Through uniformly applied transcription one appears to try to find out whether babbling resembles speech by assuming that babbling resembles speech. From the perspective of the new approach, this is shoe-horning, the circularity by which we are tempted to pretend that there are phonemic units in the protophones of infancy, the crowing of roosters, and the oinking of pigs.

THE BLINDING NATURE OF PRECONCEPTION

Shoe-horning clearly played a fundamental role in the ascendance of the babbling myths, but even in its context, it should have been possible to recognize certain relations of babbling and speech, at least in terms of the similarities in common reduplicated babbling sequences and early nursery terms of speech, similarities that had been highlighted for example by Lewis (1936) in his broad review of the diary-based literature in babbling. How could Jakobson have failed to notice the phonetic relations of late babbling and speech? One is tempted to say that it was because he only reviewed an easily misinterpretable literature from a premodern era and did not directly engage in research on infancy himself. However, there may have been more involved.

The error may have been based in part on the blinding nature of orthodoxy. Jakobson approached his reading of existing literature with preconceptions that led him to notice some observations and to ignore others. He noticed when infants were said to produce unexpected sounds that were interpreted for example as trills (presumably from raspberries) or velar sounds (presumably from gooing) in the work of Grégoire. However, when it came to reduplicated canonical babbling, the most salient of the speech-like sounds of infancy, his preconceptions led him to refuse to believe it was anything but speech: "At the transition from babbling to verbal behavior, the reduplication may serve as a compulsory process, signaling that the utterances do not represent a babble, but a senseful, semantic entity" (Jakobson, 1962/1971b, p. 215).

Thus he denied that reduplicated babbling could be anything other than speech. He knew that earlier utterances of infants were more distant from speech, as reflected in his occasional comments on precanonical sounds: "The stage of babbling (*babil enfantin*) begins with undetermined sounds which observers say are neither consonants nor vowels or, what amounts to the same, are both at once" (Jakobson, 1939/1971a, p. 79). However, this recognition did not deflect him from the central goal of maintaining for child speech a special status, a position among the lawful events of language, and by implication that status required the differentiation of speech from any prior vocal act. Jakobson sought general solutions to broad problems and his approach was appealing because it maintained, at least in most regards, a crisp internal consistency. In his mind that consistency seemed to require that babbling and speech be discontinuous, but as I see it, by assigning all babbled sounds to the categories of well-formed phonetic units, he broke his own mold and undid his consistency. By assigning babbled sounds to the categories of mature speech, he implied that the sounds of babbling constituted instances of speech-like sounds. It would have been more consistent with his own model if he had rejected phonetic characterization of babbling on the grounds that babbling and speech were discontinuous.

His ability to hold fast to positions in the face of perceived contradictions was legendary. My favorite story, told to me in both affection and amazement, is the one about his classroom encounter with a student who said, "Pardon me, Professor Jakobson, but my son did not, as your theory predicts use 'ba' as his first meaningful syllable. He said 'da' instead."

Jakobson did not hesitate. "Phonetically, 'da,'" he said in his Russian accent. "Phonemically, 'ba.'"

4

Infraphonology: Overview and Central Results

FUNDAMENTAL THEORETICAL CHANGES

To understand the vocalizations of the first year of life and to comprehend the sense in which they exhibit a systematic progression toward speech, it is necessary to take a new look at them. To replace the myths about infant babbling, a different theoretical perspective is required, incorporating a method that negates the temptation to categorize infant sounds by shoe-horning them into mature alphabetical segment types.

Infraphonology specifies the ways that well-formed elements of phonology are constructed; it also specifies properties in terms of which phonological systems can be elaborated. Infraphonology provides a basis for a new way to depict the progression of normal speech-like development, a new way to achieve insights about possible disorders of development, and new ways to approach comparative ethology of communication.

The groundwork for the change in descriptive approach was established in the comparison of late babbling and early meaningful speech, through the initial differentiation between canonical and precanonical protophones. That differentiation bore fruit by bringing into much sharper focus than had been previously possible the patterns of sound preference in babbling, patterns that conformed to preferences seen in universals of phonology and child speech. The differentiation allowed recognition of a fundamental continuity in development from infancy to early childhood.

Although the recognition of continuity between late, well-formed babbling and early meaningful speech was an important step, that recognition did not by itself make it possible to discern the relations between earlier sounds of infancy and speech. The precanonical protophones had simply been set aside in the initial studies addressing the Jakobsonian myths; the protophones were not evaluated or interpreted along with the canonical syllables in the initial efforts.

60

Resistance to transcription provided no explication of the nature of precanonical protophones; it merely precluded a false explication.

AN INITIAL SKETCH OF THE INFRAPHONOLOGICAL NOTION OF CANONICAL SYLLABLE

The fact that canonical and precanonical sounds were easily and reliably differentiated across various laboratory observers suggested that there must exist, in normal language users, a systematic basis for recognition of canonical syllables. Whether or not parents and other adults possess a precise vocabulary for describing speech-like sounds of infants, they have natural reactions to them that include an intuitive judgment about the degree to which any sound they hear approximates speech (Oller et al., 1996).

Adults notice that crying, belching, and hiccoughing are not much like speech in terms of sound quality, but that protophones such as gooing are more similar in sound quality to talking. How do they make such a judgment? The question deserves analysis and reflection.

Mature listeners notice that speech-like sounds are voiced in a particular way and that they have a particular vocal quality that contrasts sharply with the kind of voicing that occurs in other sounds such as screaming, moaning, crying, hiccoughing, or even laughter. Speech sounds usually possess a smooth, comfortable tone of vocal cord vibration. Voice scientists call it *normal phonation* or modal voice (Hollien, 1974).

Listeners notice that these smoothly voiced sounds are even more speech-like if, during some portion of the period of voicing, the mouth is open and postured in a way that can be easily differentiated from the normal at-rest position of the mouth. The smooth voicing with a postured mouth yields a vowel-like syllable nucleus. Further, the sound is more speech-like if the jaw, lips, or tongue move during the period of voicing, rather than if the mouth remains in a static position, either open or closed. Closure of the tract yields a consonant-like margin to contrast with an open vowel-like nucleus. Especially, observers note that if there is a quick movement of the jaw, an opening or closing of the mouth during a period of smooth voicing, the result can be distinctly syllabic, an effect that is due to the perceived rapid transition between the vowel-like nucleus and the consonant-like margin. All these properties of canonical syllables are well-documented in a broad literature on speech science that has been developing consistently in the past half-century, since the invention of the sound spectrograph (Koenig, Dunn, & Lacy, 1946).

If the rapid movement of the mouth that constitutes a transition from consonant to vowel is repeated cyclically while voicing, an impression of a sequence of syllables can be generated, with rising and falling sound levels corresponding to the openings and closings of the mouth. The high points of sound in these sequences are the centers of voicing, the nuclei or vowel-like sounds. The low points are the margins of voicing, the consonant-like sounds.

If the movements between the high points and low points are erratic and especially if they are drawn out in time so that the rhythm of movement seems irregular, the impression of speechiness is reduced. A relatively regular pattern of rises and falls with rapid transitions is most speech-like.

These are simple, nontechnical, unquantified observations, but they are consistent with the literature in speech science, and they constitute a systematic starting point in accounting for judgments that are made by uninstructed adults about the degree to which infant sounds resemble speech. The presence of smooth voicing, the opening and closing of the mouth, and the rhythmic movements of the mouth in accord with particular timing expectations clearly contribute to the judgment of speechiness.

All these intuitive features are quickly and easily understood by parents who bring their infants to participate in laboratory research on infant vocal development, even though parents rarely enter studies with any background in linguistics or speech science. Even so, they understand the notion of canonical syllables as soon as examples are given. The descriptions of vowel-like nuclei of primitive infant syllables and consonant-like margins are easy for them to grasp. Furthermore, parents make remarkably accurate judgments about whether or not their infants produce canonical syllables the first time the question is put to them along with a few examples of what the term canonical syllable means. Listeners do not have to learn what a canonical syllable is, because they already seem to know that intuitively; they merely need to know what to call such a syllable (Oller et al., 1996; Oller, Eilers, Neal, & Schwartz, 1998).

Here then, in simple nontechnical terms, is a definition of the notion of canonical syllable, a definition that conforms to the description of intuitive factors that influence judgments of speechiness:

> A canonical syllable is a vocal sound sequence consisting of a smoothly voiced nucleus or vowel-like sound, produced with the mouth open in any of a wide variety of possible postures, along with a quick movement of the mouth, either opening to the nucleus or closing from it.

The timing of the motion is critical (the transition must not seem long and drawn out) and the nucleus itself must be of brief, but not too brief duration (somewhere in the range of 0.1–0.5 seconds; Klatt, 1976; Lehiste, 1970). A series of such syllables, if well-formed, often shows a timing pattern that corresponds roughly to the timing patterns of other rhythmic repetitive actions such as toe tapping or hand clapping. Timing patterns of syllables also conform well to other human rhythmic patterns such as the common timing patterns of notes in traditional music. The features of the definition can be laid out in a number of ways, but it is convenient to consider a four-part breakdown of principles of canonical syllable formation (there are quite a number of other principles that, for simplicity's sake, are not considered here):

1. Normal phonation: smooth voicing.
2. Articulation: movement of the vocal tract during voicing.
3. Full resonance: opening and posturing of the tract during vowel-like sounds.
4. Rapid transitions: well-timed movements from closed to open postures.

WHAT DOES SUCH A SIMPLE DEFINITION OF THE CANONICAL SYLLABLE BUY US?

Even though this definition may seem simple (it represents only a fragment of the complete definition of well-formed syllables and even a smaller fragment of a general theory of infraphonology), its advantages are notable. Through this schematic characterization of principles of canonical syllables, a key to understanding the progression of infraphonological development in infant protophones is provided. There are four fairly obvious protophone stages that need to be accounted for, stages about which a stable international consensus is now in place (see Holmgren, Lindblom, Aurelius, Jalling, & Zetterstrom, 1986; Koopmans-van Beinum & van der Stelt, 1986; Oller, 1980a; Roug, Landberg, & Lundberg, 1989; Stark, 1980; Zlatin, 1975). All of the stages (outlined also in chap. 1) had been described extensively prior to the formulation of the definition of canonical syllables. The names given to the stages have been somewhat different in the writings of different authors, but the essential facts of development are clear and undisputed (see Table 4.1):

1. The Phonation stage (0–2 months).
2. The Primitive Articulation stage (1–4 months).
3. The Expansion stage (3–8 months).
4. The Canonical stage (5–10 months).

During the *Phonation stage,* babies produce many vegetative and crying sounds, but they also produce an abundance of brief vocalizations with the same kind of smooth voicing, or phonation, that occurs in most cases in the vowels of speech. We call these protophones *quasivowels,* and the brand of voicing they exemplify is called *normal phonation* (Hollien, 1974). The name *quasivowel* is intended to emphasize that the sounds of this stage lack full vocalic status, precisely because quasivowels are produced with the vocal tract at rest, which is to say, with the vocal tract in a relaxed breathing posture (Oller, 1980a, 1995). The tract can be closed or slightly open, but in quasivowels it does not include special posturing such as lip rounding or tongue fronting, the kind of posturing that characterizes typical vowels in natural languages. In the quasivowels of the Phonation stage, the baby produces brief well-phonated sounds with no special posturing. Other vocalizations of the same period are not characterized by normal phonation.

TABLE 4.1

Infraphonological Interpretation of Protophone Stages

Stage	Protophones Typical of Stage	Infraphonological Achievement
Phonation	Quasivowels	Normal phonation
Primitive Articulation	Gooing	Limited articulation
Expansion	Full vowels and marginal babbling	Full resonance, full articulation
Canonical	Canonical babbling	Well-timed articulation

In the *Primitive Articulation stage*, infants move their vocal tracts while they produce smooth voicing both during solitary bouts of vocalization and during face-to-face protoconversations with their caretakers (Anderson, Vietze, & Dokecki, 1977; Bakeman & Goltman, 1986; Crnic, Ragozin, Greenberg, Robinson, & Basham, 1983; Jasnow & Feldstein, 1986; Masataka, 1993; Stern, Jaffe, Beebe, & Bennett, 1975). These vocal movements often result in the dorsum or back of the tongue coming into contact with the back of the throat or palate, resulting in the protophone we call *gooing* (sometimes also called *cooing*). Face-to-face vocal turn-taking of this period often involves other vocal movements as well (the lips and tongue blade are not uncommonly involved in articulation during the Primitive Articulation period), but the back articulations are the most frequent and noticeable ones, and so give the characteristic protophones of the Primitive Articulation stage their name, gooing.

In the *Expansion stage*, a great deal of new activity occurs in protophone production. Many new sounds appear, representing explorations of various possibilities of vocal tract posturing to create differing timbres or vowel-like qualities as well as various possibilities of vocalization in the domains of pitch, amplitude, duration, and vocal quality (Robb & Saxman, 1990; Stark, 1980; Zlatin, 1975a, 1975b). Among the protophones noted routinely by observers of Expansion stage infants are vowel-like productions in which the infant opens the vocal tract fully or postures the lips or tongue in special ways while producing normal phonation. These articulated vowel-like sounds are called *full vowels* in protophone terminology and are said to have *full resonance*, a term intended to encompass a wide variety of timbres that vowels may have (Oller, 1995). Many vocal postures are explored by infants producing full vowels with normal phonation in the Expansion stage. In addition, infants toy with sounds produced with the vocal tract closed. In particular, they blow through their tightly held lips in protophones called *raspberries*. As the Expansion stage progresses, full vowels and closed sounds such as raspberries are combined in sequences of articulation that form primitive syllables that are usually ill timed if they are considered from the perspective of mature speech. The movement between closure and opening is too slow, yielding a protophone type we call *marginal babbling*. Figure 4.1 provides a spectrographic display of a marginal babble with a slow (> 200 msec)transition from an initial labial closure to a vowel-like sound. The slow transition is seen in the slow rise of the second formant from 2 kHz to 3.5 kHz.

In the *Canonical stage*, infants produce closure and opening sequences with normal phonation in well-timed, often repetitive patterns. The result is so speech-like it can scarcely be missed. In the most salient patterns of the stage infants produce reduplicated sequences, for example, [baba] or [dada], and these sequences include some of the universal syllable types found in mature languages and in early meaningful speech of children. When infants reach the canonical stage, they produce syllables that could be mistaken for speech. The utterance [dada], for example, as produced by a baby in the Canonical stage,

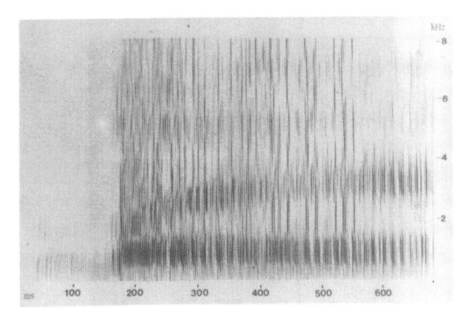

FIG. 4.1.   The spectrogram shows a marginal syllable produced by a 6-month-old infant. The initial consonant-like closure resembles [b] but is followed by a slow transition from the closure toward the vowel-like nucleus, seen in the long rise of the second formant from around 2 kHz to around 3.5 kHz. From "Pre-speech vocalizations of a deaf infant: A comparison with normal metaphonological development," by Oller, D. K., Eilers, R. E., Bull, D. H., & Carney, A. E., 1985, *Journal of Speech and Hearing Research, 28*, p. 60. Copyright 1985 by the American Speech-Language-Hearing Association. Reprinted with permission.

can count as the nursery word of that phonetic shape. Figure 4.2 provides a spectrographic display of a single canonical syllable [tat]. Note the rapid transitions of both first and second formants. The changes from a lingual closure to a vowel-like sound and then back to another lingual closure occur in less than 50 msec in each case.

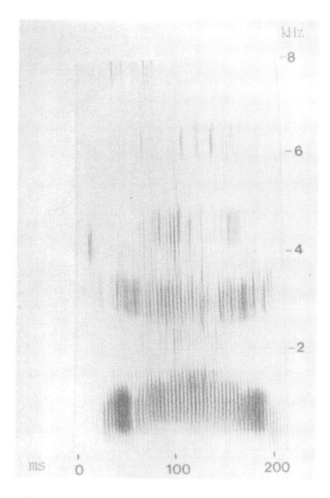

FIG. 4.2.   The spectrogram shows a canonical syllable, transcribed as [tat], produced by a 9-month-old infant. The initial and final consonant-like closures are associated with rapid transitions both at the beginning and at the end of the syllable. From "Pre-speech vocalizations of a deaf infant: A comparison with normal metaphonological development," by Oller, D. K., Eilers, R. E., Bull, D. H., & Carney, A. E., 1985, *Journal of Speech and Hearing Research, 28*, p. 52. Copyright 1985 by the American Speech-Language-Hearing Association. Reprinted with permission.

HOW INFRAPHONOLOGICAL INTERPRETATION
ELUCIDATES THE PROTOPHONE STAGES

There are at least two dimensions along which these four stages of infant vocal development need to be considered. One concerns the infant's emerging ability to use vocalizations in a variety of social and nonsocial circumstances at will—the topic of the usage of vocalizations at each stage is considered extensively in chapter 9. The other dimension, the one under consideration at the moment, concerns the infant's ability to produce sounds that resemble speech as sounds. The infraphonological definition of the canonical syllable makes that resemblance, and the progression toward it, interpretable and sensible.

Infraphonological achievements are designated in terms of principles or abstract characteristics of canonical syllables (the reader may wish to look back to Table 1.3). Quasivowels of the first stage manifest only one of these properties, normal phonation. In gooing, during the second stage, normal phonation is combined with another property, articulation, or movement of the vocal tract. In gooing, vocal tract movement is usually limited in extent, which is to say that the mouth is not moved very far from its rest position. Nonetheless the limited articulation of gooing demonstrates that infants in this stage are able to produce normal phonation and articulation simultaneously. In the third stage, the movements of the tract are made more extensive as the infant explores the range of possible articulatory postures, producing wide swings of vocal tract movement and concomitant full resonance patterns. In marginal babbling of the third stage, the infant incorporates the canonical features of normal phonation, full resonance, and fully articulated movements between full vowels and consonant-like margins in primitive syllables that are only one step away from being fully well-formed. In canonical babbling, during the fourth stage, the last feature is added to the package, as the infant produces fully articulated sequences with rapid transitions between closures and openings, yielding well-formed syllables.

The steps indicate how the simple principles of canonical syllables are systematically accumulated in the infant's repertoire of vocal productions with each stage. This progression could hardly be accidental. It shows the infant's abilities growing, differentiating, and elaborating in ways that are understandable in light of the infraphonological definition of the syllable.

In the context of the traditional transcriptional approach, we were encouraged to believe that protophones occurred at random (Mowrer, 1952; Osgood, 1953), that they were unformed and unorganized (Grégoire, 1948/1971), and that they were "purposeless, egocentric soliloquy," nothing but "tongue delirium" (Jakobson, 1941, p. 22). Such was the legacy of the alphabetic approach. The infraphonological perspective turns the apparent chaos to order and elucidates the progression of vocal development stages.

THE DISTINCTION BETWEEN VOCALIZATIONS
IN DEAF AND HEARING INFANTS IN LIGHT
OF THE INFRAPHONOLOGICAL MODEL

A primary strength of the infraphonological model is its ability to provide a stable and appropriate reference of comparison for speech-like sounds, regardless of their source, from infants, from disordered speakers, or from nonhumans. For some years prior to and during the period of development of the infraphonological model, data were being gathered on vocalizations of infants with hearing impairments. In light of the developing model, it became apparent that the traditional wisdom regarding similarities in babbling of deaf and hearing infants was of doubtful merit. That traditional view was expressed in the fourth myth noted in chapter 2, according to which deaf and hearing infants babble the same kinds of sounds, but deaf infants show a decrease in the amount of vocalization as they get older. The myth began to be challenged as soon as it was evaluated systematically in light of the protophone stage model. The very first profoundly deaf infant evaluated in the context of the protophone model (in 1972 at the University of Washington) showed several notable vocal anomalies. Most saliently, she did not begin the Canonical stage during the first year of life. No hearing child that had been evaluated longitudinally to that point within the research on protophone stages had failed to begin the Canonical stage during the first 10 months, so the deaf baby's delay in canonical babbling was conspicuous.

The delay in vocal development of the deaf infant might have been viewed as surprising because of the traditional wisdom asserting similarity of deaf and hearing infant babbling, but in fact that wisdom was itself on shaky ground, built on the observation of only two hearing impaired infants from Lenneberg et al.'s work (1965) and three hearing impaired infants from Mavilya's (1969) study. The small numbers of infants in these studies constituted only one basis for skepticism; even more fundamental concerns lay elsewhere. On the one hand, there was reason to be apprehensive about whether the infants from the prior work had actually been profoundly impaired. There had been major improvements in assessment techniques for infant hearing in the late 1960s and early 1970s (Jewitt, Romano, & Williston, 1970), techniques that were becoming clinically available in selected settings by the early 1970s. Before that time, testing of infant hearing was less reliable, and it seemed possible that some or all of Lenneberg's and Mavilya's study participants might have been less than profoundly impaired at birth, even though some of them were verified to be profoundly deaf later. Another possibility was that the particular infants studied were indeed profoundly impaired from birth but that they represented a particular subgroup of deaf infants, perhaps a group with substantial residual hearing and consequently high potential for speech development. These infants might have shown more rapid development of babbling than other deaf infants.

Mavilya's (1969) effort was stringently transcriptional, and it did not escape notice that such an approach would have rendered the primary differences between canonical and precanonical patterns of vocalization opaque. If all vocalizations were transcribed as if they were well-formed, there would have been no way to know when well-formedness came to be a part of an infant's repertoire. As far as one could tell from transcribed data, canonicity would seem to be present from the earliest sampling of sounds from every infant. Many of the example transcribed syllables at each age in Table 1.1, for example, appear to be canonical (including all those composed of at least one consonant and one vowel), even though infants at the first three ages would be unlikely to produce canonical syllables.

Lenneberg's (1967) discussion of the two deaf infants he studied engendered doubt for other reasons. He specifically rejected transcription of infant sounds in the first year of life, but he drew no distinction between the Expansion stage and the Canonical stage. The sounds of both were simply called babbling. The lack of a distinction between canonical babbling and the many precanonical sounds of the Expansion stage in his description suggested that if a difference between the deaf and hearing infants had occurred, it might have gone unnoticed.

It seemed possible that Mavilya (1969) and Lenneberg et al. (1965) missed the salient difference between canonical babbling and prior protophone types due to systematic limitations of their descriptive frameworks. Over the years that followed the observations of the first deaf infant in Washington, quite a number of deaf infants were evaluated in an effort to verify the nature of canonical babbling and its onset. Finding deaf infants was not an easy task. Even now it remains difficult to study vocal development in deaf infants because it remains difficult to identify them early in life given the low base rate of occurrence of congenital profound deafness. Referrals from collaborators engaged in screening for hearing impairment in newborns and high-risk nurseries provided access to several deaf infants. Other referrals came to a program my colleagues and I developed at the University of Miami to provide early intervention for infants and young children with hearing impairment (Oller & Eilers, 1988; Vergara, Miskiel, Oller, & Eilers, 1995). Additional referrals were made by community professionals who became aware of the research effort. In this context we gradually accumulated data at the University of Washington and the University of Miami on many deaf infants.

Results from longitudinal studies of hearing infants were compared with the outcomes for deaf infants through those years, a process that continues. The summarial outcome has been published in a sequence of studies, beginning with oral presentations (Oller, 1976, 1980b) and culminating in a series of journal articles (Eilers & Oller, 1994; Oller et al., 1985; Oller & Eilers, 1988). The results are clear-cut as seen in Fig. 4.3, where onset of canonical babbling in 100 hearing infants who have been studied longitudinally is contrasted with onsets for 37 longitudinally studied congenitally hearing-impaired infants (severe or profound).

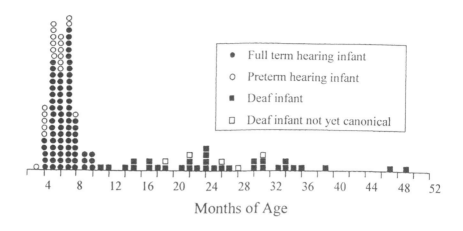

FIG. 4.3.   Onset of canonical babbling in severely to profoundly hearing-impaired infants and in hearing infants. Data on preterm infants are shown at corrected ages. From "Infant Vocalizations and the Early Diagnosis of Severe Hearing Impairment," by R. E. Eilers and D. K. Oller, 1994, *Journal of Pediatrics, 124*, p. 201. Copyright 1994 by Mosby Year Book, Inc. Reprinted with permission.

There is no overlap in the onsets for the two groups as depicted in the figure. All the hearing infants began the Canonical stage by 10 months of age, and no deaf infant began the stage that early. These results represent the largest existing body of data on babbling in deaf and hearing infants. A number of other laboratories have also reported delays in babbling of deaf infants in the context of descriptions that draw a distinction between canonical and precanonical sounds (Kent et al., 1987; Koopmans-van Beinum, Clement, & van den Dikkenberg-Pot, 1998; Murai, 1961; Stoel-Gammon & Otomo, 1986; Vinter, 1994a, 1994b).

The traditional characterization based on Lenneberg's work was misleading in suggesting that deaf and hearing infants produce the same kinds of sounds in the first year. The most notable event, the onset of canonical babbling, is so different in deaf and hearing infants that the distributions of onsets between the two groups are virtually disjunct.[1] The difference is so great and so easy to identify in the context of infraphonological description that there is reason to con-

---

[1]It is necessary to hedge because the disjunction is not perfect. Recent work indicates that onset of canonical babbling occasionally occurs in the normal range (prior to 11 months of age) for deaf infants with usable residual hearing (Koopmans-van Beinum, Clement, & Van den Dikkenberg-Pot, 1998; Oller & Eilers, 1998). The infants in the studies by Mavilya (1969) and Lenneberg et al. (1965) may also have shown normal onset of canonical babbling. It should also be noted that infants with normal hearing occasionally begin canonical babbling late (Oller & Eilers, 1998; Stark, Ansel, & Bond, 1998; Stoel-Gamon, 1989).

sider utilization of vocal development measures as a screening tool for profound hearing impairment in infancy, a possibility that is now being pursued vigorously (Eilers & Oller, 1994; Oller, 1991; see also chap. 8).

THE PROCEDURAL BREAK WITH THE PAST IMPLIED BY THE RECOGNITION OF THE CANONICAL STAGE

The modern view of infant vocalizations has a very different flavor from that of earlier eras due in part to the infraphonological style of interpretation that is increasingly taking hold since the 1970s. It is noteworthy that a distinction between a Canonical stage and prior stages is uniformly recognized by students of vocal development now, whereas it was essentially unrecognized in the primary work of infant vocal development before the modern era. Distinctions among earlier stages (Expansion, Primitive Articulation, and Phonation) are also important, but the Canonical stage proves to have extraordinary saliency and has played a major role in most recent research in infant vocal development. Consequently, it is instructive to consider the reasons that the Canonical stage was not posited in treatments of infant vocalizations prior to the modern era.

Jakobson's theory assumed that all infant sounds could be transcribed alphabetically; this approach tends to make canonical and precanonical sounds seem virtually identical. Lenneberg, even though rejecting transcription as a tool, did not address the differences between canonical and precanonical sounds, drawing a distinction only between cooing (which appears to be appropriately read as gooing in the terminology of this volume) and babbling (which was apparently meant to include canonical syllables as well as raspberries, isolated full vowels, marginal babbles, and other Expansion stage protophones).

The lack of a distinction between Canonical and Expansion stages can be traced back further than the writings of Lenneberg or Jakobson. Lewis (1936) provided the most comprehensive summary of infant vocal research in the 19th and early 20th centuries. Although his summary indicated that both he and prior authors had shown a commitment to transcriptional description, his formulation of stages in vocal development included no canonical stage and no Expansion stage. The summary based on prior research was much more oriented toward concerns of usage and social function than issues of sound content. His summary included three stages for the first year. The first stage, designated as occurring in the first 3 to 4 months of life, collapsed the Phonation stage and the Primitive Articulation stage, and focused primarily on the face-to-face interactions that occur during the latter. Lewis (1936) emphasized that during this period "the child responds to human utterance by making sounds" (p. 71). His second stage (through 9 months of age) encompassed the Expansion period and canonical babbling. He contended that a period of "pause" after the pattern of social responsiveness seen in babies in the

first stage occurs at the beginning of the second stage: "At the outset of the period there seems to be a diminution, if not an entire cessation, of the vocal responses to speech typical of the first stage; then vocal responses gradually
reappear" (pp. 71–72). The third stage, like the others, was not characterized
in Lewis' writings by acoustic features of vocalizations, but by patterns of social interaction: "The child's behavior becomes more definitely marked by
those features which are to characterize imitation during infancy and childhood" (p. 72).

Lewis' (1936) stage model thus posited that babies show three sequential
characteristics, all of which concerned vocal interaction, rather than characteristics of vocalizations themselves. The stages might be designated as follows: (a) the vocally responsive stage, (b) the vocally unresponsive stage, and
(c) the vocal imitation stage.

The model was based on an overview of the history to that point of significant U.S. and European research on babbling. The book includes phonetically based operational-level descriptions of sounds occurring at every stage,
descriptions drawn from the many available works; yet the stage model of
Lewis (1936) takes virtually no notice of sound pattern growth in infancy.
Given how conspicuous protophone stages seem in current investigations,
Lewis' failure to mention growth in sound-making capabilities is striking.

It seems likely that protophone stages were invisible to Lewis and many
prior investigators because they had chosen to view infant sounds through the
restrictive lenses of phonetic transcription. One can find illustrations of
Lewis' (1936) commitment to the transcriptional approach on almost any
page of his book. For example, he spent considerable effort describing a
"voiced velar fricative" produced by infants (presumably in gooing), arguing
that it may have had vegetative origins associated with feeding.

> If we are willing to accept the principle that there is an innate tendency in the
> child to utter a [sound] expressive of his state of satisfaction, then the facts we
> have mentioned help to show why the [sound] should take on the form of this
> specific back consonant g [Lewis' font includes a horizontal slash; the symbol ap-
> parently corresponds with gamma [ɣ] in the current IPA]. It is the vocal manifes-
> tation of the fact that the child is making guttural movements expressive of
> satiety while uttering a [sound] of satisfaction. As for the sounds x, k, g, and the
> uvular r, these are all either voiced or unvoiced variations of g [with slash], and
> have the same expressive origin." (p. 32)

The passage emphasizes both the inclination to characterize infant sounds
as well-formed, mature, operational-level phonetic units, and the simultaneous commitment to interpret the occurrence of those sounds as artifacts of
bodily need or as mechanistic responses to external events. He referred to

> Front consonants expressive of discomfort. ... There can be little doubt that the
> origin of the nasals m, n, is that they are expressive of hunger; that is, they are the

audible manifestation of the mouth movements which are bound up with that state. ...

We have found that the origin of the earlier back consonants and of the later front consonants lies almost entirely in the expression of hunger and of its satisfaction ... it is inevitable that any utterance made by the child in connection with feeding should become shaped by the movements of feeding." (pp. 35–36)

The mechanistic focus in Lewis' portrayal may help explain why sound development played such a small role in his writing, and also offers a background against which to contrast the infrastructural view of sound usage that is invoked in this volume (chap. 9 ff.). In this portrayal and that of many other current authors, the usage of sounds by human infants is seen as active and creative (see e.g., Locke, 1993; Masataka, 1993; Papoušek & Papoušek, 1984; Papoušek, 1994; Vihman, 1996). This tendency is currently seen to manifest a deep motivation in infants to develop sound-making capabilities and to constitute an indication of a species-specific interest and capability of humans.

Even in the context of his discussions of vocal patterns that correspond to the Expansion stage, where infants clearly explore dimensions of sound as sound (see chap. 5), Lewis (1936) emphasized that there must have existed some pleasure for the child, not in the act of learning to command new sound types, but in simply hearing particular sounds that he posed had come to be associated with pleasurable states through conditioning. Play, Lewis contended, was performed for the sake of pleasure that is generated when an action previously associated with a pleasurable condition is reinstated. A similar contention was also made with regard to vocal actions of the infant: "It is certainly also true of his babbling, even though it may be difficult to determine objectively at which point in his development he begins to make sounds for the sake of the pleasure they bring" (p. 63).

Modern researchers also take note of the fact that vocalizations in the Expansion stage can be produced playfully. The fact that they are is one of the indicators of the intentionality of their production (see chaps. 5 and 12). The difference between the current view and Lewis' (1936) centers around his strong emphasis on the infant's presumed pleasure in hearing sounds deemed to yield pleasurable sensation exclusively by virtue of their association with prior experiences of satiety or other bodily pleasures. He assumed that when babies vocalize, the motivation must fall into one of three categories.

We have shown ... that some order and regularity may be found in what has often been regarded as the chance and chaotic occurrence of the child's earliest sounds. We have shown that they fall into groups which may be explained by referring to three generally accepted factors—the principle of Darwinian expression [of needs], the differentiation of affective states, and the occurrence of behaviour anticipatory of a sequence of events. (pp. 36–37)

Even imitation, which was viewed as important in Lewis' (1936) model, was addressed primarily in terms of its manifestation of responsiveness to social reinforcement, not as an indication that the infant might have had an internal motivation to produce sounds that might resemble speech or that might merely resemble the sounds of other people. Lewis' conception of the motivations for infant vocalizations was thus too limiting. Some sounds were viewed as reflexive or expressive of needs and some as pleasurable by association; in each case the interpretation was mechanistic.

A more modern approach, in contrast, although accepting that mechanistic learning does occur under some circumstances, also takes notice of evidence that infants systematically pursue (whether consciously or unconsciously) the development of sounds that resemble speech. It appears that nature has provided infants with the inclination to engage in vocal actions that systematically manifest the emerging capacity for speech. A more modern interpretation allows and even encourages the search for patterns of vocal action that may represent more than "purposeless tongue delirium," and more than mechanistic response to conditioning (see, e.g., Menn, 1976; Oyama, 1993). Instead, the patterns of vocalization may reveal goals to produce sounds that infants may find interesting in and of themselves, independent (at least some of the time) of conditions of reinforcement or prior associative learning. Further, the patterns suggest infants systematically attempt to gain control over new sound types.

The fact that Lewis and his predecessors, as well the writers interested in infant vocalizations from the middle of this century, accepted phonetic transcription for infant sounds without question is consistent with the exclusively mechanistic mentality, the set of assumptions that led many to believe that infants have no independent motivations and no mastery goals in vocalization. The historically traditional transcriptional approach carried within it the assumption that all the sounds of infants are well-formed. Infants could be assumed to have no vocal development goals simply because the pinnacle of such development, speech-like vocalization, was taken by fiat of methodology to be available from the very beginning of life. In the realm of sound, the methodological filter of transcription presented the illusion that there was nothing of significance to be developed in the speech-like sounds of babies.

In the context of this history of limitation in framework of thinking, perhaps it should not be surprising that scholars failed to recognize the importance of the onset of canonical babbling. It was assumed that infants possessed no systematic intentions to acquire skills, a view that appears to have been encouraged during the early part of this century by the popularity of mechanistic behaviorism, but the view was also supported by shoe-horning categorization. Infant sounds were assumed to fit the categories of adult sounds, and thus lost both the potential to reveal their developmental progression and the potential to reveal active infant involvement in acquisition of vocal skills.

5

Keys to an Infrastructural Approach: Infraphonology as a Basis for Vocal Comparisons

DEVELOPMENT OF SCIENTIFIC INFRASTRUCTURES AND INFRAPHONOLOGY

In some cases science functions first as a descriptive taxonomic effort, and only later moves toward systematic attempts at modeling underlying systems. Yet even when taxonomy appears to come as the first step in science, assumptions have to be made about what the relevant categories of description will be, and these assumptions inevitably imply models and impose limits on the characterizations of realities that could be consistent with the descriptions (Gould, 1989).

The question is not, then, whether or not scientific description implies modeling, but rather what kind of modeling is implied. A primary focus of this work is the contrast between superficial modeling based on operational-level units (the categories of functional significance to human participants in day-to-day activities within any domain) and infrastructural modeling based on underlying realities (properties, principles, and processes that characterize the domain at a deep level). Chapter 1 introduced the notion that the study of infant vocal development has been hampered by a superficial, operational-level focus in description, and provided an example of scientific limitation in another field (chemistry) where operational-level focus once held sway and hampered understanding.

Consider another example. In human anatomy mature operational-level units include organs and other bodily structures—eyes, ears, hands, stomachs, livers, and so on. The primitive structures of developmental human anatomy include clear representatives of the mature operational-level units at some point in development, but if the process is considered from its beginning, no such structures can be found. The blastula resembles a hollow ball, but its center is not a stomach, a brain cavity, nor a mouth, but a precursor to a wide variety of mature, operational-level anatomical structures. The germ cells are an even earlier source of anatomical development, yet they have no eyes, ears, or stomachs—no mature, operational-level categories.

Still, there existed a temptation in the early years of the study of embryology to shoe-horn the structures of early development into precisely the mature operational-level categories of human anatomy. In the preformationist tradition (Bonnet, 1762), a miniature homunculus was presumed to be present in the germ cells, fully formed with eyes, ears, fingers, and toes. We know now that such a claim is fanciful and misleading, but it was defended vigorously even in the face of clear empirical evidence to the contrary in the 18th century. Bonnet argued that even if the eyes and ears were not visible under magnification in the early embryo, they must be present in a latent, if invisible form.

By now description of embryological events in terms of mature operational-level anatomical structures has been replaced with an infrastructural model of genetics, molecular biology, and macroscopic embryology. The new model is capable of providing deep insights into the nature of development and significant predictions regarding sequences of events, mechanisms of change, and abnormalities. The new model requires accepting the existence of units at various levels (germ cells, subcellular structures, proteins, enzymes, amino acids, etc.) that underlie the mature operational-level units and processes that pertain to the function of the underlying units (fertilization, meiosis, cell migration, replication, translation, uptake, etc.). Having accepted the elements of the infrastructural level of description that is required in modern embryology, numerous insights are made available.

It is my contention that describing the vocal actions of infants in the first months of life in terms of the mature, operational-level units of linguistic phonologies (segments, syllables, etc.) is no less misleading, and no less damaging to the development of genuine understanding of vocal development than was the homunculus to embryology. In proposing an infraphonological approach to the study of vocal development, we find new potentials almost immediately in explicating stages of vocal elaboration and in recognizing the nature of vocal abnormalities. This should be no surprise. The approach is infrastructural by design, and if the design is well chosen, it should be expected to yield benefits no less notable than those that have been found in other realms of understanding.

ANALOGIES AMONG INFRASTRUCTURAL SYSTEMS IN THE SCIENCES

Table 5.1 summarizes four examples of infrastructural models. In chemistry, the theoretical model that guides interpretation of physical reactions is, of course, infrastructural. Reactions in which particular substances combine to form new ones are not explained merely in terms of perceived substances, such as water, sand, stone, and so on, although these are among the categories to which we relate in everyday life; they are the operational-level units of common experience with substances and entities. Instead, the chemist's interpretation is based on a model that appeals to more fundamental elements of nature (atoms and molecules) and fundamental principles of chemical interaction. Of course, interactions producing new form, color, and elasticity of substances, indeed interactions that produce what appear to be brand new operational-level substances, are predictable based on infrastructural principles of chemistry. Yet in the absence of the formulation of basic elements and principles, the nature of the changes in chemical interaction would seem capricious. Notice that the infrastructural model does not ignore operational-level units; it accounts for them by taking into consideration underlying properties and principles of function by which changes occur. The chemical model thus makes it possible to understand the deep nature of substances and the forms they take in a variety of circumstances.

In essence, an infrastructural system for chemistry provides a deeper view of the set of chemical phenomena than can be achieved through an approach based on operational-level description alone. In accounting for biological development, infrastructural models are no less useful than in chemistry. Taking as an object of study the botanical phenomenon of flowering, one

TABLE 5.1
Comparisons Among Infrastructural Systems

Scientific Field	Operational-Level (Mature) Units	Infrastructural System	Physical Parameters
Chemistry	Earth, air, fire, water, ice, stone, …	Atomic physics, thermodynamics	Mass, form, viscosity, elasticity, color, number, …
Botany, flowering	Sepals, petals, stamens, pistils, …	Embryology of flowering plants, genetics	Mass, form, …
Developmental human anatomy	Head, eyes, limbs, digits, stomach, heart, lung, …	Human embryology, genetics	Mass, form, …
Human vocalization development	[ba], [du], [am], [i], [kuga], [daloma], …	Infraphonology	Amplitude, duration, F0, resonance, jaw opening, tongue raising, …

might choose to begin with an operational-level description focused on, for example, sepals, petals, stamens, pistils, and pollens, and one might describe these in terms of physical parameters such as numbers, colors, weights, and geometries of each. In considering development of the flower, there is difficulty in describing the embryological forms of flowers in terms of operational-level categories of mature forms. It would be foolish to try to describe the stem from which a flower will eventually emerge in terms of how many petals it has, what their colors might be, or the length of the stamen. The prebud stem does not possess the operational-level categories, and so no modern biologist would attempt to describe it in those terms.

Similarly, the seed is a flower precursor that clearly has neither petals nor sepals. To describe the seed appropriately, it is necessary to seek categories of characterization that fit structures of the seed specifically, along with structures of succeeding forms of the plant after germination, and to seek explanations of the relation among stages of development in infrastructural domains of genetics and botanical embryology. Within the infrastructural models, precursors to the operational mature units of the flower may be richly explicated; further predictions regarding stage ordering, ranges of variation in development (and across related species and subspecies of plants), and abnormalities may be formulated.

The revealing history of research in human developmental anatomy has already been noted. The same considerations apply as in the case of flower development. It can be confounding to describe precursors of mature operational-level categories by directly forcing primitive embryological structures into mature categories, but early developmental anatomists made precisely that mistake, homunculizing the germ cells and refusing to believe their own eyes when presented with microscopic images of embryological structures that did not fit the preconceptions.

The time of homunculization is long past in the realm of developmental anatomy, replaced by infrastructural approaches that allow description of embryos in terms of their own structures, precursors to mature ones. The highly developed nature of embryology as a science may not be matched in any realm of behavioral science. In psychology, for example, the difficulty of gaining acceptance for infrastructural approaches runs deep and possesses many facets. Early in the 20th century, the idea of infrastructural modeling was directly eschewed by a generation that adopted a radical empiricism in which the existence of "mind" was denied. In accord with the radical approach, the causes of behavior were sought in externally observable events only, and description was consequently focused at only the most superficial levels (see, e.g., Skinner, 1957). Operational-level description in this context was not only the norm of function; it was the explicit dogma of inquiry.

It is ironic that even after widespread rejection of radical empiricism as a model, operational-level description of behavioral development persisted. In the ontogeny of human vocalizations, the temptation to use mature operational-level categories of language in description was intense (even after the mind had been reinstated in the model of behavior), and investigators often gave descriptions for the embryological form of vocal action that were no less misleading than descriptions of seeds in terms of the operational-level units of flowers, or of blastulae in terms of homunculi.

My suspicion is that behavior, elusive as it is, not consisting of objects that can be weighed in and assayed, but coming and going in time's ever-changing panorama, provides a target that is particularly hard to sight and peculiarly difficult to pin down, so that observers are often left with limited resources to recognize its deeper forms. Animal behavior has chaotic properties in all its manifestations, and whatever its regions of regularity, these are invariably surrounded by swirling currents of noise and turbulence. The very complexity of the phenomena of behavior may weaken and confuse those who attempt to tie down perceptions, and may encourage description at the most easily accessible functional level of understanding. For speech or speech-like sounds, the mature operational-level description may be seductive, precisely because it represents the point of access with least resistance. This volume is exploring a modeling path where resistance may initially be high, because the terrain seems unfamiliar and the direction seems uphill. It would appear, however, that the higher vantage point afforded by infrastructural modeling has benefits that merit the climb.

HOW THE INFRAPHONOLOGICAL INTERPRETATION OF PROTOPHONES CAME ABOUT

The study of infant vocalizations began with descriptions based on operational-level units of the mature linguistic system of diary-writing taxonomists. The more recent taxonomic decision to treat infant sounds in terms of a system separate from the mature one (although potentially related to it), a system with its own protophonic categories, had profound consequences. At the same time, the consequences were complex, and a model to organize and explain the resulting taxonomic data did not arise instantaneously.

Exclusion of precanonical vocalizations from analysis at first was convenient because no model to interpret them existed, yet they sounded somewhat like speech, and they sounded progressively more like speech from the first month through the beginning of canonical babbling. The pattern seemed to call for a new model of interpretation to clarify the impression of progressive growth.

Furthermore, the very existence of protophones called for explanation. It was clear that they did not have vegetative function, and unlike fixed signals such as crying, they did not show fixed communicative values. In fact it was not clear how to understand their existence except in their apparent relation with speech. It was uncertain why they should exist, unless as vehicles for the development of the speech capacity, or at least as manifestations of an emerging capability for speech.

To provide a standard against which to judge each protophone event in terms of general characteristics of resemblance to speech, we began by compiling observations about the nature of well-formed syllables in natural languages and formulating a definition for the notion of the canonical syllable in terms of independent acoustic and articulatory parameters, a definition that would ultimately include (among others) the four principles of canonical syllable formation discussed in chapter 4.

WHY THE INITIAL INFRAPHONOLOGICAL INTERPRETATIONS OF INFANT SOUNDS WERE FOCUSED ON SYLLABLES

For a vocal and auditory communication system to function well it must have some temporal constraints on transmission units. Such constraints necessarily impose a rhythmic structure that makes it possible for speakers to produce sounds efficiently, and for hearers to listen efficiently. Without some sort of systematic rhythmic structure a listener would have no basis for adjusting windows of observation, and consequently, perception would be cumbersome and error-prone. Rhythmic structures can be analyzed naturally by reference to their minimal rhythmic units. If there are to be temporal variations, these can be specified with regard to the minimal units. For speech systems, such a minimal rhythmic unit is found in the syllable.

Initially the development of the infraphonological model focused on the syllable rather than on higher order rhythmic units such as the phonological foot, the phonological phrase, or some even higher order unit of rhythm. The initial focus was based on the fact that syllables are the minimal units of performance in spoken language, universally. Feet and phrases, and even higher order phonological discourse units, are composed of syllables. Further, phonemic-level segments and the phonological features in terms of which phonemes are constituted are presented in full syllables. For infants to begin to speak, they must be able to produce syllables, although the same requirement does not apply to higher order units. Control of higher levels of phonological units depends logically on the command of minimal units.

The fundamental nature of the syllable as the basic unit of rhythm suggests that infants might learn to produce well-formed syllables before ever producing phrases composed of more immature syllables. However, recent empirical work has revealed that infants have the capability to produce higher order units of discourse, composed of multiple, primitive, syllable-like chunks of utterance organized in clusters and phrases, from very early in life, long before well-formed syllables are under control. By the second month, there is clear evidence of phrasing (Lynch, Oller, Steffens, & Buder, 1995; Nathani, 1998; Oller & Lynch, 1992). Therefore, to say that there is a logical presupposition of syllable control in any child having control over higher order phrases does not mean that syllable control must be fully mastered before higher order units can appear. Primitive syllables can be used in phrases before well-formed syllables have been mastered.

The focus on the syllable rather than the segment in the early work on infraphonology is paralleled by trends in phonology in general over the past two decades. The heavy focus on segmental phonology in prior eras has given way to autosegmental or nonlinear approaches to phonology (Goldsmith, 1976; Liberman & Prince, 1977) where higher order rhythmic units play much more significant roles. The syllable is particularly prominent as a focus of analysis in phonology, including child phonology (Bernhardt, 1992; Stemberger, 1988).

PHYSICAL PARAMETERS, OPERATIONAL-LEVEL UNITS, AND INFRASTRUCTURAL MEDIATION

Infrastructural models specify the relation between physical parameters and operational-level units, and in so doing offer a characterization of the physical organizational principles that yield the entities to which we relate operationally. The physical parameters in the case of speech can be either acoustic or articulatory, but in either case they represent dimensions of potential description that are logically independent of speech. In acoustic descriptions, it is possible to account for durations, amplitudes, frequencies, and spectral properties of sounds. In articulatory descriptions, the factors that can be invoked are position, direction, and rate of movement for various structures of the mouth (jaw, tongue, lips, etc.) and other actions of the respiratory musculature and larynx. Neither acoustic nor articulatory descriptions are intrinsically associated with speech, because sounds can be nonspeech, and the vocal apparatus can produce nonspeech actions. A primary goal of infraphonology is to relate the relevant independent physical parameters to the realm of operational speech sounds, the contrastive elements of phonological systems (Fig. 5.1).

Infraphonology specifies the limits of the indefinitely large class of contrastive phonetic units that can occur in natural languages in terms of physical parameters. Speech syllables, for example, such as [ba], [stɬ], [Uˊ], and [ɓo], are all specified by infraphonological definition, and other kinds of sounds not occurring in speech are explicitly excluded. All the sounds included in the IPA must be specified (at least by implication) in infraphonology along with indications regarding relative prototypicality or markedness of each.

Infraphonology is not of course limited to syllables. Ultimately it must specify the contrastive sounds of languages at each of the tiers of human phonological function: phonological features, segments, syllables, feet, phrases, and even higher order rhythmic units. Figure 5.2 presents a fragmentary dia-

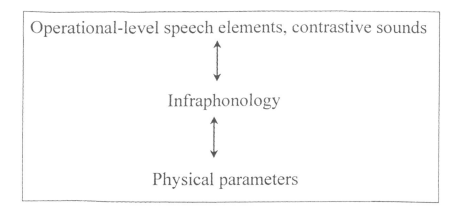

FIG. 5.1.   Infrastructural systems mediate between physical and operational levels.

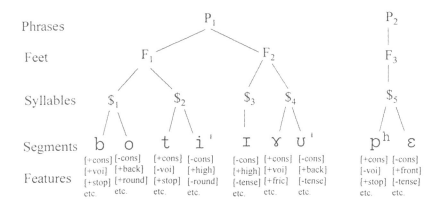

FIG. 5.2.   Operational-level phonological units are organized in tiers.

gram exemplifying the layering of operational-level units in human phonologies. The utterance portrayed consists of a series of potential syllables, all canonical, that might occur in some natural language.

In infrastructural terminology, the term *levels* is used to differentiate the operational level of function from the infraphonological level and the physical level. In speaking of phonology, the terms *segmental tier*, a *featural tier*, and so on, are used (Goldsmith, 1976). This segregation of terminology is intended to limit confusion regarding different sorts of layering.

The infraphonological approach to the study of speech or speech-like systems provides a reference against which sounds can be judged in terms of their relation with speech, without requiring that sounds be forced into mature operational-level categories to which they do not pertain. A key reference point for comparison consists of the infraphonological elements of definition that specify limits on well-formed units of speech. The reference does not represent an arbitrarily chosen replacement for operational-level categories. It is a logically necessary one, because it consists of elements that govern speech units and determine their form.

In the infrastructural description of the sounds of another creature or sounds of an immature human, we begin with operational-level descriptions of the sounds within their own system. In describing vocalizations of another primate, for example, we might refer to particular sounds as pant-hoots, contact calls, and so on, referring to sound qualities or functions, but always doing so in terms that seek to characterize the animal system on its own terms. Similarly, in describing human infant sounds, we attempt to treat them as an ethologist should, looking for the functional operational units of the infant system. In the early months of life, these include cries, laughter, vegetative sounds, and a variety of protophones, all of which are describable without reference to external systems such as speech.

The operational-level units of prespeech or nonspeech vocal systems have their own infrastructures, and ultimately it is useful to specify those infrastructures in the comparative enterprise. In evaluating nonspeech or prespeech sounds in relation to mature human phonological systems, the most enlightening point of comparison is at the infrastructural level. Attempts to relate systems at the operational level should usually be avoided because across systems, operational-level units are not of analogous dimensions, and cross-categorization can only be conducted at that level by shoe-horning. Consequently, Fig. 5.3 has no arrow between operational levels of mature human speech and infant protophones. Instead, both operational levels relate (as indicated by arrows) to infraphonology.

Comparisons can also fruitfully be made directly between infrastructural levels for human or nonhuman systems of communication as suggested in chapter 1. It would not be appropriate to revert to direct operational-level comparisons of widely different communication systems any more than it would be appropriate to revert to homunculus-based descriptions after the development of genetic and embryological models.

What exactly would be compared across communication systems at the level of infrastructure? There appear to exist at least two general kinds of possibilities that are suggested by the distinction between properties and principles (chap. 1). First, systems can be compared in terms of the extent to which they incorporate the elements of the infrastructural properties hierarchy in

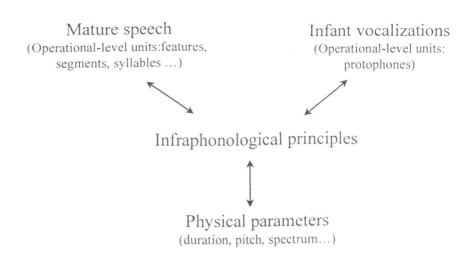

FIG. 5.3.   In the infraphonological framework standards of reference change.

terms of which communication systems appear to evolve (see chap. 12). For
example, one communication system might include the property of
Arbitrarity whereas another might not. On the other hand, the two might
both command the property of Recombinability. Second, systems can be
compared in terms of the extent to which or the ways in which each property is
implemented in terms of a set of principles. For example, two communication
systems might both command the Syllabification property, but might differ
in the nature of principles of implementation for it. One might include a principle requiring that canonical syllables include rapid spectral changes (as in
human speech), whereas another might require that syllables include rapid
shifts in a fixed whistle or narrow band of noise. Two systems might both
command a primitive property of Signal Dimensionality, but might differ in
how the dimensions are defined. Chapter 12 provides examples of the first
kind of comparison with examples drawn from human and nonhuman primates and chapter 14 offers a preliminary view of the second kind, again with
examples drawn from human and nonhuman primates.

WHY A PURELY PHYSICAL PARAMETER-BASED
APPROACH DOES NOT REPRESENT A SOLUTION
TO THE INTERPRETATION OF BABBLING SOUNDS
OR VOCALIZATIONS OF NONHUMANS

Before providing a fuller account of aspects of infraphonological theory that are
useful in interpreting infant vocalizations, it is important to specify that one of-

ten proposed option to supplant transcription of infant sounds or vocalizations of nonhumans will not, by itself, provide a solution to the problems posed by shoe-horning. When instrumental acoustic analysis became a central method in speech science after World War II, the possibility was raised that spectrography might soon generally replace auditorily based analysis of speech.

There is no denying that spectrographic analysis played a critical role in the growth of new understandings of the physical nature of speech (Koenig et al., 1946; Peterson & Barney, 1952; Potter, 1945; Stevens & House, 1961). But instrumental analysis of speech sounds tends to lead up a blind alley when applied in isolation from a perspective on the phonetic and phonemic content of speech. Similarly, instrumental analysis of nonhuman vocalizations tends to proceed without direction when applied in isolation from a perspective on the infrastructural requirements of the nonhuman vocal systems. Spectrograms provide quantifiable, visible information about physical parameters of sound—durations, intensities, pitches, resonance peaks—but quantified information on physical parameters cannot by itself specify an interpretation; nor can spectrographic analysis, by itself, provide a clear basis for determining the extent to which sounds of infants or of another species resemble speech.

To illustrate, suppose an early protophone vocalization (specifically, a brief sequence of two quasivowels) is analyzed spectrographically to produce a display as in Fig. 5.4. Suppose the goal is to specify ways in which the sound resembles speech and ways in which it does not. Finally, suppose the spectrogram is measured to produce a table of quantified values representing characteristics of the utterance as sound. In the absence of any theory of the nature of speech to guide the tabulation, the values might appear as in Table 5.2.

The results provide quantification, but they supply no obvious answer about the extent to which the baby vocalization resembles speech. The duration of the utterance is specified, but to make sense of that duration, it is important to know what durations are acceptable or perhaps common in speech. The matter is not simple, because speech includes a wide variety of possible durations for sounds and noises of various sorts. It is not sensible to ask merely what durations are possible. Rather, it is necessary to ask what dura-

TABLE 5.2

Approximate Physical Parameter Values for the Utterance Represented in Fig. 5.4.

Duration	*Total = 670 msec*
Fundamental Frequency	Average = 360 Hz, Peak = 485 Hz
Amplitude	Average = 70 dB, Peak = 100 dB
Resonance peak	Maximum = 750 Hz, Bandwidth = 450 Hz

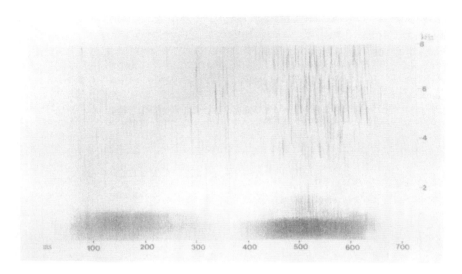

FIG. 5.4.   The spectrogram shows a two-syllable sequence of quasivowels produced by a 6-month-old infant. The two syllables show a compact resonance pattern characteristic of quasivowels with the great majority of energy concentrated below 1kHz. The interpretation of the spectrographic display is dependent upon an infraphonological theory (see text). From "Pre-speech vocalizations of a deaf infant: A comparison with normal metaphonological development," by Oller, D. K., Eilers, R. E., Bull, D. H., & Carney, A. E., 1985, Journal of Speech and Hearing Research, 28, p. 53. Copyright 1985 by the American Speech-Language-Hearing Association. Reprinted with permission.

tions are possible for each of a number of possible speech event types. Therefore, to interpret the duration of the baby sound, it would seem we need first to categorize that sound as one of a number of possible speech event types. The purely acoustic information provided by the duration of the utterance does not indicate the extent of the utterance's resemblance to speech. An infraphonological theory of the nature of possible speech sounds is necessary to render the duration interpretable. It would, for example, provide a basis to notice that a duration of 670 msec is beyond the normal range for canonical syllables (upper limit of about 500 msec). The theory would further suggest that it would be wise to measure durations of additional events, in particular the durations of any formant transitions, which must fit within a narrow range (25–120 msec) to meet the requirements of canonicity. The purely acoustic approach provides no perspective on what durations are appropriate for speech nor on what particular measurements of duration should be taken to determine the speechiness of analyzed sounds.

The other parameters (fundamental frequency, amplitude, resonances), if viewed in isolation from speech theory, offer no more revealing information about the infant sound in terms of its possible relation with speech than the duration information does. The parameter values for the infant sounds in fundamental frequency, amplitude, and resonance can be given useful interpretation only in the context of a general theory of the nature of possible speech types. Otherwise the tabulation offers only a set of arbitrarily obtained characteristics of the sound. The general theory that would specify limits on such parameter values is infraphonological in nature.

Even the specific values represented in the tabulation are subject to question. The measurement of each parameter requires choices that must be made by the experimenter. For example, the value 670 msec is not the only possible total duration that might have been assigned to the utterance. The value is based on one observer's measurement of the time from the first visible appearance of sound (as differentiated from background noise) to the time where signal merges with background noise. Perhaps, however, one should have begun the measurement not from the first visible point of differentiation of signal from noise, but rather from some point at which a presumed auditorily significant departure from the noise background occurs. How should a significant departure be defined? What criterion should guide such a decision? Acoustics, by itself, provides no answer to these questions. Further, instead of measuring total duration, the observer might decide to consider subsegments of the utterance. If so, how should such segments be selected? Perhaps each glottal pulse (represented by the many vertical striations in the spectrogram) should be measured, and an average should be taken. Perhaps the total duration of noisy portions (the dark part of each striation) of the pulses should be considered, or perhaps the focus should be on pulse-to-pulse intervals. Or maybe the segments selected for attention should be of much greater duration than individual pulses. Perhaps contiguous sequences of pulses of similar amplitude should be grouped together and measured. The list of possibilities for ways of measuring durations in this single spectrogram is endless, and a similarly unending list of ways to make measurements can be generated for the other acoustic parameters.

Given the clear necessity of providing principled grounds for measurement in acoustic analysis of speech and speech-like sounds, it might seem unlikely that spectrographic investigation of infant sounds as precursors to speech would ever have been conducted in the absence of a general theory of speech. But in fact, acoustically based studies of infant sounds have been pursued without any important grounding in a theory of speech. Lynip (1951) attempted to supplant the transcriptional approach of Irwin by supplying tabulations of data based on spectrographic analysis of infant sounds. The work was often cited as a critique of Irwin's transcription-based approach, but the results of the study had little impact because they were not sufficiently interpreted. It was not clear how the numbers illustrated relations between infant utterances and speech.

Lenneberg (1967) also presented results of acoustic analysis without any indication that the effort had been guided by a theory of speech. Although he generally rejected phonetic transcription of early infant vocalizations, the spectrographic displays presented in his work did little to assist in the understanding of infant sounds as precursors to speech. The perusal of the displays yields no insight because the displays are presented in the absence of principles by which to choose among the near limitless possible observations that might be made about them, and Lenneberg's own observations offer no basis for clarification.

The problems of utilizing unguided acoustic analysis in infant vocalizations was cogently critiqued by Koopmans-van Beinum and van der Stelt (1986), who questioned, "what are we going to measure? Which are our segmental units and what determines our choice?" (p. 38). These critics designated infant studies utilizing an acoustic approach (Kent & Murray, 1982; Pierce, 1974) and indicated that when one takes formant frequency measures of vowel-like sounds, one specifies a vowel-like space for the sound producer, but does not indicate whether the sounds of the infants are well-formed, well-articulated, normal, or delayed.[1]

The fact that there are innumerable ways to measure or display any physical phenomenon should not, of course, sidetrack the potential interest in physical, quantitative evaluation. But quantification is most valuable and perhaps only valuable in the context of theory to guide its interpretation. In the case of sounds produced by infants, the potential value of acoustic analysis is unrealizable in the absence of a theory of the nature of speech, specified in acoustic terms.

All the same observations about the potential validity of acoustic analysis apply *mutatis mutandis* to the evaluation of nonhuman sounds. If one wishes to compare nonhuman sounds with speech, then acoustic analysis can most fruitfully be conducted in the context of an infraphonological theory of the principles that speech sounds obey. If one wishes simply to understand the nonhuman system independently, it is necessary to construct an infrastructural model for the nonhuman system. The model building can greatly profit from acoustic analysis, but the effort requires theoretical organization that goes beyond the immediate tasks posed by recording, spectrography, and measurement taking. An example of infrastructurally oriented evaluation of the vocal system of the squirrel monkey is provided by Winter, Ploog, and Latta (1966). In chapter 14, themes from the squirrel monkey work are considered in the context of potential infrastructural comparisons with human vocalizations. In the context here, it is important to emphasize that the comparisons that are most useful are not directly acoustic, but are instead medi-

---

[1]The criticism notwithstanding, Kent, in particular, has made important contributions to framing acoustic measures of infant vowel-like formants in ways that prove infrastructurally interpretable. For example, he focuses on "bark" scale transformations and other normalizations that may underlie adult interpretations of infant vowel-like sounds. These transformations provide an acoustic model of the continuum that appears to mediate between infant sounds and the operational-level sounds of mature speech.

ated by the infrastructural systems posed for both the human and the nonhuman systems. The infrastructural systems incorporate acoustic information about the sounds of each species, but the proposed comparisons have the advantage of presenting acoustic information in a way that is referenced to the internal functioning of each system, formulated in terms of the universal set of possible infrastructural properties and principles.

Although the study of infant sounds and nonhuman vocalizations in terms of physical parameters has most commonly been conducted in the realm of acoustics, it is possible to approach the issue from the standpoint of articulation. This approach has been uncommon, in part because it is exceedingly difficult to conduct speech physiology experiments with infants and nonhuman animals—adult humans are more willing to suffer electrode insertions, pressure transducer attachments, and movement inhibition clamps. Institutional review boards for subject protection have been hesitant to approve such work with infants, and they show increasing resistance to animal research that requires physical restraints or sedation. However, even if one did address the description of infant or nonhuman sound production articulatorily, infrastructural interpretation would still be necessary. Data resulting from physiological monitoring, by itself, provide no clearer information about how movements or postures relate to speech or any other infrastructural system than do raw acoustic data. Both require a perspective based on evaluation of the nature of speech or some other infrastructural system.

In any domain of science, description at a purely physical level suffers from limitations of interpretation that can render the effort inert. Until an infrastructural model is formulated to account for relations between physical parameters and underlying phenomena, there is no basis for making sense of measurements. The natural sciences in general seek to determine the deep properties of phenomena, and meter readings are not the ultimate goals of description. They merely provide data to be explained, and even the methods by which readings are taken and instruments are utilized must be guided by the possible explanations envisioned by the investigator.

THE ROLE OF REAL PERCEIVERS
IN INTERPRETATION OF ACOUSTIC DATA

To provide principled choices in spectrographic interpretation, it is necessary to reference the choices to the reactions of real speech perceivers. For example, in considering the measurement of duration of speech or speech-like sounds, a significant departure from background noise can best be defined in terms of the degree of departure that is deemed significant by listeners in the process of speech perception. This is not a purely acoustic matter, because it must be resolved through the study of auditory reactions and judgments. Through such study, it might be determined that the fairly low amplitude portion of the beginning of the utterance depicted in Fig. 5.4 is noticed by listeners. Such information would provide a solid basis for including the low-amplitude beginning of the utterance in the total duration value, rather than leaving it out on some arbitrary basis such as, for example, that it accounts for only a small portion of the root mean square amplitude of the utterance. Measurement of other acoustic parameters can be similarly guided by principles developed in the study of speech perception by real listeners.

INFRAPHONOLOGY AS A MEDIATOR

The study of the physical properties of sounds cannot, then, by itself provide insight regarding the sounds' relation with speech or any other infrastructural system. The study must be supplemented by a theory based on the capabilities of real speech perceivers. At the same time, the review of past history of infant vocalizations research has revealed that real speech perceivers (unless they are instructed not to) tend to characterize infant sounds in terms of operational-level categories of their mature linguistic systems, a tendency that could easily run counter to the goals of infrastructural modeling. In the development of the infraphonological approach it is necessary to recognize the danger of shoe-horning by real perceivers and to model principles of canonicity on listeners' judgments of degrees of well-formedness rather than on their tendency to assign sounds to operational-level categories.

By defining operational units of speech systems in terms of physical parameters, infraphonology sets the stage for meaningful comparisons of baby sounds with mature sounds, because the baby sounds can be referenced to the infraphonological principles themselves rather than being consigned to equivocal description in terms of arbitrary physical units or operational-level units. The proposed approach does not do away with either physical or operational-level phonetic analysis—instead it provides a way of utilizing both at appropriate times and integrating their results in a coherent account. As suggested in Table 5.3, previous descriptions have tended to provide either acoustic and articulatory or phonetic descriptions, but have not united the descriptions in a coherent frame.

UNIVERSAL CHARACTERISTICS OF SYLLABLES
IN NATURAL LANGUAGES: THE EMPIRICAL BASIS
FOR A CANONICAL SYLLABLE DEFINITION

In chapter 4, certain principles of canonical syllable formation (normal phonation, articulatedness, full resonance, rapid transitions) were presented. These represent a revealing, although incomplete, list of properties that natural phonological syllables possess. It is useful to review more fully the characteristics of syllables in natural languages to clarify that there is an empirically identifiable general basis for delineating the universal nature of the minimal rhythmic units of speech.

TABLE 5.3

Contrasting the Infraphonological Approach with More Traditional Ones

Previous Approaches	Proposed Approach
Phonetic transcription of operational-level units, in particular "phones" or "segments"	Operational-level units (well-formed syllables, phrases, etc.)
	↕
	Infraphonology
	↕
Acoustic analysis or articulatory analysis	Physical parameters (acoustic or articulatory)

Durations of Syllables

In the search for universal characteristics of syllables, it is worth noting that all natural languages are rhythmically structured in similar ways. This similarity and consistency is critically important to speech perception and learning. Without such temporal consistency, it is hard to imagine how a learner would begin the process of making sense of the complex stream of speech. Relatively consistent syllable durations provide a frame of focus for perception, allowing the listener to perform analysis on limited chunks of information rather than requiring unrestricted analysis that could prove unwieldy. Consistent rhythmic structure, then, would seem to constitute a critical feature of any temporally organized communication system. Speech builds its rhythmic structure around syllables.

Through investigations that have measured durations of syllables as the intervals between peak amplitudes for syllable sequences in languages, the vast majority of syllables are found to fit within the range of 100 to 500 msec, with a consistent median somewhere around 200 to 300 msec depending on speech rate. This pattern yields a rate of three to five syllables per second, which is consistent for numerous languages (Delattre, 1966) and is presumably universal.

The natural pace of syllable production is not peculiar to speech, as other rhythmic motoric phenomena, such as finger tapping, operate within similar time frames (Thelen, 1981). The time frames are limited, providing a clear basis for identification of speech-like rhythmicity across any sound type that might be presented to a listener.

Amplitudes of Nuclei and Margins in Syllables

The rise and fall of amplitudes in syllable sequences can be illustrated in a canonical sequence such as [tʌtʌtʌt] (exemplified spectrographically by an infant reduplicated babble in Fig. 5.5), where the tongue closures correspond to low points of amplitude (silences corresponding to blank spaces in the display) and the openings to peaks (corresponding to the three filled portions of the display, each around 150–200 msec in duration). Such a sequence is prototypical of speech forms, and could constitute a word in virtually any language, as long as the phonetic sequence is assigned to a meaning.

The peaks of the syllable sequence are referred to as *nuclei* (or vowels) of the syllables, and the valleys (typically 10 dB or more lower than the peaks) correspond to *margins* (or consonants). All languages distinguish between consonants and vowels in this way for prototypical units. The degree of differentiation in amplitude between peaks and valleys in syllable sequences

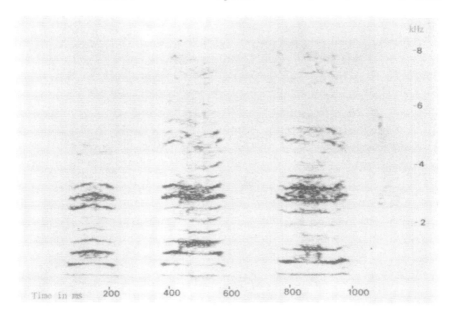

FIG. 5.5. The spectrogram shows a three-syllable sequence of reduplicated babbling [tʌtʌtʌt] produced by a 9-month-old infant. The display is based on a narrow band analysis. The syllables are each brief, with high amplitude nuclei of about 200 msec interrupted by silences of less than 200 msec, corresponding to the closures for the consonant-like elements. From "Pre-speech vocalizations of a deaf infant: A comparison with normal metaphonological development," by Oller, D. K., Eilers, R. E., Bull, D. H., & Carney, A. E., 1985, *Journal of Speech and Hearing Research, 28*, p. 52. Copyright 1985 by the American Speech-Language-Hearing Association. Reprinted with permission.

depends on both the particular vowel quality (for low vowels such as "ah" [ɑ] peak amplitudes are higher than for high vowels such as "ee" [i]) and the particular consonantal type (for glides such as [w], amplitudes are higher than for stops such as [b]). But in general, the amplitudes of consonantal margins are lower than the amplitudes of adjacent nuclei, a pattern that is common to syllables in all natural languages.

Phonatory Patterns in Speech

Syllable nuclei of natural languages, in the great majority of cases, involve a phonatory pattern (i.e., a pattern of vibration of the vocal cords) that is characteristic of (although not entirely unique to) speech. *Normal phonation* (also called *modal voice* or *chest register*; Hollien, 1974; Titze, 1994) is produced with periodic vibrations of the cords, based on a particular posturing of the glottis, showing "full involvement of the vocal fold body in vibration" (Titze, 1994, p. 256), a pattern exemplified in a videostoboscopic recording in Fig. 5.6. Other kinds of phonation are possible, and are characterized by different postures and different kinds of periodicity (or lack of it). For example, falsetto voice involves an "elongated and stiffened cover" (Titze, 1994, p. 256) of the vocal folds resulting in a near doubling of the fundamental frequency. Vocal fry, or creaky voice (sometimes called *pulse register*; Hollien, 1974), is produced through yet another posture resulting in very low frequency, so low in fact that listeners can sometimes perceive gaps of silence within each glottal cycle. The ability of listeners to identify speech as speech and to produce speech as distinct from other kinds of vocalization is in part due to their ability to produce and recognize normal phonation.

The ability to recognize normal phonation and to distinguish it from other kinds of phonation (Hartelius, Buder, & Strand, 1997) is carried to its logical extreme in some languages, where differences in phonation type are utilized phonemically. An individual syllable in such a language can be pronounced with two different vocal qualities, producing two different meanings.

> A pathological voice quality in one language may be phonologically contrastive in another. Putting it more colloquially, one person's voice disorder is another person's phoneme. This is evidenced by the fact that there are several languages that contrast not only voiced and voiceless sounds, but also additional phonation types, such as "breathy" voice (in Gujerati) or "creaky" voice (in Hausa), which would be considered strongly stylistically marked or pathological if used by speakers of a language such as English. (Ladefoged, 1983, p. 351)

The existence of phonemic voice quality in languages strongly supports the assertion that acoustic differences between vocal qualities can be detected quite systematically. In a visual illustration of distinctions (Fig. 5.7), Ladefoged (1983) presented a waveform diagram indicating differences between a vowel produced with the normal phonation pattern (called "voice" in

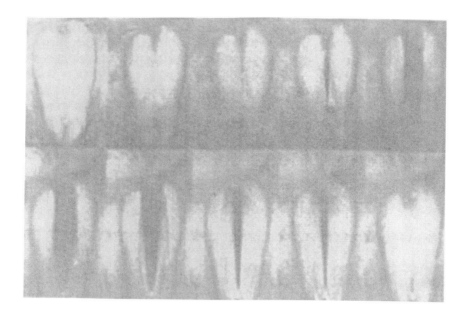

FIG. 5.6.   A series of videoframes of vocal chord movement during a normal glottal cycle. Photograph by Debra K. Klein, The University of Iowa Hospitals and Clinics. From *Principles of Voice Production* (p. 81), by I. R. Titze, 1994, Englewood Cliffs, NJ: Prentice Hall. Copyright by Debra Klein. Reprinted with permission.

the figure) and one produced with a pattern called "murmur," a type of breathy voice, in which "the vocal cords vibrate without coming completely together" (p. 352).

The waveform shows that the patterns are fundamentally different, providing listeners with straightforward acoustic information by which to differentiate the two types of voicing. It is important to emphasize that the existence of systematically utilized non-normal phonation types in languages does not change the fact that listeners recognize the normal form as the basic, canonical form of phonation. All languages have the normal form and only some languages utilize other options to contrast phonemically with the normal form.[2] Distinct acoustic patterns and related auditory discrimination capabilities provide the basis for intuitive differentiation of canonical speech-like sounds (characterized by normal phonation) from less speech-like sounds (characterized by other kinds of phonation), or abnormal forms of phonation (see Monsen, 1979).

---

[2]For example it is estimated that only 10% of the world's languages contrast normal voice with *laryngealization,* a type of creaky voice (Maddieson, 1980).

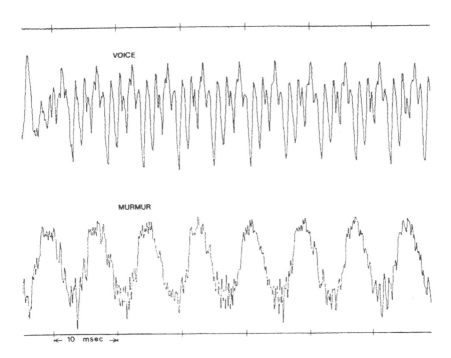

FIG. 5.7.   Voiced and murmured vowels. Parts of the waveform near the midpoints of the vowels in the Khosian words //áa and !ào from one of the Khosian languages of Africa. From "The Linguistic Use of Different Phonation Types," by P. Ladefoged, in *Vocal Fold Physiology: Contemporary Research and Clinical Issues* (p. 355), by D. Bless and J. Abbs, 1983, San Diego, CA: College Hill Press. Copyright by Peter Ladefoged.. Reprinted with permission.

Pitch Patterns of Syllables in Natural Languages

Fundamental frequency (F0) of vocalization, heard as pitch, also plays an important role in the ways listeners judge margins and nuclei in languages. F0 tends to rise along with the typical rise in amplitude toward the peaks of syllable nuclei. The range of possible F0 in spoken language is determined in part by the speaker's laryngeal dimensions. Men have lower mean F0s (around 100 Hz) than women (around 200 Hz), who tend similarly to have lower F0s than children, whose values vary, of course, with age. Newborn infants typically show F0s in crying from 300 to 600 Hz (Karelitz & Fisischelli, 1969; Lieberman, Harris, Wolff, & Russell, 1971; Murai, 1963; Zlatin-Laufer & Horii, 1977).

Speakers of all ages can produce sounds that deviate dramatically from their mean F0s. A potential range of two octaves or more is common, especially if falsetto voice is included on the high end. The key point here is that for the nuclei of syllables in speech, such a wide range of potential pitches does not occur. Instead, syllable nuclei and transitions between margins and nuclei are focused within an approximately half-octave range around the individual speaker's mean F0. In recognizing syllable nuclei and margins, listeners interpret rises in F0 as movements toward syllabic centers and falls as movements toward consonantal edges. Canonical productions of syllable nuclei can thus be characterized in terms of typical speech-like F0 patterns.

Resonance Patterns and Formant Structures of Syllables

Resonances of the vocal tract yield characteristic patterns of energy concentration in spectrographic displays. These patterns, yielding areas of energy concentration called *formants*, are predictable based on the changeable tubular structure of the vocal tract. Each change in vocal tract shape (accompanying such actions as tongue raising, jaw lowering, or lip rounding) produces different concentrations of energy and different formant patterns. With the vocal tract open and the vocal cords vibrating, one sees a particular pattern of formants that corresponds to the particular shape of the tract. Listeners tend to interpret acoustic patterns that show three clear formants as syllable nuclei, whereas patterns that show fewer formants are more likely to be interpreted as consonants.

Figure 5.8 (Baken, 1987) shows spectrographic displays of a variety of vowels from English. Note that each vowel shows a particular pattern of formant frequency, corresponding to its particular vocal tract shape. [i] and [e] have high second formants, whereas [o] and [u] show essential fusing of first and second formants at relatively low frequencies. Note also in Fig. 5.9 (representing the well-formed utterance "Joe took father's shoe bench out") that clearly defined formants tend to disappear during periods of consonantal vocal tract closure. Noise (aperiodic energy) may be present (as during the fricative sound [ʃ] as in *shoe*), but even in this case, no clear formant pattern is discernible.

Formant Transitions and the Rapid Transmission of Speech

The articulations that produce the changes from peak to valley in syllables yield acoustic transitions, seen spectrographically in rapid changes in formant structure, transitions that prove to have special importance in speech transmission (see Studdert-Kennedy, 1980). Such transitions are clearly visible in Fig. 5.9. In fact listeners use the acoustic information in the transitions between peaks and valleys as primary cues to the identity of both consonants and vowels in all natural languages (Delattre, Liberman, & Cooper, 1955; Lindblom, 1963). In rapid speech, there is virtually no steady-state information provided (Nelson, Perkell, & Westbury, 1984). The formant transitions carry the great majority of the relevant cues.

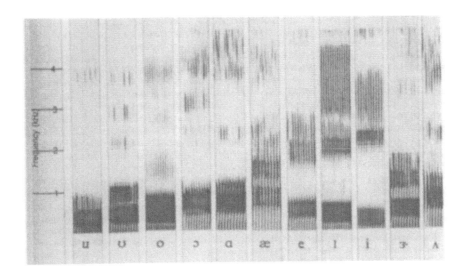

FIG. 5.8.   Formant patterns of the English vowels. From *Clinical Measurement of Speech and Voice* (p. 359), by R. J. Baken, 1987. Boston: College Hill. Copyright by R. J. Baker.. Reprinted with permission.

Consonant–vowel transitions have been noted to foster the remarkable ability of human speakers to transmit information fast, much faster than would be possible with a purely vocalic system or with an artificial communication system such as Morse code (Liberman, Cooper, Shankweiler, & Studdert-Kennedy, 1967). Syllables can be transmitted at three to five per second, and the distinction between consonantal and vocalic information embedded in syllables allows a dramatic increase in information transfer. The consonant–vowel transitions of speech provide the mechanism for encoding of both consonantal and vocalic information in time frames that would otherwise be limited largely to vocalic information (Delattre et al., 1955; Liberman, Delattre, Cooper, & Gerstman, 1954).

The ear appears to be amazingly well-tuned to the rapid acoustic changes that correspond to consonant–vowel transitions and to slight variations in their form. The transmission power of formant transitions is exploited in all natural languages. In formulating the infraphonological definition of the syllable, special note has been taken of this critical feature of speech systems. The definition of canonical syllable needs to be directly referenced to the acoustic and articulatory characteristics of syllables that enable the formation of a natural communication system with an unparalleled bit rate.

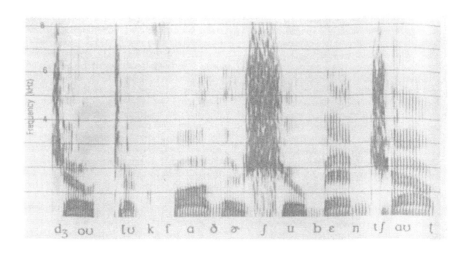

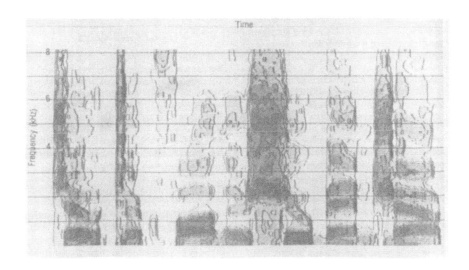

FIG. 5.9. Standard (a) and contoured (b) spectrograms of the utterance "Joe took his father's shoe bench out." From *Clinical Measurement of Speech and Voice* (p. 342), by R. J. Baken, 1987. Boston: College Hill. Copyright by R. J. Baker. Reprinted with permission.

A MORE FORMAL, BUT STILL SCHEMATIC DEFINITION OF THE NOTION OF CANONICAL SYLLABLE

The canonical syllable definition presented earlier is intended to permit characterization of protophones not merely as categories of vocalization, but as representatives of infant vocal acts that either obey or do not obey specific criteria of the definition. It is not assumed that infants consciously attempt to meet the standards of the definition. Rather, the definition provides a way to assess the extent of the infant's conformity to principles. In the same stroke, the definition offers a systematic basis on which to judge the extent to which any sound resembles speech, a fact that immediately suggests a new way to conduct comparisons among communication systems of various species.

The elements of a schematic definition for the canonical syllable are provided in two columns in Table 5.4. The first column provides a formal description of each principle and the second column provides a more informal characterization.

The canonical syllable definition is intended to specify the characteristics of the most commonly occurring syllables in natural languages, but not

TABLE 5.4
Elaborated Definition of Canonical Syllable

Principle Number	Formally Speaking, a Canonical Syllable Must Include	Informally Speaking, a Canonical Syllable Must Include
1	A single center (nucleus) delivered with normal phonation	A vowel-like element with the kind of voicing that occurs most commonly in the vowels of speech, not the kind that occurs in crying, screaming, squealing, and so on
2	At least one margin (articulated element resulting from movement of the vocal tract)	Movement (articulation) of the vocal tract (the lips, tongue, or jaw) to produce at least one consonant-like element (the margin), along with the vowel-like element
3	Full resonance in the nucleus	A vowel that is produced with the vocal tract in a special vowel posture, not merely in the at-rest configuration
4	A rapid, uninterrupted, full transition from margin to nucleus	A quick movement between the consonant and the vowel

properties of all syllables of languages. To gain an intuitive grasp of the definition, it may be easiest to consider examples. [bɑ] and [mɑ] are phonetic renderings of two common canonical syllables that occur in infant babbling and of course in adult speech as well. The words *bah* (as in "Bah, humbug!") and *Ma* (as in "Bah, humbug, Ma!"), are English representatives of these canonical categories. The most common canonical syllables in babbling consist of one plosive or nasal consonant-like element and one vowel-like element, pronounced with quick articulation between the consonant and the vowel. Infants in canonical babbling often produce strings of reduplicated canonical syllables that are transcribed as [mama ...], [dada ...], [baba ...] and so on, although canonical syllables in infancy also occur in isolation or in mixed combinations.

ON THE INDEFINITE SIZE OF THE POTENTIAL REPERTOIRE OF CANONICAL SYLLABLES

The definition specifies a class of potential syllables that is of extraordinary magnitude. In fact there is no useful way to designate a limit on the number of potential canonical syllables in possible languages. Different languages utilize different consonants and vowels to construct syllables. The IPA catalogs a large number of both consonant and vowel options from which languages choose. There are no fewer than 70 fairly commonly occurring consonant options, and no less than 25 commonly occurring vowel options. Now if we merely form CV syllables from these, we can see immediately that there are 70 $\times$ 25 = 1,750 possible syllables. But remember that languages can also form syllables with additional shapes such as CVC, CCV, CCVC, VC, and so on. For each of the 1,750 CVs there should be 70 additional CVC options (yeilding 122,500 syllables), multiplied by perhaps 40 additional CCVC options (less than 70 because not all consonants can be clustered conveniently), yielding nearly 5 million syllable types. And we have only just begun the multiplications. The numbers of possible syllables are obviously extraordinary.

Furthermore, the number of possible consonants and vowels is not limited by those that occur commonly. If we begin to introduce the very rare consonants and vowels into the discussion, the numbers explode further. The infraphonological definition of canonical syllable does not restrict the range of possible syllables to a short list, but instead characterizes the principles through which an indefinitely large class of potential well-formed syllables can be formed.

ON MARKEDNESS OF CANONICAL SYLLABLES

To say that the definition of canonical syllables specifies an indefinitely large class does not indicate that each of the millions of possible canonical syllables is equally likely to occur in babbling or speech. On the contrary, certain syllable shapes are highly preferred (especially the CV shape) and certain nucleus and margin types are similarly preferred (see discussion in chap. 3 of commonly occurring well-formed syllables).

In general, whatever forces guide choices of speech sounds in natural languages (e.g., anatomical and physiological limits) produce a preference for syllables of simple construction, one consonant and one vowel, in that order. Plosive consonants (those that involve complete closure of the vocal tract, as in [b], [t], or [k]) and nasal consonants (those that involve opening of the nasal airway but closure of the mouth by lips or tongue; e.g., [m] and [n]) have special appeal, and a small corpus of contrastive vowels is similarly favored.

Linguists have a special term for the general tendency in languages for certain structures to be favored over others—*markedness*. Favored phonological structures are said to be unmarked in accord with the fact that they are symbolized with base characters, and no special additions, whereas less favored structures are commonly *marked* with diacritic indicators of their specialized status. Thus the consonant [m] as in *meet,* is unmarked, compared with its voiceless counterpart [m̥], a rarely occurring consonant in languages, marked by the subscript to indicate its voicelessness.

The definition of canonical syllable provided here incorporates the flavor of markedness theory, because one goal of the definition is to reflect the tendency of languages to utilize some structures more commonly and in more central roles than others. But the approach of infraphonology goes beyond addressing the ways that various syllables that actually occur in languages may or may not be favored in linguistic systems, and takes account of the ways that any kind of acoustic event or articulatory action can resemble speech, which is to say the ways such events and actions do or do not abide by the fundamental rules of construction inherent to the units of phonology.

ON THE OCCURRENCE OF NONCANONICAL SYLLABLES IN MATURE LANGUAGES

Of course, even though an indefinitely large class of operational-level canonical syllables is specified by the principles just listed, and although the great majority of syllables performed in real speech are of canonical form, both adults and infants can and do produce noncanonical syllables. For example, one can speak in falsetto voice and say "bah," in which case the first principle of the canonical syllable definition (normal phonation) is violated; in a well-formed syllable, the voice quality must be normal, the kind of voicing that occurs in the great majority of speech events. One can also produce isolated vowels, in which case the second principle is violated (because isolated vowels require no articulatory movement during their production). If one does not open the mouth for the vowel, but instead produces phonation with the vocal tract at rest, the third principle is violated (because full resonance depends on posturing of the tract). Finally, if one draws out the movement from a consonantal closure (e.g., the lip closure for the [b] in "bah") to the vowel, beginning voicing just as the closure is released, but moving the articulators very slowly toward the vowel, phonating all the while, then the outcome violates the fourth principle. All these noncanonical sounds have relations with speech, but each one deviates from key principles that give speech sounds their special character and their remarkable power of rapid information transmission.

Words in natural languages can be purposely rendered in noncanonical form or can be accidentally misarticulated, especially if we speak with our mouths full. Thank you, parents of the world, for teaching us not to do that, because it is not only impolite, but it also thwarts the potentials of speech communication that depend on well-articulated transitions. Given that canonical syllables display the key characteristics that give speech its uniqueness and remarkably rapid transmission powers, one might imagine that noncanonical syllables would be avoided by languages the way cats are avoided by sparrows, but not so. Some syllables in natural languages tend to be systematically noncanonical. Phonologies are built in such a way that the core canonical units form a basic contrastive set augmented by secondary types that diverge in various ways from the canonical forms.

Thus, although the substantial majority of syllables that occur in natural languages are canonical, there are notable examples, enumerated here, of syllable types that do not abide by all the definitional principles for canonical syllables.

1. Isolated vowels: An isolated vowel [ɑ] (as in "Ah! What a humbug!") is not canonical. Why should the canonical syllable definition exclude it? Because the quintessence of speech is movement of the vocal tract (producing rapid formant transitions), and isolated vowels are (or at least can be) produced in a stable supraglottal configuration with no necessary articulation. Isolated vowels occur quite rarely as words in English, a pattern of paucity that is found generally in languages, the logical necessity of the fact that many more syllables can be composed of combinations of consonants and vowels than of vowels alone.

2. Syllabic consonants: Some syllable nuclei are consonantal in some languages, as in the second syllable of the American English rendering of *button* [bʌtn̩] (the diacritic mark below the [n] indicates its syllabicity) where the tongue never leaves the alveolar ridge (the structure just behind the front teeth) after the closure for the t. We also have syllabic [l] in American English in the word *cattle* [kʰætl̩]. These types of syllables are present but still uncommon in American English. Many languages have no syllabic consonants at all. Even other dialects of English use fewer syllabic consonants than American varieties do. Notice that in British pronunciations of the word *button*, the second syllable includes a vowel, [bʌtən].

3. Reduced syllables: The lowest stressed (or reduced) syllables in languages (English has lots of them) can be rendered with vowels that lack the special resonance qualities they would have under higher degrees of stress (Lindblom, 1963), especially if they occur in nonfinal utterance positions, where syllable durations tend to be shortest (Lindblom, 1968; Oller, 1973). Such syllables can be deemed quasivowels[3] in our terminology. At the point of the nucleus of reduced syllables, the resonance patterns often resemble those of a vocal tract at rest. Consider the first vowel in *banana*, pronounced at a conversational rate, and note that if that vowel quality is drawn out, it differs substantially from that of any of the vowels of stressed syllables in English. We transcribe it with the nasalized schwa [ə̃], in *banana* but even this characterization can overplay the pronunciation as it occurs in rapid speech, where it can be reduced to a sound with the quality that results from phonating with the mouth at rest (closed or slightly open). It might be said, in these circumstances, that the first syllable of *banana* is pronounced with a quasivowel. Languages often include reduced syllables, but these always function as context-sensitive modifications of the more basic canonical forms found in more highly stressed syllables.

4. Syllables with glottal consonants only: The consonant *h* and its relative the glottal stop (which occurs as a sharp cessation of voicing between the two vowels of *uh oh* [ʌʔo]) are produced without supraglottal articulation, and consequently they do not count as articulated consonants. The glottis itself creates the noisy sound of "h" (in, e.g., *happy*) as well as the break

---

[3]Another quasivowel usage by adult speakers can be found in certain semilexical items that appear to exist in a variety of languages. For example, in *huh*, *uh huh*, and *uh uh*, we have the option (but not the obligation) of including nuclei with quasiresonance. The mouth can be left slightly open with the tract lax and unpostured. Normal phonation can be initiated for items such as "huh" without modification of the supraglottal configuration. The resulting sound of "huh" can be somewhat variable although usually the nucleus will sound nasal with compact formants corresponding to central and mid- to high tongue position. Although it is not obligatory, the mouth can also be closed entirely in production of semilexical items such as "huh," in which case the air flow is altogether nasal, and phoneticians might refer to the nuclei as syllabic consonants (phonetic renderings in the IPA for the three examples would be [hm̩], [m̩hm̩], and [m̩ ʔm̩]). Perhaps it is important to reiterate here that the term *quasivowel* can encompass vocalizations that could be interpreted as syllabic nasal consonants as well as normal phonatory productions of an open vocal tract at rest.

Perhaps surprisingly, we also have the option on *huh* and its relatives *uh uh* and *uh huh* to pronounce crisp fully resonant vowels of the mid central type [ʌ] (like the one in the words *rut* or *puck*). This remarkable variability in allowable pronunciation causes one to hesitate in referring to *huh* and its friends as *words*. They function on the margin of the lexicon because unlike other words, they do not possess fixed phonological representations. *Rut* and *puck* must be pronounced with the English midcentral vowel. They cannot be correctly pronounced with quasivowels or syllabic nasals. The variable nucleus of *huh*, on the other hand, can be pronounced as a full vowel or a quasivowel. Its nucleus is a chameleon, and it is one of the very few cases where a putative word of our lexicon includes pronunciation possibilities that do not have the status of phonemic elements in the English repertoire. This is one of the ways that quasivowels prove their marginality within the operational-level units of mature languages.

in phonation of the glottal stop. Glottal consonants are common in natural languages, but they constitute special cases. Whereas contrasts among canonical syllables typically are cued by differences in formant transitions, the acoustic reflections of vocal tract movement, syllables that have only glottal consonants show no transitions because they involve no necessary supraglottal movements.

Of course as noted earlier, even among the canonical syllables, some are favored over others. So the canonical syllable definition provides a core point of reference in evaluating infant sounds; still, the pattern of vocal production even in adults includes noncanonical syllables, and the pattern even in infants includes preferences for certain canonical types over others.

THE INTUITIVE BASIS OF INFRAPHONOLOGICAL STRUCTURES

The ordering and interrelations of the elements of the canonical syllable definition are instructive in the comparison of infant vocalizations with speech. All the properties of the canonical syllable can be identified auditorily with good reliability, presumably because natural language listeners have to be able to differentiate speech from other kinds of sounds. Otherwise, how would they know when to treat sounds as speech and when to try to interpret them otherwise? If a strange fellow approaches, speaking an unfamiliar language, one does not turn to one's companion and ask, "What is this fellow doing?" No matter what language he is speaking, he is clearly talking, so any speaker of a natural language knows what he is doing. A more plausible question to one's companion might be "What is this fellow saying?" or "Do you have any idea what language he is speaking?" To be a mature human speaker of any natural language is to be a person capable of recognizing speech when it occurs, regardless of the language presented.

There must exist a systematic basis on which human listeners recognize what is speech and what is not. Human listeners must, thus, possess intuitive awareness of principles that determine what can count as a speech sequence. The canonical syllable definition is intended in part to provide a systematic specification for this intuitive knowledge of human listeners.

THE NEED FOR EXTERNAL DEFINITIONAL ELEMENTS—AVOIDING CIRCULARITY

Although listeners are capable of making very reliable judgments regarding the speechiness of a wide variety of sounds, and can learn quickly to do so in terms of the individual principles stated in the canonical syllable definition, the purposes of a theory of infraphonology require that elements of speech must be specifiable entirely in terms of parameters that are independent of phonology, external to linguistic systems. The external parameter criterion is required to preclude circularity in the model. If one is not watchful, it can be seductive to define phonological elements of speech as those elements that occur in syllables and phrases, a definition that amounts to the doublespeak that speech elements are the elements that occur in speech.

The very structure of the infraphonological approach precludes such circularity. Within the model, well-formed operational-level units are defined in terms of independent physical parameters. The same parameters can be utilized to define infraphonologically ill-formed units, or units of other systems of sound or articulation. To exemplify, Principle 1 of the definition of canonical syllable, accounting for normal phonation, must specify the manner in which well-formed voicing is performed physically. Using the same parameters of reference, all sorts of other ill-formed kinds of voicing or other actions of the larynx can be similarly described. To the extent that voice science provides an empirical basis for differentiating normal (or modal) voice from other vocal registers or actions of the larynx, infraphonological theory incorporating the voice science perspective is easily equipped to avoid circularity of definition regarding the nature of normal phonation.

The same is true of all the other principles of canonical syllable formation. In each case the nature of well-formed speech-like actions of the vocal apparatus and the acoustic effects can be described in physical terms and can be contrasted with other kinds of actions and acoustic effects. Consequently, the infraphonological approach provides a basis for definitions that are inherently free of circularity.

INFRAPHONOLOGY IN THE PERSPECTIVE
OF THE NATURE–NURTURE MATTER

Inevitably, we are faced with questions about where infraphonology resides and whence it arises. Does infraphonology reside in the brain or in some combination of the brain and the vocal tract, and if so, how did it get there? To what extent are there innate predispositions that make infraphonological principles as they are, or to what extent must they be learned or developed in the context of experience? To what extent might infraphonological principles arise by self-organization in the absence of any specialized speech-oriented brain mechanisms? To what extent might infraphonological principles constitute eternal conditions on how a phonological system might be constructed, conditions that might be totally universal and independent of humanity? If independent eternal principles do play a major role, then human phonological systems would surely reflect them, but the ultimate source would be localized not in the mind (neither the current mind of humanity nor any previous mind), but in unchanging conditions of the universe.

Such questions are unavoidable in the long run, and thorough understanding of the nature of the language capability requires development of well-constructed responses to them. At the same time, there are important functions that an infraphonological framework can serve in the absence of any commitments regarding the nature–nurture controversy or the possibility that infraphonological principles embody totally universal conditions on potential phonological systems. The model that infraphonology presents serves as a standard, allowing comparison of sounds from a variety of sources with the sounds of speech. In providing a standard of comparison, the model provides a guidance system for tracing the development of speech capabilities in infants and for the characterization of relations among sounds of humans and other creatures. The standard is useful regardless of its source or location in nature.

Having stipulated that the infraphonological standard is useful no matter what its source, I nonetheless briefly consider the questions posed previously. First, where does infraphonology reside? There is a sense in which speakers of natural languages have infraphonological knowledge; they can judge the speechiness of sounds, and so must possess knowledge (perhaps tacit knowledge) that guides the judgments. In this regard, one might assume that infraphonology is an aspect of what linguists have called *langue* (de Saussure, 1968), *content* (Hjelmslev, 1963a, 1963b) or *competence* (Chomsky, 1957, 1965)—these conceptions focus on the knowledge of speakers or idealized speakers of natural languages. The conclusion that infraphonology may be a kind of knowledge of individual speakers is supported by the fact that we utilize intuitive judgments of real listeners to help formulate infraphonological principles and to test their appropriateness. After all it is real listeners who must be the ultimate determiners of what counts as speech and what does not.

It is clear, then, that individual speakers do possess at least some kinds of infraphonological knowledge, and that we can study many aspects of infraphonology by evaluating that knowledge. These facts do not imply that infraphonology must be conceived of ultimately as a property of the mind or brain exclusively. That the mind possesses such information does not prove that the information originated in the mind. Over ontogenetic and evolutionary time, the mind may assume a form that it needs to assume to perform certain functions. The principles that guide the mind to take on these forms may constitute, at least in some regards, unchanging characteristics of potential phonological systems of any creature.

It is also important to emphasize that infraphonology is not best directed toward characterization of individual capabilities, but of the species as a whole. In the infrastructural notion of phonological capability, the ultimate goal is specification of universal governing patterns of language. As a consequence the model takes account not merely of existing phonetic units in languages, but of all possible phonetic units in human languages. Infraphonology thus pursues goals consistent with a long-standing tradition of interest in Universal Grammar, an Enlightenment tradition reviewed by Chomsky (1966) and extended in many of his recent works (e.g., Chomsky,

1981, 1993). The tradition encourages inquiry into abstractions regarding the language capacity in its most general form, a form that must encompass information accessible to individuals but must transcend individuals in its focus on capabilities of the species.

Because the notion of universal principles characterizing a specieswide capability is abstract, one may be tempted to question the reality of infraphonology (and other principles of Universal Grammar). It might be thought that infraphonology is merely a heuristic for comparing sounds of mature humans and other creatures, and consequently, that it could be replaced in the near future by another ad hoc model of linguistic capability. The concern is a legitimate one insofar as there may be fundamental errors in the formulation of the model. However, if the model is well-formulated, such a potential reversal of orientation would seem unlikely, because however abstract its components may be, the model is not ad hoc, and its components are not merely heuristic. Infraphonology addresses a reality in the sense that it takes note of how systems of phonology function. Infrastructural systems in general, not just in the domain of language, posit abstractions that account for empirically discernible patterns. Ultimately, in spite of their abstractness, they justifiably come to be viewed as constituting realities as long as they make useful predictions and account for a wide variety of phenomena.

It is easy to point to major historical examples of how infrastructural modeling seeks abstractions that come to be viewed as realities. When Newton posited the existence of the gravitational force, he made a leap of judgment regarding the apparent universality of the mutual attraction of masses even if they are separated by great distances. He posited an infrastructural abstraction, but in so doing he did not divorce himself from the consideration of reality. On the contrary, he sought deeply to characterize it. By the same token, the abstractions embodied in Universal Grammar (and infraphonology as a subheading within it), if they are accurately formulated, address realities that should prevent them from becoming obsolete.

Much of the hubbub about nature–nurture has to do not with just where language resides, but with how it develops. The contention that language is a property of a mental organ (Chomsky, 1986) and that it develops rather than being learned provides a strong nativist perspective on the ontogeny of linguistic capacity. According to the strong nativist view, the child's language grows in the mind in much the same way that the brain develops the capacity for binocular vision or the child undergoes puberty at a certain stage of maturation. Language acquisition is something that happens to a child placed in a certain environment, not something that the child does (Chomsky, 1993). It is not currently taken seriously that language might be exclusively a product of highly structured experience, because linguistic structure is extremely complex and delicate, and language experience of learners is commonly believed to be incomplete and characterized routinely by ill-structured input (Pinker, 1994).

Still, a non-nativist account is increasingly being entertained by philosophers of development (see, e.g., Oyama, 1990) and investigators of dynamic systems modeling and connectionism. The idea is that much of the linguistic capability that develops in children may be the product of self-organization in very general (not language-specific) mental substrates, yielding unexpectedly rich structures in the absence of language-specific predispositions, and even in the context of incomplete or messy input (Bates et al., 1998; Elman, 1993). In this view, linguistic structure is not treated as less rich than in the nativist account, but the origin of structure is taken to be a product of interaction between a powerful learning system (which may have predispositions, but not necessarily language-specific ones) and rich, although nonideal, experience in the context of solving certain problems. In this context, grammars, in all their richness, are thought to make up the class of solutions to the problem of mapping the great complexity and many dimensions of linguistic meanings onto a temporally ordered, low-dimensional linear channel of speech sound sequences (MacWhinney & Bates, 1989). The structure of language emerges in this account from the interaction of an intelligent learner, a rich experience, and inherent constraints on learning within the specific domain of mappings between meaning and sound sequences.

If we assume that language is an emergent capacity rather than an innate one, it can be argued that language may have the consistency it does in part because there exist unchanging infrastructural properties and principles that determine how potential communication systems can be formed and elaborated. In the context of this interpretation of emergentism, structures are self-organized not by magic, nor by virtue of innate knowledge, but in accord with possibilities imposed by infrastructural natural logic. For example, if a creature develops a syllabic system of communication, there are a variety of reasons that reanalysis of the syllabic units as a two-tiered system of syllables and segments (consonants and vowels), can provide a tool of greater power, with more efficient storage and retrieval. Therefore the documented emergence of segmental properties in neural network modeling of phonological learning may be an indication that even very simple systems are able to find logical potential solutions to real problems of function (Lindblom, 1992). The structure that results is rich and complex, but the process that builds it is not necessarily wholly innate. We do not know how much of the logical structure of potential phonological systems is specifically built into the human mental capacity and how much must be developed through interaction with environment in the pursuit of communicative goals that may impose ultimate structure by virtue of ageless principles determining the ways that powerful communicative systems might be formed.

It is reasonable, then, to ask whether the infraphonological capability that develops in children is self-organized or innate. In the long run, some kind of answer to this question is necessary. However, the fact that no firm answer can be given at this time does not obviate the importance of the infraphonological formulation. Similarly, if a grand unifying theory of cosmology ultimately shows that the gravitational force derives, along with other forces, from some previously unimagined condition of singularity in a primitive universe, the new formulation will not obviate the importance of reference to gravity in the context of the current universe. Whatever their degree of abstraction and whatever their ultimate sources, if they are properly formulated, infrastructural properties have timeless value.

To say that infraphonology is a part of Universal Grammar implies, at the present time, neither an acceptance nor a rejection of claims regarding innateness of universal grammatical principles, and similarly, neither an acceptance nor a rejection of claims regarding emergentism. The source of infraphonological principles is a topic of great interest, but the current dispute over how universal principles of linguistic structure arise will not, in my estimation, be resolved by pure theoretical argument, nor purely by evidence that is currently available. In the meantime, the infrastructural models themselves can be elaborated consistent with available or obtainable empirical evidence, and they can be utilized in guidance of research that should lead to deeper understanding of the function of systems independent of their ultimate origins.

THE SCHEMATIC AND PROVISIONAL NATURE OF THE INFRAPHONOLOGICAL PROPOSAL

Much about the specifics of the infraphonological proposal outlined here have been, and I presume will continue to be, treated as uncontroversial because they represent a summary of much common knowledge in the speech sciences. At the same time, there is no reason to be strict about the quantitative specifications suggested. For example, the particular indications of how long formant transitions can be in canonical syllables are both debatable and provisional. The durations of stop-consonant-to-vowel transitions in normal speech are typically 25 to 50 msec; longer transitions are associated with glides, perhaps up to 120 msec. Transitions longer than 120 msec tend to sound too slow for well-formed single syllables, but the matter proves not to be absolute.

Alan Cobo-Lewis and I conducted a perception experiment with synthetic syllables of varying transition duration to try to tie down the distinction between canonical and marginal syllables. The 11 synthetic syllables of the continuum we constructed were heard as [ba] at the shortest durations and as [wa] at the intermediate ones with a fairly sharp boundary between the categories; the longest durations were heard either as [wa] with a noticeably drawn out transition (which could be specifically noticed by listeners), or as [ua] (two syllables). However, the perceptual results showed that there was no clear categorical boundary between glide syllables and syllables with the longest transitions. The boundary between canonical and marginal syllables appeared to be fuzzy (distinctly more fuzzy than that between [ba] and [wa]), although all the subjects judged the syllables with the longest durations as being something other than [ba] or [wa]. Thus although marginal syllables could be identified reliably in extreme cases of long formant transitions (e.g., 200 msec or greater), the boundary between marginal and canonical syllables was not sharp.

As a consequence, when a value such as 120 msec is provided to indicate the limit of formant transition durations for canonical syllables, it should be understood that the value represents a mean boundary for certain syllables that have been tested in a particular laboratory setting. There are surely variations in the value of the mean boundary for other vowel sounds, other speaking rates, and perhaps other voices. Futher, it is clear that the boundaries are fuzzy. A more elaborate fuzzily logical form of an infraphonological proposal would include more detailed accounts of quantitative limits associated with principles.

Furthermore, phonological systems are extremely complex objects, and the proposal considered thus far treats only a fragment (albeit a centrally important one) of infraphonology by addressing well-formedness of syllables. That it is possible to elucidate key aspects of the development of the speech capacity and to lay the groundwork for significant achievements in characterization of abnormalities with such a schematic model provides a broad suggestion of the many advantages that may be obtained through further development of the approach.

THE DIFFICULTY OF ADOPTING
THE INFRAPHONOLOGICAL VIEW OF DESCRIPTION

The transcriptional temptation in observation of sounds produced by babies and nonhuman creatures appears to derive at least in part from the inclination to imitate speech-like sounds as a first approximation to systematic characterization. Whether or not one is a talented sound producer, it may be easy to become snared in a self-made web, to be confused into believing in the accuracy of poor mimicry. Such problems of self-deluding imitation are revealed in foreign language use where speakers often think they can pronounce the words of a foreign language perfectly (perhaps because they try so hard), but native speakers of the language still recognize their accents. It may be impossible for foreign speakers to recognize the extent of their pronunciation errors, and consequent accent, because even if native speakers try to explain how pronunciations have failed, perceptions are limited by personal experiences as language users, and foreign speakers cannot completely abandon their personal linguistic perspectives. The target language's sounds are inevitably filtered through the individual's perceptual system from the prenatal period forward (DeCasper & Fifer, 1980; Fifer, 1987; Moon & Fifer, 1990), and perceptions are shaped based on a different language or languages. (See Best, 1994; Werker

& Tees, 1984; or see Vihman, 1996, for a review of studies on early speech perception experience and how it shapes discriminability.)

When the same kinds of perceptions are applied in adult phonetic-like imitation of baby sounds or the sounds of monkeys or birds, the description flounders similarly, but babies and other creatures are not able to point out the problem nor explain its nature the way foreign language speakers can. Observers relying on imitation as a description may be left to assume that their phonetic imitations are appropriate, or at least sufficiently appropriate to be useful.

It would seem that extreme cases of mismatch between phonetic characterizations and actual sound qualities should be obvious to everyone. "Cockadoodledoo" is only one of many possible ways to characterize a rooster sound phonetically, and none of them works well. But once phonetic description begins to be applied to nonspeech sounds, the method seems to insinuate itself to new nonspeech sounds, and the habit redirects perceptions toward acceptance of the transcriptional illusions.

Infraphonological description provides an escape from the trap, but it may be difficult to seize the opportunity given prior predispositions. For phoneticians, the shift of approach requires consigning well-studied, highly practiced skills as IPA transcribers and teachers to a secondary role in description. Immediately from the point at which the shift is made, principles from which units are formed begin to play a major role in description and interpretation; operational-level units of mature speech, which to that point have dominated categorization, must play a background part. The descriptive product does not directly tell what an utterance is, but focuses instead on how well the utterance performs with regard to the principles and how well it conforms to abstract requirements.

Perhaps another reason the infrastructural approach in vocalization study seems more difficult to adopt than in other sciences is that operational-level linguistic units are themselves very highly structured in hierarchical tiers that include phrases, syllables, segments, and so on (see Fig. 5.2). It might seem that no further structure is needed. Still the infrastructure of a linguistic system is not the same as its richly structured operational system. The infrastructure of human language is capable of generating an infinite variety of linguistic operational systems for different languages. Infant vocalizations at each stage of development as well as vocal systems of other species have their own infrastructures, sharing certain properties with human language, but not including all the components required to make phonetic and other operational-level comparisons appropriate.

6

The Grounding of Vocal and Gestural Development in Biology and Experience: Physical Foundations for Speech and Sign Language

EVIDENCE OF CANALIZATION IN MOTORIC DEVELOPMENT

In light of infraphonological interpretation, protophones have come to be recognized as a set of universal developmental forms, viewed as a flowering foundation for speech. The protophones increasingly tend to be seen as growing and maturing in the way other biological systems grow and mature. There is increased interest in the biological foundations for protophones and clarification of the ways that experience affects the unfolding of the natural speech capacity. To evaluate infant vocalizations in terms of both nature and nurture, it is useful to take a step back and look at babbling in the context of other developmental phenomena.

The development of locomotion and other gross motoric capabilities follows a distinctly similar path in infants all over the world. In general children show control of raising their heads within the first 2 months, rolling over by the second or third month, sitting without support by 6 or 7 months, crawling at about the same age as unsupported sitting, pulling to a standing position by 8 or 9 months, standing alone at 11 months, and first steps around the beginning of the second year (Bayley, 1969; Cobo-Lewis, Oller, Lynch, & Levine, 1996). This developmental sequence is virtually universal, even though there do exist exceptions imposed by childrearing practices that limit child movement explicitly, as in societies where infants are bound and carried for most of the first year. Even when infant movement is severely restricted by confinement to a cradle board during the early months of life, the age of onset for walking seems minimally delayed (Dennis & Dennis, 1940).

The timing of motor development is clearly a phenomenon of biology, showing relative imperviousness to experiential deficit, but there are also notable ways in which experience can be shown to affect the ages of onset for the milestones of motor development. Visual experience, for example, appears to be critical to the normal onset of locomotion. Blind infants begin to walk with a delay of about half a year in comparison to sighted peers (Fraiberg, 1977). The delay appears to be related to the fact that infants' awareness of their location in space is normally dependent, especially early in life, on a combination of vision and information from other sensory modalities. The ability to utilize sound alone as a cue to location in space shows a relatively late onset in infants, both blind and sighted, as indicated by experiments indicating that if infants can hear but cannot see objects, they do not reach for them until the end of the first year of life (Wishart, Bower, & Dunkeld, 1978). Walking and other forms of locomotion appear to be delayed in the absence of vision, then, because visual awareness facilitates infants' abilities to map space, and the confidence instilled by solid understanding of relative locations encourages attempts at navigation.

One might protest that late onset of walking in blind infants could be the result of an experimental confound, because blind infants usually have additional handicaps beyond those of limited sight. Perhaps so, but Fraiberg's (1977) studies provide other sources of support for the idea that sensory experience relevant to the mapping of space plays a major role in the onset of walking. Parents in the studies were encouraged to give their blind infants special experiences including systematic noise making with objects in various locations with respect to the infant as well touching of and by the infant of heard objects and persons. These experiences were designed to facilitate the integration of auditory and tactual information, and were intended to accelerate the blind babies' awareness of their location in space even in the total absence of visual information. The interventions worked well, and blind infants who were given the special experiences showed earlier onsets for walking than blind infants who were treated as usual.

The patterns of development in normally sighted and blind infants indicate that experience does play a role in walking. At the same time, however, even blind infants (with and without intervention) do go on to walk, as do infants who spend much of the first year on a cradle board. It is the relative imperviousness of the development of locomotion to experiential deficit that inspires the characterization of walking as a maturational phenomenon. Walking and other motor milestones are said to be *canalized*, a term (Waddington, 1957) that emphasizes that such developmental events are difficult, although not impossible, to deflect from a biologically preordained course. It is possible to overemphasize the canalization of emerging motoric processes, but it remains a cardinal observation that development is sometimes guided along narrow biologically determined tracks.

BABBLING IN THE GENERAL CONTEXT OF MOTORIC DEVELOPMENT

Babbling development appears to be similarly canalized, a conclusion that is supported by a number of parallels with patterns of development in nonvocal realms of physical action. Although babbling manifests an emerging capacity for speech, it is also important to take account of the senses in which babbling is part of a more general development and shows patterns of growth much like those of gross motor and locomotion skills. Canonical babbling is particularly interesting in this regard because it can be viewed, especially in its reduplicated form, as a rhythmic stereotypy involving jaw and/or tongue movement coordinated with vocal cord vibration. Other such stereotypies (e.g., kicking while lying supine in the crib) that have been systematically studied show patterns of onset and stabilization (Thelen, 1981; 1994) that substantially resemble those of reduplicated babbling (Masataka, 1996b). Rhythmic hand banging (as when an infant is seated at a table) shows not only a similar rate of repetition to that of reduplicated syllable sequences (one to three per second), but also shows a nearly identical mean age of onset to that of canonical babbling (Eilers, Oller, et al., 1993a) just short of 6 months of age. Even the extent of delay in onset of rhythmic hand banging and canonical babbling are similar in infants with Down syndrome (Cobo-Lewis et al., 1996). Further, it has been demonstrated that rhythmic hand movements often occur synchronously with rhythmic babbling in the early Canonical stage (Ejiri, 1998a, 1998b; Ejiri & Masataka, 1996b; Masataka, 1996b), suggesting that the motoric grounding of babbling runs deep. In addition, an important stage in the development of the right-hand preference appears to emerge just at the point of rhythmic syllable babbling (Ramsay, 1984, 1985).

The delicacy and precision of speech articulation is a topic of great interest when addressing the fluent discursive abilities of mature speakers, but it should be noted that reduplicated babbling, however important it may be, is a relatively more simple act than mature speech. Each syllable in reduplicated babbling sequences appears to be essentially identical to its neighbors. Even if subtle differences can be heard among syllables in sequences, it is unclear that infants intend to produce functionally distinct syllables in reduplicated babbling. The syllable-to-syllable variations in perceived phonetic-like elements in reduplicated babbling may be no more significant to infants than the beat-to-beat variations in their rhythmic pounding on a table. The act of reduplicated babbling, then, by virtue of its repetitiveness, is patently simpler than fully elaborated speech production. Commonly the action is primarily one of rhythmic jaw movement coordinated with phonation (Davis & MacNeilage, 1995; MacNeilage & Davis, 1990a, 1990b; MacNeilage, 1998). The stereotypical reproduction of syllables in this simple pattern appears to reflect infants' systematic control over the form of (a limited range of) jaw and tongue movement (along with phonation) just as other motoric stereotypies, when they begin to occur, reflect infants' consolidated control over leg movements or arm movements (Thelen, 1981, 1989). Prior to showing stereotypical movements associated with consolidated control, infants show periods of less coordinated and temporally erratic patterns of action, in both limb control and in jaw movement as we see it in reduplicated babbling.

The widespread appeal of the notion that speech is special (Liberman, Delattre, Gerstman, & Cooper, 1956; Liberman & Prince, 1977) might lead one to believe that a sharp division should be maintained between motoric precursors to speech and precursors to other motoric capabilities. However, the parallels among patterns of emergence for various types of motor action argue against a sharp dichotomy. Even though babbling resembles speech in many ways, even though infants may intend babbling as an approximation to what they understand speech to be, and even though speech clearly has some important special features that make it unique and remarkable, there remain important reasons to take account of and reflect on the similarities in form and pattern of canonical babbling and other motoric stereotypies.

Ultimately the infrastructural characterization of vocal development will profit from taking account of the commmonalities between speech-like actions and other kinds of physical capabilities. Properties and principles of speech in the context of the ultimate infrastructural characterization should be transparently related to the infrastructural properties and principles that underlie many other complex actions, including locomotion, gymnastics, typing, sewing, musicianship, gesture, and sign language.

LIMITS ON BABBLING CANALIZATION

The Role of Auditory Experience in Vocalization Development

As with other motoric developments, the speech capacity emerges in a way that is both canalized (as shown later) and also undeniably affected by experience. The claim that deaf and hearing infants babble alike (aside from differences in overall frequency of babbling by the end of the first year of life) has been overturned (Eilers & Oller, 1994; Stoel-Gammon & Otomo, 1986; Vinter, 1987, 1994a, 1994b). It is now clear that hearing plays a critical role in the emergence of the Canonical stage (see chap. 4). A wide range of infants with hearing impairment, many of whom have been selected specifically because they showed no significant secondary handicaps, have shown extraordinary delays in comparison with their hearing peers. Because the distinction between deaf and hearing infants in babbling applies even when deaf infants are singly handicapped (i.e., they have no other major impairments of mind or body), there is solid basis for the conclusion that restricted auditory experience, and not some mental or motoric deficit that commonly accompanies deafness, is at the root of the major delays in canonical babbling.

Nevertheless, the precise nature of the role played by experience in vocal development remains uncertain. Whether normal development requires infants to hear the sounds of mature speakers or merely to hear the sounds of their own voices is undetermined. The suggested role of self-audition is surprising to many who first encounter the evidence of canonical babbling delay in deaf infants, but in fact, there is empirical justification for the suspicion that auditory feedback from the self may play a critical role in development.

One reason for the suspicion derives from the important role played by auditory feedback in normal adult speech. If speakers attempt to read a passage while wearing headphones that present their own voices with a short delay (approximately the duration of a short syllable), their reading can be dramatically disrupted (Lee, 1951; Yates, 1963). As a participant in experiments in delayed auditory feedback during my years as a student, I learned directly how disruptive delayed audition of my own voice could be. During the delayed auditory feedback experiments, the sounds coming through the headphones, even though they were the product of my own voice, were out of sync with my speech. They were recorded and played back as I attempted to read aloud. I stuttered and stammered and found it impossible to speak normally except in short phrases. Fluent reading aloud was impossible. The experience proved to my own satisfaction (and similar experiments form the basis for the widely held conviction) that motor control of speech is deeply influenced by hearing one's own voice, presumably because the auditory information provides speakers with a basis for making subtle adjustments in movements of the vocal tract. It follows that normal development of speech-like vocalization could similarly depend upon experience with hearing one's own voice. This possibility is supported by evidence that delayed feedback has greatest effects in children, a fact interpreted to mean feedback may be especially important during acquisition of language (Siegel, Pick, & Garber, 1984).

That normal development of rhythmic movements in general may in part depend on auditory feedback is also suggested by studies tracking the rhythmic shaking of either an audible standard rattle or a noiseless rattle in normal infants (Ejiri, 1998b; Locke, Bekken, McMinn-Larson, & Wein, 1995). The shaking of both types of rattle increases in frequency up to the middle of the first year of life, at around the onset of rhythmic hand banging and canonical babbling. After that point, the shaking of noiseless rattles decreases markedly and the shaking of audible rattles continues, suggesting that after a crossroad point in development, auditory feedback may begin to play an especially important role in rhythmic stereotypies. Because deaf infants begin to be easily differentiated vocally from hearing infants at about the same crossroad age, it seems possible that deaf infants do not produce canonical babbling normally in the first year of life because they lack the auditory feedback loops that would support the growth of rhythmically produced syllables and perhaps other rhythmically controlled repetitive actions as well.

At the same time, the fact that auditory feedback is important in mature speech or in the development of certain motoric rhythmic patterns does not prove conclusively that it plays a critical role in development of the ability to produce well-formed speech sequences. The point of this discussion is to highlight one of the ways that audition could affect the onset of vocal milestones, while recognizing that there are multiple possible influences.

Another possible explanation for the delay in canonical babbling among the deaf is the one that has been more often assumed, namely that lack of experience in hearing other persons' voices prevents infants from achieving their full vocal potential. Still another possibility is that some combination of auditory experience with others' voices and experience hearing one's own sounds is needed to lay foundations for or to trigger the onset of canonical babbling. Thus, although there is clearly some role for audition in vocal development, the precise nature of that role remains uncertain.

The Role of Motor Practice in Vocal Development

Furthermore, the precise role played by the activity of vocalization, the physical act of making speech-like sounds, through all the typical stages of vocal development is likewise somewhat ambiguous. Although infants appear to practice vocalization systematically, especially from the Expansion stage onward, it is not clear that the activity is necessary to development. From what is now known, the activity could be interpreted as a manifestation of development, a by-product of an emerging capacity, or merely as the exercise of a capability without consequences on the capability itself. Studies of infants tracheostomized at birth provide the most revealing natural experiment on the issue of the possible role of vocal practice in development, because such infants are restricted, if not entirely prevented, from vocalizing during a substantial period that would normally be devoted to vocal activity. The impediment to vocalization is usually surgically removed at some point in the lives of such infants, allowing production of vocalizations, the form of which may be assumed to be influenced little if any by prior vocal practice.

Tracheostomy is a procedure in which a breathing tube, or cannula, is inserted directly into the airway below the level of the larynx. The procedure is required when abnormalities of the airway preclude normal respiration and a correction of the anatomical defect is inadvisable until a later age. While the cannula is in place, normal vibration of the vocal cords is for the most part precluded because air passes in and out of the trachea without ever going through the glottis, which is the source of phonation, the action that produces periodic energy for the voiced sounds of speech. Surgical correction of the breathing problem is accompanied by decannulation—including the removal of the breathing tube—and other adjustments, after which the patient begins oral and nasal breathing, air passes through the glottis and vocal cord vibration becomes possible.

Infants decannulated in the second year of life after tracheostomy in the first months or days of life commonly show relatively prompt acquisition of early words (Locke & Pearson, 1990; Ross, 1983; Simon, Fowler, & Handler, 1983). It would not, however, be correct to claim that no delays occur in vocal development after decannulation, nor that absolutely age-appropriate vocalizations are present as soon as the infant is out of surgery. Age-appropriate babbling and early speech typically appear within a few weeks or months after normal breathing is restored, but many tracheostomized patients show speech and language delays, sometimes including signs of vocal or articulatory pathology, later in life (Bleile, Stark, & McGowan, 1993; Ross, 1983; Simon et al., 1983).

Could speech and language retardation in tracheostomized individuals be the result of other handicaps resulting from medical problems unrelated to vocal exercise per se (or lack of it)? Perhaps so, but even if tracheostomized patients were to begin to produce perfectly age-appropriate babbling and speech on the very day of decannulation (an unlikely situation in any case given the trauma associated with the medical procedure), it would be unwarranted to conclude that vocal practice is unnecessary to the development of speech production abilities or babbling. The uncertainty of the conclusion is unavoidable because the natural experiment of tracheostomy provides an imperfect test of the role of practice in babbling and speech development.

The key problem is twofold. First, many infants who are tracheostomized can, at least under some circumstances, produce vocalization with the cannula in place, by obstructing the tube with a finger or hand. How much patients practice vocalizing using this method is hard to gauge in the absence of specific long-term studies of many individual infants, but the fact that they vocalize at all while tracheostomized precludes the contention that vocalization practice is absent in tracheostomized infants, and permits only the weaker supposition that practice is reduced with the cannula in place.

The second problem is perhaps even more confounding for the presumable natural experiment of tracheostomy: Relative lack of vocalization in cannulated infants does not indicate lack of motoric activity with the vocal tract. The lips, jaw, and tongue can all be postured, adjusted, and articulated in speech-like gestures prior to decannulation, and it is unclear what role practice in silent (or relatively silent) vocal movement might have in the later ability to babble and speak. Systematic research on the movements of the supraglottal vocal tract in tracheostomized infants have not, to my knowledge, been conducted, so there is no basis even for an estimate about relative amounts of supraglottal vocal movement practice in infants developing normally compared with those who are tracheostomized from birth. On the other hand, research with normally developing infants shows clearly that silent practice with vocal movements does occur, and that silent movements resembling reduplicated babbling (sometimes intermixed with sequences of canonical syllables), in particular, are a common feature of infancy (Meier et al., 1997).

As a consequence of these interpretive restrictions, the results of research on tracheostomized infants leave us with only a weak conclusion. The development of the vocal capability appears to be relatively canalized, showing relatively minor perturbations as a result of deprivation in vocal action experience imposed by physical airway limitations and impediments to phonation within the first year of life. At the same time, research results do not preclude the possibility that some practice and exercise with the vocal tract and the glottis are necessary for the normal development of the ability to produce speech-like sounds.

INFRASTRUCTURAL MODELING AND THE RELATION BETWEEN VOCAL AND MANUAL BABBLING

One of the most intriguing issues that has been raised in recent research on babbling concerns what happens with deaf infants who are exposed to sign language early in life. Do they perform a sort of substitute babbling in the manual domain? The answer appears to be positive (Petitto, 1991; Takei, 1996, 1998), although there is some dispute about whether the tendency to babble manually is very strong or merely reliably discernible in some infants exposed to sign language (Cormier, Mank, & Repp, 1998; Meier & Willerman, 1995). In any case, infants exposed to sign language are seen playing with their hands in gestural motions that resemble sign language.

The excitement that has been generated around this issue owes to the interpretation that babbling may be an amodal phenomenon that is so deeply a part of the human makeup that it tends to emerge even in the face of major sensory impediments. This research suggests an extraordinary degree of canalization. The whole output system for precursors to communication appears to be switched from mouth to hands if necessary to keep the required development of communicative foundation building on course.

One of the most interesting areas of work for the future of sign babbling research, in my opinion, will address a thorny issue for which the only lasting solution will be to develop an infrastructural model of potential sign languages, a model that would be parallel with that proposed here for spoken languages and would incorporate the same or similar properties and principles (as outlined in chap. 12) in many cases. The problematic issue concerns the differentiation between hand actions that are not inherently sign-like and hand actions that could be specifically brought to the service of a potential sign system. When investigators study babies' gestural actions and other stereotypic motor behaviors, how will they tell which actions are precursors to sign?

Consider rhythmic hand banging as a particularly important example. In hearing infants, hand banging begins at about the point that canonical babbling does, and other noiseless rhythmic hand movements seem to accompany many rhythmic babbling sequences at the same age (Eilers, Oller, et al., 1993; Ejiri & Masataka, 1996). If a deaf infant begins rhythmic hand banging on schedule (and Meier et al., 1997, reported that they seem to, based on observations of a small number of individuals) are we to interpret the action as manual babbling? Because it resembles reduplicated vocal babbling in both age of onset and rhythmic structure, it seems possible that hand banging should be taken to be the gestural equivalent of vocal canonical babbling.

However, in the case of vocal canonical babbling there exists an externally justified model indicating what principles well-formed syllables must obey to function as speech. This model of infraphonology provides reasoned criteria by which to judge when a sequence is canonical and when it is not. It is thus known that a sequence properly transcribed as [dadada] is canonical. On the other hand, a sequence of vocalization interrupted rhythmically by glottal stops (e.g., [aʔaʔaʔaʔ] or [əʔəʔəʔ]) does not count as canonical because it lacks one of the key characteristics of canonical sequences, rapid formant transitions. Glottal stops require no articulation above the level of the larynx, so they produce no formant transitions. It is notable in this context that deaf infants often produce glottal sequences with excellent rhythmic control long before they begin genuine canonical babbling (Koopmans-van Beinum et al., 1998; Oller, 1991; Oller et al., 1985). The model of infraphonology provides a basis to differentiate a very speech-like rhythmic structure (reduplicated babbling) from a less speech-like rhythmic structure (glottal sequences).

The study of sign language babbling would be enhanced by a similar model that might be called *infracherology,* taking off on the term coined for the contrastive signaling units of sign languages, *cheremes* (Stokoe, 1960), which are composed of physical features including various possible hand configurations, hand movements, and bodily positions for the configurations and movements. The infracherological system would provide a natural reference point against which to determine whether hand banging should count as canonical manual babbling. Perhaps as a prerequisite for canonical manual babbling it will be determined that a particular subset of possible canonical hand configurations is required during the performance of rhythmic hand movements, or that a particular canonical relation between configuration and movement is required. Such principles of canonicity in sign could be expressed in a manner analogous to the four principles of canonical syllable construction (see, e.g., Table 1.3).

A similar issue of differentiation concerns pointing and other natural gestures that seem to constitute fixed signals the way crying or laughter constitute fixed signals in the vocal realm. Infrastructural modeling helps provide a systematic basis for treating fixed vocal signals differently from protophones along with a systematic basis for recognition of the fact that the use of both involves some common properties and principles. Infrastructural modeling should be able to play a similar role in interpretation of manual communication. Gestures such as pointing or reaching, with universal or near-universal functions in the world's cultures, would seem to be interpretable as fixed signals just as crying and laughter are. Other early manual gestures that have no universal communicative functions might be viewed as protocheres, precursors to sign, in ways that might parallel the way protophones are viewed as precursors to speech. Protophones emerge in stages. If a variety of early protocheres can be shown to emerge in stages in the first 6 months of life in deaf infants exposed to sign, the parallelism between spoken and manual babbling would be shown to be even richer than it has thus far been shown to be. The demonstration will depend on formulation of an infrastructural model capable of providing an independent basis for identification of protocheres as distinct from other gestural motoric actions, and also capable of explicating the progression that may be found across protochere stages.

Another important benefit of infrastructural modeling in the gestural and sign arenas would be the formulation of a more powerful basis for comparison for speech and sign in general. As with other cross-system comparisons considered in this volume (see in particular discussion around Figs. 1.3, 14.7, and 14.8), the optimal point of reference appears always to be found at the level of infrastructural systems. Sign languages and speech have an enormous amount in common, both in mature structure and in development. Comparison of the two systems at the infrastructural level would help to illuminate that commonality.

7

Canalization Results:
The Stability of Protophone
Development in a Variety of Contexts

SIGNIFICANT OUTCOMES OF INFRAPHONOLOGICALLY
INSPIRED RESEARCH ON VOCAL DEVELOPMENT

The infrastructural interpretation of protophones has raised theoretically
and practically significant questions about potential abnormalities of development in the foundations for speech. As soon as normal protophone stages
came into focus, there was interest in turning the camera toward events of environment or biology that might perturb their development. In part the special interest in possible aberrations of protophone development owes to the
fact that they appear so early in life. If their progress is perturbed early, and if
it is possible to detect such perturbation, then it might be possible to identify
potential abnormalities long before they would otherwise be noticed: the earlier, the better. It appears that early intervention attenuates or eliminates the
effects of many disorders (Guralnick, 1997; Ramey & Campbell, 1984;
Resnick, Armstrong, & Carter, 1988; Robinshaw, 1995; Schweinhart,
Weikart, & Larner, 1986; Yoshinaga-Itano, Sedey, Coulter, & Mehl, 1998).

A series of efforts to identify groups of children who might show delayed
onset of protophone usage, especially canonical babbling, has produced a surprising result. Instead of finding delays, the studies have usually found that
infants at risk or presumed to be at risk for developmental disorders begin canonical babbling and use precanonical protophones at least as early in life as
infants not presumed to be at risk. The result proves more potentially useful
than might be thought at first glance. The canalization of protophone development (suggested by its relative imperviousness to risk factors) places limits
on the numbers of infants who are likely to show late protophone development. The small number of infants who do turn out to be delayed—for in-

stance, the ones that do show late onset of canonical babbling—may prove to be at substantially higher risk for later language disorders than infants deemed at risk for other reasons such as prematurity or low socioeconomic status (SES). Because disorders of language occur in only a small subset of infants, even among those deemed at risk, the determination that some of them are delayed in canonical babbling may help focus attention on a particular group of infants to whom intervention ought to be administered.

The robustness of babbling in the face of risk factors turns out, then, to be useful in practice because it furnishes a background against which it may be relatively easy to focus on a foreground of infrequently occurring abnormalities. Furthermore, the robustness of protophone stage development as seen in the studies to be described in chapters 7 and 8 provides additional evidence of the maturational stability and biological depth of the emerging speech capacity.

RESULTS ON CANALIZATION OF BABBLING

The Role of Low SES

Children who suffer inattention and neglect are often expected to show delayed milestones of development (see, e.g., Hoff-Ginsberg, 1991). Indeed, speech and language deficits are known to occur reliably, although not uniformly, in children born into poverty (Hart & Risley, 1981), a condition that is assumed to be associated with inattention and neglect. In fact, the familial pressures of poverty do appear to be associated with measurably lower rates of vocal communication from parents and other caretakers to infants and young children (Harris, Barrett, Jones, & Brookes, 1988). The neglected child is slow in learning to talk (see Snow, 1995; see review in Locke & Snow, 1997). Even the particular lexical items a child hears repeatedly have a direct impact on the particular vocabulary that the child acquires (Hart, 1991; Jouanjean-L'Antoëne, 1994). Thus it seems reasonable to conclude that children born into poverty are at risk for being delayed language learners.

As an initial test of the possibility that rate of protophone development may be affected by SES, healthy, full-term infants in a series of longitudinal studies were compared in two subgroups: middle SES (MSES) and low SES (LSES). This initial test did not actually address infants growing up in conditions of poverty. The LSES group was selected to show lower SES than the MSES group, but in fact the LSES families were not impoverished in the normal sense of the term. The assignment to groups was based on information supplied by the parents in questionnaires, according to a combination of criteria from Hollingshead (1978) and Nam and Powers (1983). In accord with the system, the MSES families in general had white-collar or professional occupations, college degrees, and two parents living at home. LSES families in general had blue-collar or manual occupations, high school degrees, and either one or two parents living at home. Both these groups can be contrasted with very low SES

(VLSES) families who are genuinely impoverished. These are generally one-parent families in which the parent is unemployed and uneducated.

The study was based on samples of vocalizations tape-recorded at monthly intervals along with parental interviews throughout the study. Onset of canonical babbling was determined by methods that have proven to be reliable in the sense that parent report of onset can be confirmed in the vast majority of cases by independent laboratory-based judgments of infant canonical status (Eilers, Oller, et al., 1993; Lewedag, 1995; Oller et al., 1996).

The results of the research indicated that LSES infants of similar ethnicity and language backgrounds to the MSES comparators were not in any obvious way delayed in the onset of developmental stages for protophone categories (Eilers, Oller, et al., 1993). For example, the onset of canonical babbling was 26 weeks for 14 LSES infants and 29 weeks for 15 MSES infants, differences that favored the LSES group but were not statistically reliable. Other protophone stages similarly appeared to occur on time in both groups with no clear effect of SES. All the infants produced quasivowels, gooing, and many Expansion stage vocalizations prior to the onset of canonical babbling.

Similarities in vocal development milestones across the two groups were matched by similarities in general motoric development. Rolling over, reaching, sitting up, standing, walking, and rhythmic hand banging all began at about the same ages in the two groups.

The quantitative analysis of recordings subjected to protophone categorization and transcription when appropriate also showed substantial similarities across the MSES and LSES groups. Figure 7.1 (top panel) based on data from Oller, Eilers, Steffens, Lynch, and Urbano (1994) shows ratios of canonical syllables to all syllables for the two groups 4 to 16 months of age. The groups show great similarity. Higher scores indicate increasing speechiness, and the absolute levels and patterns of growth across time are similar.

There was only one factor monitored in the study that revealed a reliable difference between the SES groups, and this was a factor that did not pertain to the quality of production of canonical or precanonical sounds at each age. Infraphonologically the groups appeared to be indistinguishable, even in terms of the relative proportion of usage of different protophone types at each age. However, the total amount of vocalization in protophone categories of any kind, per unit time, did differ and it showed the MSES group to be the more voluble, with 7.5 utterances per minute compared with 6.0 for the LSES group (Fig. 7.1, bottom panel). The results are notable because they suggest SES does affect infants' tendencies to engage in vocalization in the laboratory sessions. At the same time the results do not suggest that SES affects the development of the basic infraphonological structures that determine the kinds of sounds infants produce when they do vocalize. The protophone stages themselves appear to be robust with regard to SES differences.

However, the differences in SES in this longitudinal study may be insufficient to produce the kinds of differences that one might expect based on major

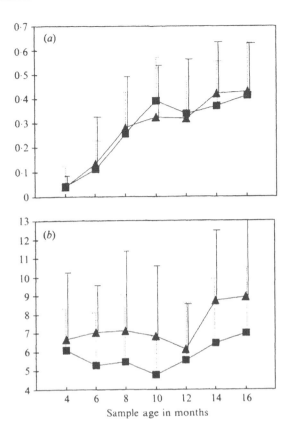

FIG. 7.1.   (a) Canonical babbling ratio for infants of LSES and MSES matched at corrected ages. (b) Volubility (or utterances per minute) for infants of LSES and MSES matched at corrected ages. ■-■, LSES; ▲-▲, MSES. From "Speech-like vocalizations in infancy: An evaluation of potential risk factors," by Oller, D. K., Eilers, R. E., Steffens, M. L., Lynch, M. P., & Urbano, R., 1994, *Journal of Child Language, 221*, p. 50. Copyright 1994 by Cambridge University Press. Reprinted with permission.

discrepancies in family resources and education. The amount of variation between the MSES and LSES families in terms of ability to survive and maintain reasonable comforts may be trivial compared with the kinds of variations that have occurred throughout human history. Perhaps in VLSES families, where deprivation has clearer effects on day-to-day living, there would be more dramatic differences in treatment of offspring, and consequently perhaps there would be observable impact on vocal development, an issue considered in a subsequent section of this chapter.

The Role of Prematurity

Another evaluation addressed the role of physical risks for vocal development, risks previously presumed to exist in infants born prematurely. There are empirical reasons to expect such infants to be delayed in various developmental domains including those of communication (see, e.g., Goldfield, 1999), even when comparisons are made between full term infants and preterm infants at gestationally corrected ages (Crnic et al., 1983; Greenberg & Crnic, 1988; Zarin-Ackerman, Lewis, & Driscoll, 1978). In research on preterm infants, age corrections are made by obtaining medically based estimates of the number of weeks by which each infant was prematurely born (DiPietro & Allen, 1991), and subtracting that number from the chronological age in weeks. Using this method infants born at term (40 weeks gestation) and infants born prematurely (less than 40 weeks) can be matched on gestational age at any point. Because results of research on various developmental fronts suggest delays in age-corrected premature infants, it was deemed likely that protophone development would also be delayed in premature infants.

Because the goal of the work was to evaluate infants that were born ahead of schedule but for whom major medical complications had not occurred, infants with intraventricular hemorrhage or major events of anoxia were excluded. Selection criteria also ruled out significant congenital defects such as craniofacial anomalies. The preterm infants were estimated to have been born an average of 7 weeks early. Preterm babies are born less mature than their full-term counterparts and consequently their early experiences are assimilated to a less mature mind and body. The question is what effects such differences in the interaction between maturity and experience have on development.

The results of the study offer further indications of the robustness of infraphonological development. The physical risk of premature birth did not, as predicted, produce a general delay in the occurrence of vocal or other motor milestones during the first year of life (Eilers, Oller, et al., 1993). In fact, after gestational age correction, there was no discernible delay in the onset of any of the factors evaluated statistically (canonical babbling, hand banging, rolling, reaching, sitting up, standing, and walking). Perhaps surprisingly, the data suggested accelerated onsets in preterm infants for both hand banging ($p < .01$) and canonical babbling ($p < .053$). Why early birth might accelerate certain developments is a matter of interest, because there have been other reports suggesting that early experience in nonhumans can trigger unexpectedly rapid development (Foreman & Altaha, 1991; Licklighter, 1990a, 1990b). It would appear that rhythmic motoric developments such as hand banging and canonical babbling (especially in its reduplicated form) may be triggered by experiences that accumulate across the first months of life.

The fact that deaf infants begin to produce canonical babbling late seems to provide further evidence of an important role for early experience. It is reasoned that deaf infants accumulate the necessary experience more slowly (through limited residual hearing and other sensory modalities) than their hearing peers (see Lynch, Oller, & Steffens, 1989). The evidence from the study of preterm infants suggests that any delaying factors associated with prematurity are outweighed by the accelerating factor of early experience. Eilers et al. (1993) reasoned that the robustness of canonical babbling onset may have reflected a biological premium within the human species to keep physical developments related to speech communication on course.

The apparent canalization of canonical babbling onset as seen in robustness of development in preterm infants appeared to be matched in the occurrence of other protophone categories. Developmental patterns in the Eilers et al. study provided no evidence at all of delays in gooing or Expansion stage vocalizations among the preterm infants.

The quantitative evidence based on recordings subjected to protophone categorization also showed basic similarity between the preterm and full-term infants for various protophones (Figs. 7.2a, 7.2b, 7.2c). One might have expected that because the preterm infants had shown accelerated onsets for canonical babbling, their proportions of production for canonical syllables would have been higher than for age-matched peers. The lack of such a difference suggests that when preterm infants begin canonical babbling early, they do so with less vigor than full-term infants.

The results suggest that early triggering of the onset leaves its mark in patterns of usage (and see Goldfield, 1999). By the same token, other evidence suggests that late onset of canonical babbling in deaf infants (Oller & Eilers, 1988) and in infants with Down syndrome (Lynch, Oller, Steffens, Levine, et al., 1995) may be accompanied by differences in the session-to-session pattern of usage of protophones available in the infant repertoires. In particular, less stability of production of sounds deemed to be in the current repertoires has often been noted across samples for handicapped infants.

The results from premature infants suggest canalization in one sense; prematurity does not seem to slow protophone development. If anything it speeds it up a little. The special mix of maturation and experience found in preterm infants does, then, appear to have special effects—early triggering and, apparently, slight reductions in rate of production of canonical syllables once they appear.

The Role of Combinations of Extreme Poverty and Prematurity

Another effort addressed a group of infants who were both preterm and LSES. To the extent that low SES and prematurity are taken to be risk factors, these infants were doubly at risk. Previous research has suggested that risk factors sometimes compound (Barocas, Seifer, & Sameroff, 1985; Barocas, Seifer, Sameroff, Andrews, Croft, & Ostrow, 1991; Malatesta, Grigoryev, Lamb, Albin, & Culver, 1986; Sameroff & Seifer, 1983; Scott & Carran, 1987) to pro-

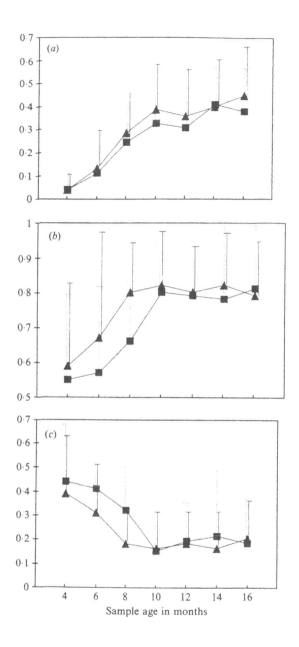

FIG. 7.2. (a) Canonical babbling ratio for preterm and full-term infants matched at corrected ages. (b) Full vowel ratio for preterm and full-term infants matched at corrected ages. (c) Quasivowel ratio for preterm and full-term infants matched at corrected ages. ■-■, preterm; ▲-▲, full-term. From "Speech-like vocalizations in infancy:

continued on next page

duce deleterious outcomes in health and development. It might be imagined that prematurity alone or low SES alone might produce negligible ill effects, but the two working in concert might yield major delays in onset of speech-like vocalizations. The results did not confirm such a prediction, however, as LSES preterm infants developed vocally without delay with respect to full-term MSES infants (Eilers, Oller, et al., 1993).

Still, the differences in SES between the two groups may have been insufficient to reveal the potential effects of social deprivation. Indeed, even though the parents of the LSES infants were less highly educated and less highly employed than their MSES counterparts, they were no less actively involved in the study, and there was no indication that they were less committed to their infants. Gross differences between the MSES and LSES groups in factors such as nutrition or household safety did not appear to be present. It is possible that the selection of families for a study requiring long-term commitments created a bias in participant recruitment. Perhaps LSES families that volunteered to participate were not entirely typical of all families meeting the assignment criteria, but were especially interested in the welfare of their infants, sensitive to needs of care taking, and so on.

In an effort to create a more extreme test of the roles of SES and of multiple risk, another study was conducted allowing comparison with a group of preterm infants from circumstances of extreme poverty (VLSES; Oller, Eilers, Basinger, Steffens, & Urbano, 1995). The data indicated again that social setting, even extreme poverty, does not appear to throw the development of canonical babbling off course. By 10 months of age (corrected for prematurity), it appeared that virtually all the VLSES infants were in the canonical stage. The data suggested striking similarity between VLSES infants and infants of higher SES and suggested no important differences in protophone development.

Evaluation of the proportion of canonical babbling produced among the infants in all the groups also revealed no reliable differences. Consequently, in terms of canonical babbling stage attainment and proportional production, the VLSES infants were not discernibly delayed as a group.

The one VLSES infant that did appear to be delayed (based on failure to produce a canonical sample at either 10 or 16 months) was very ill, with multiple hospitalizations during the period in question (see Oller et al., 1995). On the other hand there were four infants among the VLSES sample that were known to have been exposed to crack cocaine prenatally, and for whom the data showed no evidence of delay in onset or performance of canonical babbling.

Other aspects of the evaluation of protophone production also suggested substantial similarity among the infants of all the SES groupings. Evaluations of full vowel ratios showed no indication of depressed performance in the VLSES infants. Other protophone types (raspberries, squeals, etc.) were also produced similarly among the three SES groups. Extreme poverty thus played no obvious retarding role in the development of infraphonological capabilities.

Volubility data presented a different picture. The depression of quantity of babbling per unit time that was observed in comparing the LSES and MSES infants was seen again with the VLSES infants.

The results of the study suggest that infraphonological capabilities are indeed difficult to deflect from their preordained course. Babbling outcomes proved to be little if at all affected for infants living in very low socioeconomic conditions. In such conditions of extreme poverty, important deficiencies in familial interaction are presumed to occur (Harris et al., 1988; Hart & Risley, 1992; Osborn, 1968). Furthermore, because the VLSES infants were also prematurely born, the study confirms again the robustness of protophone development with regard to multiple factors that constitute risks to development in general.

The Role of Exposure to Different Languages and Bilingualism

The babbling drift hypothesis expresses the expectation that different kinds of language exposure might yield differences in babbling. Indeed, differences have been reported among infants from different language communities (de Boysson-Bardies et al., 1984; Hallé, de Boysson-Bardies, & Vihman, 1991; Levitt & Utman, 1992; Levitt & Wang, 1991; Vihman & de Boysson-Bardies, 1994), but it should be noted that such differences have not focused on infraphonological parameters or protophone development directly. Instead they usually focus either on differences in canonical syllable production as indicated in transcription or on acoustic differences that can be monitored spectrographically.

Even though infraphonological parameters must, by definition, have substantial universality, it remains an empirical question whether language experience might alter the course or change the rate of infraphonological development in the first year of life. We know that infants must be affected vocally by their ambient language experience at some point. Is it possible that such experience could affect the rate or form of emerging protophones?

A longitudinal study of monolingual English- and Spanish-learning infants in Miami showed no differences in the development of infraphonological capabilities (Oller & Eilers, 1982). Differences in language background yielded no obvious differences in rate or content of protophone development. Gooing, raspberries, squeals, and growls were all present in both groups, and canonical babbling began in both at about the same age.

An additional study (Oller et al., 1997) addressed the possible role of multiple language exposure on infraphonological development. There was no way ahead of time to know what kinds of effects to expect, as bilingualism in general has been claimed variously to be beneficial or harmful (see Ben-Zeev, 1977; Ianco-Worrall, 1972; Lambert, 1981; Macnamara, 1967; Peal & Lambert, 1962; Torrance, Wu, Gowan, & Aliotti, 1970). Taking the cue from such contradictory claims, if there are effects of bilingualism on babbling, they could be either accelerating, because the richer phonetic experience of children growing up bilingually might stimulate special developments, or retarding, because the extra burdens of hearing a wider variety of sounds might prove confusing to infants.

The results of the research, however, provided no reason to believe that bilingualism has any effect on rate or quality of infraphonological development, even for infants from bilingual families in the LSES category and even if the infants were born prematurely. The onset of canonical babbling, for example, was slightly earlier in the 29 bilingual infants than in their 44 monolingual counterparts, and the differences were so small (an average of less than a week) as to suggest no reliable effect. All the other patterns seen in the monolingual samples regarding canonical babbling seemed to be mirrored by the bilinguals. The premature bilinguals at corrected ages began canonical babbling a little earlier then their full-term counterparts, and outpaced the full term infants by about the same magnitude (3.5 weeks) as in the case of monolinguals. The LSES bilinguals did not show any delay in onset with respect to their MSES counterparts; instead the LSES group began the canonical stage a little (although not reliably earlier) than the MSES group, the same pattern that had been observed with monolinguals. The results on canonical babbling onset suggested no basis for any contention that bilingualism, either functioning alone or in concert with other factors (prematurity or low SES), constitutes either a risk or an advantage for vocal development. Instead, the onset of the stage of canonical babbling seems to be robust with respect to language environment.

Although other stages of vocal development were not evaluated in the study at the same level of detail, the outcomes of the work also suggested grossly similar patterns of appearance in the other protophone stages across monolingual and bilingual children. All major categories of protophones appeared in both groups at about the same ages.

The quantitative analysis of transcribed tape recordings also failed to detect either retarding or accelerating effects for bilingualism. Canonical babbling ratios and vowel ratios were statistically indistinguishable across monolingual and bilingual groups. Furthermore, analysis of the volubility of infants in the two groups as expressed in the sessions showed no tendency for bilingual infants to vocalize either more or less than their monolingual counterparts. The study of infants growing up in bilingual homes provided further support for the idea that the development of speech-like vocalizations across the protophone stages is highly canalized.

8

Limits on the Disruption
of the Canalized Pattern of Babbling

WHY HEARING IMPAIRMENT DISRUPTS BABBLING
BUT DOES NOT PREVENT IT

Given the extensive evidence of canalization in the development of infraphonological capabilities, it is worth taking a somewhat deeper look at circumstances that delay or otherwise disrupt the process. Congenital deafness produces severe delays in the onset of canonical babbling, and it can be concluded, as a consequence, that hearing experience normally plays at least a role in triggering the events that lead to well-formed syllable production. Yet it is worthwhile to ask why deaf children ever go on to babble if hearing is so important to the process of development.

The best guess currently is that hearing-impaired infants achieve a stage of canonical babbling only after they have accumulated sufficient experience to trigger the onset. Because they have only residual hearing, it takes longer for that accumulated experience to reach its threshold level than it does in hearing children, or so we have reasoned.

There are several kinds of important evidence relevant to the reasoning. First, there is the correlation between canonical babbling onset and age of amplification in congenitally deaf infants (Eilers & Oller, 1994). For most of the deaf infants for whom age of onset of the canonical stage has been obtained, there is also information about when they first started using hearing aids, the "age of amplification." Although amplification is usually of significant assistance to deaf children if it is accompanied by aggressive auditory training, the degree of assistance depends in part on the degree of residual hearing. Children with very little residual hearing benefit less from hearing aids than those with more residual hearing. Still, almost all deaf children do benefit to a measurable extent. It stands to reason, consequently, that the sooner one begins amplification with deaf infants, the sooner they may accumulate the necessary experience to trigger onset of canonical babbling. Similarly, it stands to reason that deaf infants with more residual hearing should accumulate the necessary experience sooner than those with less. Very few of the deaf infants that have been followed longitudinally had much residual hearing, and the numbers of infants studied have proven too small to conduct a useful test of the role of degree of residual hearing in protophone development. However, there was major variation in the age at which hearing aids were fitted among the infants in the study, and this variation allowed a correlational test.

The correlation between age of onset of canonical babbling and age of amplification in deaf infants was positive, significant, and very high ($r = .69$, see Fig. 8.1). Nearly half the variance (48%) in onset of canonical babbling was accounted for by age at amplification. The correlation strongly suggests, although it cannot prove, that the enhancement afforded by aided hearing speeds the onset of canonical babbling, presumably by speeding the rate at which auditory experience is accumulated in deaf children.

The magnitude of this empirically determined correlation is remarkable, but the real correlation between age of onset of canonical babbling and age of amplification could be higher. Error in measurement for any two phenomena limits the ability to recognize any potential relation between them, because the error tends to attenuate the correlation that can be empirically determined. Consequently the real relation in nature may be higher than the correlation that can be determined empirically, and there is no way to tell how much higher the real correlation might be. The obtained correlation often provides only an estimated lower limit on the real correlation.

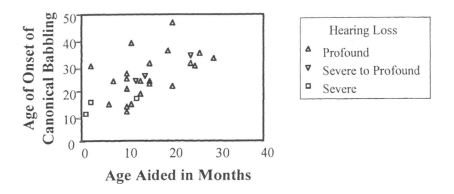

FIG. 8.1.   Relation between age of onset of canonical babbling and age at auditory amplification in hearing-impaired infants and young children. From "Infant Vocalizations and the Early Diagnosis of Severe Hearing Impairment," by R. E. Eilers and D. K. Oller, 1994, *Journal of Pediatrics, 124*, p. 202. Copyright 1994 by Mosby Year Book, Inc. Reprinted with permission.

Substantial error of measurement is clearly involved in the obtained correlation between canonical babbling onset and age of amplification. First of all, the age of onset cannot be measured perfectly even when infants are seen often in longitudinal work. The age of onset determined for each infant can be incorrect by weeks or months, depending on the size of the interval between contacts with the infant or infant's family. This inaccuracy of determination was likely to have been particularly high with the deaf infants, because their onset ages appear to have been less reliably assignable than in studies of hearing children. One reason is that canonical babbling in hearing-impaired children appears to begin less abruptly than in hearing infants. Instead of beginning to produce canonical syllables repetitively on one day and then continuing to do so essentially every day thereafter, deaf infants often seem to start the Canonical stage on one day and then leave off, producing no more canonical syllables for days or weeks. Eventually, but sometimes months later, the stage is firmly established and canonical syllables are produced consistently. The Canonical stage onset, therefore, cannot be easily assigned to a single day or week in deaf infants, but shows inevitable measurement variance that may be a month or greater (Oller & Eilers, 1988).

Interpretation of the correlation between age of canonical babbling and age of amplification is also complicated by the fact that age of amplification is only a proxy variable used to determine the amount of accumulated auditory experience. Age of amplification is not a perfect measure of the amount of accumulated auditory experience, because there is considerable variation in the extent to which hearing aids are utilized with deaf infants after they are provided. Infants often remove their hearing aids, and it is then necessary for parents to intervene to reestablish amplification. Only with consistent attention from family members can consistent usage of hearing aids be attained with infants, and consequently there is large variation in how much usage occurs with individual infants.

A better measure of accumulated experience, if it could be obtained, would be based on the number of hours of usage of amplification prior to the onset of canonical babbling. The proxy measure, age of amplification, provides only a noisy estimate of the degree of auditory experience, and the greater the noise, the greater the potential attenuation of the correlation between canonical babbling onset and the variable of interest, the amount of accumulated auditory experience.

Finally, although all the deaf infants in the study were at least bilaterally severely impaired, there was some variation from infant to infant in the degree of residual hearing available. These differences in degree of residual hearing constitute yet another limitation on the correlation, because there is every reason to believe that the measure of age of amplification and the amount of accumulated auditory experience have complex relations to the degree of residual hearing.

Granted, a correlational relation does not prove a causal relation, but there are reasons to suspect in this case that a threshold level of accumulated auditory experience may indeed constitute a requirement of canonical babbling onset. All in all the high correlation obtained between onset of canonical babbling and age of amplification suggests the possibility that auditory experience plays a surprisingly strong role in triggering protophone development. Nearly half the variance can be accounted for even though the measures being correlated are themselves imperfect due to several major sources of measurement error.

DEVELOPMENT OF PROTOPHONES
IN A COCHLEAR APLASIA

The results of the studies reviewed suggest that accumulated auditory experience may play a triggering role in vocal development, but they do not create an airtight case for the idea that auditory experience is required for canonical babbling to begin. The various results suggest that a child with absolutely no hearing, and consequently no potential for auditory benefit from amplification, would either begin the Canonical stage very late or not at all, but the results do not clearly determine which possibility is correct. If a child with absolute deafness never began to produce canonical babbling, it would seem to suggest that some kind of auditory experience, however limited, is necessary for infraphonological development to occur. On the other hand, if such a child eventually did begin to produce well-formed syllables, it would suggest that audition is not the only kind of sensory experience that can trigger progress in protophone development.

Cases of total lack of hearing are found in *cochlear aplasia,* a rare condition where the primary organ of hearing simply does not develop. One deaf infant with cochlear aplasia was studied systematically by Lynch et al. (1989). The infant had shown no discernible response to his hearing aids at 2 years of age, and was consequently evaluated through computerized axial tomography (CAT) revealing the condition of cochlear aplasia. The child was permanently and totally deaf, and hearing aids were in principle incapable of transmitting auditory information to him.

The child had been nearly silent up to the point when first referred for treatment, vocalizing little in any of the protophone categories other than quasivowels. The child's pattern of production was atypically primitive even for a deaf child. It was clear that if this child ever reached the Canonical stage, the event would provide incontrovertible evidence that canonical babbling onset does not depend on auditory experience, even if auditory experience is particularly well suited to triggering it. The result would suggest that experience in other sensory modalities could, under extreme circumstances, provide a sufficient, although imperfect, substitute for hearing.

After the diagnosis of cochlear aplasia, clinical treatment provided to the child was modified to focus on his visual and tactile capabilities. Lipreading was emphasized, and the child was fitted with tactile aids utilized routinely with deaf children in the project where he was being educated. *Tactual vocoders* (see Brooks, Frost, Mason, & Gibson, 1986; Cowan, Blamey, Galvin, Savant, Alcantara, & Clark, 1990; Eilers, Vergara, Oller, & Balkany, 1993; Miskiel, Özdamar, Oller, & Eilers, 1992; Özdamar, Oller, Miskiel, & Eilers, 1988; Vergara, Miskiel, Oller, & Eilers, 1995) are devices that receive sound through a microphone, divide the sound into a number of channels based on acoustic frequency, and then use the information in each channel to drive a stimulator on the skin. The fingertip-sized stimulators are worn in a linear array on the skin (the arm, abdomen, or forehead are favorite locations) with the high-frequency channels at one side and the low-frequency channels at the other. As sound occurs in the environment, the microphone picks up acoustic information and the tactual vocoder transmits the information in real time to the skin of the wearer. The device is a simple, real-time spectral display on the skin.

A few months after the cochlear aplasic child began receiving tactile speech training, his vocalization pattern changed distinctly, and shortly after he began wearing a tactual aid during his entire school day, he began the Canonical stage. By 32 to 34 months of age the child produced richly canonical samples of vocalizations consistently.

The results of the research with the cochlear aplasic child provide clear evidence that deafness, even total deafness, does not preclude canonical vocal development. Experience does appear to play a role in vocal development, and auditory experience seems to have a privileged role in providing useful experience, but other kinds of experience appear to be substitutable under extreme circumstances.

The results did not show unambiguously that the tactile experience played a significant role in the child's vocal development. At least two important changes took place when the child entered treatment. One concerned intensive, face-to-face vocal therapy, consisting primarily of attempted elicitation of protophones through verbal and social interaction. The second concerned an attempt to highlight sensory information that was available to the child through emphasis on facial actions, lip movements, and utilization of the tactile aids. Either one or both of the changes in the child's treatment could have played an important role in his development of canonical sounds.

In fact there is no way to rule out the possibility that the onset of the Canonical stage would have occurred even without intervention. The only certain conclusion from the study of the infant with cochlear aplasia is that auditory experience did not play a role in the onset of the Canonical stage. As an existence proof, the study shows that audition is not absolutely necessary in the development of canonical babbling.

THE INTERPRETATION OF HEARING IMPAIRMENT AS A LIMITED DISRUPTOR OF VOCAL DEVELOPMENT

The fact that canonical babbling is delayed in deaf children indicates a limitation on the robustness of protophone development, but the fact that canonical babbling begins at all in a case where a primary triggering mechanism is absent suggests a limitation on the limitation. Protophone development is disrupted by hearing impairment, but other sensory modalities seem to be able to take the place of audition, supplying the necessary experience to spur development on, a fact that provides another view of canalization. The human organism seems to be set to find a way to produce canonical babbling in the face of many obstacles. Multiple channels appear to be available to meet nature's apparent babbling imperative. If sign language is available in the deaf infant's environment, then the canalization tendency appears to be reflected in manual babbling (Petitto, 1991).

Other facts about the limited nature of the disruption in canonical development under the influence of hearing impairment provide further indications of the vigor of human vocal development. Major disruptive effects of hearing impairment on protophone development appear to be restricted in two ways: delays are limited to cases of substantial auditory loss, and disruptions are relatively hard to discern prior to the age at which the Canonical stage usually begins in hearing infants. Concerning the first limitation, it should be noted that the various studies of late onset canonical babbling (Eilers & Oller, 1994; Kent et al., 1987; Murai, 1961; Oller & Eilers, 1988; Stoel-Gammon & Otomo, 1986; Vinter, 1987) in the hearing impaired have all focused on infants with at least severe impairments. Hearing impairment is traditionally categorized as mild, moderate, severe, or profound. Sometimes, individuals found to show deficits that are near the boundaries of the categories are characterized by a dual term, such as severe to profound. Although categorization systems differ to some extent from author to author, infants in the studies just noted have virtually all been in the severe to profound or profound categories. Because they were both congenitally and at least severely to profoundly impaired, they are commonly referred to as *deaf.*

Demographically speaking, there are fewer deaf infants in the population at large than infants with less substantial impairments. Compared to the deaf, the more numerous children with mild and moderate hearing impairments are not the focus of so much research and media attention in part because their more limited impairments produce effects that are much more subtle (see, however, Feagans, Kipp, & Blood, 1994; Friel-Patti, Finitzo-Hieber, Conti, & Brown, 1982; Teele, Klein, & Rosner, 1984; Wallace, Gravel, McCarton, & Ruben, 1988). Although moderately impaired children may have difficulty hearing their teachers unless they sit close to the front of the class, they do not typically need to be educated in self-contained classrooms for the hearing impaired, and they do not need sign language interpreters to assist them—indeed, they usually do not learn sign language. They speak intelligibly and understand speech fluently as long as the signal-to-noise ratio is reasonably good. Deaf children, on the other hand, typically suffer major difficulties, and most often do not learn to understand speech well enough to attend lectures without an interpreter, nor to carry on a complex conversation with a stranger, not even with a familiar individual at a normal rate of speech.

Somewhere near the boundary between moderate and severe hearing impairments, there is a threshold beyond which a relatively minor impairment suddenly becomes a major one. At about the same threshold point in degree of hearing loss, it appears there is also a threshold for major delays in the onset of canonical babbling. Research to date suggests that bilateral hearing impairments in the mild and moderate range do not usually retard the onset of canonical babbling beyond 10 months of age (Oller & Eilers, 1998) whereas impairments in the severe-to-profound and profound ranges do produce delays in the great majority of infants (although there are a few exceptions, especially among infants with the greatest degree of residual hearing).

Systematic research on vocalizations of infants with more minor hearing impairments has been extremely limited. Evidence that mild and moderate impairments rarely produce major disruption is based on a few individual infants who have been followed. For example, one longitudinal case study evaluated an infant with congenital bilateral atresia, a condition in which the external ear canal is found to be closed at birth; the canal must be surgically opened at a later point. Atresia produces a hearing impairment roughly equivalent to the kind that would occur with perfectly fitting earplugs, allowing no acoustic leakage. The reader can simulate the conductive hearing loss of bilateral atresia by covering both ears very tightly. Notice that sound is not eliminated, but merely attenuated, because sound is transmitted to the cochlea, although imperfectly, through the tissues and skull.

In the case of the infant in question, his atresias were not surgically corrected until he was well past a fully Canonical stage, which he had begun right on schedule for normally hearing infants, in the middle of the first year of life. His vocal development seemed perfectly normal.

Infants who suffer from intermittent conductive hearing loss due to otitis media, the middle ear blockage that is one of the most common conditions encountered in pediatric practice, also offer an opportunity to evaluate effects of mild hearing loss on protophone development. Antibiotic treatment normally speeds recovery from otitis, but many infants are prone to reinfection. Although there is much ongoing research on the effects of otitis media on language development in general, including published reports of notable delays in vocabulary and other communicative capabilities in children who as infants suffered from recurrent bouts of middle ear infection (Feagans et al., 1988; Friel-Patti et al., 1982; Gravel & Wallace, 1992; Kavanagh, 1986), I know of no reports indicating late onset of canonical babbling or other protophone disturbances in such cases. Individual cases of infants with many bouts of otitis media in longitudinal studies at the University of Miami have produced no cases of late onset canonical babbling that were attributed to the middle ear problems.

A currently ongoing study will provide a more rigorous test of the possibility that mild or moderate hearing impairments may have some discernible (although relatively subtle) effect on vocal development in the first year of life. The research will address both infants with recurrent otitis media and, more importantly, infants with stable losses (i.e., sensorineural losses) in the mild or moderate range. At least two infants with bilateral hearing impairments in the moderate range have shown delayed babbling onset, although it remains uncertain that these infants showed their delays because of hearing impairment as opposed to other risk factors (Oller & Eilers, 1998).

Another way that protophone development is robust with respect to hearing impairment is seen in the fact that deaf children produce essentially the full range of Expansion stage sounds at appropriate ages. The pattern of rich Expansion stage vocalization was reported for an infant with a congenital profound loss as a result of Waardenburg's syndrome, an autosomal dominant genetic syndrome that often produces hearing loss, but is not associated with mental handicaps (Oller et al., 1985). The girl's vocal development was of particular interest specifically because if her vocalizations differed from those of hearing children in important ways, the differences could not be attributed to mental retardation. Indeed she was an intelligent, lively infant who vocalized freely. Contrary to a traditional expectation of relative silence in deaf infants, she was quite vocal in face-to-face interaction, and it was not difficult to elicit rich and varied samples of protophones. Other recent studies have also reported no difference in the amount of vocalization in deaf and hearing infants either at comparable ages (Koopmans-van Beinum et al., 1998) or at comparable vocal development stages (Nathani, 1998).

The most notable feature of the sounds themselves was their Expansion stage variety. The infant produced all the typical protophones of the stage—including raspberries in abundance, squeals, growls, full vowels, marginal babbles, yells and whispers—but in addition, she produced quite a number of other sounds sometimes produced by hearing infants, including ingressive-egressive sequences (vowel-like syllable sequences produced alternately on breathing in and breathing out in quick succession) and clicks.

There was one feature of her Expansion stage repertoire that stuck out, and that has since been observed as a typical feature of deaf babbling in the Expansion stage (Koopmans-van Beinum et al., 1998; Oller & Eilers, 1988). This feature was the frequent production of *glottal sequences*, syllabic sequences that lack any supraglottal articulation (see Fig. 8.2). The timing of the sequences is unremarkable (showing syllable nuclei of around 200 msec duration separated by a glottal interruption, resulting in a silence of roughly similar duration), but because there is no supraglottal articulation, there are no formant transitions (note the flat formants in Fig. 8.2). The vocal tract assumes a posture and maintains that posture while the glottis and diaphragm perform the syllable output through alternation of phonation and cessation of phonation. A subsequent case evaluation with a deaf infant (reported in Oller, 1991) indicated that glottal sequences were produced frequently and in many sessions throughout a period of months in a pattern that resembled the usage of canonical syllables by hearing infants. The report presented the speculation that glottal sequences were a sort of canonical babbling substitute for the infant, who could not hear formant transitions, but who could, through residual hearing and taction, sense syllabic sequences based on the beats of each syllable nucleus.

As a simple illustration of the basis for the speculation, it is useful to consider the nature of residual auditory input to deaf listeners. To simulate perceived sound in most cases of severe or profound loss, it is instructive to use low-pass filtering, which yields a pattern of acoustic energy that resembles the

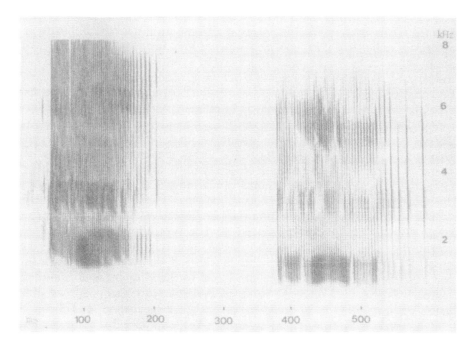

FIG. 8.2.   The spectrogram shows a glottal sequence of two-syllables produced by a 8-month-old deaf infant. The two syllables are separated by silence corresponding to a glottal stop. Notice that the first and second formants both before and after the glottal stop are flat, indicating no significant movement of the supraglottal vocal tract. From "Pre-speech vocalizations of a deaf infant: A comparison with normal metaphonological development," by Oller, D. K., Eilers, R. E., Bull, D. H., & Carney, A. E., 1985, *Journal of Speech and Hearing Research, 28*, p. 58. Copyright 1985 by the American Speech-Language-Hearing Association. Reprinted with permission.

presumed perceivable input for the impaired listener. After low band-pass filtering, canonical sequences such as [bababa] and glottal sequences such as [ʔaʔaʔa] sound very much alike, apparently because most of the acoustic information associated with formant transitions is severely attenuated. It can be reasoned that glottal sequences may sound like canonical syllable sequences to most deaf infants, and may be used as substitutes for canonical sequences by deaf infants at the age at which canonical babbling would occur in hearing infants. Glottal sequences have now been observed in many additional deaf infants and appear to be one of the most common Expansion stage sounds in the deaf even though glottal sequences are only occasionally produced in hearing infants.

The explanation of why glottal sequences occur so frequently in vocalizations of deaf infants remains somewhat incomplete and uncertain. Perhaps a maturational event occurring around the middle of the first year of life presses infants to produce well-formed syllables (in much the same way that maturational pressures seem to spur infants to sit up, crawl, and perform hand banging at about the same age). Perhaps the deaf infant initially attempts to satisfy the maturational imperative with glottal sequences. So why do deaf infants not continue with glottal sequences instead of advancing into a true Canonical stage? Formant transitions are critically important to well-formed syllables, and deaf infants can perceive the movements of jaw and lips that produce formant transitions in other speakers. Perhaps accumulated visual experience ultimately provides the deaf infant with sufficient additional basis for a final canonical advance that adds articulated, well-formed transitions to sequences that are otherwise deployed without movement on the part of the supraglottal tract.

There is more to be discovered about the role of hearing impairment in babbling, and there is a need for studies of vocal development in infants with other sensory impairments, especially blindness. It is undeniable that infants have a biological propensity to develop protophones, but the role of experience cannot be ignored. As we characterize that role empirically, we provide an anchor point for the understanding of the biological imperative for speech and its precursors.

RESULTS ON CANALIZATION OF BABBLING: THE ROLE OF MENTAL RETARDATION

The first reports that directly addressed the speech-like vocalization development of infants with Down syndrome (Dodd, 1972; Smith & Oller, 1981), appeared to provide an indication of extreme canalization in canonical babbling development. Dodd (1972) noted similarities in quantity and quality of babbling production in 10 normally developing infants and 10 infants with Down syndrome. The similarities were so salient that she speculated babbling may not be learned; otherwise the slow learning that is associated with Down syndrome would surely have slowed the development of babbling.

Smith and Oller (1981) directly compared onsets of canonical babbling in 9 normally developing infants and 10 infants with Down syndrome studied longitudinally, and found them to be statistically indistinguishable as groups, although 1 Down syndrome infant was delayed in onset. He began the Canonical stage at 12 months, presumably delayed as a result of major health problems, including repeated events of heart failure, from which he died during his second year. Smith and Oller were inclined to follow the lead of Dodd (1972) in speculating that because normally developing and Down syndrome infants showed such notable similarities in vocal development, babbling must be little affected by learning. The empirical outcomes of both studies were surprising because babbling and speech are clearly related and because Down syndrome is characterized by very major delays in speech at later points in development (see review in Miller, 1988).

However, later research provided evidence of differences in the onset of canonical babbling for normally developing and Down syndrome infants (Lynch, Oller, Steffens, Levine, et al., 1995). The research followed 13 infants with Down syndrome. The methods in this research differed from those of Smith and Oller (1981) in that the earlier study involved a 3-month sampling interval, whereas the more recent one involved 1-month intervals. Accordingly, it seems reasonable to assume that the data from the more recent study may have provided greater resolution in measuring the onset of vocal stages. The results reported by Lynch and colleagues indicated a delay in onset of canonical babbling of about 2 months in the Down syndrome infants as a group, a result that seemed to conform to the outcome of a concurrent effort indicating relatively low proportions of canonical syllables in 16-month-old Down syndrome and normally developing infants (Steffens, Oller, Lynch, & Urbano, 1992).

The more recent effort provided an indication of delay in Down syndrome, but the delay was surprisingly small. Most of the infants with Down syndrome began canonical babbling within the range that has been found for hearing infants (from 4–10 months). Of the 23 infants with Down syndrome in the two studies, only 3 showed onsets later than 10 months.

In addition, canonical babbling onset is much less delayed than several other motoric factors in Down syndrome, as indicated by another concurrent study with the same groups of infants studied by Lynch and colleagues (Cobo-Lewis et al., 1996). The investigators evaluated the parent diaries and laboratory observations of onsets for motoric milestones and reported that infants with Down syndrome were delayed by many months in sitting, crawling, standing, and walking, but they were delayed reliably less in canonical babbling and hand banging, two phenomena of development that may be viewed as rhythmic stereotypies. Thus, although canonical babbling is delayed in Down syndrome, it can be said to be delayed relatively little in the context of motoric development generally. This may be yet another indication of the especially solid canalization of the development of precursors to speech, the apparent human tendency to keep the growth of the capability for talking on course.

A separate cross-sectional investigation has been conducted with 17- to 62-month-old communicatively impaired children with severe or profound mental retardation. The research, based on protophone categorization of tape-recorded laboratory samples, generally showed the children had fully canonical speech-like sounds, even though they had no meaningful speech (Oller & Seibert, 1988). The great majority of the children (29 of 36) showed fully canonical samples, but only five of them were able to produce any meaningful words. Words that were produced were prereferential, transmitting social functions but not referential meanings (see chap. 12 for a discussion of referentiality). It is also notable that all of the children with meaningful speech had relatively high canonical babbling ratios, all showing values within the range found for 11- to 13-month-old normally developing infants. The results suggested that not only must a child be able to produce canonical syllables to learn to talk, but apparently it may be required to have established a *firm* command over canonical syllables before one can begin to talk. This interpretation is supported by subsequent results indicating that normally developing infants begin to talk only after they have been producing canonical babbling for months (Oller, Levine, Eilers, & Pearson, 1998).

The central importance of canonical syllables in speech production may be a factor that helped to foster the canalization of infraphonological development in the evolution of the human species. That mentally retarded children of preschool or kindergarten age continue to utilize canonical sounds extensively even in cases where functionally rich speech communication is unlikely ever to be possible suggests a sort of fossilization, a freezing in time of the canalized capability to produce playful but meaningless speech-like sounds.

THE POSSIBILITY OF SCREENING FOR DISORDERS BY EVALUATING PROTOPHONE DEVELOPMENT

Inspired by infraphonological theory, the evaluation of protophone stage development in infants at risk and in infants with various abnormalities began with the intention of determining whether protophone development might be delayed or otherwise disrupted in infants who later show delayed or deviant development of language and language-related abilities. The results of the various studies have yielded a surprisingly crisp picture, suggesting potentially important applications of protophone evaluation in infancy. On the one hand, deaf infants are notably delayed in onset of the most salient of the protophone stages, canonical babbling. On the other hand, other infants, whether at risk for developmental disorders or not, rarely show delays in canonical babbling. The critical age according to the results appears to be 10 months. Babies that begin canonical babbling after 10 months can be assumed to be at extreme risk for profound hearing impairment. This crisp picture suggests it might be possible to screen for hearing impairment based on an evaluation of canonical babbling at the end of the first year of life.

What about other disorders that specifically affect spoken language capabilities or related abilities such as reading? Would they not also be predicted by late onset of canonical babbling? The results to be reviewed next suggest that other disorders may indeed be predicted by delayed protophone development. Furthermore, the results suggest that delayed onset of canonical babbling can be determined through an efficient and inexpensive method based on an interview with parents at the end of the infant's first year of life.

DISORDERS OF SPECIAL INTEREST FOR SCREENING

It is currently impossible to identify individuals with language or language-related disorders until the point at which a delay in language or language-related function can be measured directly, usually in the third year of life or beyond. The categories of infants that it would be most valuable to identify as being at risk are precisely those that show no other obvious disorders, who appear at birth to be healthy and normal, but who later show significant language-related handicaps.

Four groups are of special interest. One group has specific language impairment (SLI), a category that may or may not be well named. By definition, the group consists of children for whom only language disorders and no other categories of disorder are present. It is, however, acknowledged by students of the handicap, that children diagnosed with SLI often have additional intellectual deficiencies (Johnston, 1988; Kahmi, 1993; Leonard & Schwartz, 1985). Related to SLI is the group of disorders that are presumed specific to phonology, including apraxia (Pollock & Hall, 1991; Velleman, 1994), dysarthria, and developmental phonological disorders (Dinnsen, Chin, Elbert, & Powell, 1990; Edwards, 1978, 1995; Elbert & Gierut, 1986; Gierut, 1989; Grunwell, 1982; Hodson, 1980; Hodson & Paden, 1981; Shriberg & Kwiatkowski, 1980, 1994). Again the phonological disorders frequently show comorbidity with other handicaps of language or cognition (Catts, 1986). A third category of interest is a specific learning disability, dyslexia. Dyslexic children may speak intelligibly and understand speech relatively well, there is reason to believe that many have fundamental phonological handicaps that affect their ability to process alphabetically coded information (Catts, 1986; Ehri, 1989; Tunmer & Rohl, 1991), a speculation that is supported by the fact that phonological awareness (e.g., the ability to create rhymes or to pronounce the first "sound" of a word) is highly predictive of reading ability (Webster & Plante, 1992). A final category of interest is autism. Autistic children are typically profoundly impaired in vocal communication, even though there are a variety of intellectual and emotional anomalies associated with the disorder (Nishimura, Watamaki, Sato, & Wakabayashi, 1987; Rutter, 1978).

These four groups are of such interest in the context of research on vocal development because none of them can presently be systematically identified early in life. SLI, phonological disorders, dyslexia, and autism are conditions that can be reliably diagnosed only after significant handicaps reveal themselves in the third year of life or later. In all four cases, it would appear to be likely that late onset of canonical babbling may, at least sometimes, mark the emerging disorder long before traditional symptoms can be reliably identified. Children with SLI, phonological disorders, and dyslexia typically have problems with phonological processing and with complex coordination of linguistic units in coherent sequences. To reach the Canonical stage, infants must coordinate infraphonological parameters, previously explored independently in the Expansion stage, to create coherent syllabic nuclei and margins in well-timed sequences. This development appears to form the foundation for all subsequent phonological capability. If it develops late, it may signal trouble in all things relating to processing and production of sequential speech-like information. The role of phonological awareness in reading is well-established (Liberman, Shankweiler, Fischer, & Carter, 1974), and late development of foundations for phonological awareness may foretell long-term difficulties.

With autistic children, the reasons for suspicion that canonical babbling onset may be delayed are partly empirical, although the information is scanty and anecdotal. Two reports have come from parents of autistic adults, who were asked retrospectively to describe the vocalizations their children produced as infants. They both reported that the children did not produce sounds such as [baba] or [dada] until years after other children, and in both cases the reports were provided without any prompting. Of course reasoning from such information may still be precarious, and there is reason to suspect that different autistic children may show very different patterns of development. Onset of autistic-like symptoms is sometimes reported to occur after a period of apparently normal development (see, e.g., Short & Schopler, 1988). Two-year-olds who do not seem exceptional in speech development (which is to say they have developed at least a minimal intelligible spoken vocabulary) sometimes appear to regress in the ability to talk with the beginning of autistic behaviors (Harper & Williams, 1975; Short & Schopler, 1988). It seems possible that children showing this presumed late onset of autism may differ in protophone development from children in whom autism is assumed to have begun much earlier. In any event, there may be cases of autism that can be identified very early based on late onset of canonical babbling.

The scientific literature includes three reports providing four cases of normally hearing infants who began the Canonical stage late, after 10 months. Two of the four children showed significant later anomalies, one with significantly late onset of vocabulary acquisition (Stoel-Gammon, 1989) and the other with apparent reading problems in the early school years (Stark et al., 1988). A third child showed no obvious developmental delays, but did show an atypical pattern of articulation within his babbling (Stoel-Gammon, 1989). The fourth infant with delayed canonical babbling showed no significant disorders later in life as far as could be told (Koopmans-van Beinum & van der Stelt, 1986). Thus, two of the four were verified as delayed, suggesting the possible utility of evaluating the onset of canonical babbling as a potential screening tool for significant language-related developmental disorders. Furthermore, research on SLI suggests that it may be accompanied by anomalies in babbling patterns (Whitehurst, Smith, Fischel, & Arnold, 1991).

SPECIFIC SCREENING STUDIES BASED ON THE EVALUATION OF CANONICAL BABBLING ONSET

To assess the potential use of late onset of canonical babbling in early identification of language-related disorders, it is important to take several additional steps. These are requirements for a practical and important screening procedure:

1. To show that the method can be applied in practice, it is important to determine that infants who are delayed can be accurately identified at low cost.
2. To determine the magnitude of the screening task, it is necessary to gain perspective on the rate of late onset in the population at large, independent of cases involving severe or profound hearing impairment.
3. To ensure that late onset of canonical babbling is actually associated with language-related disorders, it is necessary to conduct follow-up research on infants found to show late onset canonical babbling.

A series of studies have been addressing these issues since the mid-1990s. A long-term study has recently been completed (Eilers, Neal, & Oller, 1996; Oller & Eilers, 1998; Oller, Eilers, Neal, & Cobo-Lewis, 1998; Oller, Eilers, Neal, & Schwartz, 1999) evaluating the rate of late onset in a sample of more than 3,000 infants at about 10 months of age (corrected for prematurity when necessary). Most of the infants were born at risk for developmental disorders, but all of them had passed initial screening for hearing impairment based on averaged brain stem response audiometry. In a telephone interview, parents were asked simply to describe their infants' vocalizations. Interviewers recorded judgments about the infants' stage of protophone development based on the parents' statements. After the telephone interviews, all parents with infants for whom the recorded judgment was precanonical were invited to come to the laboratory for a recording and laboratory evaluation of the baby's babbling.

Judgments based on parents' descriptions of infant babbling were remarkably accurate whenever infants were categorized as canonical. Ancillary studies confirmed that parents are in general extremely good at giving descriptions that suggest their infants are in the Canonical stage (Oller et al., 1996; Oller, Eilers, & Basinger, in press). Laboratory evaluation rarely contradicted parent-based assignment of infants to the Canonical stage.

Judgments based on parents' descriptions of infant babbling whenever infants were categorized as noncanonical were not as accurate (about half proved accurate), but this inaccuracy is not disturbing. Optimal design of screening evaluations minimizes misses and allows a moderate rate of false positives. It is important not to miss individuals that have the condition one screens for (late canonical babbling), and so it is extremely important that parents give accurate information when they indicate their infants are in the Canonical stage. If a parent's description yields a false canonical judgment, the screening procedure misses an infant toward which the procedure is targeted. On the other hand, it is not so worrisome if parents are mistaken in saying an infant is noncanonical. This is a false positive error that increases the size of the group of infants that must be evaluated again. However, as that number is relatively small, the error is of relatively little significance.

The conclusion here gives a hopeful response to the first requirement of a practical screening method listed earlier. The parent interview method works well, yielding tolerable levels of misses and false positives (which probably can be reduced with further modifications of procedure). Parents appear to be excellent informants about their infants' babbling (and see Lyytinen et al., 1996), suggesting that it should be possible very inexpensively and efficiently to identify the great majority of infants who start canonical babbling late.

The remarkable ability of parents who have not been tutored in the facts of babbling or language development, and who in many cases are uneducated, to offer accurate descriptions of their infants' babbling conforms to the idea that humans are intuitively gifted in their evaluation and treatment of infants. Papoušek and Papoušek (Papoušek, 1994; Papoušek & Papoušek, 1987) offered evidence that human nature includes not only the ability of infants to produce species-specific gestures, facial displays, and vocalizations, but also the ability of parents to make sense of those infant expressions. Parents have to be able to respond effectively to infant cues, according to the reasoning, and nature appears to assist by facilitating the development of intuitive parenting abilities. When, for example, infants begin canonical babbling, parents quickly shift intuitively from treating the infant sounds as playful exercises or social games to treating them as potentially referential. They do not have to think about the shift; they just do it. As a result, infants may learn vocabulary more rapidly. The canalization of vocal development may, according to this reasoning, be paralleled by a natural ability of parents to recognize and respond appropriately to infant actions.

With these observations in hand, there is reason to be confident that the study provides a sound basis for estimating the rate of late onset canonical babbling, responding to the second requirement for a screening procedure listed at the beginning of the section. It appears, based on the research, that 3% or less of infants in the population at large without hearing impairment begin canonical babbling after 10 months of age. These infants are the ones that may be deemed at risk for certain language-related disorders based on their canonical babbling performance. I report the figure as 3% *or less* because the population of the study is skewed in such a way that infants at risk due to factors such as prematurity, low SES, and a variety of prenatal conditions are disproportionately (although not uniquely) represented.

Perhaps the most important results of the study concern the relation between late onset canonical babbling and other disorders. Fewer than half the 26 late canonical babblers that participated in the follow-up proved to have important medical conditions including cerebral palsy, epilepsy, hypotonia, and heart disease. Three of these conditions were diagnosed only after the infants in question were designated as late onset babblers and subsequently referred for medical evaluation. It would therefore appear that late onset of canonical babbling may be a useful addition to a general screening battery because it provides a basis for initiating early diagnosis of otherwise undetected medical (particularly neurological) conditions.

A small group of late canonical babblers were followed up through 30 months of age to assess their language development, and they were compared with a group of infants who had begun canonical babbling on time. The groups were similar because all the infants had originally been contacted through the telephone study. The infants in the control group were selected at random from the more than 3,000 infants. The two groups had similar low rates of significant medical problems. The follow-up has shown that productive vocabulary (based on the MacArthur Communicative Development Inventory; Fenson et al., 1991) was notably delayed in most of the late canonical babblers when compared with the control group (Oller et al., 1998). Receptive vocabulary was not delayed.

Consequently, it would appear, in response to the third requirement of a screening procedure listed at the beginning of this section, that late onset of canonical babbling does provide an indication of delay in speech acquisition. The delays seen are of sufficient magnitude to warrant intervention. The fact that the delays appear to be limited to speech production suggests that the screening method based on late onset of canonical babbling may help to identify infants at special risk for linguistic problems related to the output or retrieval of phonological units that are required in early vocabulary. Delays in output or retrieval of vocabulary or phonological information required in the child lexicon could have long-term consequences in domains such as expressive vocabulary, sentence production, and reading, in which the ability to retrieve and manipulate phonological information is believed to play a key role (Liberman et al., 1974; Webster & Plante, 1992).

These data suggest the possibility that the infants may indeed be at high risk for SLI, phonological impairment, dyslexia, or autism. It is extremely expensive to conduct follow-up research, and consequently it was not possible to follow the late onset canonical babblers long enough to determine whether they would show any of the indicated disorders. More than 90% of them were, however, either significantly medically involved or delayed in vocabulary development. It is important that about half of them would not have been identified as at risk by any standard medical criteria. Thus the evaluation of infant babbling appears to be an effective way to identify infants at risk who would be missed by other standard methods.

It is also important to reemphasize that the method of evaluation suggested by this study could be cost-effective, as it could be based on a telephone interview in the great majority of cases, and on follow-up evaluation only in cases in which risk is already determined to be high due to indicated late onset of canonical babbling. In the U.S. health care system, implementing the method of screening suggested by the study would require that all parents of infants 10 to 12 months of age be contacted (either by phone or in a face-to-face interview) by a health care worker. Presumably it would be most cost-effective to conduct a series of evaluations at that time, one of which would include the questions about babbling (especially the open-ended ones). Such an approach could be used to screen for profound congenital hearing impairment in addition to other possible language-related disorders.

Currently, hearing screening is conducted in many neonatal wards with audiological methods based on evoked potentials or otoacoustic emissions (Bess & Hall, 1992; Weber, 1988). There is good reason to consider screening all newborns, but in most places, screening is applied only with infants already designated at risk. Only about half the infants that actually have significant hearing losses are designated at risk, and as a result, about half the infants with hearing impairment cannot be identified through a screening approach that focuses on at-risk infants only. Screening by the vocal development interview method would be less costly (assuming it could be incorporated into a new "end-of-the-first-year" evaluation) and consequently more feasible to apply to all children who have not already been screened.

Practical application of results from infraphonological interpretation of protophone development is growing. Clinicians in many settings around the world are now on the lookout for infants with late onset of protophone development, especially canonical babbling (Koopmans-van Beinum et al., 1998; Stoel-Gammon, 1989; Vergara et al., 1995; Vinter, 1987, 1994a). Children who show severe speech delays for any reason are often assessed in a way that references the protophone model, and intervention plans are often formulated to encourage development through protophone stages in anticipation of more traditional phonetic or word-based training. The possibility of widespread screening for language-related disorders based on parent interviews about babbling represents another potential application. All of these applications are enhanced by converging information regarding the robustness of protophone stages and the specific roles played in their disruption by biologically based handicaps and experience.

9

An Expanded View of the Landscape in Infant Vocalizations: Infrastructure for Sounds and Functions in Babbling

TWO ASPECTS OF INFRASTRUCTURAL MODELING IN VOCAL DEVELOPMENT

To this point, the focus of this volume has been the development of the human sound-making capability, an infraphonological matter. From this point forward the treatment incorporates issues of the usage of potential signals, an infrasemiotic matter. To illustrate the distinction between signal and usage in protophone development consider the nature of vocalization in the Primitive Articulation stage. The various articulations and vocalizations that occur in gooing reveal something about infraphonological development, but gooing interactions also tell us something about how babies connect with other people vocally and facially. Babies use gooing to do something important. Through the interactions that include gooing, they establish and build a relationship with their caretakers. Similarly, the Expansion stage is a period during which babies perform important functions with vocalization. On the one hand they pursue social usage of sounds, but they also use Expansion stage protophones for practice in vocal control.

Keys to the understanding of vocal development are, then, to be found both in infraphonological interpretation and in the recognition of the emergence of infrastructural properties of vocal action that underlie communicative function. These elemental properties include Interactivity, as manifest in gooing, and Contextual Freedom of sound production, as manifest in the practice-like playful usage of vocalization in the Expansion stage, along with a number of other properties to be considered. The formulation of a model of infrastructural properties constituting the underpinnings of communicative signal and function (in chap. 12) will provide a backdrop not only for understanding of infant vocalization development, but also for comparison of vocalization systems across species.

TWO KINDS OF PROPERTIES THAT MUST BE COMMANDED BY ANY SPECIES SEEKING TO COMMUNICATE POWERFULLY IN THE VOCAL DOMAIN

The properties to be discussed in more detail in chapter 12 are intended to represent timeless aspects of potential phonological systems and potential semiotic systems for any species. It is posited in this treatment that in the course of development or evolution of a vocal system these timeless properties must be systematically incorporated in accord with certain logical constraints in order for the system to progress. However, the ways that the properties are incorporated may take on system-specific or species-specific character.

The properties of potential vocal communicative systems (both on the phonological and the semiotic side) are related to each other within a network of presuppositions. Development of command over one property often presupposes command over others. In accord with this presuppositional logic, it is possible to develop or evolve a simple vocal communicative system commanding only a subset of the properties. As infants develop infraphonologically and infrasemiotically, they can be seen to introduce the properties systematically in accord with the natural logic of presupposition. At each stage of development, additional properties or principles of implementation for properties are added to the growing infant system. The system of infrastructural properties provides a reference point for interspecies comparison because it allows a systematic characterization of the extent of evolution of any vocal communication system along a developmental sequence that all evolution must follow to advance. Species may differ both in the extent of their evolution along the logical sequence of properties and in terms of manners of implementation of command over properties. It is my belief that by formally itemizing the key infrastructural properties and specifying their presuppositional relations, it will be possible to clarify greatly the discussion of comparative ethology and our evolutionary history in speech.

Partly then as a prelude to the discussion of comparative vocal ethology in primates it will be useful to survey the landscape of human infant communication more broadly than in chapter 4, with special emphasis on the utilization of the infant vocal repertoire in a variety of social and nonsocial contexts. The discussion is infrastructural on two fronts, one related to growth in sound-making abilities (interpreted in terms of potential infraphonological properties and human specific well-formedness constraints) and one related to growth in usage of sounds (interpreted in the context of posited control over infrastructural properties underlying communicative function). With the landscape of infant vocal development in full view, the way will be prepared to contrast the development of human vocalizations with communicative actions of other species at a variety of ages.

THE LAY OF THE LAND IN INFANT VOCAL COMMUNICATIVE ACTION: SOUNDS OTHER THAN PROTOPHONES

To put matters in a perspective that will aid interpretation of functions of vocalization, we consider not only protophones, but also other significant vocalizations and gestural and facial communications that may accompany them. Among nonprotophone vocalizations to be considered are vegetative sounds, crying (along with its facial counterpart of grimacing or frowning), and laughter (along with smiling).

Table 9.1 provides a summary to which the survey refers.

Vegetative Sounds

Vegetative sounds such as sneezing, burping, or coughing have been given little investigative attention as communicative signals. Stark (Stark, Rose, & McLagen, 1975) was one of the few to address their role in the development of a capacity for vocal communication. Nevertheless, parents systematically take note of vegetative sounds in interpreting infant state. A parent who hears the baby cough may decide to pat the baby's back. A parent who hears hiccoughs may give the baby a bottle. These sounds can be said to have an indexical communicative value (Peirce, 1934) because they index a state that the observer can interpret, even though the communications thus achieved may have been unintentional on the part of the sender. Of course any action (even the lack of action) can be interpreted indexically, and so vegetative vocalizations (which in the nominal case are produced unintentionally) are typically not included in the discussion of precursors to a specific linguistic capacity. Their role in the discussion of language owes to two facts: First, vegetative sounds are produced by the vocal system (and here Stark offered insights about the relations between production capabilities for vegetative sounds and other vocal signals), and second, even vegetative sounds are sometimes produced voluntarily for specific communicative effect.

Perhaps the experience of getting attention for coughing and other vegetative sounds inspires babies to take advantage of presented opportunity. Perhaps biological heritage supplies infants with abilities to use vegetative sounds communicatively. In any case, by the middle of the first year of life, during the Expansion stage, infants often show voluntary vocalizations of vegetative form, presented playfully or instrumentally to gain attention. My daughter Jenna in her second half-year of life used to cough and smile at adults, then laugh uproariously with them when they realized that she was pretending. She is an adult teacher of children herself now, and still finds ways to surprise a crowd.

TABLE 9.1

	New Vocal Types Occurring: Protophones	New Vocal Types Occurring: Other Sounds	Infraphonological Achievement: Principles of Well-Formed Syllabification in the Human System	Infraphonological Achievement: Properties of Potential Phonological Systems	Infrasemiotic Achievement: Properties of Potential Semiotic Systems
Phonation stage	Quasivowels, sometimes with glottal adjustments	Vegetative sounds; crying	Normal Phonation	Very Primitive Syllabification And Rhythmic Hierarchy	Contextual Freedom (production of quasivowels under no external stimulus control), primitive Free Expressivity
Primitive Articulation stage	Gooing		Articulatedness (movements of the vocal tract during normal phonation, creating primitive consonant-like margins)	Primitive Signal Analysis as seen in extremely variable production of sounds in gooing	Directivity (vocalizations with eye contact), Interactivity (use of gooing in turn-taking interactions)
Expansion stage	Full vowels, squealing, growling, yelling, whispering, raspberries, marginal babbling	Laughter	Full resonance of nuclei, creating well-formed vowel-like centers for syllables	Signal Analysis (exploration of pitch, intensity, resonance types), Categorical Adaptation, primitive Recombinability in marginal babbling	Elaborate Free Expressivity (use of cry, vegetative sounds and protophones in playful self-expression), early Imitability
Canonical stage	Canonical babbling, reduplicated babbling, variegated babbling		Well-formed transitions between margins and nuclei	Fully well-formed Syllabification, early Recombinability of syllables, early Rhythmical Hierarchy, Hot/cool Synthesis	More elaborate Imitability, Designation
Integrative stage	Gibberish, mixing of early speech and babbling		Elaboration of babbling and speech	Further Recombinability, and early Segmentation	Conventionality, Arbitrariness, early Semanticity, Displaceability, Propositionality

Vegetative sounds thus begin at birth, and infants appear to gain voluntary control over them with time. Eventually, at least by the late Expansion stage, infants may pretend to emit vegetative sounds in fun, they may imitate such sounds uttered by adults, or they may merely produce them repetitively, out of apparent interest in the sounds themselves, with no obvious social intent, indicating Contextual Freedom of vocalization. Under such circumstances, there is no external stimulus required to elicit these sounds and no necessary internal state to inspire them. The ability to produce sounds in new situations with expressive intent manifests an infrasemiotic property of Free Expressivity. The baby not only produces the sounds at will, but also does so in ways that express the child's current state, whatever that might be. In cases where the infant produces vegetative sounds voluntarily with eye contact, the property of Directivity is manifest, and when a back-and-forth exchange ensues, there is evidence of Interactivity. Thus by the middle of the first year of life, vegetative sounds, those lowly, scarcely studied relics of bodily states in the usual case, come to be controlled by Expansion stage infants to an extraordinary extent, yielding elaborate events of voluntary communication.

Crying as a Communication: Sometimes Accidental, Sometimes Intentional

In the moments after birth, infants cry reflexively in a manner that appears to be culturally universal (Barr, Konner, Bakeman, & Anderson, 1991), and although this newborn action clearly fits within the same category as crying that occurs later in the first year, indeed, throughout life, the actual sounds of crying change notably in physical character and usage (Barr, Chen, Hopkins, & Westra, 1996; Lester & Boukydis, 1992; Stark & Nathanson, 1974; Stark et al., 1975; Wolff, 1969). By 3 to 4 months of age, the function of crying is also often different from that which obtains at birth. By the later ages, infants cry not only reflexively in response to pain or hunger, but also to some extent voluntarily to attract attention (Emde, Gaensbauer, & Harmon, 1976; Papoušek & Papoušek, 1984; Prechtl, 1984). By the second half of the first year of life, infants cry identifiably in fright or anger, they call for attention, and when the intensity of feeling is low, they may choose merely to fuss. Fussing and crying appear to represent the weak and strong ends of a physical and functional continuum (Green, Gustafson, & McGhie, 1988; Wasz-Hockert, Lind, Vuorenkoski, & Valanne, 1964; Wolff, 1969).

Crying appears to be unintentional in newborns, but it serves an indexical communicative function in any event because caretakers recognize infant need through it (Acebo & Thoman, 1995; Green, Jones, & Gustafson, 1987). Even newborn cries are accompanied by facial expressions indicating distress (see Fig. 9.1). Crying proceeds to attain more elaborate communicativeness after modifications imposed by infants themselves on the physical form of crying (e.g., the rhythmic nature of cry syllables becomes more variable) as well as the form of accompanying gestural and facial actions produced within contexts that prove interpretable to caretakers. By the middle of the first year of life, infants clearly use crying for their own identifiable purposes (Bell & Ainsworth, 1972; D'Odorico, 1984; Green et al., 1987; Gustafson & Green, 1991; Lester & Boukydis, 1992; Wolff, 1969). The elaborate constellation of facial expression, gesture (often including reaching), and vocalization can be adjusted by the child to transmit frustration, anger, or impatience, and to communicate requests or demands. These characteristics of crying by the

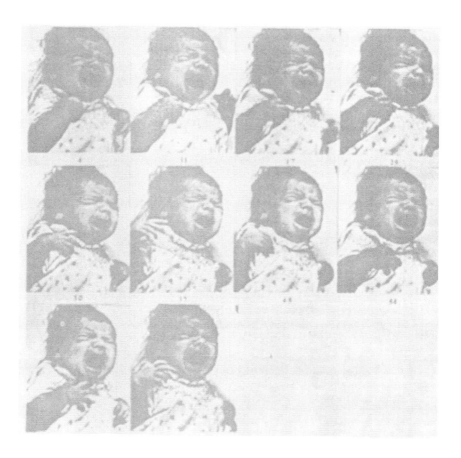

FIG. 9.1. Infant facial expression during intense cry bouts in unmistakably distressful. From "Spontaneous cry in the newborn infant; sounds and facial gestures" by Stark, R. E., & Nathanson, S. N., 1974, in J. F. Bosma (Ed.), *Fourth symposium on oral sensation and perception: Development of the fetus and infant*, p. 339. Bethesda, MD: U.S. Government Printing Office. Reprinted wi th permission.

middle of the first year of life show that in crying as in vegetative sounds, infants come to command important infrasemiotic properties, particularly Directivity and Free Expressivity.

Crying has been given much attention as a communicative signal in research, in part because aberrations in the physical character of the newborn cry can signal distress or physical abnormalities in the infant (Zeskind & Lester, 1978). A very high-pitched cry, especially one of low volume, is typical of infants born prematurely. One serious congenital anomaly, *cri du chat*, is named after the sound of the cry heard at the birth of infant victims of the syndrome. Parental reactions to infant crying have also been studied extensively, providing support for the idea that parents can recognize different categories of crying (particularly pain and hunger). Another line of research has provided suggestive evidence that if parents accurately assess their infant's medical status based on cry sounds, the intellectual outcome years later is better than if the assessment is inaccurate. This relation appears to be independent of whether the baby is actually sick or well at the time of the assessment. The parent's perceptiveness about cry seems to matter more than the infant's immediate condition. Perhaps the accuracy of judgment reflects parenting talent or attentiveness, a factor that may play a major role in developmental outcome (Lester, Boukydis, Garcia-Coll, Peucher, McGrath, Vohr, Brehm, & Oh, 1994).

Laughter and Smiling

Facial expressions play a major role from the beginning of infant communication. Smiling begins within the first weeks of life. Pediatricians used to claim that infant smiling was caused by gas, a strange claim, as gas does not as a rule cause the rest of us to make a face that resembles smiling. The physical form of the newborn smile is not especially ambiguous (Andrew, 1963; Eckman, 1994; Fischer & Lazerson, 1984). It has very much the same physical topography as the later smile, involving a conjunct of eye and lip corner movements that are easily identified (Emde et al., 1976; Sroufe & Waters, 1976).

The gas hypothesis is not taken very seriously anymore, but it has an implication that is still worth considering. The implied notion is that early infant smiling is reflexive, that it constitutes a mechanistic response to some unseen internal stimulus. Although gas probably has nothing to do with it, there is reason to believe that the earliest infant smiles are indeed involuntary, in particular because newborns usually smile while they are asleep. By 6 weeks of age or so, the same topography of smiling occurs in wakeful face-to-face interaction with adults (Emde et al., 1976). In these early interactions, the infant smiles responsively. As the weeks and months pass, however, infants come to use smiling actively to initiate or to maintain interactions and to indicate comprehension.

A key affective companion of smiling in the vocal domain is laughter, which flowers around 4 months of age (Sroufe & Waters, 1976). Infant laughter has been studied much less than crying, perhaps because it is not so easy to elicit in the laboratory. However, its interest in the search for roots of communication capabilities of humans should be no less. Laughter begins, as crying and vegetative sounds do, with a general topography that suggests reflexiveness. This early topography includes a quick and sudden burst of laughing in response to an external stimulus such as tickling, and the burst ends without repetition.

At this early stage the infant does not initiate bouts of laughter. Across the first year of life, the pattern of laughter usage changes, and as with vegetative sounds and crying, infants come to emit laughter more purposefully, sometimes playfully, often themselves initiating events of interactive communication, pretending to laugh (Nwokah, Hsu, Dobrowolska, & Fogel, 1994; Papoušek & Papoušek, 1984). Sometimes older infants utter laugh-like short syllables in social interactions with adults in such a way as to suggest recognition or interest. For example, when an adult shows an object, the infant may emit a quick syllable [ha], accompanied by a smile, as if to say, "I've seen that before" or "That's interesting." When a laugh is utilized in this way, it typically transmits a positive tone. Not only do infants indicate "I've seen that before" with a voluntary laugh syllable, but simultaneously they indicate that they take some pleasure in the experience.

Across the first year, both laughter and smiling are utilized systematically by the infant in social interactions that become increasingly elaborate. For the purposes of this work, the key feature of this elaboration is that infants begin with smiles and laughs that occur in restricted circumstances and appear to be more or less reflexive, but across the first year they gain increasing control over smiles and laughs, allowing action that can be adjusted to social circumstances. The elaborate use of laughing manifests Directivity, Interactivity, and Free Expressivity in the first year of life.

THE LAY OF THE LAND IN INFANT VOCAL COMMUNICATIVE ACTION: THE PROTOPHONES AND THEIR USAGE

Quasivowels and Grunts

The occurrence of crying, laughter, and vegetative sounds such as sneezing or coughing in newborn infants forms a backdrop for other vocalizations that are more closely related to the speech capacity. It may appear paradoxical that these critically important sounds, the ones that specifically presage the linguistic capacity, often seem initially less communicative than crying or vegetative sounds. I termed these earliest occurring speech-relevant sounds *quasiresonant nuclei* or more simply, *quasivowels* (Oller, 1980a, 1986), sounds that characterize the Phonation stage, the first of the protophone stages discussed in chapters 1 and 4. Quasivowels sound a lot like grunts, which also occur from the first week of life. Grunts, however, are reflexive sounds (in my usage), happening artifactually in the context of bodily movement or physical straining. As a consequence, grunts include a sharp (or glottalized) onset, whereas quasivowels can occur with either gradual or abrupt onset. Both early quasivowels and grunts are short in duration and are produced with the supraglottal vocal tract (i.e., the mouth) at rest. The tract is not postured to produce any special resonance that would accompany a wide open mouth, spread or rounded lips, or any specialized tongue position; the at rest position contrasts with the way the vocal tract might be postured in speech for the production of a particular vowel sound. In quasivowels, the vocal tract is left in no special position, and the infant vocalizes with normal phonation, the kind of phonation that later will be the hallmark of speech production.

Quasivowels differ unmistakably from crying, reflexive laughter, or vegetative sounds in the quality of their phonation. Only quasivowels include normal phonation with its smooth tones and formants, whereas the others include varying degrees and types of dysphonation or hyperphonation, patterns that yield the impression of vocal tension or raspiness. Crying and vegetative sounds also often include phonatory discontinuities (breaks in the stream of vocal cord vibration) that do not often occur in quasivowels. The special qualities of the voice in these infant sounds play important roles in their identification and interpretation (see, e.g., Zeskind & Barr, 1997).

Another way that quasivowels resemble speech is that they occur as quick syllable-like productions. The duration of quasivowels is commonly a few tenths of a second, just the length of quickly articulated syllables in natural languages. Even in the first 2 months of life, quasivocalic sounds of infants show patterning of durations that resemble speech (Lynch, Oller, Steffens, & Buder, 1995). Crying, laughter, and vegetative sounds, on the other hand, include special timing properties and (optionally) repeating units that are discernibly different from those of speech (Provine & Yong, 1993; Stark et al., 1975; Truby, 1965).

Whereas grunts (as I use the term) always indicate a condition of physical strain or movement, and other sounds such as crying or coughing indicate other states of the body or the emotions, quasivowels appear to be free of predefined communicative potential. In the first week of life infants produce them with no obvious intent and no obvious externally eliciting stimulus. Consequently, quasivowels may be the first sounds uttered by human infants with Contextual Freedom. Although these sounds are not required to serve any social function, our research suggests that by the middle of the first year of life, quasivowels may be the most frequently occurring single category of vocalization in infants (Oller et al., 1994). They occur in a wide variety of circumstances, some clearly communicative (see McCune, Vihman, Roug-Hellichius, Delery, & Gogate, 1996; Vihman, 1996) and some with no social intent; indeed, quasivowels often occur when the infant is alone.

The communicative roles that do come to be served by quasivowels, especially in the second half-year, include some of the same ones found in voluntary laughter. Thus, quasivowels may be employed as markers for assent or recognition: "I see," or "Yes, that's the same thing I saw before." Even adults use quasivowels in such ways, as in the usage "hmm." A central difference between quasivowels, even when they are used communicatively, and laughter events is that the latter necessarily involve an affective expression, whereas the former are free to express unencumbered intellectual interest. *Free* is the key word here, because quasivowels can be employed as the infant chooses. With a smile and a rising–falling intonation, they can indicate interest and pleasure. With a frown and a quick falling intonation, they can indicate disinterest or disgust. With a blank face and a falling intonation, they can indicate an intellectual response (e.g., recognition) free of affective valence. At the beginning of the first year of life, it is not easy to interpret infant quasivowels, but as the year progresses, the infant uses the sounds increasingly systematically, and the interpretation becomes increasingly clear, determined by precise presentation in context. This pattern of growth in the use of quasivowels in infancy and early childhood was described and discussed by McCune and Vihman (McCune et al., 1996; Vihman, 1996), who referred to the quasivowels as grunts, in accord with the common parlance usage of the term.

Human language, of course, has the infrasemiotic property of Free Expressivity. Linguistic communications can express whatever emotions or attitudes we have in our hearts or minds. A wide variety of sounds can be used to perform the expressions. This freedom of expression may be first seen in infants through their use of quasivowels. In mature language, words or sentences can be made to bear dramatically variable communicative contents under the influence of subtle changes in intonation or context. Ultimately in adult communication, even the sound of crying can be used ironically and laughter can be derisive. Human infants come to be able to utilize quasivowels in at least primitively similar ways, the expression of a wide variety of intents depending on social context, facial expression, gesture, and intonation. In infant quasivowels, intentional vocal acts free of affective content are found in the first weeks of life, and from these primitive, often scarcely noticed sounds, babies begin down a path of vocal communication that leads to talking.

It should also be noted that quasivowels in the first months of life function as primitive rhythmic units within a hierarchy that includes primitive phrase-like groupings of quasivowels (Lynch, Oller, Steffens, & Buder, 1995; Nathani, 1998). Thus, although these early vocalizations are limited in terms of their adherence to principles of syllable well-formedness, they do provide a stable temporally defined unit of approximately adult syllabic duration from which higher order groupings can be constructed.

Gooing and Face-to-Face Vocal Interaction

By 2 months of age infants not only smile responsively, but they also engage in remarkable dialogues in face-to-face interaction, wordless but full of rich social content. These dialogues are typical of the Primitive Articulation stage discussed in chapters 1 and 4. During these interactions, parents hold infants facing them, gain eye contact, smile, and raise their chins and eyebrows (Papoušek & Papoušek, 1987; Papoušek, 1994; see Fig. 9.2). Accompanying this facial display, parents commonly speak to the baby in a high-pitched special register with extended durations of syllables and wide sweeps of intonation (Fernald et al., 1989). The infant may smile in response, maintaining eye contact, and then, in a moment that never seems to fail to delight, the baby goos. The patterns of adult interaction are stable with varying body postures of infant and adult and persist in various infant emotional states (see Figs. 9.3 and 9.4).

The sound of gooing is hinted at by its onomatopoetic name, because these sounds often include tongue articulations at the back of the mouth, yielding sounds that at least vaguely resemble the *g* of the word *goo*. Furthermore, the vocalic sounds that typically accompany the back articulations are frequently quasivowels, produced with little or no posturing of the tract, a sound that vaguely resembles the vowel in the word goo, although lip rounding is involved

FIG. 9.2.   Split-screen video research conducted at the University of Miami exhibits a mother on one screen holding direct eye contact with her three-month old baby Janelle shown from another camera on the adjacent screen. The mother shows the characteristic intuitive parenting signs of early interactions including smiling, eyebrow and chin-raising. The baby is gooing. Printed by permission of the mother, Jennifer Ross.

FIG. 9.3.   This still photograph shows the author with his grandson, Liam, at 2-months of age. Eyebrow raising is notable for both participants in this interaction. The infant vocalizes resonsively though being held upright. Printed by permission of the parents, Jenna and Andrew Bradley. Photograph by Peter Lafreniere.

in *oo*, but not usually in the infant sounds, and tongue positioning may be quite different. (I hasten to reemphasize, however, that the resemblance of gooing sounds to the word *goo* can be greatly overstated in phonetic transcription as gooing sounds rarely incorporate all the principles of syllable well-formedness found in mature speech and consequently phonetically transcribed versions of gooing syllables cannot pass the phonetician/reader test; see chap. 1).

FIG. 9.4. This still photograph shows the author's son-in-law, Andrew Bradley, with Liam at 2-months of age. The infant is fussing, and the father shows eyebrow-raising. Printed by permission of the parent. Photograph by Peter Lafreniere.

The sound quality of gooing is important because it includes both normal phonation and in the same utterance, limited but discernible tongue action. Speech ultimately requires extensive and highly coordinated actions of the voice and the supraglottal vocal tract including tongue, lips, and jaw. In gooing, we see that the infant by 2 months of age can produce articulations that vary substantially from event to event (Zlatin, 1975a, 1975b). Sometimes there is no articulation, but other times the infant begins with a quasivowel and follows with a friction sound at the back of the mouth. The reverse may also occur, with the back articulation beginning the vocalization and the quasivowel following it. Many additional variations also occur. Infants do not appear to have a rigid formula for how the sounds of gooing are to be produced. Sometimes there is friction in the articulation and sometimes there is not. Sometimes the quasivowel part comes first, and sometimes the articulation, or consonant-like part does. Sometimes the infant deviates from the quasivowel pattern by opening the mouth during the normal phonation period, yielding a more identifiable vowel-like sound, and other times the lips and jaw remain essentially immobile.

The variability of vocalization in gooing contrasts with the sound patterns of vegetative sounds and with communicative signals such as crying or laughter. It would be wrong to imply that the latter include no variation (see, e.g., Green et al., 1998), but it is important to note that the variation that does occur in vegetative sounds and communicative signals is constrained by the functions that these sounds serve. The physical character of vegetative sounds and communicative signals is bounded because in the former case the sounds are artifactual (the natural result of bodily conditions) and in the latter case their role in communicating particular affective states necessitates precision and clarity of presentation.

Gooing, on the other hand, is free to roam. Its function is unhampered by predetermined affective functions. As a consequence, while infants are engaged in face-to-face interaction, they produce gooing sounds that appear to range expansively at the infant's will. Whereas in the case of quasivowels we emphasized a freedom in communicative function, in the case of gooing, we note a greater tendency for the sounds themselves to vary freely in quality and form. Quasivowels are usually short in duration and usually involve simple falling intonation during the early months of life, but gooing sounds can be produced at a wide variety of durations and can express a number of intonational patterns. With gooing the infant seems to have launched into a new realm of free-roaming sounds that can be adjusted to the infant's whim and possible social intentions. This beginning of the exploration of sound-making capabilities and their potential range represents the onset of command over an infraphonological property of Signal Analysis.

The most salient usage of gooing is in the face-to-face circumstances of vocalization (indicating the earliest clear cases of Directivity in vocal action in humans) and turn-taking (indicating the earliest clear cases of vocal Interactivity) that have been so extensively studied (Anderson et al., 1977; Ginsburg & Kilbourne, 1988; Kaye & Fogel, 1980). Parents and researchers alike have noted that infants are responsive to interaction at 2 months of age and engage in what appear to be protoconversations where gooing sounds are prominent. The very roots of communicative dialogue are often assumed to be foreshadowed in these vocal and facial interactions. Yet to understand the breadth of the significance of gooing as a phenomenon, it is critical to take note of the fact that babies can produce these sounds in a wide variety of other circumstances as well. Sometimes, 2- and 3-month-old babies goo when they are all alone. Sometimes somewhat older infants goo in ways that suggest they wish to attract attention. In such cases it is they who are the initiators of interaction and the adults who become the responders. Smiling may or may not accompany gooing. As with quasivowels, the affective qualities that can be included in gooing are optional to the baby, again indicating that vocalization in the human infant manifests Free Expressivity.

Gooing interactions may represent the earliest social uses of vocalizations without specific, necessary affective quality. The infant seems to be interested in the human face, the voice, and the entire conjunct of the social connection. There may be no obvious pleasure displayed, yet the infant pursues these interactions actively and vigorously. It is clear that infants are motivated to look at people and to "converse" with them (see Trevarthen & Marwick, 1986; Trevarthen, 1979).

Excursus on Infant Play in Humans and Other Mammals: A Background to Discussion of the Expansion Stage of Vocal Development

By 3 or 4 months of age, infants begin to diversify vocally, in the Expansion stage of protophone development. A wide variety of new sounds begin to occur during this period in a veritable explosion of new types. So great is the vocal activity during the Expansion stage that many have referred to it as a period of vocal play, invoking the many repetitive and exploratory actions of infants and young children that appear to represent active attempts to master motoric actions and understand the nature of the world (Stark, 1980; Zlatin, 1975a, 1975b). The extraordinary Contextual Freedom of vocalization in the Expansion stage is matched by the tendency for vocal actions to show exploration in Signal Analysis where infants appear to develop systematic control over a variety of acoustic and articulatory dimensions.

Before proceeding to describe some of the vocalizations of the Expansion stage that illustrate the infant's control over Signal Analysis, I provide a brief empirical justification for the claim that human infants do indeed attempt to master new capabilities through play. This excursus will be redundant for most developmental psychologists or biologists familiar with the facts to be noted, but it may be useful for others to lay out reasons to believe that infants are in many regards active, playful learners. Here I do not entirely reject an older developmental psychology assumption that infant actions are sometimes produced unintentionally by a developing motoric system that evolves mechanistically, either through genetic preprogramming or by a stimulus–response learning system that operates without infant intention. Nevertheless, I suggest adding a critical component to the behavioristic characterization: playful, directed action.

After a presentation I made at a small conference in 1979, an internationally prominent developmental psychologist contested my contention that infants in the Expansion stage vocalize with purpose. He noted that although infant boys show penile erections, it would be unreasonable to assume that they intend to engage in sexual acts at such a tender age. By the same token, he argued, the fact that infants vocalize does not indicate that they intend to engage in any kind of social act, and it does not indicate (according to his view) that their vocalizations represent an attempt to learn to talk. Vocalizations appear to occur at random, and there is no empirical reason, he claimed, to think there is any purpose in them.

He saw human infant vocalizations as passive and mechanistic and found no justification for the assumption that infants, through their vocal actions, systematically pursue mastery. His view was surprising because many infant actions are clearly purposeful. For example, it is impossible not to notice that infants grasp and explore objects (Fischer & Lazerson, 1984; Piaget, 1969; Tamis-LeMonda & Bornstein, 1991) by reaching out for them systematically by 6 months of age; holding them, as if to ask what they feel like; examining them visually and rotating them to gain a view of all sides as if to ask what they look like; mouthing them, as if to ask what they taste like; and shaking them vigorously, sometimes banging them on available surfaces, as if to ask what they sound like (see Fig. 9.5). The systematicity of this exploratory action makes little sense unless we assume that the infant is engaged in an active attempt to understand objects.

When infants begin to crawl or scoot, they clearly practice the activity, not merely for the purpose of attaining new objects to explore, but also for the pur-

FIG. 9.5. This still shows a 6-month old infant handling a toy just provided by the mother. The baby Shelby produces a raspberry sound while examining the object through various sensory modalities. Printed by permission of the mother, Sue Reamer.

pose of scooting itself. Crawling infants sometimes go up and down stairs, for example, repeatedly accomplishing nothing more than getting from one place to another. Similarly, as infants learn to cruise (walking while holding on to a stable object) and then to walk, they often perform repetitive locomotory actions, leaving little doubt that they are trying to walk, because they are trying to walk, not because they are trying to get somewhere walking—they could do it easier by crawling at that point. Infants seem to delight in just knowing how to get around. My son spent many hours in my office as a 4- and 5-month-old on the carpeted floor. While I was writing about infant vocal development, he was scooting from place to place, taking off if the door was left open. My publication productivity was distinctly limited during that era.

Infants seem to have a tremendous desire to control things and to master new capabilities. Even in the first weeks of life, infants can learn to control the presentation of sights or sounds (Eimas et al., 1971; Siqueland & DeLucia, 1969) through adjusting their pattern of sucking on a pacifier rigged to control a tape recorder or picture presentation system. In addition, they can learn to turn their heads to the side of a crib to control the presentation of a sound (Papoušek, 1967). By 2 months of age they can learn to kick to make a mobile move, and can remember what they learn about the connection between kicking and the mobile's movement days or weeks later (Rovee-Collier, Sullivan, Enright, Lucas, & Fagen, 1980). By 6 months of age, infants seated on their mothers' laps will turn their heads as many as 50 times toward a speaker each time a sound occurs in order to control the activation of an animated toy (Moore, Thompson, & Thompson, 1975). The tendency of infants to take repeated systematic action to control the occurrence of an event (even if the event is as apparently uninteresting as a mere a bleep or tone pip) suggests that infants have a deep-seated propensity to seek control of their environments.

Much infant and young child play is interpreted as goal-directed practice, developing skills and understanding (for a general review, see Bornstein & Lamb, 1992). Of course play is not limited to human infants and children. Mammals in general are extraordinarily prone to systematic and sometimes mischievous play. From rat pups to goat kids to baby chimps, little mammals spend enormous effort in play, wrestling, butting heads, mouthing objects, and climbing on whatever structure can be treated as an obstacle (Fischer & Lazerson, 1984; Loizos, 1969; Morris, 1967). It seems natural to conclude that play may have a key role in the development of a variety of capabilities in mammals. Evolution tends to provide behaviors that have survival value, and given its ubiquity and persistence throughout childhood (even into adulthood in many species), play is recognized as a crucial factor in preparation and maintenance of skills. Natural selection appears to have instilled in mammal species the internal motivation to seek mastery through exploratory activities and fun.

There are, of course, more formal and measurable ways to address the issue of intentionality in infant actions and in chapter 12 I consider some of these. Some infant behaviors are reflexive, but much like other actions of infants, vocalizations in the first year of life are often structured in ways that make clear that mastery motivation drives their production. Even before the Expansion stage, it appears that quasivowels and gooing can be performed by infants at will, in circumstances that suggest no external stimulus has elicited them and where the only internal stimulus that seems plausible as a source of them is infant interest in the sounds themselves.

Exploratory Play in Squealing and Growling

By the beginning of the Expansion stage of vocal development, the activity of sound exploration by infants can easily be verified by merely keeping track of sound types that are produced by babies and the circumstances under which they occur. During this stage squealing occurs, usually abundantly. Research has not made clear whether squealing begins as a reflexive response to tickling or some other social stimulus; sometimes squealing does occur in such circumstances (see Fig. 9.6). However, by the middle of the first year, squealing occurs frequently as an event initiated by babies. It is characterized by high pitch, often in a falsetto register (the kind of voice used by Mickey Mouse). Sometimes squeals include alternation between falsetto and full voice, and usually they show substantial vocal tension.

Sometimes infants may seem to be expressing delight or frustration in squealing, as indicated by facial expression, but most often they seem to produce sequences of squeals for no obvious reason other than the interest in exploring the sounds themselves. In such cases, facial affect may remain neutral, whereas the vocal activity ranges broadly, including or not including articulations, and the vocal quality changes sharply, often entering and leaving falsetto register. Infants do not obviously intend squealing to express delight, but parents often love to hear babies squeal, nurturing the production of the sound by imitating it or trying to elicit it with interactive play.

During the same time period in which squealing is so prominent in the repertoire of infant vocalizations, during the Expansion stage from the fourth month or so through the middle months of the first year of life, infants engage in an additional vocal exercise that appears to be the opposite of squealing, and often generates a rather opposite response on the part of parents. This vocal type is called *growling,* and here the production is rarely assumed to be reflexive in infants. Growling often appears with neutral facial expression (see Fig. 9.7), or can occur accompanied by a look of strain, or even smiling. The sound quality of growling often includes "creaky voice" (sometimes called "vocal fry") and typically involves very low pitch and high degrees of vocal tension (Oller, 1980a; Oller et al., 1985). As with squealing, however, the physical characteristics of growling can vary extensively, including or not including vocal tension or fry and various articulations such as those occurring in gooing.

The very low pitch and noisy vocal tension of growling is somewhat comical, because it seems surprising that an infant can produce such a low sound,

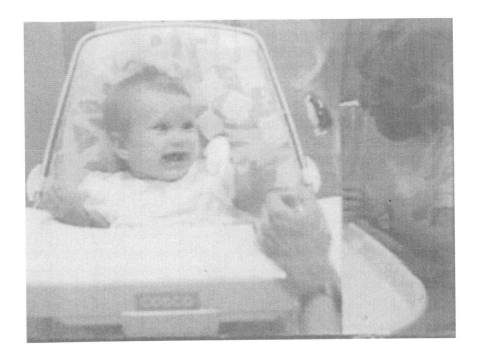

FIG. 9.6.   This still shows 6-month old Shelby squealing in apparent delight as a toy is being presented by the mother. On other occasions the same sound may be produced in circumstances that include no social interaction at all, accompanied by a neutral facial expression. Printed by permission of the parent.

and it has a flavor that might be interpreted as anger, although the facial expressions of anger seem usually to be missing and the goal-directed focus of anger does not appear to be present (again, see Fig. 9.7). Unfocused as it is, growling in infants can have an ominous tone. The mother of one infant who growled more than most asked me one day to tell her please that the child was normal, as we listened to his voice in the background from his crib, growling in long strings, loudly. Horror films seemed to have gotten to this mother, who was reassured when I insisted that babies all over the world make that kind of sound and eventually stop, even without an exorcist.

One parameter that seems to tie squealing and growling together is pitch. The two sound types represent extremes of the continuum of pitch, and infants explore them both (Kent & Murray, 1982; Robb, Saxman, & Grant, 1989), producing fundamental frequencies that are 10 times higher in squealing than in growling. All the other sounds of the infant vocal repertoire are

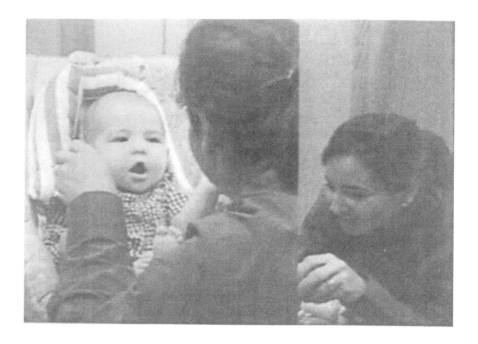

FIG. 9.7.   The infant Claudia is growling loudly, but the facial expression is neutral even in the context of maternal eye contact. On other occasions the same sound may be produced with a look of disgust or even delight. Sometimes the same sound is produced in circumstances that include no social interaction. Printed by permission of the mother, Ceci.

produced in between squealing and growling in terms of pitch, usually at two to four times the pitch of growling (Oller, 1980a). In part, it is the obvious conceptual connection between squealing and growling in the realm of pitch that first inspired the speculation that infants might be systematically exploring their vocal capabilities during the Expansion stage. The conclusion that they are indeed engaged in exploration becomes nearly inevitable when we take stock of the way infants seem to practice these sounds, sometimes producing one or the other in long strings while occupied in solitary activities, or systematically alternating between the two sound types for no apparent reason other than the interest of toying with their contrastive natures. The natural development of contrastive functions or structures is posited in the notion of *epigenetic selection* (Sachs, 1988). Both squealing and growling appear to be epigenetically selected and emerge as contrasting, complementary features in a developing domain of pitch and vocal quality.

FIG. 9.8. In this split screen shot, the mother has been instructed to sit passively looking away from the infant Sebastian in a "still-face" pose, after a prior period of free interaction. The 6-month-old infant reaches and cries intentionally, attempting to regain the mother's attention, a common pattern of normal infant action during the still-face period. Printed by permission of the mother, Sabrina.

The tendency of infants in the Expansion stage to produce stable sequences of squeals and other sequences of growls suggests the intentional development of contrasting types of sounds produced with Contextual Freedom. Furthermore the exploration of the pitch dimension suggests command of Signal Analysis, and by virtue of the apparent creation (or at least solid command) of new categories contrasting along the pitch dimension, it suggests Categorical Adaptation, the ability to create new categories of vocal function.

Expansion of the Repertoire With Yelling and Whispering

The exploratory character of infant vocalization is also seen in the appearance of yelling and whispering during the Expansion stage. In yelling, infants explore the ability to produce sounds of maximum amplitude, and in whispering they delve into sounds of minimum amplitude. Both kinds of vocalizations can be adapted to special social purposes, of course, but when these sounds are performed during the middle of the first year, infants as a rule appear to be engaged in nothing more than sound play.

Loud crying for attention is utilized during the same period of time (see Fig. 9.8), but the vocal quality of crying as well as the patterning of its sequential elements is quite distinct from that of yelling. In the latter the infant normally produces a single, long, and very loud syllable, with the mouth wide open, and often with normal phonation. If the yell is repeated, it may be done with different vowel-like elements or different durations at the infant's discretion. Crying, whether voluntary or involuntary, tends to follow a pattern that includes repetition of chains of base units, with cry-typical dysphonation (Green et al., 1998; Zeskind & Barr, 1997). The chains of base units or episodes are organized in a way that makes it easy to identify crying and differentiate it from yelling. One of the key features of infant crying is that there is an ingressive breath between each minimal rhythmic unit and substantial stereotypy in timing of the repetitive chains of units. Yelling does not necessarily include repetitive units.

Yelling occasionally generates a response in parents not unlike that of growling: "Why, in heaven's name, does he yell when he doesn't need or apparently want anything?" True enough, but of course the infant also uses screaming purposefully on some occasions.

In our own laboratories, we discovered that whispering occurs quite frequently in infant vocal development well after we already knew that yelling existed as a playful and practiced sound. The reason for the delay in the investigative recognition of whispering was that the latter is produced at an amplitude that makes it often hard to hear in tape recordings. We had originally instituted a policy of categorizing only those sounds that could be easily (and reliably) identified during review of tape recordings (Oller, 1980a), and that policy had included a proviso that transcribers should include only the sounds that could be heard clearly and distinctly. As a result, the great bulk of whispering in our baby vocalizations tapes had been passed over in our transcripts.

The discovery of whispers resulted from the hypothesis that was suggested by the symmetry between squealing and growling. It had been hypothesized that these symmetrical sounds might represent attempts on the infant's part to explore the pitch dimension at both ends. Yelling was already on the list of commonly occurring sounds of infants, and it seemed likely that a symmetry might obtain with respect to yelling as well. We then looked back to tapes of infants recorded longitudinally at 4, 5, and 6 months of age, and applied a new criterion of transcription in which low-amplitude sounds were not ruled out. With the new procedure it was found that whispering was present in much the same way as yelling (Oller, 1986). Infants appeared indeed to maintain the symmetrical exploratory pattern, evaluating their abilities with amplitude at both ends of the dimension, again in a pattern consistent with the model of epigenetic selection. As with squealing and growling, yelling and whispering reveal that infants command vocal Contextual Freedom, Signal Analysis, and Categorical Adaptation.

Exploration of Vowel-Like Sounds

Another dimension of exploration that starts around the fourth or fifth month of life and elaborates throughout the Expansion stage concerns resonance capabilities of the vocal tract. Vowel-like vocalizations occur in abundance during this period, as the infant appears to experiment with the production of sounds with differing timbres (Lieberman, 1980; Stark, 1980). The mouth may open wide for an [a]-like sound or the lips may be rounded and tongue brought forward with the jaw low for a vowel that resembles the [o]-umlaut of German or the even lower front-rounded vowels of Danish. Sometimes the jaw is simply lowered slightly to produce a schwa-like articulation (as in the first vowel in the American pronunciation of the word *banana*).

Speaking any natural language requires the ability to manipulate the resonances of the vocal tract systematically to create different vowel sounds. As infants practice a variety of vowel-like articulations through these fully resonant nuclei (or full vowels) they explore the acoustic and articulatory space that languages utilize to form contrastive vowels. Again Signal Analysis and Categorical Adaptation are seen within the dimensions explored by infants of the Expansion stage.

In emitting these vowel-like sounds, infants often utilize normal phonation, the same kind of phonation that is found in quasivowels, and of course the same kind that is the primary form found in real speech. At the same time, infants are not restricted to producing fully resonant nuclei with normal phonation. Sometimes the pitch and vocal quality that accompanies a fully resonant nucleus is such as to justify categorizing it as, for example, both a squeal and a fully resonant nucleus. Typically in the vocal play of squealing, growling, yelling, and whispering, the vocal tract assumes specialized postures that can be heard as vowel-like sounds, although the vocal qualities of these specialized infant productions may become the most salient aspect of the productions. The fact that an individual vocalization can represent more than one protophone category reveals the inherently featural definition of protophones.

Fully resonant nuclei of the Expansion stage are often produced as prolonged syllables, as much as 1 sec in duration, but sometimes the articulations are much shorter. Occasionally, the syllables composed of vowel-like sounds are produced in a quick sequence, punctuated by glottal interruptions (Holmgren et al., 1986). The English word *uh oh* has such an interruption (or glottal stop) between its two syllables. Such an utterance can be termed a *glottal sequence* (Oller et al., 1986). The timing of production of glottal sequences is much like the timing of real speech syllables, a further indication of the growing relation between these infant sounds and speech.

Not uncommonly, fully resonant nuclei occur in social interaction either with or without eye contact (see Fig. 9.9). However, as with the other sounds of the stage, these vowel-like sounds are often produced by an infant engaged in solitary play. I remember particularly observing my son alternately producing high and low vowels while seated in a high chair, with no apparent intent other than his own amusement. "Ah, ah, ah," he seemed to say, gazing into space, then hesitating before continuing "ih, ih, ih."

The nearly transcribable character of the vowel-like sounds in the Expansion stage is often seductive (as reflected in the last sentence) in part because cases of infant alternating production suggest an emerging contrastive system. However, the infant's intentions in producing such contrasts may invoke only the grossest of dimensions (e.g., high vs. low jaw position) whereas alphabetical characterizations or phonetic transcriptions suggest a much richer featural phonetic framework. For this reason it remains important to resist uncautious transcription of precanonical sounds.

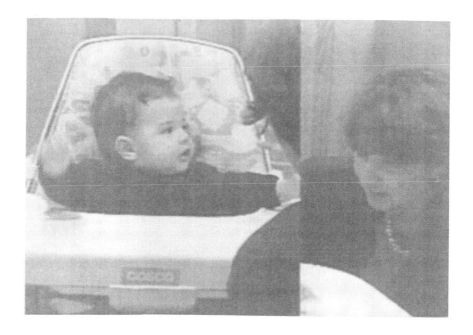

FIG. 9.9.   In this split screen shot, the mother is trying to engage the 6-month-old infant Sebastian visually, but the latter looks away, producing a full vowel-like sound, deemed to have a mid to high-quality. At other points in the same session, the infant shared gaze with the mother and vocalized interactively. These patterns of interaction are common in the Expansion stage of vocal development. Printed by permission of the parent.

Raspberries

Among the most striking sounds of infancy are "Bronx cheers" or raspberries. Infants use their lips (or a combination of tongue and lips) to produce noisy friction sounds, sometimes with voicing, sometimes without, sometimes with trilling of the lips, and sometimes only with friction (Oller et al., 1985). To substantiate the argument that infant vocalizations are internally motivated, created by the infant rather than being learned, it is convenient to focus on raspberries. Parents not uncommonly detest them, not just because they may sound a bit ill mannered, but because babies often seem to choose the moment of high chair feeding, with a mouth full of cereal, to try out their raspberry capabilities. Consequently, parents who otherwise might be held under the sway of the rigid notion that babies learn everything by social reinforcement usually adapt quickly to a more liberal and at least partly maturationist view when they note that their babies produce raspberries without any training or encouragement at all.

Raspberries are produced, like the other sounds of the Expansion stage, in sequences of practice and play that may or may not involve other people. Infants in this period are clearly in control of their vocal actions, exploring, experimenting, and gaining a grasp of what their lips and voices can do.

To recognize how raspberries directly manifest the growth of a linguistic capability, we need to look into the structure of phonological systems. In the formation of syllables, languages utilize both vowels and consonants. In acoustics and articulation, consonants and vowels are not strictly delimited, but rather seem to be woven together in a seamless sequence of overlapping and integrated cues for speech segments. Usually the cues listeners use to interpret speech segments involve the quality of sound or change in the quality of sound, but in other cases they involve silences occurring between segments of vocalization or noise. Vowels form the nuclei of syllables, and in their prototypical form they involve normal phonation and full resonance. Consonants are attached as margins to vowels, blending with them through transitions of resonance, and showing their special consonantal characteristics through the nature of those transitions and distinguishing sound properties. Margins of syllables can be characterized by a variety of features including noise, lower amplitude than adjacent vowels, more compact resonance, and sometimes an absence of sound. To refer to consonants as sounds is thus partially misleading, because silence often plays an important role in their perception. On the other hand, many consonants do involve sound, often noisy, friction-based sound.

Consonant-relevant noises, entirely unlike the fully resonant nuclei discussed earlier, are created by the lips or tongue, and in raspberries, the infant explores the ability to produce precisely such sounds. In gooing during the first few months of life, the back of the tongue begins to be involved in articulations that have some of the properties of certain consonants, but the sounds of gooing tend to be soft and gentle. Raspberries are raucous, with noise or trilling, with lips and sometimes tongue protruding. They leave no room for doubt that they are intentional, and that the infant is engaged in gaining command over potential features of sound. The production of raspberries, then, suggests the properties of Signal Analysis (because a new feature of friction is being explored) and Categorical Adaptation (because raspberries represent a novel category that appears to be created by the infant).

Marginal Babbling

That raspberries are precursors to the consonant capability is especially revealed in the fact that they commonly are combined with fully resonant nuclei in the late Expansion stage to form primitive syllables. In the first occurrences of infant syllables that adult ears perceive as including both consonants and vowels, there is a great deal of variability. In particular, the timing of these primitive syllables is scattered much more widely than the timing of syllables in speech (see Oller, 1980a). In mature syllables, the mouth moves from relatively closed positions for consonant-like segments, toward relatively open positions for vowel-like segments. In mature speech, these movements, observable in instrumental acoustic displays as formant transitions, are controlled within a narrow time window. Most formant transitions occur very quickly, within about 50 msec. Long ones can be 100 msec or so, patterns associated with particular classes of consonants, the glides (such as w and y), sounds for which the primary distinguishing property is precisely long formant transitions (see, e.g., Miller & Liberman, 1979).

The human vocal tract can, of course, produce much longer formant transitions, but when it does, the result seems awkward and unnatural, perhaps immature. All other things being equal, long formant transitions (beyond about 120 msec) yield an impression that is less speech-like than short ones. During the Expansion stage, especially late in it, human infants explore the possibility of putting potential consonant-like units (formed, e.g., from raspberry articulations) together with potential vowel-like units. These primitive syllables are constructed with transition times that are too long to be characteristic of speech. The syllables seem ill articulated and drawn out, even though in terms of phonation type and articulatory complexity they resemble mature syllables.

These slowly articulated primitive syllables are called *marginal babbling* (Oller, 1980a), a term formulated tongue-in-cheek, one might say, because it is intended simultaneously to imply that such sounds are less acceptable as speech than prototypical mature syllables, and that they include specific consonant-like margins. Marginal babbling is not extremely frequent and is not produced repetitively in sequences of similar syllables the way many of the other Expansion stage sounds are. This difference between marginal babbling and other sound types explored during the Expansion stage seems to suggest that infants in beginning to form primitive syllables are continuing, consistent with the stage, to explore their vocal capabilities, but in this case the exploration takes the specific form of attempts at recombining elements of their existing repertoire of individual utterances. Prior to this point, fully resonant nuclei are in the repertoire and have been practiced. Similarly, raspberries are in the repertoire and have been practiced. In marginal babbling the two elements of the repertoire are joined to form novel combinations.

The property of Recombinability is a key feature of human languages (Hewes, 1983). Without Recombinability, a communicative system would be formed from a group of prime elements, each of which would transmit a particular message. The number of messages transmissible within the system would be restricted by the number of prime elements—and these would have to be few in number because there is some practical limit to how many prime elements can be effectively discriminated and recognized in any real communication system.

Recombinability opens the bottleneck. A small number of prime elements are combined and recombined sequentially to form many new (although possibly longer) transmission units. To exemplify, if an infant has two discriminable vowel-like articulations and a raspberry, he can be said to have three possible prime communication units. By recombining the three into syllables, however, the infant can have the three prime units, plus the raspberry (in syllable-initial position) combined with vowel one, the raspberry combined with vowel two, and each vowel combined with the raspberry (in syllable-final position). Four new transmission units are thus formed by combinations of the primes. As the number of primes increases, the number of potential transmission units that can be formed through recombination increases multiplicatively. Infants in fact may command a number of different raspberry-like articulations as well as several vowel-like articulations. Furthermore, marginal babbling is formed from a variety of additional articulations. Not only movements of the lips (as in raspberries) but also of the tongue may come into play as the infant appears to experiment with combining opening and closing gestures of the vocal tract. The hallmark of marginal babbling is its variability.

Recombinability, and the variability of articulation that it implies, is clearly one of the properties that made it possible for language to show explosive power as a tool in the possession of our distant ancestors. Recombinability was a necessary (although not the only necessary) element in the creation of lexicons of unlimited size. Sequences of recombined syllables formed the basis for vocabularies without bound. In taking stock of the human endowment for speech communication, it will be useful to keep in mind that infants create recombined sequences of prime elements from their vocal repertoires by the time they are 4 to 6 months old, a pattern of vocal action that appears to be essentially absent in other primates at any age (but see chap. 12 on Recombinability).

It is important to stipulate that not all syllables produced during the Expansion stage are properly called marginal syllables. Some of the recombinations yield well-formed or canonical syllables, sequences that are well-timed, sometimes with transitions of 50 msec or even less. However, during the Expansion stage, such syllables occur rarely and sporadically rather than repetitively and systematically. They appear to occur because infants produce a great variety of primitive syllables during marginal babbling, with a wide range of formant transitions. Most of these are too long to be considered well-formed, but on the edge of the distribution of durations for primitive syllables produced in the Expansion stage, a few of the experimental syllables are found to have been articulated rapidly, and they sound like well-formed syllables. It makes some sense to think of these well-timed occurrences as accidents. In any case, the sporadic occurrence of varying durations during this period suggests the infant is not concerned about restricting formant transitions during the Expansion stage. As we define stages of development in the human vocal capability, we focus not on sporadic occurrences that represent probes of experimentation, but on the more tightly controlled production of sounds as evidenced in repetitive, consistent production.

Marginal babbling does not, of course, represent the very first attempt on the infant's part to produce articulated utterances (i.e., utterances showing movements of the vocal tract during phonation). The first such attempts are found in gooing, a phenomenon that occurs 2 to 4 months earlier than marginal babbling. Yet marginal babbling represents a clear advance over gooing in that the former systematically includes fully resonant nuclei, whereas the latter typically manifests quasivowels as nuclei. Thus, in marginal babbling, the extent of movement of the vocal tract during phonation is typically ample and consequently the formant transitions found in marginal babbling are often wide and dramatic, whereas in gooing the movement from a consonant-like closure in the back of the mouth toward a quasivowel is minor and may go essentially unnoticed. Still, even in gooing, occasional well-formed syllables can be heard. Again, however, as in marginal babbling, such occurrences are sporadic and do not appear to be intentional. The gooing infant produces a range of postures of the vocal tract although most of the postures deviate little from the at-rest position. On the edge of the distribution of postures, however, are a relatively small number of goos that show a relatively open vocal tract, and when these happen to be combined with a quick articulation of the back of the tongue against the palate or other structure of the tract, the result may be perceived as a well-formed syllable or even a bisyllable *aga* or *uhguh*. Thus it is fair to say that occasional canonical syllables occur even as early as the Primitive Articulation stage and also during the Expansion stage (Oller, 1980a; Zlatin, 1975a, 1975b). Because these syllables occur sporadically rather than repetitively, they are treated in the protophone stage model as accidental.

Early Imitation in the Expansion Stage

The earliest clear evidence of selective imitation of vocal sounds is reported for the Expansion stage (Kessen et al., 1979; Masataka, 1992). These indications are found in infants who produce vowel-like sounds with intonations that systematically resemble modeled vowels of varying intonation. Some earlier indications of imitation (Papoušek & Papoušek, 1989) are less certain because they do not result from experimental presentation of sounds; in such naturalistic observation it cannot be determined whether the infant imitates the parent or vice versa. Very recent experimental work (e.g., Kugiumutzakis, 1999) offers more hopeful indications of early vocal imitation. In any case, it is clear that across the first months of life, infants not only come to be capable of vocalizing with Directivity and Interactivity, but they also come to match vocalizations specifically, showing the property of Imitability.

The Canonical Stage: The Emergence of Well-Formed Syllables

The developments of gooing and the Expansion stage clearly distance humans from their primate relatives, but it is not until the subsequent Canonical stage that infants begin to produce sounds in a way that parents identify unambiguously as being related to speech. The production of canonical syllables is seen most distinctly in reduplicated sequences that sound like "baba," "dada," or "mama." It is surely no accident, that nursery terms for father, mother, grandmother, and so on are typically drawn from this very repertoire of reduplicated canonical syllable sequences (Jakobson, 1962/1971b; Lewis, 1936; Oller et al., 1975). Infants all over the world produce such reduplicated sequences, and languages all over the world draw on them to compose the most fundamental names that pertain to an infant's experience.

When babies produce canonical babbling, they produce sounds that can count as words, assuming that the language in question happens to include words composed of the syllables the babies produce. Usually nursery terms provide such words (Lewis, 1936). To say that canonical syllables are well-formed is to say precisely that they have the potential to count as words. Prior to the Canonical stage it is rare that infants produce utterances with this potential. With the onset of the Canonical stage, such syllables are routine, occurring many times daily. They show that the infant has commanded well-formed Syllabification.

A canonical utterance, in the usage here, consists of one or more well-formed syllables. The vast majority of syllables produced in real speech are canonical. The relatively few exceptions to this rule represent specialized modifications of the prototypical frame provided by canonical syllables.[1] To

---

[1] See chapter 5, section titled "On the Occurrence of Noncanonical Syllables in Mature Languages."

count as well-formed, the syllable requires a fully resonant nucleus produced with normal phonation, at least one margin (or consonant-like element), and a rapid formant transition between the margin and the nucleus. This definition is a central component of the theory of infraphonology elaborated in chapters 4 and 5. A canonical syllable includes a vowel and at least one consonant pronounced quickly, without breaks in phonation or drawing out of transitions. A well-formed syllable is snappy, whereas its antithesis, a marginal syllable, is slow in getting underway, so slow that the mature listener notices the temporal retardation of articulation. Untrained human listeners are very competent at identifying the syllables we designate as canonical (see Oller, Eilers, Neal, & Cobo-Lewis, 1998). If mature listeners could not recognize well-formed syllables, they would be in a difficult position when attempting to differentiate speech from nonspeech. The understanding of language clearly depends on an ability to identify speech as opposed to other kinds of sounds, vocal or nonvocal.

The appearance of canonical syllables, once the Canonical stage is underway, is hard to miss. Parents recognize it immediately and apparently make adjustments in their interactions with infants to account for the fact that the sounds the baby has come to command resemble speech enough to be exploited as speech. Parents immediately try to impose conventional lexical interpretations on the baby's sounds: "Oh, yes, you said 'baba'; here's the bottle." In so doing, parents appear to shape infant vocal usage, molding its occurrence toward linguistic function (McCune, 1992; Papoušek, 1994).

Yet the first occurrences of controlled, repetitive canonical syllables, announcing the onset of this most salient and crowning stage of infant vocal development, do not appear to bear communicative intent any more than the vocal explorations of the Expansion stage. At the beginning of the Canonical stage, infants produce well-formed syllables with no apparent purpose other than that of mastering the capability to do so. My son entered the stage at a typical age of 7 months, saying something that sounded more or less like "bababa" and then "bababababa." It was clear that he did not intend these syllables to be treated as communications. In later months he imitated canonical syllables already in his repertoire when we attempted to elicit them from him, but at the beginning, canonical syllables were merely his spontaneous invention and plaything. This interpretation of child action as play is consistent with observations of parents that have been in the developmental literature for more than a century (Taine, 1877/1971).

The onset of canonical babbling is a topic that has inspired considerable research (Eilers, Oller, et al., 1993; Lynch, Oller, Steffens, & Buder, 1995; Oller & Eilers, 1988; Smith & Oller, 1981; Stoel-Gammon & Otomo, 1986; see also chaps. 6–8). Most infants appear to begin canonical babbling rather suddenly. Laban, for example, began on a particular day noted in my diary when he was 7 months old, and from that day forward, canonical syllables produced in reduplicated form were the most salient aspect of his repertoire of vocalizations every day for months. Other children sometimes appear to have a more gradual onset for the Canonical stage. Some appear to begin the stage without using reduplicated sequences. Instead, individual well-formed syllables appear, consisting usually of one consonant-like element followed by one vowel-like element (a CV syllable); or two-syllable sequences may occur, consisting of a vowel-like element, a consonant-like element, and another vowel-like element (VCV). The key to identifying the onset of the stage is sufficient repetition of these well-formed syllables to yield a clear impression that infants are producing the syllables deliberately, not accidentally as a part of primitive syllable exploration that might be characterized primarily by marginal syllables.

In Laban's case, there was a strong preference for a canonical syllable "ba" from the beginning of the Canonical stage throughout the remainder of the first year of his life. Later in the year, however, he did explore syllables with a lingual articulation, sounding like "da" or "dih." Other infants have other preferences. In longitudinal studies we have recorded preferences for quite a number of possible syllables, including "da," "dih," "ma," "na" and "ya."

Reduplicated strings such as "baba" mark the Canonical stage and seem to constitute the primary criterion on which parents base the opinion that their babies are ready to start talking. However, apparent reference does not necessarily constitute actual reference. Often the baby looks off into space while babbling all alone in the crib. At the beginning of the stage, the baby does not necessarily show any interest in using well-formed syllables communicatively. Long reduplicated sequences are produced as if they constitute a pure motoric exercise.

During the Canonical stage infants produce both reduplicated sequences and variegated sequences of canonical syllables (Mitchell & Kent, 1990; Smith, Brown-Sweeney, & Stoel-Gammon, 1989). In producing strings of canonical syllables that are systematically different, infants manifest Recombinability of syllables. This property ultimately allows the formation of a wide variety of phonological words. Furthermore, in canonical babbling infants produce strings of syllables that are clustered in phrases, indicating that control over a property of Rhythmic Hierarchy of syllables is being developed. To add to the remarkable complexity that emerges in the Canonical stage, infants weave intonational variations into their sequences of hierarchically structured syllables, variations that appear to code affective information. Thus Hot–Cool Synthesis, the graceful merging of affective (hot) values of communication with potentially informational (cool) ones (Locke, 1993), is introduced to the infant repertoire.

Imitability of vocalizations is seen only as a flash of color in the Expansion stage but flowers fully in the Canonical stage. By late in the fully consolidated Canonical stage, infants selectively imitate contrasting well-formed syllables.

The Integrative Stage and the Onset of Real Speech

Canonical babbling continues for many months after its onset and indeed continues well after the onset of real speech, with the two forms of vocalization integrated to the point that it is hard to tell in many infants what is speech and what is babbling (Elbers & Ton, 1985; Vihman & Miller, 1988). The problem is partly one of definition and partly one of inherent ambiguity in actions of infants along with variability of parental interpretations. First, a word about the definition of real speech. We have already seen that in the broadest sense, communication occurs at birth. Some innately available sounds, such as crying, have communicative value, even if it is not intended. Their value is natural and universal to the human species. The meaningful units of real speech do not have this universality. Each word is defined by convention, so when babies begin to talk, they either have to learn words defined by prior convention, or (and this is where some serious difficulties of categorization begin for students of child language making behavioral observations) they have to make up new words and get their parents to accept them. Either way they introduce the infrasemiotic property of Conventionality into their repertoires. Now, people who study child language accept that infants do use made-up words, and their definition of real speech is generally broad enough to encompass words based on conventional forms as well as made-up words. I use this current meaning of real speech.

The methodological difficulty with made-up words owes to the fact that their earliest appearances are not necessarily clear, neither regarding the child's intentions nor the parents' interpretations (Dore, Franklin, Miller, & Ramer, 1976; Vihman, 1996). To make matters worse, even infant pronunciations that appear to be based on conventional forms are often ambiguous regarding whether or not the utterances are intended as meaningful by the child, and if they are, then ambiguities often obtain regarding what conventional word the child is attempting to produce. When babies say "baba," they can mean *big boy* or *bottle* or *buggy*, or they can mean nothing at all. To add to the difficulties, infants in the Integrative stage of vocal development often produce strings of syllables, some of which appear to be words and some of which appear to be pure babble.

Figuring out what babies mean during the growth in verbalization that is seen in the Integrative stage is quite a task both for parents and researchers. Of course the difficulties of interpretation of infant actions are not entirely insurmountable, and we can be sure this is so because eventually the child and the parent do understand each other. The fact that they do not understand each other perfectly at the beginning does not mean that early speech cannot be studied, but rather that it must be studied with tools that adapt to the ecological facts of parent–infant communication, and take account of the inherent ambiguities in the process.

Real speech in children, then, begins not with a bang but with a sputtering, composed of vocal probes by infants that must be deciphered with ingenuity and shaped toward some potential meaning by parents. The study of very early vocabulary items in children shows that some of them are composed of syllables that are not even canonical. Laban, for example, produced a consonantless imitation of a cat's meow, and used this utterance as a primitive word during his very early speech. Our daughter Jenna's very first word (according to Rebecca) was pronounced "ah," meaning roughly *hi*. Another report indicates an infant had an early word pronounced "mm," meaning loosely, *animal* (Quay, 1993). Other research shows infants using vocalizations very loosely to communicate such functions as assent, or generalized questions utilizing quasivowels referred to in this context as grunts (McCune et al., 1996; Vihman, 1996). Such words are precanonical inventions of the child, and parents must notice the systematic spatial and temporal connection between the utterances and their contexts of usage, as well as noticing the child's gestures, facial expressions, and gaze direction, to know that the infant intends something by them. In some cases when infants initially produce such sounds without communicative intention, parents may impose interpretation, encouraging children to make a meaningful connection between sound and context. Perhaps sometimes infants understand the parents' goal. It is hard to be sure. It is clear, however, that the earliest words sometimes represent a sort of negotiation between parent and child over how to say things.

The ambiguity of very early vocabulary is also seen in homonymy. Eventually the syllable "ba" played a remarkably central role in Laban's early speech repertoire (through about 14 months of age). At one point he had a wide variety of words that were pronounced "ba," including *Beth* (his eldest sister), *bath, ball, book, boy, big,* and *bird*. All these words had clearly distinguishable meaning for him—he could point to appropriate pictures when any of these words was pronounced for his identification.

Canonical babbling had clearly provided a frame for Laban on which linguistic meanings could be hung during the Integrative stage. As he elaborated his canonical babbling, he developed new frames for communication. By the middle of the second year, he had various syllables (ba, da, ni, to, ma, and a few others) that could be strung together, although Recombinability was limited as evidenced by the fact that reduplicated sequences of syllables were used extensively and preferentially. Among our favorite Laban words in that era were *helicopter*, pronounced "DAtototo," and *elevator*, pronounced "Edadada."

Across the first half of the second year of life, infants acquire a variety of new words. Some of these clearly possess not only Conventionality, but also Arbitrariness of connection between signal and value. Whereas a meowing sound hints at the cat that it might be used to represent, the word *edadada* bears no notable resemblance to elevators. The latter word would thus be said to possess Arbitrariness. By the end of the second half-year of life, infants use words they have acquired in remarkably analytical ways, making reference to classes of entities independent of any particular social intention. A word can be used to refer to the class while asking for it, naming it, refusing it, and so on. This dissociation between social intentions (corresponding to illocutionary forces) and meanings (corresponding to analytical references) reveals the development in the infant repertoire of the property of Semanticity.

In addition, across the Integrative stage infants often produce very elaborate babbling sounds of a variety termed *gibberish*. Here, canonical syllables of substantial variety are mixed with syllables that might be deemed precanonical by virtue of their reduced stress status. The sequences are often long and elaborately intoned. A common circumstance of gibberish production is seen in infants playing "telephone." They seem to be imitating what they understand telephone talk to constitute—unintelligible jabber, rapidly produced, and lots of it. Gibberish shows considerable expansion of control over Recombinability of syllables as well as Hot–Cool Synthesis as manifest in the rich intonations expressed.

By the end of the Integrative stage, many infants recombine segment-sized elements of well-formed syllables to form new syllables. The elements of [ba] and [dɪ], for example, are recombined to form [bɪ] and [da]. This extension of the property of Recombinability yields a new property, Segmentation.

The coexistence of babbling and real speech in the Integrative stage provides an intriguing indication of the continuing exploratory involvement of the infant. Vocalization by this time has become a flexible tool, commanding ideas, and delivering thoughts entwined with feeling. Still, in addition to the potential of sounds for transmitting communicative values, vocalization is also still a plaything and an object of intrinsic interest. Through at least 18 months of age, babbling continues in most infants to occupy a role of honor, and so it should. Infants raise their voices from primitive beginnings eventually stating, in well-formed sounds we cannot mistake, that they too are human.

THE UNIVERSALITY OF INFANT VOCALIZATIONS
AND THE NATURALNESS OF THEIR RECOGNITION

The existence of everyday terms to describe categories of significant vocalizations in babies, both protophone categories and other sounds, may be taken to suggest that the foundations of vocal interaction between caretakers and infants has biological, not merely cultural roots. To the extent that the terms for these sounds occur with moderately good translatability across a variety of natural languages, the suggestion is strengthened. Babies all over the world perform similar vocal actions, and parents all over the world appear to understand them at least at a global level.

At the same time, there appear to exist some notable cultural differences in the treatment of the sounds of infancy both in terms of categorization as sounds and in terms of interpretation of intended communicative functions. Some protophone categories that are well named in English do not appear to have corresponding terms in other languages. In Hindi, for example, it appears that there is no common term for "babbling." Of course Hindi-speaking persons know what babbling is, but when talking about it, they tend to refer by example, saying [bʌbʌ] or [dʌdʌ]. In Mandarin Chinese raspberries and squeals produced by infants can be described in long phrases, but do not appear to be represented by common simple terms. My informant (Shih-fen Tu, University of Miami) says that the Chinese try to ignore such sounds, thinking them a bit impolite, and perhaps this is why the language appears to lack special terms to describe them, even though Chinese parents are perfectly aware they occur. In my *Petit Larousse* (French/English) dictionary, *raspberry* is given the translation *faire pfft* and is categorized specifically as a "rude sound." So the opinion seems to have gotten around.

Table 9.2 provides a summary of terms found in several languages for just a few of the infant vocal actions considered within descriptions of protophone stages. I have loosely transliterated the Chinese, indicating tones numerically according to the Mandarin standard (1 = high/flat, 2 = rising, 3 = dipping, 4 = falling, 5 = light).

To be sure, words in natural languages are utilized with great flexibility, and words that describe infant vocalizations are no different in this regard. The word *growl*, for instance, is sometimes used to refer to a sound that implies a threat when produced by, for example, a dog. The same term is, on other occasions, applied to vocalizations of humans, sometimes implying threat, and sometimes not. The sound quality of certain infant vocalizations of the Expansion stage inspires utilization of the same descriptive term, even though infants' abilities to use growls socially may be very different from abilities of adults. Thus, the potential intentions and the potential interpretations of the intentions of growling can be rather varied. As a conse-

TABLE 9.2
Terms for a Few Infant Sounds in Six Languages

English	Spanish	French	German	Chinese (Mandarin)	Czech
Cry	Lloro	Cri	Schrei	Ku(1)	Křik
Laugh	Risa	Rire	Lachen	Siaw(4)	Smich
Goo	Gorgojeo	Roucoulement	Gurren	Tsitsigugu(1)	Vrkat
Squeal	Chillido	Cri aigu	Quietschen	?	Pistěni
Growl	Gruñido	Grognement	Brummen	How(3)	Mručeni
Raspberry	Trompetilla	Faire pfft	Prusten	?	Prskani
Babble	Balbuceo	Babillage	Plappern	Yaya(1) Sueh(2) Yi(3)	Žvatlani

quence of such complications, the terms listed in Table 9.2 must be understood as nontechnical. Accordingly, they are not easy to define in a strict way. Both within languages and across languages there are inevitable ambiguities in how the terms are used, and inevitable imperfections in translating them. For example, the term *gruñido* in Spanish is often used to mean grunt as well as growl, and in English *gooing* is sometimes called cooing or gurgling, terms that have their own special connotations that are not portrayed in identical ways in other languages.

Having laid out these provisos, it is important not to lose sight of the quasi-universality that is implied by the information in Table 9.2. Mature humans use primitive communicative displays including laughter, crying, growling, and squealing and all over the world, these displays are recognized as manifesting particular emotional content (Darwin, 1873; Eckman, 1994; Emde et al., 1976). Babies all over the world cry and laugh, and parents all over the world know how to refer to those actions. Babies goo, and similarly parents recognize the gooing and react to it both with deeply felt emotion and with communicative actions of their own, especially smiling, eyebrow raising (Papoušek & Papoušek, 1979, 1987; Papoušek, 1994), and verbalizations that babies do not precisely understand, because they surely do not understand the spoken words or sentences. Yet there is something rich in these interactions, something undeniably communicative and apparently universal, in the sense that we all seem to have the capability to engage the baby with subtle, intuitive vocal and facial signals.

The baby sounds in Table 9.2 that produce the most difficulty in translation (squeal, growl, and raspberries) deserve special comment, because, as we have seen, they are not used in infancy primarily to communicate. Instead they are typically explored as pure sound in the play of babies, who seem not to care if any one is listening at the time. This playful action manifests properties of vocal control that underlie communicative function even though the actions themselves do not constitute intentional communications. Babies (and other communicators) need to be able to produce sounds in any context whatsoever. Only when they have such a capability can they use speech-like sounds at will as a form of self-expression and as a contextually appropriate communication for a wide variety of situations. Playful usage of vocalizations illustrates the emergence of control over Contextual Freedom.

Perhaps it is infants' lack of communicative intent in the use of Expansion stage sounds in play that has inspired some cultures to leave these sounds out of their lexicons, apparently hoping that such antisocial action will go away. In a few months it does seem to, although the study of infant vocalizations long ago led me to believe that these ephemeral sounds of the first year do not exactly disappear. The bud of a flower does not exactly disappear when it blooms. Rather, it transmogrifies. So it is with the vocalizations of the first year of life: They do not actually disappear, but rather grow into something remarkable.

10

Protophones and Other Vocalizations

PROTOPHONES, THE MYSTERIOUS VOCALIZATIONS
OF HUMAN INFANCY

Protophones include (among other categories) quasivowels, goos, fully resonant nuclei, raspberries, and both marginal and canonical babbling. Why do
such sounds exist? Protophones do not, in early stages of development, transmit specific linguistic meanings, and thus they are not communicative in the
full sense that speech is communicative. When babies produce protophones,
it often appears that their only purpose is play or practice, although on other
occasions the same sounds can be utilized expressively and socially. Are these
expressive uses of sufficient value to justify the existence of protophones in individual infants? Is it possible instead that protophones are artifacts of the
process of development or even relics of our evolutionary history?

Research suggests that babies all over the world produce these sounds, and
they appear to be recognizable to both adults and children. It is my impression that protophones are unique to humans, but in fact this is a matter that
can only be evaluated through empirical consideration of vocal sounds that
occur in other species. Protophones can be best understood in contrast with
fixed signals and vegetative sounds, vocal types that clearly do occur in many
other species. Contrasting protophones with fixed signals and vegetative vocalizations is useful in terms of providing a perspective on the origins of the
protophones, and further on the origins of vocal systems in general, at varying
degrees of complexity. The nature of human vocalizations will thus be clearer,
and the way will be prepared for more powerful infrastructurally based comparisons across species.

THE FIXED VOCAL SIGNALS

The usages *fixed signal* and *fixed vocal signal* adapt the terminology of ethological investigation, where the phrase *fixed action pattern* (Hinde, 1970, 1983) is
used to refer to recurring motoric sequences that vary little from individual to

individual within a species. A subheading under fixed action pattern, the term fixed signal encompasses recurring motoric displays that specifically transmit communicative functions.[1]

In the ethologist's usage, particular fixed action patterns or fixed signals are typically elicited by particular *sign stimuli*, events that play important roles in the species' environment. For example, the reliable tendency of a human newborn to suck in response to light touch on the lips is taken to constitute a fixed action pattern, a species-typical behavior that is important in early feeding (Eibl-Eibesfelt, 1970). Similarly, grasping in infancy may be viewed as a fixed action pattern because it is reliably elicited in response to light touch on the palm of the hands in many primates, including humans. The grasping reflex may be related to the need of infants in various primate species to hold on to caretakers or objects to prevent themselves from falling. Fixed signals bear resemblance to other fixed action patterns in the stability of their forms. For example, many primate species have a particular fixed vocal signal that (especially in conjunction with a particular facial expression) is associated with threat, another associated with appeasement, and so on. Each fixed vocal signal may be presumed to be elicited by a sign stimulus as well, although the stimulus often must be assumed to be an internal state of the organism rather than a tangible external stimulus. Facial expressions and postures often provide the clues that ethologists use to determine the emotional state that may be the internal stimulus for a particular vocal display.

All primates that have been studied possess a group of fixed vocal signals (see review in Sutton, 1979) that can be elicited with varying degrees of flexibility by specific events or emotions (e.g., pain or sudden fear), and that consequently signal those events or emotions specifically, but flexibly. One aspect of the flexibility of fixed signals is seen in the fact that they are often, perhaps typically, produced with obvious intention both in humans and nonhumans. Often they are directed toward listeners and produced persistently until a desired effect is achieved (see chaps. 11 and 12 for further consideration of intentionality in signaling). Further, given that there is often no external sign stimulus to elicit them, fixed signals appear to be produced for signaling purposes by the individual animal in a variety of species.

Conspecifics react in biologically significant ways to fixed vocal signals (e.g., a fright signal may be read as warning), and it can be presumed that there is survival advantage for the species in the fact that the signals are produced and understood. The values or functions of fixed signals are the

---

[1]Because fixed action patterns are produced with substantial flexibility in many species, the term fixed action pattern has been challenged, and some have advocated the use of the alternative, *modal action pattern* (Barlow, 1977). The proposed change in terminology is intended to emphasize that fixed action patterns often do not possess the unchanging character of physical reflexes such as the knee jerk, but rather constitute more flexible capabilities. The use of the terms fixed action pattern or fixed signal in this volume is conservative, maintaining the traditional usage, but there is no intention to deny the flexibility of fixed actions or signals.

classes of emotions or intentions they express, plus the states of affairs they may denote.[2]

To the extent that the range of intentions and interpretations is delimited by nature, fixed signals can be said to have immutable values. Obviously the values are not perfectly immutable because intelligent animals show flexible production of signals. Adult chimpanzees are sometimes said to produce alarm calls teasingly toward conspecifics (Fischer & Lazerson, 1984), and infant nonhuman primates sometimes produce alarm calls at inappropriate times and are punished by members of their troop for doing so (Cheney, 1984). Monkeys sometimes also inhibit the production of fixed signals in the context of appropriate sign stimuli, as in the case of individuals who remain silent after finding a food source that in other cases elicits a call announcing the find. Such individuals may be beaten up by the troop if they are caught in this act of hoarding (Hauser, 1996). Further, many primate species express signals in varying degrees of intensity, depending on circumstances (Marler, 1976; see also chaps. 12 and 14). There is evidence that flexibility is even greater in interpretation of signals than in their production (see Seyfarth & Cheney, 1997, for examples of this special flexibility in primates).

Still, in the repertoire of a species the range of possible expressions or interpretations for each signal type is limited by the need to maintain distinctiveness with other signal types both in sound and in function. Presumably, natural selection constrains any shift in either sound or function that would cause a signal to impinge on the domain of one of its neighbor signals unless the survival relevance of the other signals also changes. In some cases, as for example with certain alarm calls, it is presumed that natural selection favors evolution of rigid acoustic clarity of signal and narrow interpretation possibilities as long as ecological conditions do not change. To allow change in alarm signals is to run the risk of thwarting the potentially critical function of, for example, inciting flight or defensive action in cases of real danger.

For purposes of definitional clarity, it is important to recognize that fixed signals have no obvious biological functions other than those associated with signaling. Fixed signals presumably exist (in an evolutionarily ultimate sense, Tinbergen, 1952) primarily because they have signaling value, and because the transmission of those values enhances in some way the potential for survival of the species. Fixed signals are thus specialized to the purpose of

---

[2]There is an important distinction to be maintained between the producer's expressed emotion or intent and the receiver's interpretation, a distinction emphasized in the assessment/management model of Owings and Morton (1998). The producer of fixed signals typically has regulatory or management intentions in producing vocal or gestural displays, whereas the receiver may have discrepant goals and consequently may not assess the signals as the producer intends them to be assessed. Both the assessment and the management side of signals are presumed to be products of natural selection in the Owings and Morton model, but they are distinct because they are often subject to different forces—the assessor and producer do not always have the same interests.

communication, and any communicative system that has fixed signals can be said to incorporate a property of Specialization.[3]

THE VEGETATIVE SOUNDS

In contrast to fixed signals, vegetative sounds (such as burping, coughing, or hiccoughing) have origins that are not primarily associated with signaling, and therefore do not show Specialization. Vegetative sounds result from bodily functions associated with respiration, swallowing and digestion. To the extent that they have signaling values, those values are incidental, imposed by the observer after the fact. To say that vegetative sounds have incidental values does not, however, necessarily imply that the interpretation of them is unimportant from the standpoint of survivability. In a species capable of rich interpretation of actions, the occurrence of a vegetative sound (e.g., a fit of coughing) may provide the basis for social assistance ("Does anybody know the Heimlich maneuver?"). The intelligent assessment of vegetative sounds by animals appears to be natural, and consequently vegetative sounds may have social significance in many species. For example, sneezing by one member of any mammal species, which clearly has a respiratory function, could serve an additional social function by signaling to other members of the species the presence of a substance (a chemical, dust, or pollen) that is potentially dangerous. To the extent that a species possesses the ability to interpret sounds or gestures that are not specialized for communication, it can be said that the species possesses a communicative property of Indexicality. Because vegetative sounds are produced at least to some extent by all advanced organisms, and because intelligent organisms such as mammals interpret and adapt to a wide variety of actions of both conspecifics and other organisms, it seems likely that the property of Indexicality for vegetative sounds is present by virtue of interpretation in a very wide variety of animals.

THE APPARENT EVOLUTIONARY RELATION
BETWEEN FIXED SIGNALS AND VEGETATIVE SOUNDS

The line between vegetative and fixed signals may not always be clear, especially in the deep time of evolution. The distinction assumes that as fixed signals evolve they are shaped by virtue of their communicative function, generally through a process that has been called *ritualization* (Lorenz, 1963). Vegetative sounds are presumably shaped by bodily operations such as respi-

---

[3]Hockett and Altman (1968) posited the existence of a design feature called Specialization. Here, I propose a redefinition of his term to encompass any kind of display that serves primarily communicative function. In the prior usage, Specialization was restricted to systems that also possessed Conventionality, a property implying learned signal-value associations.

ration and swallowing. Fixed signals may, however, have vegetative roots. For example, whereas screaming clearly represents a fixed signal in modern humans, its predecessor in deep time may have been a vegetative sound (perhaps of very different form) that resulted incidentally from the bodily reaction to pain. Through natural selection, the sound may have been shaped so that it became louder in successive generations or came to possess acoustic characteristics that would allow it to carry better through forests, and so on. Fixed signals may, then, be evolutionary exaptations (Gould, 1983) whereby bodily responses that originally occur for one purpose are adapted through natural selection for another. Fixed signals may have origins in bodily responses originally associated with needs unrelated to communication but through natural selection they may be molded to the purposes of communication. (This is not a new idea, but see a recent review of relevant issues in Owings & Morton, 1998). When we draw the distinction between fixed signals and vegetative sounds, we are required to tolerate ambiguity given that vegetative responses can be interpreted as signals, and it is not clear that they have not also been shaped to some extent through evolution to facilitate their interpretation as signals, in spite of their continued role as reflexive expressions of bodily conditions. Perhaps the two types of sounds should be thought of as ends on a continuum where the fixed signals have been maximally shaped to fit communicative purposes and where vegetative sounds have been little modified for communicative purposes.

Even in development we see changes that might be thought of as movements along the apparent continuum. The newborn human cry, for example, appears entirely reflexive at birth. It seems to be a response to discomfort or pain, and shows no intentionality. However, as the months pass, the infant begins to use crying more communicatively, and may produce cry-like sounds to get attention (see chap. 9 for references). The sound that begins ontogenetically as an apparent bodily reflex comes more and more to have the characteristics of flexible fixed signals, detached from the bodily origins that originally incite its production.

In keeping with the definitions I observe, both vegetative sounds and fixed signals are relatively immutable (in the evolutionary short term) on two accounts. First, their form, the character of the sound quality of each of them, is relatively constant, at least constant enough to be identified and to be distinguished easily by members of a species from other vegetative sounds or fixed signals utilized by the same species. Second, their signaling values are relatively constant. Connections between particular signals and particular values cannot be reversed; thus a growl, which signals threat in canines, cannot be reinterpreted by a new generation of unmutated canines as having some value distinct from threat. Modifications of value that do occur for any signal within species or individuals must be contained within specific regions of value (by gradation for example) so that the fundamental distinctions among different signals can be maintained.

FIXED SIGNALS AND VEGETATIVE SOUNDS IN HUMANS
AND OTHER CREATURES

Humans, whether infants or adults, are similar to other primates (and many other mammals) in possessing both vegetative sounds and fixed vocal signals. Other mammals cough, sneeze, and burp much as we do—the sounds are relatively identifiable across species. The fixed vocal signals are, on the other hand, more species-specific in terms of sound quality. Sounds that serve similar functions across primate groups, for example, may not sound alike. In humans the fixed vocal signals include crying and laughter (and see chap. 14 for more extensive portrayal of human fixed signals). These vocal types appear to reveal an important aspect of our evolutionary history, because just as in monkeys and great apes, they can be elicited by specific stimuli, they appear to be produced (at least in some cases) involuntarily, and they have relatively fixed forms and communicative functions. They are in a sense, biological givens. People do not learn to laugh, nor do they learn the meaning or functions of laughter. Rather, they develop these capabilities naturally. We do not learn to understand an infant's first cry (although we may indeed learn how to respond to it as caretakers). The reaction, unified and intuitive, occurs in an involuntary instant.

To be sure, fixed signals in monkeys, apes, and humans are flexible, but the flexibility seems especially notable in humans, who produce fixed signals at will, laughing ironically, scoffing, pretending to laugh, and so on. Even human infants, as noted in chapter 9, sometimes utilize laughter (or laughter-like syllables) to communicate understanding. Further, in pretend play, crying or other fixed signals can be faked by very young children. Vegetative sounds also can be faked in humans, just for fun or for communicative purposes, as when we cough or clear our throats to announce our presence to an inattentive clerk. Flexible vocalization usage in nonhuman primates is studied specifically because ethologists are seeking to determine the extent of free usage of vocalizations in other primates. In humans such occurrences are entirely commonplace beyond early infancy and have not often been deemed necessary to study.

Even though special uses of fixed signals do sometimes occur, neither in humans nor in other primates is it fundamentally possible to change the values of fixed signals nor vegetative sounds. Even ironic laughter obtains its special meaning against a shared background of natural understanding about the prototypical communicative value of laughter, and even a fake cough still implies a respiratory function.

HOW PROTOPHONES ARE DIFFERENT
FROM OTHER SOUND CLASSES

In contrast, the protophones of human infancy, the sounds that have been the primary focus of much recent research in vocal development, have no biologically specified values as signals (with limited exceptions in squealing and growling).[4] They are generally not elicited by sign stimuli and no emotional states are specifically associated with them. Unlike human fixed signals and unlike the sounds of other primates in the main, protophones have the potential to be molded to situations, and thus given new, flexibly adapted communicative functions or meanings within each infant. This is a primary feature of language in its embryonic state, a feature of Conventionality. Associations between particular protophones (especially the advanced babbling sounds of the second half-year of life) and particular circumstances or intentions can be remembered. Infants can learn to produce the sounds in a consistent association with particular intentions or circumstances. Protophones, in this manner, cut a path on the way to a lexicon. To say that infants can learn primitive lexical associations does not precisely require that the associations be taught. In fact, the first associations between protophones and intentions tend to be made up by the child rather than provided in examples from the parent language.

Another feature of protophones is Contextual Freedom. Babies producing protophones in the first months of life show themselves capable of producing sounds that do not have to be produced; when they are produced, they do not have to be produced within a narrow range of acoustic parameters. No specific stimulus elicits them obligatorily, and they are freely produced in the absence of any external stimulus. Even emotional conditions of the infant appear to vary substantially day to day and moment to moment during production of each protophone type.

Normally developing babies spend a substantial portion of their early lives producing protophones before they go on to create the primitive lexicons that launch their lives as talkers. They coo and goo in interaction with their caretakers and they engage in long bouts of vocal play daily during the Expansion stage. Often this play occurs with no apparent intent to communicate.

DEFINING THE CATEGORIES OF VOCALIZATION

Formally, protophones are defined partly positively—they are the specific precursors to speech—and partly negatively—they are not vegetative sounds, nor are they fixed vocal signals (both of which are more distantly related to

---

[4]Both squealing and growling appear to be associated with values that are relatively, although not entirely, fixed. Infant squealing occurs in response to tickling and seems to express delight in many early occurrences, but infants utilize squealing in other ways as well, sometimes expressing frustration, sometimes merely practicing the sounds themselves. The fact that adult humans sometimes produce sounds that might be called squeals in circumstances such as tickling suggests that squealing has been transferred during development into the protophone system from the fixed signals. Squealing thus has a dual identity. Growling, similarly, functions as a protophone in the Expansion stage, occurring in pure vocal play. In adulthood, however, it appears that growling (of substantially similar form to that of infancy) occurs in response to frustration or anger as a fixed signal. Again the protophone system appears to draw on fixed signals, and growling has a dual identity.

speech), nor are they speech per se. Table 10.1 provides a summarial account of the broad categories of human vocalizations with examples.

Vegetative sounds are present from birth. Fixed vocal signals evolve across life, with crying being present from birth, and various other subcategories emerging later; laughter, for example, typically appears at 4 months of age (Masataka, 1996a; Sroufe & Wunsch, 1972). The developmental changes in form of human fixed signals are notable, but it is important to note that the changes do not prevent us from recognizing a cry or a laugh at any age. Protophones have a schedule of appearance encompassing the first year of life, and speech usually begins at the end of that year.

The terms for subcategories provided as examples in Table 10.1 under each of the four broad categories are mostly drawn from the common parlance, but they are utilized in a variable research literature, and consequently the terms carry ambiguities that in some cases need to be disentangled through technical definition. The ambiguities tend to make some of the subcategories appear as if they should belong to more than one of the broader categories—for example, *grunt* is often used to refer to communicative vocalizations indicating assent or understanding. In our usage, such a vocalization would be called a quasivowel, and the *grunt* would be limited to cases of reflexive response resulting from other bodily action. Table 10.2 provides formal definitions utilized here.

SIGNIFIANT ET SIGNIFIÉ

In the first three columns of Table 10.2, categories are considered in terms of their signal and value characteristics. The distinction between signal and value has, in different terminology and with slightly different focus, been fundamental in linguistic theory since the teachings of de Saussure (1968), whose lectures from the 19th century were provided to us through transcribed notes from his students. De Saussure's French terms were *signifiant* and *signifié*,

TABLE 10.1

Broad Categories of Human Vocalization With Examples

Vegetative Sounds	Fixed Vocal Signals	Protophones	Speech
Coughing	Crying	Quasivowels	Made-up words
Sneezing	Laughing	Gooing	Real words/sentences
Burping	Moaning	Fully resonant nuclei	Discourses
Hiccoughing	Sighing	Raspberries	Singing
Gulping	Others	Marginal babbling	Others
Reflexive grunting		Canonical babbling	
Others		Others	

loosely translated as symbol and meaning, the two parts of what he called *le signe*, or the linguistic sign, roughly equivalent to the word or morpheme. Ambiguities of the term *meaning* are considered later; in the interim I shall use *value* in its place.

In the appraisal of the evolution of linguistic systems, it is important to maintain the distinction between signal and value because it helps to clarify basic properties that differentiate more primitive and more advanced forms of communication. This volume has already offered detailed characterizations of the ways that the sound quality or signal characteristics of protophones come to resemble those of speech progressively across the first year of life (see chaps. 3–5). It is also important to consider the ways that protophones come to resemble speech in terms of the types of communicative values that are transmitted.

As indicated in Table 10.2, the values of individual vegetative sounds and fixed signals are predetermined, in the former case by the nature of the bodily functions that are indexed, and in the latter by the natural history of the species, which we presume, includes—or included at some point in evolution—survival advantages owing to the ability of members of the species to transmit and understand a repertoire of innate signals.

In the terminology of de Saussure, the symbol–value connection in both vegetative sounds and fixed signals is not arbitrary. However, the nature of the connection in the two cases is fundamentally different because in vegetative sounds the vegetative function that produces the sounds is itself responsible for the value that can be applied to the sound, whereas in fixed signals, the values that go with particular signals are set by natural selection. Fixed signals do not have to be associated with particular bodily functions and thus have the potential (through natural selection) to transmit a wide variety of potential values. It is empirically clear that natural selection can shape both the form of the signals and the values they transmit, if for no other reason, than that among different animal species there exist signals of quite different form that transmit similar values, and there also exist relatively similar forms that transmit different values. Humans who care for captive chimpanzees must learn to understand some of the facial expressions and vocalizations of chimpanzees, because these signals and their signal–value connections are not identical to those of fixed signals in humans. Of course some of the signals of humans and other chimpanzees (indeed, of other mammals) are similar in both form and value, a fact that is presumably indicative of common heritage. The fact that fixed signals are set to values by natural selection implies, of course, that they can appear, from the perspective of other species, to have the design feature of Arbitrarity in de Saussure's terminology. However, this is not actually what de Saussure had in mind with the term. I follow his intent and limit the application of Arbitrarity to cases in which values are set by convention in a species. When specific values are set for particular signals by natural history, I say that the signals show Specialization, because they have been molded for communicative purposes. Both speech and fixed signals show

TABLE 10.2

Definitions of the Broad Categories of Human Vocalization

	Signal Characteristics	Value Characteristics	How Values and Signals Are Connected	Properties, Intentionality
Vegetative sounds	Small repertoire, relatively immutable in form	Indexing a small number of bodily functions only	Bodily functions preset the potential values for each sound	Indexicality only, no Specialization, no Recombinability, no Free Expressivity
Fixed signals	Small repertoire, relatively immutable in form	Signaling a small number of socially significant values	Natural history selects the values for each signal	Indexicality and Specialization, but no Recombinability, little Free Expressivity
Protophones	Small repertoire, changeable form	Relatively free associations with values	Values can be set in play and interaction	Indexicality, Specialization, some Recombinability, some Free Expressivity
Speech	Unlimited sized repertoire, strong adaptability of form across cultures and individuals	Entirely free associations with values	Values can be set through many kinds of learning	Indexicality, Specialization, Recombinablity, Free Expressivity, Conventionality, and many other properties

Specialization because both are driven by communicative forces in evolution. On the other hand, only speech has Arbitrarity under normal circumstances.[5]

Protophones provide examples of potentially communicative acts that can be produced independent of any signaling value. Consequently, protophones have the potential for association with new values. They provide a launchpad for arbitrary associations of signals and values. In human ontogeny, protophones themselves are used in a variety of communicative and noncommunicative ways, but the early associations of signal and value are made somewhat gradually and their numbers are relatively small. In speech, the connections between signal and value are unlimited in number. They become entirely free, to be defined by convention and learned.

DEFINITION OF SIGNALING VALUE

The distinction between symbol and meaning was extended to include a subcategorization of different kinds of values by Austin (1962), who brought to our attention the fact that the notion of meaning is ambiguous in everyday usage. Meaning sometimes designates semantic functions such as reference, where symbols are connected analytically to mental representations, typically conceptual classes of entities, events, actions, or attributes. On other occasions meaning refers in the common parlance to what Austin called *illocutionary force*, the pragmatic function served in the process of transmitting semantic messages.

To exemplify the distinction between illocutionary force and meaning consider an example. If I am walking through the zoo with my sister, and seeing a lion, I say "lion," I do two very different things in the same act. On the one hand, I unequivocally invoke a class of beings that are in English designated by the word lion. The reference is unequivocal because I do not (and cannot without redefining the term) invoke other classes of beings or objects such as wildebeasts or brick pavers. I invoke a particular semantic connection by saying "lion." On the other hand, in the same event, I perform an illocutionary act with a number of possible forces. For example, the force might be that of an announcement, which could be made clearer by elaboration: "I see a lion over there in its cage." Or the force might be a warning, which could also be elaborated: "A lion has escaped from its cage; let's run into the concession to save ourselves from harm." Or the force might be that of a correction: "You must need glasses if you think that creature over there is an antelope. It's a lion."

---

[5]I hasten to reiterate that humans are capable of using fixed signals freely and of applying new functions to them if they wish. One might, for example, decide to produce a fake laugh as a signal to start a race. If everyone in the race agrees, then the new communicative value of laughter could be utilized in this arbitrary manner routinely. However, laughter would still maintain its nonarbitrary natural function in other circumstances. Speech units have no nonarbitrary natural functions, and so can be assigned by convention to new values without being required to carry along the baggage of prior assignments.

Which of various possible forces is transmitted in any speech act is determined in practice by a number of factors, including, but not limited to, tone of voice and prior linguistic context (Cole, 1975; Gordon & Lakoff, 1975). For example, yelling suddenly "Lion!" leads more naturally to an interpreted force of warning than casually reciting "lion" in a monotone. Similarly suppose my sister has just said "I think that's an antelope over there," and I respond "lion." Here it is natural to interpret the force of my utterance to be that of a correction. On the other hand if she asks "What is that?" my response of "lion" will likely be taken as an informative answer to the question.

Regardless of the illocutionary force that is assigned to the utterance "lion," the semantic content of the act remains constant. The class of beings, lions, is necessarily invoked in all the possible circumstances of force where the word is uttered. The distinction between force and meaning is present in every event of communication that includes a semantic component. It is always important to be clear that the distinction between illocutionary force and semantics requires the recognition of two levels or layers of representation in possible communicative systems. Hereafter when, I write *meaning* I intend semantic meaning, not force.

In primitive communication systems, no distinction between force and meaning obtains. Fixed signals in nonhuman primates clearly transmit forces, but do not—with rare and interestingly restricted exceptions (Gozoules, Gozoules, & Ashley, 1995; Marler, Evans, & Hauser, 1992; Struhsaker, 1967; see also chap. 12)—have distinguishable semantic properties. Similarly, human fixed signals transmit forces but not semantic features; so, for example, when we laugh, we respond to an event and indicate a reaction (an illocutionary force of pleasure or social affiliation),[6] but we do not refer in a semantic sense to anything. Of course we may laugh at some object or event (e.g., a painting), but laughter does not refer to the particular painting or to the class of paintings under other circumstances. On another occasion we may laugh at a totally different object or event. Laughter does not refer to a painting or to the class of paintings the way the word *painting* does. Laughter maintains its social illocutionary force regardless of what is laughed at, but laughter does not inherently refer to anything. It can be said that laughter possesses Indexicality but not Semanticity. The noun *painting,* on the other hand, always refers to the class of paintings, and can do so in utterances of the word with varying illocutionary forces. In general both words and fixed signals have forces, but only words have semantic meanings. Words can transmit ref-

---

[6]The illocutionary force of human laughter is somewhat diversified. Provine (1996) argued that the primary function of laughter is social affiliative, and does not depend on humor. On some occasions, of course, laughter does occur as an expression of a sense that something is funny. Still the social affiliative function of laughter may be the primary one. Events and words that are not at all funny may produce laughter in situations where social affiliation is being pursued. In fact, according to Provine's research, the great majority of laughter at social gatherings is produced in response to statements that are not in the least funny.

erential information both indexically (e.g., they can point to entities) and semantically (e.g., they can do so independent of circumstances), but fixed signals can only transmit referential information indexically (they cannot point to entities independent of particular circumstances).

It is worth noticing that we tend not to laugh when we find the producer of a joke offensive. Jokes seem to release the signal of laughter in circumstances where social affiliation is being pursued, but not in circumstances of hostility. Still, we may laugh when we are all alone at an event that tickles us, so humor does have an independent role in inspiring laughter in some cases. From an evolutionary perspective, it may be that laughter developed because it transmitted the illocutionary force of social affiliation, and that humor became one of the kinds of communicative actions that could inspire the expression of affiliation through laughing. Humor may have subsequently acquired an independent status as a releaser of laughter even in nonsocial situations.

Early protophone usage is also restricted to the transmission of forces. Semantic meanings are not involved. Further, early made-up words of infants, drawing signals from among the protophones, always have forces, but may lack Semanticity (Dore et al., 1976). Even some words in mature human languages have conventional forces, but lack referential meaning. Consider the so-called performative terms such as *hello* and *wow*. They perform functions and transmit illocutionary forces (greeting, expression of surprise), but they do not refer to entities or events any more than laughter does (Bates, Benigni, Bretherton, Camaioni, & Volterra, 1979). On the other hand the nouns and verbs of human languages refer specifically to entities, events, processes, and so on. When each noun or verb is used, it always invokes its particular semantic referent class, but it also always transmits an illocutionary force that may vary from utterance to utterance of the very same word.

Throughout this work I utilize the term *value* systematically to encompass both force and meaning, as reflected in Table 10.2. I use value to refer to both in order to have a convenient way to discuss the evolution of systems of communication that proceed from having a single level (with force only) to having multiple levels (including at least force and meaning).[7]

In addition, value is used here to encompass interpreted consequences of actions that are not produced with communicative intent, but that yield communicative outcome. Thus vegetative sounds, which are not produced in normal circumstances with any intent at all, can be interpreted as bearing information about the respiratory or digestive condition of the producer or some quality of the environment that may have occasioned the condition of the producer. Such indexical information, like the indexical information transmitted by fixed sig-

---

[7]Additional levels of value obtain in the human system where, for example, meaning includes both literal and metaphorical layers, as well as additional layers that devolve from the semantic implications of statements (Cole, 1975). In addition to illocutionary force, there are further layers of value that are associated with conversational role and motives.

nals such as laughter, is clearly not the same thing as meaning, but it is included within the purview of the notion of value as I use the term.

Of course indexical information can be transmitted by any action. Everything we do has a variety of kinds of potential significance that can be gleaned indexically. The interpretation of actions can involve a diversity of creative strategies in the observer. These interpretive processes are different from the comprehension of meaning in that the latter entails a specifically linguistic and semantic network of conventionally defined relations among words (or other symbols) and conceptual categories, whereas indexing invokes no such network, and consequently, a very different kind of procedure for comprehension.

Illocutionary force also can be attributed to actions that have no communicative intent within the producer. An observer can mistakenly credit intent where it does not exist, or can impute intent incorrectly. Vegetative sounds can, thus, be taken to have forces. That forces can be attributed to vegetative vocalizations in humans owes in part to the fact that human beings have voluntary control over their vocal systems and can produce excellent replicas of vegetative sounds such as coughing or hiccoughing in the absence of the normal circumstances that cause the sounds to occur reflexively. A cough may thus be utilized intentionally to attract attention, to warn a speaker that they may be treading on dangerous ground, to indicate nervousness, and so forth. However, these are special uses of coughing that do not supplant its basic indexical status. Even when produced intentionally, a cough still indexes a condition of the respiratory system, even if only by pretense. Words are radically different on this account. Instead of indexing conditions obligatorily, they make reference arbitrarily, yielding a kind of value that is different in both content and in the process by which it is derived. The utility of the term *value* resides in the fact that it encompasses the broad scope of interpretations that can be given to actions. Indexical import, force, and meaning are all contained within its purview.

ON THE SIZE OF ILLOCUTIONARY FORCE REPERTOIRES

It is notable that the number of prime illocutionary forces is very small compared to the number of prime elements of any natural semantic system. Semantic systems can embrace any aspect of knowledge or awareness, and consequently a great many dimensions fall within the reach of semantics. Illocutionary forces are restricted to the acts that can be performed in the process of communication, and consequently only those features of actions that pertain to communication itself (as opposed to the world of objects, actions, qualities, etc.) are involved. An essentially exhaustive listing of illocutionary forces used in human communication is short (limited to a few score, including requests, comments, criticisms, refusals, etc.; see, e.g., Fraser, 1975), whereas a listing of semantic elements would include at least thousands and might be of unlimited size, depending on how prime elements of semantics are defined. The limited size of illocutionary repertoires seems to reflect the fact that communicative interaction has natural bounds imposed by the nature of possible communicative forces, and at least to some extent the possible forces are held in common across species.

Fixed signals never occur in large numbers within a species (see chap. 14 on the size of fixed signal repertoires). The restriction in size of inventories may be merely a reflection of the fact that each signal transmits a single force, and there are only a small number of prime forces to transmit. In Table 10.1, the list of fixed signal examples in humans is short. The list is not exhaustive because there are intensity gradations of categories that seem to justify independent titles (e.g., chuckle, laugh, guffaw, etc.) but the list of dimensions of fixed vocal signals that occur in our species does appear to be limited to perhaps five or six. Lists of fixed vocal signals (constructed to refer to graded dimensions) from other primate species may be similarly short (see chap. 14).

Another possible reason for the brevity of lists of fixed signals within species is that the signals themselves are not recombinable to form new possible signals (see chap. 12 on Recombinability). Each fixed signal must be distinguishable from each other fixed signal by virtue of gestalt features usually transmitted in a single burst of a half-second or less, and if longer, the expression tends merely to be extended without major variation, or repeated without variation other than that afforded by gradation of intensity. The number of such signals that can be easily discriminated is limited, and consequently the number of signals that can supply survival benefits may be limited.

It is not obvious whether the limited size of fixed signal repertoires owes more to limitations in the discriminability of unrecombined signals or more to limitations in the natural size of illocutionary force inventories. The enormous advance in potential numbers of communicative elements that occurs in speech as opposed to fixed signal systems clearly depends on the introduction of semantic elements, along with the distinction between force and meaning, as well as the utilization of recombined signaling elements, namely syllables and their component units in mature speech, phonemes and phonemic features. With the addition of these phonological elements, it is possible to compose lexicons of unlimited size. The importance of protophones in the emergence of the speech capacity can be seen in the fact that protophones offer recombination, albeit in a somewhat primitive form, and at the same time offer the potential for adaptation to a variety of new potential communicative forces and meanings.

THE SCALE OF VOCAL COMMUNICATION TYPES AND THE ROLE OF PROTOPHONES IN COMPLEX COMMUNICATION

Vocal systems seem to be naturally scaled in terms of the kinds of sounds they use. Vegetative sounds are relatively simple as communicative devices. They possess the property of Indexicality but not that of Specialization. Fixed signals are more complex in that they possess both properties; they can index entities and they are specialized to the purposes of communication. Because systems that possess fixed vocal signals appear always to possess vegetative sounds as well, and because fixed signals may represent exaptations of prior vegetative sounds, it would appear that a system with fixed vocal signals would represent an advance over a system with vegetative sounds only.

Both vegetative sounds and fixed signals can be utilized by humans in ways that suggest greater complexity. They can both develop ontogenetically to include properties such as Contextual Freedom, Conventionality, and even Semanticity. Even though they cannot give up their inherent forces, they can be assigned new forces or even meanings by humans. The extent to which such flexibility of usage in vegetative sounds and fixed signals is possible in nonhuman primates is a subject of inquiry.

Protophones display both Indexicality and Specialization, but in addition they provide a point of expansion from which additional properties are added to the human communicative system. Contextual Freedom appears in the earliest protophones, and additional properties are added progressively. There is no obvious point in the process of development when one can say that speech is unequivocally present in humans because the incorporation of infrastructural properties proceeds by steps, each of which brings the system closer to mature language.

Yet it is not empirically clear that the production of protophones is required for speech to develop (see chap. 6, on limits on babbling canalization and the role of motor practice in vocal development). There may be other possibilities to explain why protophones exist. Perhaps the protophones are, at least in part, an evolutionary relic. As the human organism matures, they emerge, but perhaps only because the system of speech is in the process of flowering. Protophones clearly manifest an emerging capacity for speech in infants even if they are not required for development (see chaps. 4 and 5). Perhaps the protophones provide a sort of evolutionary trail, hinting at a sequence of steps through which humanity proceeded on the way to modern language.

I doubt that the story is so simple. My guess is that protophones are partly the product of pure physical and mental maturation and in that sense may include certain indications of our natural history. However, we have seen that protophones come into being ontogenetically both in the context of active infant exploration of vocal capabilities to produce sounds and expressive capabilities to use sounds (see chap. 9). The structure of the sounds may provide clues regarding the evolutionary trail, but I suspect these are indirect clues. I reason that the infrastructure of potential complex communicative systems imposes limits on both ontogeny and phylogeny. According to this reasoning, the origin of the protophones may be found in both places.

Tinbergen (1951) taught that it always pays to recognize the distinction between proximate and ultimate causation of behavior. In the former case we seek to know why a particular organism performs an action at a particular point in time. In the latter case we seek to know how and why a species of organisms comes to be able to produce actions in general. For the protophones, as for many other capabilities of complex organisms, it would appear that causation can be interpreted from both perspectives. Protophones appear to be developed in the proximate sense in many individual events of vocalization in infancy; in an ultimate sense they appear to have been developed by the human species in the course of the creation of language.

11

Primate Vocalizations in the Perspective of Infraphonology and Infrasemiotics

HISTORICAL ROOTS OF SPECULATIONS ON THE ORIGIN OF LANGUAGE

Although it is not clear when it began, the study of human language origins has a history that dates back at least to the ancient Greeks, and likely much further. To say that language origin has been studied for a long time is an understatement comparable to the suggestion that life has been studied for a long time. Aarsleff (1976) offered a cogent representation of the depth and timelessness of the interest:

> This, at least, is certain: since the possession of language and speech has always been considered the chief characteristic of the human species, the question of origin has also been considered fundamental in any attempt to understand the nature of man and what distinguishes him from other animals. Most major philosophers and most philosophical systems have dealt with the problem in one way or another; in fact, so universal has this interest been that its absence, as in Kant, has been cause for wonder. Plato, Aristotle, the Stoics, the Epicureans, the Church Fathers, Thomas Aquinas, Luther, the German mystics, Jacob Boehme and Robert Fludd, Marin Mersenne, John Locke, and following him, most eighteenth-century philosophers would readily have understood the question [of the relevance of studying language origins] in its present formulation. (p. 4)

It is also true that from early in the time of modern thought consideration was given to the communication capabilities of nonhumans, and especially nonhuman primates, a topic assumed to be germane to human linguistic origins. This interest provides one of many indications that intellectual communities accepted the notion of evolution (even human evolution) long before they accepted the idea of natural selection, a conception that was originated more than a century later in the works of Darwin and Wallace.

Although prior to the 20th century little empirical work was actually done to evaluate communicative capabilities of nonhumans, by the 17th century there was influential speculation about the nature of and reasons for the lack of speech and language capabilities of great apes. The history of this reasoning was reviewed by Aarsleff (1976), who took note of the fact that the nature of ape abilities was widely bantered about in intellectual circles even though little empirical information was gathered until the early portion of the 1900s.

Perhaps surprisingly, even after active ethological work with apes was well underway, the 17th-century speculation continued to capture the attention of influential writers in linguistics:

> In fact, as Descartes himself quite correctly observed, language is a species-specific human possession, and even at low levels of intelligence, at pathological levels, we find a command of language that is totally unattainable by an ape that may in other respects surpass a human imbecile in problem solving ability and other adaptive behavior. (Chomsky, 1968, p. 9)

The essence of the Cartesian formulation included the assumption that animals could not speak because they did not have the minds for it, an idea that is reflected in modern nativist, especially Chomskian, views about human intellect and linguistic gifts. The contention that apes did not have the mouths or the vocal capabilities necessary for language came later (see, e.g., Keleman, 1948). Descartes sought a characterization of humankind that would differentiate us radically from our nearest relatives, and whatever the current motivations for asserting innateness in human linguistic capabilities, it is hard to deny the continuing general inclination, in science and in the public alike, to locate and emphasize the ways that human language capabilities exceed those of our primate relatives.

I prefer to seek a delicate balance in consideration of nonhuman communicative capabilities, for it is not enlightening, in my opinion, simply to dismiss nonhuman systems as uninteresting, or to fall back on presumed achievements of armchair philosophy, achievements that are sometimes taken to have demonstrated that the differences between our own communication systems and those of other species are so great as to obviate the utility of any comparison at all. There is no denying that the systems of communication in human and nonhuman primates are different. Furthermore, there is no denying that the differences have something to do with the mind. They may also have a fair bit to do with the body, especially the mouth and tongue. Yet how human language and nonhuman communication systems are different, in precisely what ways, and for what reasons pose questions that may lead to insight about our origins and may help establish a perspective useful in shoring up our apparently fragile self-concept as a species.

There are a few essential observations about ape communication abilities that seem to have been understood very early in the history of such interests that have changed recently only in details, but not in overall form. I argue that the lasting achievement found in these observations owes to the isolation of key infrastructural properties of potential communication systems. Seventeenth-century thinkers sought and found underlying properties that differentiate humans from apes. These properties, considered at length in chapter 12, turn out to have an enduring utility, because they can be applied in comparisons among other systems of communication that might be encountered, for example, the systems of human infants, of some new species of primate, or even of creatures from another planet. The potential utility of these infrastructural properties was not fully realized in part because the development of a general theory of properties was not pursued. The few properties that were isolated did, however, form a permanent core of important theory on which revealing comparisons could be made.

To grasp the essential observations we begin with a salute to a French philosopher, Condillac, who, according to Aarsleff (1976), has been given far less than his due in current characterizations of the history of linguistics. Following up on Locke's *An Essay Concerning Human Understanding* from the previous century (there are many recent editions, e.g., Locke, 1965, from Dent Publications in London), Condillac (1756) pointed to three key categories of "signs" in his *Essay on the Origin of Human Knowledge:* accidental signs (which can be understood to refer to the class of communicative acts that bear only indexical values), natural signs (which can be read as fixed signals), and instituted signs (genuine lexical items of the referential sort). This breakdown was not entirely new, because it drew at least in part from Locke, but it was enormously influential in the 18th century and was passed down many decades later to Saussure through his teacher Bréal, who was deeply influenced by the French idéologues, among the main beneficiaries of Condillac's reflections. Key modern concepts regarding the basic properties of human language were considered explicitly by Condillac: One was that ideas and sounds are arbitrarily connected in human languages (the word *rose* refers to the category of roses, but the sound of the word has no inherent relation with roses). This Arbitrariness property would prove to play a powerful role in the comparative enterprise. The three-way distinction in categories of signs (accidental, natural, instituted) clearly prefigures 20th-century semiotic developments, notably from Peirce. For our purposes the three-way distinction among sign types is referred to with the more modern terms *indexical, fixed,* and *arbitrary.* The infrastructural properties of potential communicative systems that are implied by the three terms are Indexicality, Specialization, and Arbitrariness.

Condillac's idea of most consequence for this discussion was that animals, possessing certain rudimentary forms of thought, and possessing the capacity to interpret indexical signals and to both produce and interpret fixed signals, did not have the capability that humans possess to form arbitrary signs. Humans, in contrast, were recognized as sharing with other primates the capability to manage indexical and fixed signals, exceeding other creatures in the domain of arbitrarily formed vocabulary. There is little room for doubt, then, that his tripartite characterization was perfectly parallel to recent characterizations of vegetative acts (interpreted indexically), fixed signals, and linguistic vocabulary items. For example, Condillac's characterization of natural signs makes explicit his understanding of emotional expression in fixed signals, when he referred to them as "the cries which nature has established to express the passions of joy, or fear, or of grief, etc." (cited in Aarsleff, 1976, p. 10).

The reader may have noted that crying is not only nonarbitrary in its association with its emotional value, but that, in its pristine state, crying lacks meaning altogether, in the same way that laughter lacks meaning. The distinction between force and meaning, an additional necessity in clarifying human and nonhuman styles of communication (and implying the introduction of the infrastructural property of Semanticity), would not assume prominence in the discussion of communication until more than two centuries later, under the influence of Austin (1962). For Condillac, the focus in discussing natural signs (fixed signals), such as crying, was on the fact that such signals were immutable in value and that conventions of society (and by implication, learning) played no significant role in their establishment. By contrast, he emphasized that linguistic signs did have to be learned, that they were established not by nature but by convention, and were therefore, changeable by convention, a pattern he deemed impossible for other animals.

Locke too, decades earlier, noted the Arbitrarity principle of human vocabulary, emphasizing that languages of the world would not have had different words to denote the same meanings were it not true that ideas could be assigned by convention to sounds or gestures among humans. It was believed that no other creature could do as much, and Locke, Descartes, and Condillac agreed that the capability for signal-value Arbitrarity formed a critical basis for the superiority of human reasoning over that of any other creature. We can (and in what follows I do) update and substantially expand the reasoning of the 17th- and 18th-century philosophers with empirical evidence from a rapidly growing literature on the possibilities of communication in nonhuman primates, evidence that was not available to Condillac. Further, the treatment here is expanded to specify a variety of additional infrastructural properties of potentially workable communication systems, some of which have already been noted in prior chapters.

VOCAL GIFTS OF HUMAN INFANTS AND THE HISTORICAL DISTINCTION BETWEEN HUMAN AND NONHUMAN COMMUNICATION

It bears stipulating that although the mastery of arbitrary signs appears to be the unique province of humans, this advantage is not manifest throughout human life. Only after about a year of infancy does learning of lexical items become unambiguously possible. Yet even if this capacity takes a year or so to emerge, it is remarkable that such an immature member of our species as a toddler appears to show greater gifts of vocal communication than the most advanced primate of any other species. Much of the following chapter is devoted to specifying precursor properties of a rich communication system that enter the repertoires of infants in the first 18 months of life, many of them before the onset of meaningful speech.

From the first instants after birth, human infants can be said also to possess communicative capabilities that include all the presumed features of the general primate pattern, capabilities implied by the notions of both accidental and natural signs, the properties of Indexicality and Specialization. Human vegetative vocalizations (accidental signs) are interpreted indexically from the first day of life by parents, and the fixed vocal signal of crying (a natural sign showing the property of Specialization) is commonly present with the first breath of life. Other fixed vocal signals (notably laughter) emerge across the early months of infancy.

Had Condillac chosen to take particular account of the communicative skills of the human infant, he might have noted that they had only accidental and natural signs in their repertoires, and that consequently they began life with vocal capabilities similar to those of apes. The science of language and communication has vastly underplayed the elaborateness and delicacy of differentiations in vocal communication between humans and nonhumans that begin to appear during the first months of human life. Even very recent authors have primarily emphasized ways in which human infants up until perhaps 18 months of age resemble not only other primates, but other mammals in general. In this context early human development is said sometimes to fit into a pattern that, according to the characterization, is not just panprimate, but panmammalian (Scarr, 1983). I hold, by contrast, that the existence of similarities among many mammals in early development should not prevent us from recognizing special features of human action and capability that occur from the first months of life, features that presage the development of even more elaborate capabilities, including those of speech communication, and features that may prove us to be distinct from our primate relatives in vocal communication at a point far earlier than has generally been acknowledged. Condillac and many modern authors appear to acknowledge only certain broad distinctions among communication capabilities of adult humans and nonhumans, distinctions that apply, on the whole, only after the end of the first year of life. Such an approach misses the opportunity to recognize human uniqueness during the first months of life.

INFRASTRUCTURAL PROPERTIES (OR DIMENSIONS) OF COMMUNICATIVE CAPABILITY AND THE COMPARATIVE ENTERPRISE

There is much more to be said, then, about language and species, both developmentally and synchronically, than could be provided by the Enlightenment philosophers. The early thinkers insightfully isolated the infra-structural property of Arbitrarity in assignment of words to meanings and correctly[1] noted that this property was unique to humans. There are, however, many additional, isolable, yet beautifully interrelated properties that may or may not obtain within nonhuman communication systems and that deserve consideration in making cross-species comparisons.

These infrastructural properties pertain to two realms: to signals them-selves and to the values transmitted by signals. As for signals themselves, we of course refer to the relevant properties as infraphonological. In chapters 4 and 5 an introduction to the property of syllabification was provided, includ-ing an account of the principles by which syllables are specifically formed in speech. A number of additional infraphonological properties are considered as we continue. These properties constitute natural components of signal sys-tems, components that can be systematically incorporated into an auditory and vocal signaling system to lend it power. In the context of a species-inde-pendent theory of infraphonological properties it is possible to make insight-ful comparisons among differing systems.

In addition to a theory of signal properties, we also need an account of infrasemiotic properties that can be transmitted by signals, an account that encompasses ways potential signals can be used and manipulated, including ways that yield indexical, iconic, arbitrary, and richly syntacticized acts of language. Again, such an account of properties can offer a species-independ-ent backdrop for comparison. Any species that evolves a communication sys-tem is required to gain control of infrasemiotic properties if its system is to have flexibility and power. The Enlightenment thinkers had usefully formu-lated certain infrasemiotic properties, but a general theory of infrasemiotic values was not available to them, and a theory of infraphonology had not been envisioned at all.

There have been several forays during the 20th century into the formula-tion of properties or design features of communicative systems, formulations that offer perspectives on fundamental aspects of both signals and values. One of the most extensive attempts was made by Hockett, whose several articles on properties of linguistic systems offer a framework within which important comparative work has been pursued in modern times. Second, the theory of signs (or semiotics), developed most notably by Peirce, provides crisp clarifi-cations of distinctions regarding types of value that are possible in communi-

---

[1]Of course they did not know about sign language learning in great apes (Gardner & Gardner, 1969), nor about certain learning capabilities of cetaceans (Tyack & Sayigh, 1997). Arbitrarily as-signed meanings prove learnable by other animals in some circumstances, but the conditions of such learning appear to be tightly circumscribed. Humans can, in some cases, teach other crea-tures arbitrarily paired symbols and meanings. On the other hand, if other creatures develop arbi-trary signs in the wild, it has yet to be reliably reported. That one chimpanzee may pass on human-taught signs to another in captivity (Fouts, Fouts, & Van Cantfort, 1989) does not funda-mentally change the point that the use of arbitrarily formed signs is a primary characteristic of the human species, and as far as can be told, no other.

cative systems. Third, recent work of Bickerton supplies a modern view of certain fundamental properties of language, including many referenced by Hockett, but also encompassing the rich patterns of human syntax embodied in modern views of universal generative grammar.

My overview in the next chapter of the comparative communicative capabilities of humans and nonhumans attempts to incorporate and expand on insights of the three sources mentioned, except that my treatment ends well before reaching a characterization of richly syntacticized language properties. I focus on more primitive communicative abilities and the properties that underlie them. From the vantage point of these more primitive properties of potential vocal language, there is the opportunity to survey more profoundly the relations among different communication systems and to evaluate the emergence of the human capacity for speech as it may have appeared in various stages of differentiation from its general primate background.

Although my overview stops prior to rich syntax, in other regards, it attempts to expand the perspectives afforded by those who have offered prior design feature outlines. Still, the treatment is less than comprehensive, since communication, even primitive communication of human infants, is by nature a highly structured matter. The goal is to focus on highlights of the emergence of that structure in contrast with structures of nonhumans and in terms of a design feature or infrastructural properties approach.

The approach is founded on the idea that it is possible to specify properties that may or may not occur in particular communication systems, or that may occur in varying degrees within different systems. If properly formulated, these properties may constitute a stable set of logical possibilities from which systems of communication choose, and may constitute a species-independent, universal system of limits on the ways that vocal communication can be developed.

Of course, the system is context sensitive in the sense that the nature of the limits is determined in part by the physical nature of organisms, including their anatomies as well as their sensory and motor capabilities. Comparative descriptions in terms of abstract, universal properties should yield lasting insights. Sebeok (1968) noted that similarly motivated approaches to comparisons across communicative systems may have been somewhat hampered in recent history by the fact that although there have been a number of attempts to develop semiotic models, these have not resulted in an entirely coherent, widely accepted theory: "Even today, semiotics lacks a comprehensive theoretical foundation but is sustained largely as a consistently shared point of view" (p. 7).

To the extent that attempts to delineate potential properties may differ across authors, I maintain the hope that the differences result largely from superficial terminological discrepancies or from focus on different degrees of generality by different authors (e.g., one author may differentiate a particular set of closely related design features that another author may collapse under a single heading). The basic features that have been formulated are, I think, naturally occurring components of function that exist independent of our formulations. As such, they appear to constitute eternal possibilities. Of course, postulation of things eternal is risky. Whether these design features are universal primes or convenient contrivances, however, there is much to be said in the context they provide about how humans and apes are similar and different communicatively. This comparison also yields a useful perspective on the possible steps of linguistic evolution that may have been taken between ape-like ancestors, ancient hominids, and modern humans.

Properties as used here does not indicate strictly binary features. On the contrary, many of the properties represent dimensions along which communication systems may differ. Therefore human and nonhuman systems may differ importantly on individual properties without differing absolutely on them. Similarly, the progression of hominid development toward modern linguistic capabilities may have been accompanied by incrementally increasing capabilities along many of the dimensions to be discussed.

A COMMENT ON THE WIDELY PUBLICIZED SKEPTICISM ABOUT INTERSPECIES COMPARISON

The interspecies comparisons we make may be viewed skeptically in the light of Chomsky's (1967) widely cited disdain for any attempt to juxtapose human and animal communication systems. To do so in a way that is not meaningless, he said, we must establish a level of abstraction where there are "plenty of other things incorporated under the same generalizations which no one would have regarded as being continuous with language or particularly relevant to the mechanisms of language" (p. 73). Countering this contention, Sebeok (1968) said that the goal of semiotics is precisely to provide a level of abstraction that would allow the sort of insightful comparison portrayed as uninteresting in the preceding passage. That the generalizations may encompass matters that are not, from everyone's perspective, relevant to language may be more a comment on the restrictiveness of the preferences of some regarding what should be called language, than on the potential value of comparison. Many of us do, after all, seek to understand the connections between ourselves and our distant ancestors. Acceding to the resistance expressed in the preceding passage would leave us little opportunity to investigate such connections. My contention is that an infrasemiotically and infraphonologically rich system of design features can provide a workable and lasting system for comparison.

THE POPULAR CURRENT COMPARISON OF HUMAN AND NONHUMAN PRIMATE VOCAL COMMUNICATION SYSTEMS IN TERMS OF PROPERTIES

The modern characterization of human and nonhuman communication systems has, of course, not failed to take note of the fact that Arbitrariness of signs is a human function. However, during the second half of the 20th century, the focus in such comparative efforts has taken some bold new turns. Most notably, current authors have emphasized that no other species has been shown to have a full-blown syntactic system of the sort found in human language, whether spoken or signed (for reviews see, e.g., Bickerton, 1990; Pinker, 1994). This has been the predominant issue raised in the recent literature aimed at differentiating humans and nonhumans in communication. It has been argued convincingly that the primary infrastructural features of human syntax (grammatical categories and hierarchical syntactic phrase structures as specified in x-bar theory, recursive application of rules, various characteristics of government and binding, etc.) are entirely absent, as far as can be told, from the communication systems of any other species (Bickerton, 1981; Chomsky, 1966).

A second issue presumed to distinguish human communication from that of other species has also been argued strongly, although less successfully, in a widely cited recent literature. It concerns the posited idea that language exists only in humans because only humans possess the required anatomy for certain (presumably) necessary sounds of natural languages (see Crelin, 1959; Laitman, 1984; Laitman & Heimbuch, 1982).

Both these issues—the presumed syntactic and the presumed anatomical uniqueness of humans—ultimately deserve consideration in the comparative enterprise. However, it is surprising how much attention has been paid to them, given that there are many other logically prior and more primitive properties to consider that offer a more telling perspective on both the differences and the similarities among species. They may also provide a richer view of how our system of communication developed through evolution.

On the issue of syntactic capabilities, it is undeniable that the richness of human syntax represents a remarkable feature of differentiation from other species. Yet before a creature can be expected to form advanced linguistic structures (e.g., hierarchical phrasing, center embedding, anaphoric reference, and complex agreement patterns), the creature needs a whole series of more basic capabilities that can be expressed in terms of design features that are essentially ignored in the widely noted literature on syntactic superiority or uniqueness of humans. These largely ignored basic capabilities can form a more substantial basis for illustrating the relations in power and in evolutionary distance between human and nonhuman communication. By utilizing the model provided here, based initially on infant development of infraphonological capabilities and infrasemiotic functions, it is possible to enhance the perspective on how primitive language capabilities may have emerged in human history and may have laid the groundwork for later evolution of the capability for linguistic syntax.

On the issue of anatomical differences that may have played a role in language evolution, it is my belief that presumed limitations of nonhuman primates have been dramatically overplayed. To be sure, potentially important anatomical differences may exist, but limitations in the vocal periphery of other primates do not in and of themselves preclude the development of a rich linguistic system that could have a great many properties pertaining to human language, properties that do not in fact occur, at least not to the degree they do in humans, in any nonhuman primate. Many additional design features are absent (or present only in weak form) in nonhuman primates aside from those that might be explained by peripheral anatomical limitations, and again, in my view, these should be accorded precedence to the anatomical matters addressed in the popular literature speculating about language evolution. I do not deny a possible role for the popularly discussed anatomical limitations in linguistic evolution, but the absence of other design features of human phonological capability deserves far greater attention than the absence of rather special vocal anatomy at this point, as it is logically possible for a creature to develop a richly complex linguistic system (even including fully syntacticized structures) with the peripheral vocal anatomy of a bird. Chimpanzees are and Neanderthals were surely in a better position to produce speech-like utterances than birds are, if we consider only peripheral vocal anatomy, and yet some parrots and blackbirds do a remarkably effective job of imitating speech (see, e.g., Pepperberg, 1990; West, Stroud, & King, 1983) whereas chimpanzees do not. It is fair to say, contradicting the currently popular claim, that we simply do not know how elaborately Neanderthals might have been able to talk.

The existing literature that emphasizes anatomical uniqueness of human speech organs (Lieberman, 1975; Lieberman & Crelin, 1971), acknowledges that both nonhuman primates and our hominid ancestors may have possessed the anatomical structures necessary to produce many speech-like sounds, but it is emphasized in the writings that nonhumans and early hominids could not produce all of the vowels currently found in human languages; in particular, it is presumed they could not produce [a], [i], and [u], the so-called *point vowels*. An essential aspect of the argument is that language began only after the hominid larynx descended to a position lower in the throat than in any other primate, and as a consequence of that lowering, point vowels became possible.

The overstatement manifest in the argued importance of such anatomical factors can be seen clearly if we simply consider the fact that these point vowels are only 3 out of 20 or more possible vowel elements from which languages may choose. Languages do not need to have a large number of vowels, as evidenced by the fact that many languages have very few vowels of any kind, as noted by Wescott (1976):

> There are languages such as Wishram (Amerind, Chinookan)... that can be analyzed as being univocalic and systemically, therefore, vowelless. And there are many other languages—perhaps as many as 10% of contemporary vernaculars—that have fewer than the five to twelve vowel phonemes that characterize a majority of the world's languages. (p. 111)[2]

---

[2]It is important to recognize that such analyses are phonemic in nature. All natural languages have phonetic vowel nuclei, as a necessary part of canonical syllable structure. The question is how many phonemic vowels (contrastive vowel elements) does each language employ, and here there appear to exist huge differences, perhaps ranging from zero to a score.

Pinker (1994) captured the point this way: "E lengeege weth e smell nember ef vewels cen remeen quete expresseve" (p. 354).

It is thus clear that giving up the three point vowels would not, in and of itself, prevent a creature from having a rich and varied linguistic system that could enormously surpass any known communicative system of nonhumans. Consequently the claim that language began only after the hominid larynx descended to a position lower in the throat than in any other primate, and as a consequence point vowels became possible, constitutes an unjustifiable assertion about the possibilities of linguistic evolution. We need a broader view than that implied by Lieberman's anatomically restrictive contention, a view that encourages evaluation of the steps of linguistic emergence that may have preceded the full phonemic inventories of modern languages. Similarly, we need a view that seeks to determine language origins prior to the development of elaborate syntactic structures.

The consideration of design features in the next chapter illustrates ways that nonhumans, and primates in particular, are indeed communicatively less capable than humans. The human system is richer and more varied, incorporating many properties from the universal possibilities that are not present in any other primate species or incorporating these properties to greater extents. The surprise is that long before human children begin to speak in conventional words, long before they reach the arbitrary sign learning criterion set by Condillac, they already show an enormously superior vocal communicative capability when compared with nonhuman primates of any age.

12

Infrastructural Properties of Communication in Human and Nonhuman Primates

THE IMPORTANCE OF INFRASTRUCTURAL COMPARISON

Similarities and differences between humans and nonhumans in vocal communication can best be seen in the light of deep characteristics of their systems. By basing comparison on fundamental features of the systems, we acquire the ability to see more clearly the nature of connections and divergences. Superficial comparisons can, in contrast, prove confounding. Consider the opinion of Hockett and Altmann (1968):

> We might note, of written English, that some words begin with the letter "A" and others do not. Do gibbon calls have this property? An affirmative answer seems to be false, a negative answer misleading rather than true. A system cannot either have or lack this property unless it has such things as words, and such things as letters, and unless one of the latter is the letter "A." The question is meaningless because neither answer is verifiable. (pp. 61–62)

Hockett's complaint was not directed at a straw man. There was a tendency in much of the literature of his era to pose near-meaningless questions about primate communication capabilities by attempting to shoe-horn the categories of communication systems of other animals into the categories of mature human language. Sebeok (1968) reviewed the literature, concluding that "descriptions of other sign systems tend to more or less slavishly imitate—despite occasional warnings ... —and more often than not quite erroneously, the narrow internal models successfully employed by linguists" (p. 8).

We have seen, starting in chapter 1, how confusion can be engendered by comparing infant and adult vocalizations through imposing the superficial operational categories of the adult system on the infant one. Alphabetical-level speech sounds are not present in sounds of very young infants and to describe the baby's efforts in those terms is to run the risk of mischaracterizing the facts. It is more productive to compare the adult and infant systems in terms of deeper principles of unit formation, principles that can be shown to be systematically acquired by infants across the first months of life. Similarly, it is more useful to compare human and nonhuman primate systems in terms of deep properties and principles of potential unit formation. In this infrastructural approach, it is possible to pose sensible questions about similarities and differences among species.

The formation of syllabic units can be characterized in terms of principles that specify how physical parameters of articulation and acoustics are manipulated to yield well-formed Syllabification. Individual speech syllables are physical events, but the property of Syllabification is an abstraction, as are the human infraphonological principles that specify its implementation in speech. If another creature develops a syllabic system with the power to generate an indefinitely large inventory of morphemes, that creature will be required to implement the abstract property of Syllabification in some way. Some set of principles of minimal rhythmic unit formation (another name for Syllabification) must be established in any system of vocal communication.

Each property to be discussed in this chapter represents an abstraction that will ultimately require a rich specification in terms of particular principles of implementation within each system of communication, human or nonhuman. These properties can provide a reference for comparison across species, a reference that highlights potentially significant questions about the fundamental relations among differing communication systems.

THE INHERENT ABSTRACTNESS OF INFRASTRUCTURAL PROPERTIES OF COMMUNICATION

When we seek evidence of the presence of a particular property in a communicative system, we cannot directly observe its corresponding principles. Consider Fig. 12.1, where two properties, X and Y, are shown to be implemented by a set of principles, each of which is evidenced by certain concrete actions. The properties are defined to be abstract characteristics of capability, the principles to be systematic methods of implementation of the properties, and the actions to represent concrete event categories manifesting command of corresponding principles. The evidence provided by the actions can be used to determine whether or not, or to what extent, a property is present in a system of communication. In the case of the property of Contextual Freedom, for example, command can be demonstrated by several possible action types (spontaneous [unelicited] production of sounds, exploratory vocalization, etc.), each of which could be thought of as indicating command of a principle

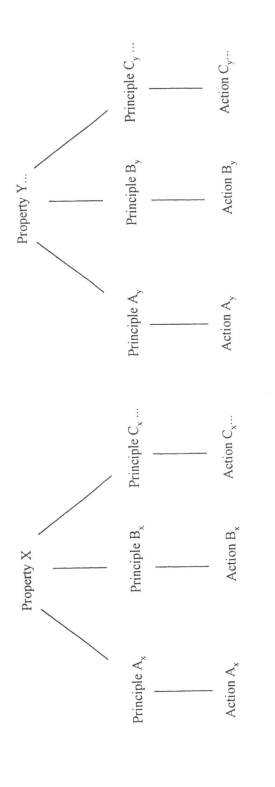

FIG. 12.1. Properties, principles, and actions.

217

(e.g., vocal spontaneity, vocal systematicity, etc.) that implements an aspect of the property of Contextual Freedom.

Human capabilities, within this focus, can be seen to be manifest in a wide variety of human-typical action types. Limitations on communicative systems and consequent lack of control of individual properties (in infants or in another species) may be manifest in a limited degree of control over actions of particular types or in context limitations on how actions are implemented. For clarity's sake, in this volume properties are capitalized (Interactivity, Directivity, etc.), and principles and actions are presented without capitalization (spontaneous vocalization, resonance control, etc.).

The distinctions drawn among properties, principles, and actions are meant to emphasize the fact that there are many routes along which species may be differentiated in the evolution of communicative systems. Even within the realm of a particular property there is potential domain specificity of specific principles and actions that may manifest its development. The current literature in learning includes a major focus on the fact that generalization of acquired capabilities or properties does not always occur as we expect it to. For example, Barasch (1977) illustrated the point in experiments with squirrels and dogs, the latter being demonstrably more intelligent (i.e., able to learn new tasks) than the former in most circumstances. Barasch demonstrated the point by tying a dog on a leash and running the leash around a post, then fastening it to the side of the space at a point so that the dog could not reach a food bowl that was right in front of it. To reach the food, the dog had to go backwards around the post to obtain a more direct line between the point to which it was tied and the food. The dog struggled, pulling at the leash, unable to reach the food. The dog succeeded in getting to the food, but only after having struggled for some time and then in a moment of apparent surrender, having wandered around the post. This slow pattern of solving the leash and post problem is typical of dogs. In contrast, the otherwise dull-witted tree squirrel, similarly tethered, will make one pull on the tie, then look at it and understand immediately to run around the post. Tree squirrels, according to Barasch, are adapted by virtue of living in trees to this domain-specific ability. To get food they can see in a nearby tree, they often have to begin by going backwards along one limb, then down to the ground, then up another tree and out another limb. Going around a post to get a better angle on a food bowl is no challenge. According to this reasoning, intelligence and learning capabilities that seem to pertain to general realms (such as navigation) are often developed within very specific domains.

Such domain specificity appears to apply to all creatures, the higher primates included. Common chimpanzees, among the most intelligent creatures we know, show certain surprising gaps in their abilities to learn. For example, Boysen, Bernston, Hannan, and Cacioppo (1996) found that chimpanzees show a notable inability, in a two-choice task, where the object is to learn to choose the smaller pile of a desired food as a condition for being given a larger pile. The adult chimpanzee fails on this task, whereas human children over 2 years of age succeed easily. In other domains, chimpanzees show remarkable intellectual abilities.

Research has indicated, further, that when a creature shows poor ability in a particular domain, it remains possible that a change in circumstances will make it possible for the creature to perform much better. For example, if the white-crowned sparrow is allowed to listen to tapes of the song sparrow, it fails to learn the song. If, on the other hand, it is allowed to be tutored by a live song sparrow, it does learn the song. It appears that the apparent learning limitation can be overcome with a change in the domain of exposure (Baptista & Petrinovich, 1986). West, King, and Freeburg (1997) also provide evidence of context sensitivity in the learning of song by the brown-headed cowbird.

Domain specificity of learning capability indicates that a workable properties model must include room for flexible implementation of principles. The model provides a general framework for interpretation of communicative systems, but there remain wrinkles within the fabric of evolution, and a tenable model must accommodate them.

EPITOME

The chapter provides documentation on 18 properties (see Tables 12.1 and 12.2) in terms of which human vocal communication systems and nonhuman primate systems of communication can be compared and distinguished, in some cases very crisply and in others by degrees. The distinctions may be considered to be of special interest, in part because humans begin to show special capabilities during the first 18 months of life, and in some cases during the first 2 months of life. The capabilities that make us particularly linguistically powerful develop remarkably early.

The list is clearly not exhaustive, although it includes quite a spectrum of differences between human and nonhuman vocal systems that are not emphasized in the widely publicized literature on the topic. Although the goal is to define properties in a way that maintains logical distinctions among them, the properties are naturally related in an implicational hierarchy. This is to say that occurrence in a communicative system of one of these properties may imply that others are already in place, at least to some extent. The implicational hierarchy and the ladder of potential stages that it suggests are considered more extensively later.

Both infrasemiotic and infraphonological properties naturally group themselves in terms of roles they play in establishing a communication system with both power and efficiency. Consider the following infrasemiotic groupings:

1. Free use, lack of context binding: If a system is to be powerful and provide a basis for transmission of signs (especially large numbers of signs

TABLE 12.1

Infrasemiotic Properties

Roles Played by Properties or Design Features	Properties: General Design Features of Communicative Capability	Particular Actions That Manifest Capabilities in Humans Even as Infants	Conditions That Indicate Lack of Capabilities in Nonhumans Even as Adults
Free use, lack of context binding	Contextual Freedom	Spontaneous vocalization	Little spontaneous vocalization
		Inhibition of vocalization	Little vocal inhibition
		Exploration of the vocal space/vocal entertainment	Little vocal exploration
	Free Expressivity	Spontaneous instrumental use of vocalization	Vocalization limited to fixed values
		Creative playful vocal communication	Lack of creative vocalization usage
		Instrumental conditioning of vocalizations	Difficult vocal conditioning
Sociality	Directivity	Face-to-face vocal actions	Little face-to-face vocalization
	Interactivity	Vocal turn-taking	Little vocal turn-taking
	Imitability	Immediate and delayed selective vocal imitation	Little or no vocal imitation

Value elaboration and lexical openness		
Designation	Use of vocalization to support joint attention	Lack of triadic reference
	Use of vocalization to support requests and offers	Lack of joint reference in requests and offers
Conventionality	Acquisition of vocal signals with group-specific values	Immutability of vocal signals within species
Arbitrariness	Noniconic signaling	Fixed signals only
	Nonindexical signaling	Fixed signals only
Semanticity	Representation/symbolization	Limitation to fixed forces
Displaceability	Reference to the absent	Limitation to the here and now
	Reference to past, future	Limitation to the here and now
	Reference to the imaginary	Limitation to the here and now
Propositionality	Use of two- and three-term sentences (roots only)	Single, fixed signals only

TABLE 12.2

Infraphonological Properties

Roles Played by Properties or Design Features	Properties: General Design Features of Communicative Capability	Particular Actions That Manifest Capabilities in Humans Even as Infants	Conditions That Indicate Lack of Capabilities in Nonhumans Even as Adults
Intentional signal analysis	Signal Analysis	Tonality, pitch exploration	Holistic vocalization only
		Resonance exploration	Holistic vocalization only
		Intensity exploration	Holistic vocalization only
		Duration exploration	Holistic vocalization only
Dimensional elaboration	Categorical Adaptation	Acquisition of new features founded in signal dimensions	Fixed signal repertoire
Elaboration of signal units	Syllabification	Production of well-formed minimal rhythmic units obeying canonical principles	Holistic vocalization only
	Recombinability	Syllable recombination	Fixed repertoire
	Rhythmic Hierarchy	Embedding of syllables and syllable sequences in higher order units	Holistic vocalization only
	Segmentation	Generalization of discrete segments in syllable formation	Fixed repertoire
	Hot–Cool Synthesis	Intonation/syllable blending	Hot signals only

that are conventionally established), communicators need to be able to use and explore the units of transmission (the potential phonology if you will) freely, in a wide variety of contexts. For signals to be produced totally at will, it must be possible (a) for potential signals (vocalizations) to be produced with no necessary social functions (manifesting the property of Contextual Freedom); and (b) for vocal signals to be produced as expressions of values that are not predetermined by species-specific fixed signal assignments (the property of Free Expressivity).

2. Sociality: To function as a general system of social intercourse, speakers need to be able (c) to direct communications to individuals or specific groups of individuals (the property of Directivity), (d) to interact responsively in vocal communicative give and take (the property of Interactivity), and (e) to imitate selectively the vocalizations of other members of the community at will, which is to say in a wide variety of circumstances (the property of Imitability of community-determined signals).

3. Value elaboration and lexical openness: A key step that a vocal communicative system must take in value elaboration beyond pure social interaction is (f) to allow the vocalizations to support and participate in triadic reference, the pointing out of entities about which attention can be shared between two communicators (the property of Designation). To maximize the range of values that can be transmitted, the system must be capable of adaptation to communication about new ideas, new circumstances, and new experiences. Thus it must be possible (g) for members of the community to formulate and acquire new units (and here we refer to vocal signs consisting of both new signals and new values) specific to the community (the property of Conventionality). Further, for a communication system to be powerful and efficient (h, i, j), the system of values that can be transmitted must be unrestricted in terms of categories of feeling, thought, or illocution that can be delivered and in terms of the spatial and temporal frames of reference to which they may refer (the properties of Arbitrarity, Semanticity, and Displaceability). Finally, for a communication system to attain rich syntactic structures, it must (k) begin by developing primitive constructions involving multiple lexical items expressing semantic relations greater than the sum of the semantic content of the words of which the constructions are composed (Propositionality).

The system of transmission units for a powerful language (here we focus on signals independent of the values they have the potential to transmit) must be capable of elaboration and acquisition so that an indefinitely large repertoire of potential communicative units can be delivered. The infraphonological properties that are thus required are also naturally divided into three groupings.

1. Intentional signal analysis: The vocal and auditory character of speech must be structured in such a way (l) that it can be manipulated along acoustic and articulatory dimensions at will (Signal Analysis).

2. Dimensional elaboration: A maximally powerful signal system requires an indefinitely large class of discrete transmission units (phonological words, if you will, as well as a system of higher order rhythmic units in which words can be embedded). It must be possible (m) for users of the system to develop and acquire new acoustic and articulatory dimensions or fragments of dimensions that can then be used to form new transmission units (Categorical Adaptation).

3. Elaboration of signal units: (n) Minimal rhythmic units must be regulated by principles of formulation that make it easy to produce and perceive them in a complex stream of communication wherein many units are presented rapidly (Syllabification). To create openness of the system of words that can be formed, (o) it is important to allow them to be strung together in varying orders (Recombinability). (p) Higher order rhythmic units, formed of syllable strings, must also be regulated by a system of phrase structure (Rhythmic Hierarchy). If minimal rhythmic units are appropriately structured (with, e.g., a margin–nucleus distinction), (q) they can be further analyzed to create a system of higher efficiency by allowing components to be manipulated and stored independently (Segmentation). The system can be made yet more powerful if it is given (r) the potential to deliver graded affective information (e.g., coded prosodically) superimposed on and integrated with sequences of discrete (segmental or syllabic) units (Hot–Cool Synthesis).

The remainder of the chapter is devoted to a general review of ways the properties reveal features of intentional control of vocalizations, followed by an explication of each of the properties and the extent of their availability in human and nonhuman primates.

DIFFERENCES BETWEEN THE PRESENT FORMULATION OF PROPERTIES AND THE DESIGN FEATURES OF HOCKETT

The present model is substantially influenced by the founding effort of Hockett and his colleagues in formulating design features for language (Hockett, 1960a, 1960b; Hockett & Altmann, 1968). Hockett intended the features he posited to be permanent standards against which communicative systems of any species could be compared. The work has indeed provided a standard that has been widely utilized as a basis for comparing communication systems among species (for significant recent applications of the approach see Noble & Davidson, 1996; Vihman, 1996).

I share the fundamental goal to determine the basic and unchanging properties that are the prerequisites to the evolution of complex communicative systems. The present formulation of the properties of vocal communication here, however, is different from that of Hockett in certain general ways:

1. Hockett's system is binary (each design feature can be characterized as on–off), whereas the present approach is dimensional (each property may have multiple principles that implement it, and each of these may be present in a communicative system to varying degrees).
2. Hockett's approach is based on a list of features without specification of possible hierarchical relations among them, whereas the present approach is inherently hierarchical, with each property and principle fitting into a tree-like scheme of presupposition where progress in implementation of one property or principle may depend on progress in implementation of a logically prior one.
3. Some of Hockett's features represent broad categories, collapsing a variety of properties from the present approach.
4. Hockett's approach was distinctly behavioristic and portrayed meaning in a manner where words and referents were seen as directly connected, whereas the present approach has a more cognitive flavor, accepting potential roles for concepts and other mental abstractions in complex communicative systems.

The first two points of difference were recognized explicitly by Hockett and Altmann (1968) as constituting conceptual limitations within the original formulation of design features. The binarity of features (Point 1) has been critiqued as an important weakness throughout the period of Hockett's influence in ethological comparison (Lyons, 1991). Most observers agree that properties of communication do not necessarily occur in an all-or-none fashion, but rather they tend to be incorporated into communicative systems in steps and by degrees.

By the same token, hierarchical relations among properties and principles (Point 2), although not accounted for in Hockett's approach, are hard to miss once one begins to look for them. For example, the property of Arbitrarity logically presupposes that of Conventionality simply because it is not possible to assign meanings arbitrarily through learning if it is not possible to assign meanings through learning.

This approach also differs from that of Hockett and colleagues because it seeks more directly to determine optimal formulations facilitating the characterization of hierarchical relations for properties. In keeping with this intention, it is important to recognize *prime properties*, the minimal dimensions of relevance to the evolution of communicative systems. If prime properties are collapsed under broader single headings rather than being differentiated fully, hierarchical relations can be obscured. It is useful, in accord with the need to focus on prime properties, to maintain distinctions among a variety of hierarchically related properties that are collapsed under a single heading within Hockett's system (Point 3). For example, Hockett's feature *openness* (also called productivity, a feature in accord with which new messages are coined freely) appears to represent a collapsing of the presently proposed properties of Categorical Adaptation, Conventionality, Recombinability, and Propositionality, as well as even more advanced syntactic properties that have not been treated here. All of these properties contribute to the ways that a linguistic system is open to novelty and creativity. What Hockett called *duality of patterning* is a feature that represents the structurally rich nature of both sides of the linguistic sign (phonological and semiotic), a feature that is incorporated as a general organizational aspect of the present treatment, with a number of properties pertaining to each side of the sign as indicated in the epitome earlier.

Hockett's approach to linguistics was distinctly behavioristic (Point 4). One of the features of his interpretive style that has been critiqued severely concerns the tendency to view reference in a way that seems to discount a role for cognitive categories. Von Glaserfeld (1976) in particular found fault with Hockett's unwillingness to adopt a view of semantics concordant with the abstract notion of symbol: "To turn into a symbol, the sign's one-to-one relation to a perceptual 'referent' must be severed" (p. 222).

The more cognitive approach supported here and by von Glaserfeld defines Semanticity as requiring association of words with cognitive representations, not merely with external referents that can be seen and felt. The production of symbols, according to this view, invokes cognitive representations that must be recovered by the listener. There is always a distinction to be drawn, in this view, between the individual referent entities or events in any individual act of reference, and the cognitive categories to which those entities or events pertain. Semanticity results in the ability to make reference to cognitive categories independent of particular illocutionary forces (because each cognitive category can be invoked with varying illocutionary intents), and it lays the foundation for reference to categories that are not in the here and now (Displaceability).

The use here of the term Semanticity is thus quite different from Hockett's. For Hockett a semantic event is associative and denotative but it is not required that the association invoke cognition and it is not required that the communicative act denote a mental category. Instead the communicative act can directly denote a real-world object or circumstance. Even the dancing of bees is semantic in Hockett's usage because it yields an association between the action of dancing by one bee and the location of a food source by the community of bees. The dance denotes the food source directly, not mediated by any abstract category of location, but by pointing to a concrete individual place.

There are a number of ways that the dancing of bees does not meet the requirements of Semanticity as the term is used in this volume. For example, there is no evidence that bees could utilize the food-source dance for any purpose other than the location of a food source. Thus to the extent that it could be said there is an illocutionary force to the dance, there is only one possible illocutionary force. The dance is not used, for example, merely to indicate a location that the bees might reflect on; nor can the dance be used to tell bees not to go to the location of the food source, because for example there might be danger there. Semanticity refers here to the much more advanced circumstance of conventional and arbitrary communication where a distinction between meaning and illocutionary force can be justified, and where multiple functions must be possible for each meaningfully communicative unit. Because the dance of bees is limited to a single function, it cannot be said to bear meaning, and therefore cannot be semantic in nature. The fact that a group of bees flies in the correct direction to find the nectar source after witnessing the dance does not necessarily indicate that the bees have formulated any kind of cognition with regard to the dance. They have not necessarily understood anything in the normal sense of the term *understand*. The reaction can instead be interpreted as a mechanical and stereotypical behavioral response that is predetermined genetically. In general the properties model formulated here differs from that of Hockett and his colleagues in that this work, concurring with von Glaserfeld and others, often invokes cognitive categories as key intermediating aspects of communicative capability.

Some of the properties treated here appear to be defined in essentially the same way as in Hockett's work; consider, for example Arbitrarity (he called it *arbitrariness*), Conventionality (*tradition*), and Displaceability (*displacement*). Adjustments of interpretation may be necessary, however, to account for the specifically cognitive style of reasoning that is presupposed within this work, in contrast with Hockett's more behavioral approach. A variety of additional features from Hockett are also compatible with the formulation here. They represent design requirements that would seem to apply to any vocal communication system of minimal power, and consequently these features appear to be present in both human and nonhuman systems. These features are not included among the 18 properties of focus in this chapter and are not further treated in the book; they include vocal-auditory channel, broadcast transmission (signals can be heard by nearby individuals regardless of intent of the vocalizer), rapid fading (physical effects of signals are short-lived), interchangeability (in the usual case, producer and hearer both have the ability to produce and understand signals), and complete feedback (one hears one's own voice).

Other features in Hockett's system correspond to elaborations of communicative systems that surpass the levels of development to be considered in this volume. *Prevarication*, for example, is Hockett's feature characterizing the ability to pose vocal representations that do not correspond to referential fact. Prevarication is an advanced feature of vocal communicative systems because its productive presence in a system presupposes more primitive properties such as Designation and Displaceability, at least weakly. Empirically we know that children learn to tell lies relatively late in the process of learning to talk (Lafreniere, 1988).[1] There do exist, however, primitive kinds of deception that I am not inclined to include under the heading of Prevarication. For example, some nonhuman primates have been reported to show an ability to mislead their conspecifics through failing to vocalize when vocalization is normally expected (Hauser, 1996). Others have reportedly utilized vocalizations to personal advantage in ways that falsely manifest an emotional state (Byrne & Whiten, 1985). Similarly, human infants at 3 or 4 months of age cry voluntarily to solicit attention—they seem falsely to manifest a state of physical distress. There is more to say later about such cases of apparent vocal deception in human and nonhuman primates. A key point is that these represent cases of deception where the vocalization itself (or inhibition of vocalization) constitutes a crucial aspect of the deception without directly providing referential information that is false. False information is derived by the listener (through the combination of vocalization and context), but is not provided in the vocal communication directly and uniquely. To the extent that there is information referred to by the vocal act, the listener always has to figure it out, because the vocal act cannot (given that it constitutes a fixed signal) directly encode the information. Consequently, these vocal acts manifest aspects of the properties of Contextual Freedom and perhaps Free Expressivity but they do not directly manifest deception vocally: They result in a false interpretation (which may be informationally rich) of a total contextual event (including the vocal act), but it is not the vocal act that uniquely determines the interpretation. As I would define vocal Prevarication, these cases would not meet the necessary criterion of false reference to entities or events, coded directly in the vocal act.[2] In any event, acts of vocal Prevarication defined this way surpass the levels of complexity in communication to be considered in this volume.

Similarly, Hockett's feature *reflexiveness* (metacommunication) represents a very advanced property of communication systems. The metacommunicative ability to talk about language implies Semanticity, Displaceability, and Propositionality, and enters children's systems of speech very late. We know of no cases of reflexiveness in the communicative systems of nonhumans. The design feature of reflexiveness is not treated here, although Metacommunication is obviously a critical property in elaborate communication systems.

An additional difference between this treatment and that of Hockett concerns the term *discreteness*, which in Hockett's usage represents one of two key principles of the property I call Categorical Adaptation. Hockett's discrete-

---

[1] It is also notable that Lafreniere (1998) argued strongly for a natural logic approach in the interpretation of stages of deception. He pointed to recursive application of infrastructural principles of deception that produce increasingly complex kinds of prevarication in children as they mature.

[2] I am not certain whether Hockett's use of the term prevarication would have included a similar definitional limitation.

ness focuses exclusively on the categorical or quantal nature of linguistic units.[3] Categorical Adaptation also encompasses a principle of acquisition of new quantal categories.

ON THE NOTION OF INTENTIONALITY
AND THE ABILITY OF HUMANS TO SPEAK
AND TO EXPLORE VOCALIZATION AT WILL

Perhaps the most widely acknowledged difference between nonhuman primate and human vocalization capabilities concerns intentionality. In fact it has been claimed that free will is one of the features that makes humans human: "The ability to choose among ideas and possible courses of action may be the most important of all human attributes; it has probably been and still is a crucial determinant of human evolution" (Dubos, 1968, p. 142).

Mature humans are said to vocalize at will, whereas nonhuman primates vocalize only under conditions of specific stimulus control, or under the influence of specific emotional conditions (see literature review on this time-honored but rather doubtful claim in Hauser, 1996). The matter has been discussed extensively by investigators interested in the physiological basis for vocalization in nonhuman primates and in human speech. Considerable emphasis has been placed on neuronal connections that suggest a more elaborate system of vocal control in humans than in apes and monkeys, a system that involves extensive cortical, limbic, and subcortical components in humans, but shows more limited and lower level brain components in nonhuman primates (Jürgens, 1995). It may be of particular importance that motor cortex in monkeys appears to include direct connections to brain stem centers that control supraglottal muscles, but not to those that control the larynx (Jürgens, 1995). Human brains, on the other hand, do show direct connections from motor cortex to the nucleus ambiguus from which site the laryngeal musculature is directly commanded. The availability of direct connections suggests the possibility that human voluntary control of vocalization may be greater than that of nonhuman primates precisely because humans possess more extensive and well-connected cortical control systems for vocal action.

In spite of apparent differences in brain organization, it is important not to succumb to the temptation to view humans as utterly unique and unlike other animals. Griffin (1992) offered particularly persuasive arguments against the

---

[3]The quantization principle is manifest in the fact that English /b/ is distinct from /d/, /p/, and /m/ and that there are no intermediate linguistically functional categories. Subtly different pronunciations of /b/ tend to be heard as /b/ rather than "somewhere in between /b/ and /d/, /p/ or /m/." Categorical Adaptation appears to be unique to humanity, but the principle of discreteness of signals is found in many primate species, and quantization of categories appears to be the general rule of cognition across many primate and nonprimate species (Harnad, 1987). Nonhuman animals, like humans, tend to categorize continua functionally into a small number of units rather than treating all perceivable subtle differences as important.

traditional view of nonhumans as mechanical, unthinking creatures. His book *Animal Minds* critiques the tradition of behaviorism, wherein it was common for investigators to seem rather terrified by the idea of animal consciousness. Current research has made it clear that the mammalian mind is elaborate and its consciousness is hard to deny. It was once common to assume that abilities of nonhuman primates could not in any way be analogized to those of humans. More recently many have argued against any drastic schism between human and nonhuman communication. Snowdon (1982) argued with particular vigor against the presumed "dichotomy between simple, stereotyped, fixed communication systems in animals and complex, variant, and open communication systems in human beings" (p. 212).

There is much to be said about the intentionality of communication in nonhumans in general and nonhuman primates in particular. Still, I have not included intentionality in the list of properties of communication systems because I view intentionality as a complex idea that pervades the space of all the properties to be discussed. It is because *intentionality* covers too much ground, incorporating aspects of many interrelated properties, that it has provided only a vague frame for characterization of differences between human and nonhuman primate vocal capabilities. I take all the properties listed in Tables 12.1 and 12.2 to represent realms of intentionality, and increasing command of the properties can be interpreted to indicate increasing voluntary control by the organism.

INTENTIONALITY AND THE TRADITION OF TELEOLOGY

For some, resistance to considering the notion intentionality goes beyond its generality and consequent vagueness. There is a philosophical history of opinions about intentionality that even now constitutes a hurdle for anyone who addresses the matter. The empiricist orientation that was popular until at least the late 1960s and continues to hold sway in many circumstances actively espoused disinterest in the potential existence of intentions of any kind. Even the word *teleology* acquired a negative connotation. Any characterization of action that attributed purpose to an organism might be derisively called teleological, implying that attribution of intention to an organism constituted idle speculation, circular reasoning, and a waste of time.

In fact, the term teleology can conjure up more positive imaginings, for it constitutes a philosophical tradition of its own, dedicated to the study of design and purpose, and the tradition has deep roots. An interest in intentionality does not necessarily commit one to a narrow view. Frisch (1967) discusses the view of Niels Bohr who pointed out that physicists study the electron either as a wave or as a particle, depending on the conditions under which its behavior is observed. In a similar way, he noted that behavior of animals can be studied as expressions of free will or determinism, depending on the point of view of the observer.

It seems unreasonable to assume that any complex organism's actions can be well understood in the absence of a framework that incorporates the notion of purpose at its core. My attitude has been fostered by theoretical work on the motor control of speech by my graduate school mentor, Peter MacNeilage, who emphasized the notion of goal or target in movement, and espoused a model in which sensory feedback from the vocal and auditory periphery was utilized online by speakers to guide precise articulations of speech gestures. MacNeilage (1964, 1970) noted that articulations of a particular phonemic unit on different occasions required vastly different muscular contractions, depending on where the articulators were found at the moment of initiation of any phonemic movement. Accurate movement could be modeled appropriately, given the infinitude of possible starting positions, only if it was assumed that the speaker actively adjusted the articulators toward a target posture, a reasoning that implied speakers must perform actions purposefully and recheck the progress of their actions along the way.

MacNeilage cited as a primary source of inspiration, Lashley (1951), who focused on the complexity of serially ordered actions and reasoned that only complex models of purposeful action could account for them. Lashley's view was consistent with a teleological tradition that had placed the notion of purpose in complex organisms on an objective footing, even in the heyday of the empiricist influence. Hofstadter (1941) laid the prophetic groundwork for cybernetic modeling by positing that teleological actors possessed a threefold scheme of function including ends, sensitivities (monitoring capabilities), and techniques, a pattern that presaged the cybernetic terminology "reference value, sensory function, and effector function". Within such models, negative feedback played a crucial role (Rosenblueth, Wiener, & Bigelow, 1943). The role can be exemplified in the action of grasping an object: "I regulate my motion by the amount by which my task is not yet accomplished. This makes it possible to accomplish the same task regardless of my initial position and [that of] the object to be picked up" (Wiener, 1948, p. 203).

Thus whether one is grasping an object or articulating a speech sequence, it is fruitful to posit the notion of goal or target and assume that complex organisms actively seek to reach motoric targets by monitoring discrepancies between stored representations of target configurations and sensorily determined instantaneous configurations (von Glaserfeld, 1976). Any goal-directed action, in this teleological frame, is thus intentional and purposeful by definition.

Within this view of intentionality, we are required to recognize that nonhuman primate vocalizations are commonly intentional. Aggressive vocalizations of monkeys or apes, for example, are often pursued repetitively until the opponent animal submits or runs off. Such vocalizations are clearly directed (they include eye contact or body orientation toward the opponent, at least intermittently, throughout each bout of aggression) and their repetition within the context of a variety of general body postures (hanging from trees, running about, jumping up and down, etc.) suggests that the animal pursues vocal targets, accurately reproducing a similar sound again and again. So within the negative feedback model of teleology, animals in a state of aggression (and presumably in other states as well) clearly act purposefully, guiding the continuation of displays by reference to the targeted response of opponents, and pursuing the target systematically through a coordinated performance of vocalizations and other postural and gestural actions.

At the same time, in spite of the clear goal-directedness of many nonhuman primate vocal actions, there is an apparent relative lack of flexibility in the contexts wherein vocalizations can be used by nonhuman primates. It is often emphasized that there appears to be an inherently emotional component to the vocalizations of monkeys and apes (Smith, 1977). A particular vocalization is said to occur in response to a particular emotion. Without the appropriate emotion, the vocalization does not occur, according to the traditional observation, and this limitation has been viewed as demonstrating a limitation of intentionality in nonhumans.

So-called reflexive vocalizations that constitute species-specific fixed signals, whether in humans or nonhumans (e.g., crying in response to sadness, or shrieking in fear) are assumed similarly to be inspired by particular emotions. Even anencephalic (lacking cerebral cortex) human infants shriek reflexively (Monnier & Willis, 1953). To the extent that vocalizations such as those that occur in aggressive displays of primates occur in response to specific anger-inspiring circumstances, one might say that such displays are also reflexive. Still, aggressive displays inherently indicate a measure of intentionality because they are used repeatedly in the pursuit of particular goals until the battle ends. Crying and shrieking are not required to show such goal direction.

Of course there are many kinds of goals. It is possible on the one hand to focus on the goals of an organism to produce particular sounds (independent of their values); on the other hand, it is also possible to focus on the goals an organism may seek by producing particular sounds. Within each of these two domains there are many possible subheadings, many types of sounds that can constitute targets, and many types of goals that can be pursued by producing sounds. If we adopt the view that intentionality is always reflected in goal seeking, then our notion of intentionality is bound to be as complex as our notion of potential goal. Different creatures may be seen as differing in control of intentionality because they may be capable of pursuing different types of goals or may be capable of pursuing the same goals to different degrees.

The properties of communication to be discussed in what follows can be thought of as pertaining to specific domains defined by goals that organisms may pursue (e.g., social contact, interaction, imitation, etc.). The review conforms in some regards to the traditional wisdom in which nonhuman primate vocal actions are characterized as revealing limitations of intentional control within a variety of specific domains. The review also suggests that humans, even in the first year of life, show surprising control in these domains. The goal of the properties review is not, however, to prove human superiority, but to explicate a method of comparison that invokes an infrastructural properties model, a method that should offer a stable framework for interspecies evaluation of vocal communication.

PROPERTY 1: CONTEXTUAL FREEDOM

When ethologists wish to determine the functions of particular vocalizations (or displays in other modalities) within a species, they observe the contexts in which the vocalizations occur. In general, when one describes the context of any communicative display, one seeks to determine what events transpire immediately before the display, what conspecifics are present, and how these conspecifics react to the produced sound. Emotions are typically attributed to the producer based on the nature of the display itself. Thus, for example, piloerection or the baring of teeth are typically interpreted as threat displays, and accompanying vocalizations are typically interpreted as aggressive (Morris, 1967; Moynihan, 1969; Rowell, 1969; Winter et al., 1966). All these factors (events in the environment, presence of conspecifics, reactions of conspecifics, and apparent emotions of participants) constitute the context of any display. To the extent that any vocal display occurs consistently within a definable context and does not occur in the absence of the context, it can be (and traditionally has been) argued that the display is produced involuntarily or reflexively in response to the context.

Displays produced with considerable contextual consistency can be said to be bound by specific stimulus control and lack of inhibitability. Healthy human neonates cry in response to a needle stick. The stimulus (presumably pain) elicits the response virtually without exception. Thus the cry, in these circumstances, utilizing the traditional approach of ethology, can be said to be reflexive; that is, it can be said to be under the control of a specific stimulus and to be uninhibitable.

To the extent that displays can be produced in the absence of specific (fixed) stimulus control, and consequently can be utilized in contexts where no stimulus control is apparent or in contexts that are sensitive to learning, they can be said to be (relatively) intentional. Further, as intentionality becomes more elaborate, previously conditioned vocalizations are not necessarily produced even in the contexts of prior learning. They can be inhibited even if they have been conditioned to be associated with specific circumstances, if the organism has a reason to inhibit them.

These matters pertain to definitions of Contextual Freedom, and details will become more apparent in what follows. I focus on three action and contextual types that provide evidence of Contextual Freedom. Each shows an aspect of intentional control over vocalizations; in the abstract, it is possible for an organism to succeed in some of the three domains but not in the others, or to succeed in any of the domains to varying extents. There are, thus, different degrees of Contextual Freedom that might be considered in the abstract, and the ultimate judgment of the extent of human and nonhuman primate mastery of vocal Contextual Freedom can be made most insightfully in terms of degrees of apparent control in each of the three domains of action and contextual control. The surprising fact is that humans show notable development in each of the three domains during the first year of life. At first blush it appears that even the human infant may surpass the mature primates of other species in these vocal abilities. However, the matter is empirical, and the relevant data deserve scrutiny.

It is important to note that all three domains have a remarkable characteristic in common. When human infants succeed in any of the domains indicated, they break from the apparent standard primate pattern wherein vocal signals are inherently and obligatorily communicative and social. The circumstances that provide strong evidence of Contextual Freedom are precisely the circumstances that show an ability of humans, even as infants, to vocalize in the absence of social conditions, or to inhibit vocalization in the presence of conditions that might be expected to inspire a particular vocal display. The break of the human infant from the primate mold appears to be crucial to the creation of a powerful system of communication that can be adapted to unanticipated circumstances.

Spontaneous Production of Vocalization

As noted, ethologists have often contended that vocalizations of nonhuman primates are inspired by particular external events (e.g., the appearance of a potential predator) or by particular emotions (e.g., an individual is angry or hurt) that might be inspired either by external events, or by purely internal state changes. In *The Expression of Emotions* Darwin (1873) emphasized the idea that displays by a variety of animals, including human beings, are often emotionally charged. He advanced the possibility that certain acoustic properties might be inherently tied to certain emotional conditions in a way that might transcend species.[4] In particular, he argued that low pitch of the voice might be reflective of aggressive state (presumably mimicking the vocal characteristics of large, dominant animals that tend to have lower voices), whereas high pitch of voice may reflect submissive state. A recent review of empirical studies on nonhuman primate species provides general confirmation for Darwin's suggestion (Hauser, 1996).

There is a long tradition of emphasis on the idea that nonhuman primates are bound to vocalize in this way, nonintentionally, under the influence of

---

[4]This idea has been pursued vigorously by Morton and colleagues, who hypothesize that a motivation-structural code guides the development of fixed signals so that certain acoustic properties tend to pertain to certain communicative forces across a wide variety of species (Owings & Morton, 1998).

their emotions. In the howler monkey, there is a cry that inspires a rapid response from the troop. The call has been interpreted as providing an indication that an infant howler has been dropped from a tree. However, the claim has been made that "it is never purposeful. Never does the animal cry out with the motive of enlisting aid. The cry is simply an expression of mood, and the mood catches" (Ardrey, 1961, p. 87).

Similarly there have been observations that suggest that although the great apes perform many gestural actions on command when these pertain to the hands and arms, they appear to have difficulty responding when asked to produce a vocalization. Shozo Kojima (personal communication, 1996) made this observation regarding chimpanzees on my visit to the Inuyama primate facility, and Kim Bard (personal communication, 1991) has remarked similarly, indicating that chimpanzees sometimes show an expression of puzzlement and seem to exert substantial effort in attempting to vocalize.

The crux of a traditional understanding of how and why vocalizations are produced in nonhuman primates is this: Vocal sounds are presumed to be produced (virtually obligatorily) in response to certain circumstances, either external or internal, and to be virtually impossible to produce in others. This characterization is too rigid to fit the currently available facts, but it represents a first approximation that has resisted modification over many years of observation. We consider modifications that would make the characterization more accurate, but it remains indisputable that human vocalizations are more flexible, being producible in circumstances that appear to be entirely under the control of the individual. Again the characterization may be too extreme in the first place because at least in some circumstances humans, like their ape and monkey relatives, appear to use intonation and pitch to reveal emotion. The difference, though, is that in humans even the intonational characteristics of speech are not inherently and not necessarily tied to any particular emotion. Although a tendency toward emotional expression may be present, it can be overruled at will in humans, even reversed. A vocalization that is usually associated with one emotion can be produced even when the speaker feels an opposite emotion. If we choose to do so, we can express aggressive intent with high pitch and submissive intent with low pitch. By altering facial expressions, postures, and verbal content of our utterances we can override the effects of pitch or interpretation. Further, even with vocalizations that normally express emotions, many humans can perform as actors, producing excellent renditions of emotional vocalizations for no reason other than to play a role. We are not bound to any particular vocal form in any particular situation, context or emotional condition.[5]

---

[5]It may be worth noting that although it is possible to conjure up the emotional vocalizations, it may not be possible to do so without actually feeling some of the emotions that normally go with them. Thus the actor who cries aloud may indeed feel deeply sad in the performance, and a growling Elmer Gantry portrayer may indeed feel self-righteous anger.

In the virulent debate with Skinner, one of Chomsky's (1968) key battering instruments was the fact that humans manifest freedom of use of vocalizations:

> The normal use of language is not only innovative and potentially infinite in scope, but also free from the control of detectable stimuli, either external or internal. It is because of this freedom from stimulus control that language can serve as an instrument of thought and self-expression. (p. 11)

Here we witness the traditional (and obviously correct) claim that humans are able to speak spontaneously, with no emotional content, or in ways that contradict emotional conditions. The use of the term *spontaneous* in this section is intended specifically to convey this idea of actions produced independent of either external elicitors or particular internal emotional states. For the purposes of this volume, the interesting point is not so much that mature humans can vocalize spontaneously, for this fact seems obvious, but rather that the ability is manifest very early in life, a fact that was not obvious to many scholars of the behavioristic middle of the 20th century. Even so, certain careful observers emphasized spontaneity in vocal action of babies as a primary characteristic a very long time ago. Sigismund (1856/1971) described his own infant's pattern:

> In the second three months (in the case of one child in the twenty-third week, with other healthy children considerably earlier) were heard, for the first time, the loud and high crowing sounds, uttered by the child spontaneously, ... the child seemed to take pleasure in making the sounds. (p. 18)

Similarly, Taine (1877/1971) observed his daughter's vocal development and concluded that in human infancy:

> There is the same spontaneous apprenticeship for cries as for movements. The progress of the vocal organ goes on just like that of the limbs; the child learns to emit such or such a sound as it learns to turn its head or its eyes, that is to say by gropings and constant attempts ... she first made the sound *mm* spontaneously by blowing noisily with closed lips. This amused her and was a discovery for her. In the same way, she made another sound, *krauu*, pronounced from the throat in deep gutturals; this was her own invention, accidental and fleeting. The two noises were repeated before her several times; she listened attentively and then came to make them immediately she heard them. In the same way the sound *papapapa*, which she said several times by chance and of her own accord, which was then repeated to her a hundred times to fix it in her memory, and which in the end she said voluntarily, with a sure and easy execution (always without understanding its meaning) as if it were a mere sound that she liked to make ... all initiative belongs to her. (p. 21)

Finally, Darwin (1877/1971) himself made observations of one of his infant children, noting that the early crying sounds seemed entirely reflexive. Soon thereafter, however, "he appeared … to learn to begin crying voluntarily. … When 46 days old, he first made little noises without any meaning to please himself, and these soon became varied" (p. 27).

The descriptions emphasize the infant tendency, by the Expansion stage, after 3 months of age, and perhaps earlier, according to Darwin's observations, to vocalize in patterns that appear to watchful observers to be bound to no external nor internal stimuli. The claim is not that vocalizations cease entirely to express emotions. Some vocalizations continue to show emotional content, but infants begin to show the ability to vocalize in patterns that often bear no obvious relation to external conditions or particular emotions. Babies in the Expansion stage seem often to explore vocalizations for their own sake. These observations from early diary studies are entirely confirmed in many more recent longitudinal studies that have reported infants producing protophones in the absence of any obvious stimulus control (e.g., Oller, 1980a; Stark, 1980; Zlatin, 1975a).

The occurrence of quasivowels during the very first month of human life is significant precisely because quasivowels appear to possess no inherent social function. They appear to be produced by the infant, at this very early stage, for no reason at all. This I take to represent the first step in Contextual Freedom, the production of sounds that have no interactional driving function, no social *raison d'etre*. Later, of course, the very same sounds can be adapted to a variety of social purposes (McCune et al., 1996).

Such vocalizations are spontaneous, and it is in this sense that humans, from the first half-year of life, appear to be different from nonhuman primates. Apparently functionless sound making and later vocal play is a hallmark of human infancy, and it is largely absent in nonhuman primates at any age. The spontaneous production of sounds by human infants provides a key indicator of Contextual Freedom.

Now for caveats. There appears to be more spontaneous vocal activity in nonhuman primates, especially in very young nonhuman primates, than realized until fairly recently. Recent work with monkeys of the marmoset group suggests that in infancy there is a substantial tendency to vocalize in a way that suggests practice with vocalizations that later in life are destined to serve important signaling functions (Elowson et al., 1998; Snowdon et al., 1997). Marmoset infants appear to babble in species-specific vocal types, systematically alternating among repetitive sequences of vocalizations that seem to be produced for no purpose other than practice. The similarities with Expansion stage human infants in patterns of vocalization in marmosets appear to be significant.

The research on marmosets is bound to require important revisions in the traditional view of vocal play in nonhuman primates. However, the new data do not necessarily suggest that nonhuman primates engage in vocal play to the same extent as humans nor in precisely the same ways as humans. The data suggest a more moderate shift in interpretation. The appropriate level of shift may be difficult to determine because it is hard to determine the functions of vocalizations in many cases, especially in infants of any species. Consequently, when baby primates produce indistinct sounds, it is not easy to determine whether these utterances constitute immature exemplars of adult sounds, or whether they are special sounds of infants. Further, when infant monkeys and apes produce sounds in contexts that are ambiguous, it is hard to know whether they are playing with sounds or utilizing innate sounds in ways that simply have not yet been adequately understood by ethologists.

It is becoming increasingly clear that infant nonhuman primates sometimes produce sounds that appear different from those produced by adults (see, e.g., Biben & Bernhards, 1995; Newman, 1995; Symmes & Biben, 1992). An infant chimpanzee studied intensely by Kojima at the Inuyama primate facility in Japan (discussed later) produced few if any vocalizations spontaneously, but produced some vocalizations that seemed peculiar to infancy in response to human experimenter elicitation. Further, it has been argued that a sort of linguistic play may occur in cotton-top tamarins as infants when they are left alone. The sounds produced appear to include some features of adult vocalizations, although the structure of these is not rendered perfectly, and the sounds are produced out of the normal context of elicitation (Snowdon, French, & Cleveland, 1986). Whether infant tamarins truly engage in vocal exploration that would indicate a spontaneous usage or whether the sounds represent a sort of isolation calling that is simply immature in form remains undetermined. In addition, Symmes and Biben (1992) reviewed studies suggesting that "while babbling as a form of amusement has not yet been identified in nonhuman primates, it is worth noting that vocal output of an unusually variable nature does accompany social play (but not object play) in a small number of primates" (pp. 132–133).

It may be important that such play is social, and specifically does not occur in the context of object focus on the part of the infant monkeys. The limitation suggests that these species (squirrel monkey and cotton-top tamarin) may not possess the ability (or the inclination) to produce sounds for their own sake, but are instead limited to producing them in some social context. Symmes and Biben (1992) contended that the playful sounds of the youthful squirrel monkeys and tamarins included no "communicative function—that is, no role in affecting the behavior of the play partner" (p. 133). This phrasing does not rule out the interpretation that the monkeys' playful sounds are produced as an accompaniment of social play, an interactive element of the process of play. The same possibility appears to apply to the observations of playful vocalization in infant marmosets as reported by Elowson et al. (1998).

Recall now that human infant sounds in the Phonation stage often show no social characteristic, and in the Expansion stage vocalizations are clearly produced for the pleasure of the sound-making itself, with no social partners present and no social accompaniment. Human infants often vocalize while mouthing, handling, banging, or visually scrutinizing objects with no obvious intention of socially directing the vocalizations they produce during the object exploration.

Vocal actions of infant nonhuman primates do appear to be somewhat more flexible than those of adults of the same species, but it may still be that human infants show a more extensive Contextual Freedom than any nonhuman primates, as manifest in spontaneous infant sound production that is pursued for its own sake. Social functions need play no role for the human in vocalization, whereas vocalizations of nonhuman primates seem (at least usually) bound to social functions. This capability to detach sounds from social function is seen in humans by the middle of the first year of life, and perhaps earlier, and constitutes a key indicator of Contextual Freedom.

Inhibition of Vocalization

The second action type that demonstrates Contextual Freedom might be more appropriately treated as a lack of action. There are two realms in which discussion of vocal inhibition is relevant—the realm of reflexive and emotional sounds, and the realm of nonvegetative, nonreflexive sounds that bear no inherent emotional or social content, sounds such as protophones or speech. I consider these two realms in turn.

In many circumstances it is possible for humans to inhibit the production of emotional vocalizations that might otherwise occur reflexively in response to specific conditions. I once shrieked in involuntary alarm when a large frog inexplicably leapt into my lap at the dinner table. How it got into the house was never determined. This vocal action reflecting startle has been the source of endless teasing from my wife and children for 15 years. As I recall, the exclamation had a perfectly masculine resonance, but as the other members of the family retell it, the sound was a high-pitched burst of squeaking terror.

I could have inhibited that sound of alarm had I known there was a frog in the room, and this is the key point. Human adults can inhibit emotional vocalizations under many circumstances. In contrast to vegetative sounds such as sneezing, coughing, and hiccoughing, which people cannot (in their reflexive versions) inhibit easily, it is essentially possible to inhibit any emotional vocalization (the nonvegetative fixed signals) if there is forewarning and preparation. This ability to produce a lack of vocalization when a vocalization might be expected provides a further indication of the human Contextual Freedom in vocalization. The normal eliciting stimuli for a vocalization can be overruled by humans, but like our nonhuman primate relatives, we have an inclination to produce certain kinds of sounds involuntarily in response to certain releasing stimuli.

The typical ability of humans to inhibit emotional vocalizations for social purposes is supported by the fact that we designate as abnormal persons who cannot inhibit sounds. There exist specific disorders (e.g., Tourette's syndrome) in which individuals are unable to inhibit the production of vocalizations (and sometimes other motor actions). Victims of these disorders may show dramatic anomalies of social adjustment indicated in the production of involuntary tics, often including epithets and a variety of other possible exclamations. The disorders that produce uninhibitable vocal outbursts appear to be deeply biological. When the brain is injured, difficulties of voluntary control and inhibition sometimes result (Coffey & Park, 1997; Peterson & Leckman, 1998).

The fact that brain lesions can often be designated as the sources of difficulties in human inhibition of emotional vocalization offers confirmation for the contention that human mental capacities make voluntary control, including inhibition of vocalization, possible. Brain mechanisms that appear to be responsible for this capability were reviewed by Jürgens (1992). Moreover, the review provides an intriguing characterization of the differences between human and nonhuman primate brain mechanisms that can be brought to bear on vocalization. Humans appear to control vocalization from both extensive frontal cortex sources and limbic and brain stem structures. Nonhuman primates, on the other hand, control vocalization very largely from homologous limbic and brain stem structures only. The frontal cortices of nonhuman primates appear far less elaborate, occupy a much smaller proportion of the brain cavity than human ones, and show fewer connections with the lower brain centers associated with control of the mouth and larynx, facts that correlate with the apparent lesser involvement of cortical structures in the control of vocalization in nonhumans.

On the whole, it is assumed that voluntary control of vocalization is dependent on cortical mechanisms. Inhibition of emotional vocalizations is considered one of the prime manifestations of such control by neurologists. Healthy human adults clearly show the ability to inhibit speech and most emotional sounds. Nonhuman primates appear to find inhibition of vocal sounds difficult but not necessarily impossible. Goodall told the story of a chimpanzee that apparently wanted to hoard bananas he found, but could not suppress his food barks (cited in Bickerton, 1990), an outcome that is often presumed to represent the general obligatory vocalization pattern of nonhuman primates in response to appropriate eliciting stimuli.

However, the obligation does not appear to apply in all circumstances with nonhuman primates. For example, Hauser and Marler (1993), described the ability of rhesus monkeys to suppress food calls. In an experimental setup, individual monkeys found a cache of food that had been prearranged by human observers. The monkeys often scanned the neighborhood before beginning to eat without announcing the find (hoarding) or vocalizing to indicate the find (sharing as good monkeys should). The food calls could be inhibited if the monkey decided to try to hoard the find, but the animal ran the risk of being beaten, regardless of rank in the troop, if found eating at an undeclared site.

The contextual control over food calling in rhesus, according to Hauser (1996), is also manifest in the sensitivity of the animals' vocalizations to social setting. Females gave food calls more than males, and peripheral males (those not living in a group) did not call at all. A variety of kinds of research indicate that both nonhuman primates and other animals often adjust the use of food calling to their own advantage depending on what particular other animals are nearby. These audience effects suggest substantial inhibitory control over vocalization in nonhumans. Other studies have provided evidence that it may be possible to train rhesus monkeys to refrain from vocalizing (Sutton, 1979) in response to particular stimuli that have previously been conditioned for vocalization. Still, conditioning studies that have suggested the ability of rhesus monkeys to inhibit vocalizations have required substantial periods of training, and have been critiqued for providing only weak evidence of conditionability of any kind for vocalization in monkeys (Myers, 1976). In adult humans, in contrast, such inhibitory ability seems general and appears to be possible to institute on the basis of instantaneous decision, without any training at all. Although this conclusion is based on nonscientific observation, it would appear hard to dispute.

In human infants, on the other hand, the facts are obscure. It is hard to know what determines infant actions and I know of no experimental studies on the extent of human infant capability to inhibit emotional vocalizations. At the same time, I have often observed infants of 4 months of age and older to cease crying in response to an abrupt or startling event, but this sort of cessation provides only a limited characterization of the ability to inhibit crying. It does not provide direct evidence about how old a human would need to be to inhibit vocalization in, for example, circumstances of physical danger where hiding and silence may be the requirements for survival. The problem of testing broad questions about the inhibitability of crying in infants would be complicated by the fact that it is not possible to make very young infants understand conditions in which it might be desirable to be silent (e.g., danger might be avoided by silence).

To this point, this comparison of inhibitory abilities in humans and nonhumans has had the competitors on rather equal footing because I have considered vocalization types shared by both groups, namely those vocal signals that directly express emotions or needs. The human ability to inhibit vocalization is perhaps more obvious in the realm of sounds that do not necessarily express particular emotions. I see no need to prove empirically that normal humans can refrain from speaking or babbling if they choose to withhold such vocalization. The inhibitory ability follows logically from the fact that speaking and babbling (or other protophone production) are performed only when and if the speaker decides to perform them. Human infants appear to show a total command of when they produce protophones at least by the beginning of the Expansion stage, a point at which it has also been noted that infants also show the ability to control the vocal pattern of crying, producing instrumental uses of it (to gain attention, rather than as expressions of pain; Gustafson & Green, 1991; Lester & Boukydis, 1992), and showing the ability to cut off crying in response to loud sounds. Because it appears indisputable that human infants by the Expansion stage are already richly endowed with the ability to produce a set of sound types (the precanonical protophones) under no discernible stimulus control, it seems similarly indisputable that by that age, human infants can inhibit the production of a variety of vocalizations.

Exploration of the Vocal Space and Vocal Entertainment in Human Infants

Expansion stage infants provide dramatic illustrations of how early the human interest in vocalizations develops. The primary manifestations of exploration of the vocal space are seen in two forms: repetitive production of sounds under the influence of no discernible stimulus control and systematic alternation in production of different sound types, again under the influence of no detectable external events.

In our longitudinal studies we have routinely witnessed clear cases involving long sequences of a single, nonvegetative vocal type in Expansion stage infants. In addition we have heard Expansion stage infants produce systematic alternation between two vocalization types (e.g., two different vowel-like sounds), producing one type several times, then switching to the other, seemingly practicing the distinction (Oller, 1980a). Our data show many cases in which an Expansion stage infant will apparently spontaneously produce a large number (30 or more) of exemplars of a vocal type during one 20-minute session, and then produce none at all of that type, producing many exemplars of other types, in another session during the same week, even though the circumstances of recording, laboratory arrangement, and adults present appeared identical (Oller, 1991). In each case of such systematic vocal focus, the infant sound production pattern may seem to be entirely unrelated to any elicitation by other persons or to any attempt on the infant's part to direct the vocalizations toward other persons. Moreover, similarly patterned, practice-like vocalizations are often produced by Expansion stage infants who are alone. The systematic, practice-like activity of vocalization is reminiscent of locomotory practice in infancy. Parents often report that an infant just learning to navigate stairs will go up and down repeatedly, with no obvious intent other than mastery of the task.

The exploratory pattern of vocalization in the Expansion stage is often implemented with no discernible social intents, but in some cases the same vocalizations that are practiced apparently for pure egocentric pleasure are produced socially, in vocal entertainment. (In cases where vocal entertainment is pursued with vocalizations not primarily designed to function that way, both Contextual Freedom and the additional property of Free Expressivity are evidenced. Free Expressivity is taken up in the next section.) I recall watching my second daughter during the early canonical stage perform spontaneously for a group of assembled friends. The adults were seated around the living room when she scooted to the middle of the room, sat up, smiled, and—when the adults halted their conversation expectantly seeing that she seemed to have something to say—coughed and then grinned broadly. There followed explosive laughter from the multitude, which she allowed to subside, and then with exquisite timing, coughed again, resulting in further laughter. By the fourth round of this, the novelty had begun to fade, but there was no doubt that the repetitive, completely voluntary production of the vocalization had been neatly calculated to achieve its effect. Baby Jenna was a comedienne and voluntarily directed her vocal expressions; the social power provided by Contextual Freedom was at her disposal, manifest in her vocal entertainment.

As far as I know, the only report of another primate species practicing a set of vocalization types in repetitive and systematically alternating sequences is that from Elowson and colleagues (1998) who observed such sequences in infants of the marmoset group. This work may provide important enhancement to our understanding of practice-like vocal activities in nonhuman primates. Still, a paucity of vocal practice is notable for both infant and adult nonhuman primates, as emphasized by Symmes and Biben (1992).

To summarize, reports that hint at vocal practice in nonhuman primates are very limited: some investigators have noted that juvenile nonhuman primates may sometimes produce certain sounds out of their normal context, and may also produce some sounds that do not appear to occur in adults of the species. Elowson and colleagues have found that marmoset infants produce sounds that will, at a later point in life, be used with species typical functions. Such sounds have not been found to be produced in a practice-like fashion among apes, but instead vocalization appears to be tied to social functions and activities. The property of Contextual Freedom as manifest in repetitive and systematically alternating practice of sounds appears, then, to be typically human, and rarely present in other primates, especially beyond infancy.

PROPERTY 2: FREE EXPRESSIVITY

Vocalization that is not context bound can be brought to the service of unanticipated functions. Free Expressivity is the ability to produce sounds in the service of some function even though the sounds have not been designed by natural selection to serve that function. This is one of the fundamental keys to power for a communicative system. With Free Expressivity available, one can find ways to express emotions or states (and ultimately, with some additional properties, ideas) through vocalizations of any sort, produced in contexts where interpretation can be supported by other factors (facial expression, gesture, social context). I consider three types of evidence of human control over Free Expressivity in the first year of life.

Spontaneous Instrumental and Expressive Use of Protophones and Other Vocalizations

When human infants call for attention, whether through quasivowels, yells, squeals, or intentional crying, they manifest Free Expressivity (they also thus manifest Directivity, discussed later). All these sound types are utilized in other circumstances. It is completely clear that by the Expansion stage, there are voluntary uses of vocalizations such as crying and yelling for attention, a pattern of voluntary action that has been noted as developing in the first trimester postnatally within both vocal and nonvocal realms (Gustafson & Green, 1991; Papoušek & Papoušek, 1984). The goal-directedness of such vocalizations is often patently obvious, given the presence of persistent reaching and expressions of facial distress along with often immediate cessation of the sound making when the infant is picked up. The reader may wish to refer back to Fig. 9.8 showing a 6-month-old infant crying to get attention.

Quasivowels are clearly used instrumentally in interactions at some point during the first year of life. It is not clear, however, whether quasivowels may be utilized instrumentally in the first month or two of life. Similarly it is not clear whether gooing, in the Primitive Articulation stage, is produced with an attention-getting intent. My suspicion, based partly on research by Yale, Messinger, Cobo-Lewis, Oller, and Eilers (1999), is that gooing at least does show the property of Free Expressivity, because infants clearly regulate their emotional states during gooing interactions—they look away when overstimulated, and vocalize with vigor, seemingly to regain attention in some cases when parents look away from an interaction. Research by Legerstee (1991) indicated that by 7 weeks of age infants vocalized differently to people who were interactive or unresponsive, and differently yet when focused on objects.

Consider the most primitive possible event of vocal Free Expressivity: In this case vocalization would occur without social intent, and would express a state or condition without any necessary intention that the sound be heard. To meet the requirements of Free Expressivity, a single sound type would have to be able to express multiple states of emotion. I suspect this is what occurs in many cases when infants vocalize while alone in their cribs in the first 3 months of life. Free Expressivity appears clearly in Expansion stage infants. In Fig. 12.2 a 5-month-old produces a wide range of proto- phones while playing alone, focused on objects he can reach, expressing apparent delight, and on other occasions, frustration. To the extent that infants can perform free expression through vocalization (using sounds that are adapted to express different states or conditions on different occasions), they show preparation for growth of a massively powerful communicative system. They are thus freed to utilize vocalizations that are not otherwise committed to particular values (as in fixed signals), and to do so in any way that proves advantageous. With additional properties to be discussed later, this foundation permits the development of an unlimited system of communicative value.

FIG. 12.2. Five-month-old Liam is producing a wide range of protophones as he plays with objects in reach. The expressivity of the sound-making is not inhibited by the lack of anyone with whom to interact. Printed with permission of the parents.

Instrumental use of vocalization can be said to occur in nonhuman primates to the extent that fixed signals are often used in instrumental ways as inspired by the emotional inclinations of the user. Thus, for example, aggression displays are used to ward off enemies, and seduction displays are used to attract mates. What does not appear to occur often in nonhuman primates is free adaptation of sounds to spontaneous instrumental circumstances. Free Expressivity requires this adaptive characteristic, manifest in the first trimester of human infant life. Even instrumental crying in humans shows Free Expressivity through its freedom to function as complaint, request, anger, or refusal, depending on social circumstances and style of presentation by the infant producer.

There are cases that have been reported where nonhuman primates use vocalizations to instrumental effect even though the same vocalizations are normally used in other ways. Gibson (1990b) reported on such vocalizations in a cebus monkey that lived in her home. She said, "I always come in response to his alarm bark. He frequently uses the alarm bark when there is nothing alarming in the vicinity—he simply wants my attention" (p. 211).

The anecdote suggests a pattern of adaptation not unlike that seen in the 4-month-old human infant who cries for attention, even though the distress expressed is not physical. Another anecdote of interest concerns a young baboon observed to emit a cry that brought his mother running (Byrne & Whiten, 1985). She then chased off a big baboon that had been digging nearby. The offspring then immediately began digging in the location where the other baboon had been at work. It was reasoned that the young baboon used the cry of fear to bring his mother to chase away the bigger baboon that had nearly completed the digging task where edible tubers were found. If the interpretation is correct, the young baboon had used the vocalization to instrumental and deceptive effect.

Apes who have learned to communicate through sign language or through keyboard systems are apparently capable of much more obvious acts of communicative deception. The bonobo chimpanzee Kanzi sometimes asks with his keyboard to go to a particular location when his real plan is to gain access to something or someone along the way (Savage-Rumbaugh & MacDonald, 1988). For example, when a chimpanzee friend is busy in an experiment, and Kanzi knows he is supposed to stay away from the area of the experiment, he may ask to go into the forest with the caretaker. However, along the way, he pulls free and runs to play with the friend. When he is recaptured by the caretaker, he shows no interest in the forest. Of course this example is based on communication in a nonvocal modality, but it does indicate that chimpanzees can be extremely intelligent in how they communicate within the visual modality. The abilities of nonhuman primates to communicate vocally in ways that include instrumental adjustments appear to be substantially more limited. However, further research is needed to determine the extent of adaptability of vocalization in nonhuman primates for instrumental purposes.

Creative Playful Vocalization

My daughter Jenna's entertaining use of coughing at a dinner party (described earlier) when she was in the Expansion stage offers an example of creative playfulness in addition to indicating the ability to control production of sounds across contexts. Babies by this age typically use vocalization in a kind of repartee with obvious social function although there is no necessary desire to obtain any action from listeners other than perhaps recognition or vocal response. During the Expansion stage infants produce sounds creatively and initiate vocalization spontaneously. Perhaps because they are so vocally self-motivated at this point, elicitation of vocalization often proves to be difficult. During the Primitive Articulation stage, in contrast, elicitation through social interaction with infants is relatively easy. It appears that the growth of mind that accompanies the Expansion stage includes a much stronger tendency on the part of the infant to direct and control substantial aspects of any interaction. The infant seems in control, often crawling or scooting about the room while vocalizing at intervals, sometimes with social intent, sometimes apparently with mere expressive intent, and sometimes apparently with the sole intention to explore the sound-making capability. When, in the midst of such varied use of vocalization, the child stops, faces an adult, and vocalizes in a way that suggests playful interactive intent, it catches the eye of observers. During the Expansion stage, such events are hard to miss as indicators of Free Expressivity in vocalization.

To my knowledge, no nonhuman primate vocalizes with creative playfulness adapting sounds to the variable purposes of varying play circumstances. One might try to find such creativity in the vocal accompaniments of play fighting in nonhuman primates, yet as I understand it, this sort of vocalization consists of fixed signals that are transferred to the play fight based on analogy with actual fighting. The close relation between the functions of the aggressive vocalization in each instance suggests a rather limited and stereotyped kind of generalization in contrast to the free adaptation of vocalizations seen in humans. Specific research on the use of playful vocalization in nonhuman primates would seem warranted to evaluate the potential command of Free Expressivity.

Instrumental Conditioning of Vocalizations

We have seen that nonhuman primates typically use each vocalization in their repertoires to achieve a specific end or to express a specific emotion. Consequently, it stands to reason that instrumental conditioning of such vocalizations (as evidenced in an animal's learning to use a vocalization to obtain a reward not normally associated with the sound) would require a fundamental modification in the usage of the sounds. To the extent that a creature can use vocal sounds for special purposes, tailored to circumstances, and supported by ecologically unanticipated rewards that may occur in nature or in an experiment, the animal shows Free Expressivity.

The empirical question is if nonhuman primates have the ability to learn special uses for vocalizations. Can nonhuman primates be instrumentally conditioned to vocalize? A series of experiments suggest that they can, although the situations in which such conditioning is successful appear to be substantially circumscribed. A series of studies by Sutton and colleagues (Sutton, 1979; Sutton, Larson, & Lindeman, 1974; Sutton, Larson, Taylor, & Lindeman, 1973; Sutton, Trachy, & Lindeman, 1981), suggest that rhesus monkeys can learn to increase the rate of particular vocalizations, to vocalize with one sound to a particular light and with another sound to a different light, and to refrain from vocalizing to a third light. However, it is not always easy to achieve such conditioning, with failures to condition reported in some studies, and with long periods of training required in others (Myers, 1976). Further, the conditioning applies essentially only to vocalizations that are already in the species repertoire. New vocalizations cannot be added by conditioning. This is a limitation that apparently applies not only to nonhuman primates, but to many other species as well: "At present there is not a single, well-documented case in the literature to demonstrate that vocal learning by imitation takes place in mammals below humans" (Jürgens, 1992, p. 36).

Conditionability of vocalization in mature humans, on the other hand, is a matter of triviality. Every word we speak includes a history of instrumental and other uses that are defined by cultural needs and interests rather than by the biological imperatives that drive the use of fixed signals. Therefore it is unnecessary to provide empirical evidence of conditionability of mature human speech. The more interesting question concerns how early in life humans show evidence of vocal conditionability. The answer is that conditioning of gooing sounds appears to be possible in the first few months of life. A wide variety of studies have indicated that by the Primitive Articulation stage social conditioning can modify patterns of vocalization in human infants (Bloom, 1988; Bloom & Esposito, 1975; Bloom, Russell, & Wassenberg, 1987; Masataka, 1993) including the modification of the quality of sounds produced. Apparently in contrast to results reported for nonhuman primates, the phenomena of learning reported for human infants are robust. The questions at stake in such studies do not concern whether vocalizations can be conditioned, but rather how they can most effectively be conditioned through social responsivity of parents and different patterns of timing in responses or lack of responses.

Human babies prove to be very sensitive to vocal conditioning of sounds that occur naturally in the protophone repertoire. Imitative learning of sounds or sound sequences, however, may not occur until later. The middle of the first year seems likely (Kessen et al., 1979) as a beginning point, although there are studies suggesting that even infants under 6 months of age may be able to imitate pitch or vowel variations (Kugiumutzakis, 1999; Masataka, 1992). By the onset of real words (usually by 12 months of age), human infants undeniably demonstrate the ability to acquire new sound sequences through some form of social or instrumental conditioning.

Free Expressivity in vocalization is thus shown to be available to human infants in a wide variety of ways, at least by the first trimester of life. In contrast, given the results of research to date, it appears that nonhuman primates show notable limitations in access to Free Expressivity of vocalization at any age.

PROPERTY 3: SOCIAL CONNECTION THROUGH DIRECTIVITY: FACE-TO-FACE EXPRESSION IN HUMAN VOCAL COMMUNICATION

The property of Free Expressivity implies no specific social function, although expressive displays can be adapted to social functions. Fixed vocal signals in nonhuman primates, although not often freely expressive, have inherent social functions. An infant's cry inspires a protective response from conspecifics, an aggressive vocalization inspires submission or aggressive retort, and so on. Human vocalization also includes an inherently social characteristic in many cases. Even though fixed signals of humans and nonhumans yield social effects, they are not necessarily produced with the intention of obtaining social effects. The focus of Property 3 is the Directivity of communication, the tendency to produce displays with the intention of having them be observed, and by implication of having them produce social effects.

All primates show limited Directivity of vocalizations, but the social usage of vocalizations in humans includes a key feature that appears unique, or nearly unique, among the primates from the first months of life. This feature is observed in face-to-face vocal interaction among human parents and their infants during the Primitive Articulation stage.

We often think of human vocalizations as transmitting information, ideas, and disembodied thoughts. In contrast, primitive vocal communications are often utilized with purposes that do not intentionally transmit ideas or thoughts. Even in adults, language is not just a factual information delivery and reception system, but also one of the channels of interaction through which human beings connect, bond, and socialize. It appears to be crucial that communicators be able to direct their friendly (as well as their informational) vocalizations toward specific listeners. Directivity is seen in human vocal communication ubiquitously. In speech, any type of utterance can be directed through (in the prototypical circumstance) simultaneous vocalization and eye contact toward any listener.

There has been considerable recent discussion of the social connecting property of human language. Dunbar (1993, 1996), for example, emphasized that language is a tool of socialization, and took pains to note that much of human communication can be viewed as essentially contentless (noninformational) except insofar as it provides a platform for contact, friendship, and social reassurance or comfort. Locke (1993) especially emphasized the ways that language may have served such functions throughout the evolution of communication in hominids.

To place in perspective the mechanism of social language function, it is important to consider ways that social functions are expressed vocally in nonhuman primates. Classical ethologists (e.g., Lorenz, 1951; Tinbergen, 1951) make reference to displays by nonhuman animals, configurations of actions across modalities (gesture, facial expression, vocalization) that serve particular social and communicative functions. Based on the descriptions that have been made of these configurations in primates, it is possible to discern a notable gap in the nonhuman patterns of vocal communication. The gap concerns simultaneous eye contact and vocalization. Eye contact is utilized in some nonhuman primate displays that include vocalization, but the use of direct visual regard is often a sign of threat or dominance (Mitchell, 1979), and the vocal accompaniment is commonly growling (or its equivalent within each species), which may be attended by additional facial or postural signs of aggression.

For nonhuman primates, circumstances in which nonaggressive combinations of vocalization and eye contact do occur are sufficiently rare and limited in type that they deserve comment. One of the few examples is seen in some nonhuman primate young. Chimpanzee young, for example, invite play with other youngsters utilizing a combination of eye contact, a body posture that includes bobbing, a facial expression that is specifically referred to as the *playface*, and quiet guttural exhalations (Loizos, 1969). It is notable that rough and tumble play that is commonly initiated in this way is seen often in the young, but rarely in adults. The mutual eye contact that occurs under these circumstances appears to be instantaneous and fleeting, after which rough and tumble play may ensue. Vocalization, then, may be directed from the play invitor to the invitee, but the vocalizations seem to have a relatively minor role in these interactions. Although the example is presented to indicate that there may be circumstances in which nonhuman primates utilize vocal Directivity in a manner that is not, strictly speaking, aggressive, it may be important to note that the rough and tumble play that occurs under such circumstances can itself be interpreted as a form of ritualized, pretend aggression.

Extended periods of eye contact with vocalization are rarely observed in nonhuman primates. Moreover, extended eye contact that serves functions of pure or affectively positive social contact is essentially absent in nonhumans.[6] Consequently it can be said that nonhuman primates show a major limitation, even in adulthood, in how they command the property of Directivity. I take this as an important gap, because, as argued later, humans use face-to-face contact with alternating vocalizations as a primary form of social interaction in a wide variety of circumstances, and one of these circumstances involves a pattern of interaction that begins in the first months of life for infants.

The near absence of long-duration vocal interchanges with eye contact (and consequently with sustained Directivity) in nonhumans is especially notable because socially motivated nonvocal actions of long duration do appear to be a major feature of primate life. As an important observer of primate ethology, Sparks (1969) focused on mutual grooming as a key method of social contact, and a characteristic that pervades the Order: "Picking through the fur of another individual is perhaps the most characteristic of all primate behavior" (p. 193).

When grooming in nonhuman primates is observed and evaluated, however, it is notable for its lack of eye contact and its sparse utilization of vocalizations. Sparks (1969) noted that "the groomee will avoid looking at the face of the groomer" (p. 197), and that in some species, lip smacking, but not vocalization, may occur if the eyes do meet. Lip smacking occurs frequently during grooming episodes (van Hooff, 1969), for example in chimpanzees, but again the topography of the action is quite distinct from that seen in typical human

---

[6]Snowdon et al. (1997), however, reported the use of face-to-face vocalizations by adult cotton-top tamarins while they are sharing food with their young.

interactions. For one thing, lip smacking is voiceless (not involving laryngeal vibrations), whereas speech utilizes voicing widely and critically, because the syllabic structure of canonical syllables requires it. Further, among humans, even between adults and infants, eye contact is commonly utilized intermittently for extended periods of social interchange with voiced sounds. It has been noted that baboons may grunt (a vocalization that includes very brief laryngeal vibration; van Hooff, 1969) during grooming, but again the cross-modal topography of the action is different from that occurring in human vocal communication. Baboon grunts seem simply to accompany the activity of grooming, whereas in humans, face-to-face vocal interaction is a standard platform for social intercourse, where eye contact, smiling, laughing, and vocal turn-taking create a rich and varied form of connection where the vocalizations themselves constitute a primary focus.

Human vocal interactions have a remarkable characteristic, then, as seen in the general ethological context. One of their most common forms involves eye contact with alternating vocalizations that are socially motivated, and in many circumstances these include little or no element of aggression or threat. One might attribute this pattern to the fact that much of human linguistic interchange involves the transfer of information that must be shared. But at least in the primary sense of the term *information*, a great deal of what we humans do, face to face (and often side by side, especially among men) when we talk to each other, involves little information exchange. Instead, we often simply connect emotionally and socially, and in a sense we stroke each other in a pattern that might be dubbed *vocal grooming* or *grooming talking* (Morris, 1967). Morris argued for an evolutionary substitution where vocalization took over as a social mechanism from the more ancient ritual of body grooming in hominids. Morris (1967) referred to humans as *naked apes* to emphasize the functional loss of hairiness that occurred in human evolution:

> We no longer have a luxuriant coat of fur to keep clean. When two naked apes meet and wish to reinforce their friendly relationship, they must therefore find some kind of substitute for social grooming. If one studies those situations where, in another primate species, one would expect to see mutual grooming, it is intriguing to observe what happens. (pp. 165–166)

He went on to argue that smiling and face-to-face vocalization replaced the more typical primate pattern of lip smacking and body grooming. However, the social effects were deemed similar. Primates are social, group-living animals that need methods of maintaining good will among members of the troop, and vocalization, in Morris' (1967) portrayal, appears to have played a major role in this arguably critical social domain for ancient hominids. Whether the process of evolution involved a replacement of one kind of grooming with another is disputable, but what seems undeniable is that at some point in hominid evolution, vocalizations began to serve a function that did bear an important resemblance to that of mutual grooming.

One of the most extraordinary features of the human pattern of vocalization as a social bonding interaction is that its utilization begins in the first months of life. In a species-typical manner, a human mother (or other caretaker) holds a 2- or 3-month-old infant in a face-to-face posture, and either attempts to elicit smiling and vocalization through the use of smiling and vocalization, or simply waits for the infant to show a sign of recognition or greeting, and then begins to smile and vocalize in response. It is usually easy to get 2- or 3-month-old infants to engage in such visual and vocal interchanges, with extensive gooing and smiling, and the emotional effect is utterly natural and pleasing. The reader may wish to refer back to Figs. 9.2–9.4 showing just such interaction. This pattern of parent–infant visual and vocal interaction has been studied in an extensive literature (Anderson et al., 1977; Bloom, 1977; Ginsburg & Kilbourne, 1988; Kaye & Fogel, 1980; Papoušek & Papoušek, 1989; Stern et al., 1975) that suggests it is both extremely widespread culturally and quite fundamental in helping to establish social bonds within families. The conclusions of the literature are bolstered by the fact that adult humans show an intuitive knowledge about and tendency to engage in such interactions (Papoušek & Papoušek, 1987). When infants smile and goo while gazing face to face, adults respond intuitively; somewhat involuntarily and almost instantaneously, they raise their chins and eyebrows (Fig. 9.2), producing a full delighted smile, and they often vocalize in a pattern that has been dubbed *motherese* (see, e.g., Snow, 1972). Adults show difficulty in suppressing their intuitive reactions to infants smiling and vocalizing even when instructed, in laboratory circumstances, to remain impassive. In Fig. 12.3 the mother has been instructed to maintain a still-face, looking away from the infant, but she cannot resist smiling as the infant vocalizes loudly seemingly entreating the mother to interact. This tendency to interact with infants is one of a constellation of presumably nurturant adult actions that are believed to be biologically deep in our species and have been termed *intuitive parenting* (Papoušek & Papoušek, 1987).

Face-to-face vocal interaction with a social connection function, then, presents a dimension along which human and nonhuman primates differ undeniably. We resemble our primate relatives in some patterns of social interaction that include vocalization (most notably in aggression, pain, and fear displays), but we differ substantially in the displays that involve social connection. Our vocalizations in the social connection domain are more elaborate, of course, but more to the point here, they are used specifically to create and maintain bonds among conspecifics, and their crossmodal topography is uniquely human from the first months of life. Morris (1967) asserted that in all realms of display, from vocalization to facial expression, humans differ from other primates with regard to the aspects of communicative actions that are devoted to development or maintenance of friendship or familial affiliation:

FIG. 12.3. In this split screen shot, the mother has been instructed to look at a picture on the wall above and behind the infant Janelle and to maintain a still-face (no facial expression, no talking). However, she cannot resist her 3-month-old infant's entreaty to interact. At this instant Janelle growls loudly looking squarely at the mother. Printed with permission of the parent.

Although our smiling face ... is unique to our species, our aggressive faces, expressive though they may be, are much the same as those of all the other higher primates. (We can tell a fierce monkey or a scared monkey at a glance, but we have to learn the friendly monkey face.) (p. 132)

When it comes to vocalization, our differences from the other primates are extraordinary. Friendly vocalizations in humans are implemented in ways that are undeniably distinct insofar as Directivity is concerned. Nonhumans show the ability to command Directivity only under limited circumstances; humans show no such limitations, and even human infants in the first 2 months of life provide dramatic displays of socially directed, nonaggressive vocalization, a pattern of interaction that is entirely natural and amazingly easy to elicit.

PROPERTY 4: INTERACTIVITY: SOCIAL CONNECTION
THROUGH VOCAL TURN-TAKING IN HUMAN
COMMUNICATION

The social requirements of communication in humans involve at least two primitive, fundamental properties. Directivity provides the basis for establishing a tie between speaker and hearer. The other property, Interactivity, provides follow-through and continuity. In noting that turn-taking is a natural aspect of adult human conversation we require no empirical support. However, there are two matters that do deserve evidential comment. First, vocal turn-taking occurs only in limited forms in other primates, at any age, and second, human infants engage in vocal turn-taking with parents from the first months life, during the same face-to-face interactions already discussed.

It is fair to say that the topography of conversational Interactivity found in humans is essentially not present in nonhuman primates. I know of no reports of nonhuman primates taking vocal turns face to face in purely social, affiliative interaction. There are, however, exchanges of vocalizations in nonhuman primates that are worthy of mention in this context because they suggest limitations of range that appear to apply to vocal interactions in other primates. In fighting and fight preparation, both among apes and other primates, there are often both vocal and visual-postural displays that show a back-and-forth of threat and sometimes fear-related vocalizing. It seems reasonable, however, to emphasize the difference between this kind of vocal interchange and the sort that characterizes social conversation in humans. In the fight and flight circumstance, vocalizations appear to occur in a manner that is tied rigidly to a regime of territorial and defensive displays and responses. The pattern does show Interactivity of a limited sort, but it is locked into a particular circumstance.

As noted earlier, play of many primate young commonly begins with solicitation involving multimodal displays that may include vocalizations to complement postural and facial actions on the side of the invitor. Once a play bout begins, there may be additional vocalizations with a more interactive, turn-taking flavor, but these tend again to be locked to the circumstances of the rough and tumble play activity, which itself often mimics many of the features of fighting. Thus simulated anger vocalizations or pain vocalizations may be heard during the rough and tumble game.

There are those who see in the facial expressions and vocalizations of play invitation foundations for friendly facial and vocal actions in humans. It has been noted that the playface in chimpanzees may be related to human smiling, and that the soft guttural staccato exhalations that often accompany the playface may be related phylogenetically to laughter (Bolwig, 1963). Still, whatever the functions of vocalizations and facial expressions in nonhuman primate play are, they manifest only a rudimentary, context-limited capability for vocal Interactivity when compared with the context-free capability seen in humans. In human interactions, turn-taking need not be limited to any circumstance of rough and tumble play or any other social ritual. Any topic of mutual interest or imagination or any conceivable circumstance of social function can create the frame around which turn-taking vocalization may be elaborated by humans.

The richest back-and-forth vocal actions seen in the nonhuman primate world may be found in gibbons. Males and females of the species engage in a duetting of vocalization that has a song-like quality.[7] A vocalization duet is described by Marler and Tenaza (1977): "When [the female gibbon] begins her full song, the male normally stops singing until she has completed it, whereupon he adds a short coda, then pauses for several seconds before starting to sing again" (p. 1007).

According to Deputte (1982), the patterns of interactive vocalization in the white-cheeked gibbon can be quite complicated, encompassing a rich gestural and postural dance as well: "During the paroxymal phase, the female becomes progressively more agitated, jumping, shaking, and brachiating quickly in many directions. At the climax of her song, the female comes to her partner or another group member and embraces him" (p. 71).

The ritual is not entirely fixed either. Males especially seem to show vocally responsive variations that imply intentionality: "The complex antiphonal organization suggests that in addition to expressing emotion, the call may be produced under the volitional control of the male" (p. 90).

Such a pattern surely indicates control of some level of Interactivity. Similarly, it has been noted that in macaques, the acoustic structure of calls of responding individuals is dependent on the structure of the preceding calls from other individuals (Maurus, Streit, Barclay, Wiesner, & Külmorgen, 1988; Surgiura & Masataka, 1995). Vervet and rhesus monkeys have been found similarly to show patterns of turn-taking where pitch or other features may be dependent on prior vocalizations in a series (Hauser, 1992b; Maurus et al., 1988). Turn-taking vocalization has also been reported in squirrel monkeys (Biben, Symmes, & Masataka, 1986), and marmosets (Snowdon & Cleveland, 1984).

Thus the facts suggest that limited Interactivity is present in nonhuman primate vocalization. What is missing in the nonhuman cases is the ubiquitous and context-free Interactivity of the human circumstance, where eye contact and social function can be, at the will of the participants, bound together in a complex of vocally expressed intents that can, in adults, include any imaginable communicative value from social affiliation to mere sharing of information; from warning, threat, and cajoling, to argumentation and speculation; from description to fantasy and deception. In humans there are no effective limits on when and where these functions of vocalizations can be implemented.

---

[7]Deputte (1982) reviewed literature indicating that duetting is common in many species beyond the higher primates, including tropical birds, horseshoe bat, desert antelope, South American Cebidae, and tree shrews.

In human infants the range of potential communicative values is, of course, more limited than in adults, but even in the first months of life vocal interactions show rich patterns of conversational interaction expressing social affiliation (Trevarthen, 1979). Gooing interactions have been described in a prior chapter. It is worthwhile to reiterate that research indicates a progression from the first gooing interactions to those occurring just a few weeks later. The key point is that infants begin in face-to-face gooing (at 7–13 weeks) by producing vocalizations that often clash (occur in temporal overlap) with those of caretakers, whereas older (12–18 weeks) infants show a clearer pattern of alternation, suggesting they have gained greater control over sequencing of Interactivity (Ginsburg & Kilbourne, 1988), and the trend appears to strengthen in following months. The infant can thus be said to gain an ability to vocalize in unison or in alternation (Anderson et al., 1977; Stern et al., 1975). Furthermore, it is clear that eye contact plays an important role in the gooing activity because infants vocalize most frequently when they are looking attentively at a visually and vocally responsive interactor (Kaye & Fogel, 1980), and because the pattern of infant vocalization is subtly modifiable by contingencies of parental vocalization and timing within the face-to-face interaction (see, e.g., Roe, 1975; Roe & Drivas, 1997), indicating that infants are sensitive to the notion of turn by the middle of the first half-year of life (Bloom, 1977; Masataka, 1993). Infants at this age even interact with other infants in accord with the turn-taking patterns seen in parent–infant interactions (Casagrande, 1995). The subtlety and richness of these turn-taking patterns led Papoušek and Papoušek (1979) to contend that gooing interactions constitute a fundamental adaptation of our species, an adaptation that provides a foundation for social growth and kinship relational stability. Many have seen roots of language in the Interactivity of the human infant in gooing (e.g., Trevarthen, 1979).

It may be important to wrap up the discussion of Interactivity with a few stipulations about how nonhuman primates may be able to perform more interactively than we presently know. It has been noted that there are extreme variations in how species act depending on environmental circumstances. For example, play appears essentially to drop out in baboon troops that are pressured to forage constantly in circumstances of drought. Instead of playing, the infants of such troops spend their time following the group. Many other social activities are also suppressed, apparently due to the requirements of feeding (Hall, 1963). Similar depression in the appearance of play has been found in rhesus monkeys in circumstances of food shortage (Loy, 1970). Such observations have inspired caution in deriving conclusions about social activities of species: "There may be no such thing as a 'normal social structure' for a given species ... description [may be] only useful if accompanied by a description of the environment in which it occurs" (Rowell, 1969, p. 301).

The contextual sensitivity of play activities suggests that under circumstances that might be constructed artificially or found in special cases in the wild, some nonhuman primates might show far greater capabilities in Interactivity than have been reported in the existing literature. I had a special opportunity to consider this possibility in a visit to the primate facility at Inuyama, Japan, where the director of the laboratories, Shozo Kojima, has been studying the vocalizations of an infant chimpanzee. Kojima's summary of the work emphasizes that whereas the chimpanzee infant vocalized little in interaction with its mother, it was possible for humans to elicit quite a number of vocalizations from the chimpanzee infant during early periods of development. The method of elicitation was fairly simple. The experimenter interacted face-to-face with the chimpanzee infant in much the same way one might interact with a human 2-month-old, vocalizing and smiling. The chimpanzee infant responded with vocalizations that were more numerous and more variable than were otherwise observed. Further, the infant vocalizations that occurred in the human–chimpanzee interaction were in some cases distinguishable from adult vocalizations of the chimpanzee, a pattern that is consistent with the observations of flexibility in infant vocalizations in marmosets, bushbabies, and lemurs (Newman, 1995; Snowdon, 1988; Zimmerman, 1995). However, in the case of Kojima's infant chimpanzee, the variable vocalizations were elicited by human interactors rather than conspecifics.

Kojima's observations of Interactivity in vocalizations of an infant chimpanzee suggest caution in the conclusions we draw about the capabilities of nonhuman primates. The infant vocalized rarely when alone, but when stimulated by a human interactor, utilizing techniques not unlike those human parents use with their infants, the chimpanzee baby produced a notable increase in vocalizations. The lack of Interactivity seen in nonhuman primates may, then, in part be due to lack of social structure that might stimulate it. Thus the prudent conclusion is that although Interactivity in humans (even as infants) is clearly more elaborate and extensive than that in nonhumans, our knowledge of the limits on potential Interactivity among other primates remains sketchy.

PROPERTY 5: IMITABILITY: SELECTIVE MATCHING IN VOCALIZATION

Another social requirement that must be met by vocalizations that are to be used in a human-like communication system concerns adaptation to community-determined signals. Human adults, of course, are capable of imitating words they have never heard before in their own language, and to a more limited extent words from languages they do not know. This imitative action can take place either immediately after presentation of a model or later. Further, a sequence of imitative actions can be produced one after the other, replicating a sequence of differing models.

These facts of adult human capability seem routine, but they are not at all ordinary in the context of our primate kin. Nonhuman primates appear essentially unable to perform such vocal imitative actions. The literature on attempts to teach apes to communicate with humans includes the consistent observation that, even with extensive, long-term training from early in life, apes fail to produce human-like vocal sounds of any kind except in rare and sporadic cases (Gardner & Gardner, 1969; Hayes, 1951; Kellogg & Kellogg, 1933). The various attempts to teach signing to apes resulted in large measure from the early recognition of the fact that apes much more easily imitated gestural acts than vocal ones.

It is important to note that although specifically vocal sounds are not easily imitated by apes and monkeys, imitation of certain gestures of the mouth and tongue can clearly be taught in some species. For example, chimpanzees can be taught to imitate lip protrusion or lip smacking, as I observed firsthand in the colony at Inuyama where Kojima provided us with demonstrations of the imitative capabilities of animals that had been trained in studies with him and his colleagues. He emphasized, however, that although the work had been successful in establishing supraglottal imitations, consistent vocal imitations had never been achieved.

If we wish to know whether nonhuman primates are capable of vocal imitation, asking them to produce human-like sounds may not provide the appropriate test. Perhaps one should provide models of sounds from the animal's own repertoire of species-specific sounds. I know of no studies of imitation that have pursued this approach experimentally with nonhuman primates. However, there does exist observational research specifically seeking evidence of imitation of conspecific actions in stumptail macaques and gorillas. The work has suggested that vocal imitation of species specific sounds does not occur (Chevalier-Skolnikoff, 1976), or at least that the occurrence of such imitation may be quite rare. The research was conducted within the Piagetian perspective and sought to determine the sensorimotor intelligence of nonhuman primates at various ages utilizing adaptations of an assessment based on Piaget's stage model. The investigator concluded that the nonhuman primates, consistent with other literature she reviewed, were far more capable of imitation in visual and gestural domains than in vocalizations, and that human infants pulled away from the monkeys and apes in vocal imitative ability very early in life.

The only kind of vocal imitation that I know of in nonhuman primates pertains to a type that is sometimes called *vocal contagion*. When one animal produces a vocalization, other animals sometimes join in, vocalizing in the same way, but in a manner that suggests the possibility that the initiating vocalization inspires an emotion in the conspecifics, who then vocalize in a similar way based on the same emotion that inspired the original vocalization. Squirrel monkeys will produce contagious peeping even after cortical anterior cingulate lesions, which appear to limit both spontaneous production of isolation peeps and voluntary control, as evidenced by a loss of conditionability of other sounds (see review in Jürgens, 1995). Human neonates show vocal contagion as well. In the neonatal ward, one infant begins to cry, and if the nurses do not act quickly, soon the whole ward wails.

It is not vocal contagion, but selective Imitability of sounds that is of concern here. The imitative property of human communication that affords it its power is that which allows the speaker to adapt instantaneously to any new word and to switch systematically from one word or sound to another and then to another as models are presented and ultimately to reproduce previously heard sequences after indefinitely long delays, as the communicative intent that requires replicating particular sound sequences arises. It remains uncertain how early in life human infants begin to show the capability for selective imitation in vocalizations. By 6 months of age, there is good evidence of Imitability for pitch of vowel-like sounds presented to infants in an experimental paradigm (Kessen et al., 1979). However, the ability may actually be present earlier, as suggested by experimental studies (Kugiumutzakis, 1999; Masataka, 1992) and by observational research of apparent matching of intonations in the vocalizations of infants in the first 3 months of life when they interact with their mothers (Papoušek, 1994; Papoušek & Papoušek, 1989). The difficulty in interpreting the observational research is attributable to the complexity of the time series of events occurring in interactions. Matching is clearly present in the interactions, but it is difficult to tell whether the infants imitate the mothers or the mothers imitate the infants.

Studies of human infant vocal imitation have, of course, usually presented models that were presumed to be in the current vocal repertoires of the infants. Unpublished research in my own laboratories in the 1980s attempted to inspire infants who appeared to be on the verge of a new stage of vocal development (e.g., precanonical infants who appeared to be nearly ready to begin the Canonical stage) to produce progressive sounds (namely well-formed syllables) under the influence of persistent modeling. Not a single instance of such progressive, selective imitation was ever observed. Precanonical infants did not produce canonical sounds in spite of our efforts at laboratory elicitation.

On the other hand, selective imitation was commonly observed after modeling of sounds that were in the infant repertoires during the middle of the first year of life. The laboratory assistant could sometimes inspire an infant to growl by modeling growling and then could sometimes get the infant to switch to squealing by modeling squeals. The pattern of selective Imitability occurred in some Expansion stage infants but not in others, and it was not clear whether the infants who did not show the pattern would have done so if we had been able to see the infants more often, or if we had used more elaborate elicitation procedures.

By the end of the first year of life, in infants who were well into the Canonical stage of vocal development or the succeeding Integrative stage, it was also clear that some infants who commonly produced two different canonical syllable types (say [ba] and [da]) could be inspired selectively to alternate between sequences of the two syllables by alternating modeling. Again it was not clear whether all year-old infants might have been capable of such selective imitation.

By the age of 12 months many infants already produce a few conventional words spontaneously, suggesting a selective imitative capability that includes a characteristic of delay between the presentation of the model and the production of the word by the child. However, it is not entirely clear that such early words are truly acquired imitatively. The sounds used by 12-month-olds in these early words (e.g., [dada]) form part of a babbling repertoire, and it appears parents may instruct the infant to treat the sounds associatively with particular circumstances or objects. Again, it may be the parent and not the infant who does the imitating. Early word usage does not thus, in and of itself, provide a clear indication of imitative vocalization. The proof of canonical syllable imitation must, I think, be sought in the (alternating) selective imitation of particular syllables presented in sequence, as discussed earlier.

To my knowledge, such vocal imitation has simply never been reported in any nonhuman primate, at any age.[8] By the middle of the first year of life, the property of Imitability appears to be established in humans, and may be partially present earlier. By later in the first year, the capability extends to new categories of sounds, and during the following months imitative abilities of human infants expand dramatically.

PROPERTY 6: DESIGNATION: THE USE OF VOCALIZATION TO INDICATE ENTITIES IN COMMENTS, REQUESTS, AND OFFERS

One of the key features of communication in humans, vocal or nonverbal, is that it capitalizes on the human ability to share attention about objects. The ability to share reference to entities lays a critical foundation for any rich communication system. Without it, communication is limited to functions of social bonding and Interactivity, including emotional expressions and the transmission of certain social illocutionary forces (threat, entreaty, alarm, announcement, etc.). The sharing of attention is seen during the first year of human life in two domains.

Triadic Reference to Objects

By about 8 to 12 months of age, infants point to objects and follow the pointing of adults toward objects (Butterworth, 1996; Tomasello, 1996). The infant's alternation of gaze from the object to the adult makes clear that the infant is aware that attention to the object is being shared in a triadic reference (I, you, thing). In complex events of this sort, vocalization is often utilized by

---

[8]At the same time there is good evidence of vocal imitation in cetaceans (for reviews see McCowan & Reiss, 1997; Tyack & Sayigh, 1997) and of course in birds.

the infant as an aspect of the interaction, as if the vocalization constitutes a comment "look at that" or "yes, I see that." It is important to recognize that the vocal comment does not specify the nature of the object or in any way symbolize it. The same vocalization and the same gestural complex of pointing and looking can be used to reference any object. I choose to call this property of communication Designation.

Notably, joint attention of this sort is seen in very limited forms, if at all, in nonhuman primates in the wild (Leavens, Hopkins, & Bard, 1996). Bard and Vauclair (1984) suggested that when joint attention does occur in chimpanzees in their natural interactions, it appears to be limited to circumstances involving food or nesting materials, and not other kinds of objects. In interactions with humans, chimpanzees can be taught to engage in the elements of joint reference, pointing and alternating eye contact (Tomasello, 1996; Tomasello & Farrar, 1986). There is good documentation for chimpanzee pointing toward desired food items along with gaze alternation to a human caretaker in laboratory circumstances (Hopkins & Leavens, 1998; Leavens et al., 1996). Sign-language-trained chimpanzees and gorillas are very good at showing the property of Designation (Krause & Fouts, 1997; Patterson, 1978a, 1978b). Orangutans also show some joint reference abilities including gaze alternation (Bard, 1990; Call & Tomasello, 1994). In all these cases, however, vocalization is either absent from the communicative complex or appears to play little role in it, and consequently, vocal Designation is not generally evidenced.

The most interesting case resembling vocal Designation in nonhuman primates concerns alarm calls and food announcement calls of certain monkeys, thought to include a sort of referentiality (Marler et al., 1992). The vervet monkey, for example, possesses alarm calls that differentiate danger from the air ("eagle?") and danger from the ground ("leopard?"). Conspecifics react to these calls with appropriate flight away from the announced danger. It is important to note, however, that the topography of such alarms is substantially different from that of human joint reference. I do not know what sort of eye contact with conspecifics may obtain, but as far as I know, pointing is never involved. It is, however, noteworthy that monkeys do not react to alarm calls purely mechanistically. They are more likely to flee in response to a real alarm call than to a tape-recorded playback of one, and they often look around for a predator prior to fleeing (Cheney & Seyfarth, 1980; Weary & Kramer, 1995). To the extent that sharing of attention occurs among the monkeys in such situations of alarm, it would appear that it occurs within a holistic event that is always tied to alarm and potential flight. The human attention sharing need involve no fear and no alarm. The vocalization and the alternating gaze can constitute nothing more than the drawing of attention to an object.

Similarly with food calls that are specific to particular kinds of food, I am unaware of evidence that nonhuman primates show alternating eye contact or pointing. Conspecifics understand the calls and come running (Hauser & Marler, 1993), but the topography of the event involves Designation in a less specific way than is seen in humans. Rhesus monkeys clearly understand a great deal about their social situation, and they clearly understand that food found by one member of the troop is supposed to be announced. We know this because rhesus sometimes suppress the food call (after looking around to see if any one is watching). If they do, they may be beaten by the troop if they are caught eating the unannounced find. Therefore to say that rhesus monkeys lack the communicative property of vocal Designation does not suggest a general lack of mental capacity regarding entities or awareness of what other members of the troop may know or want. The limitation appears to reside in the lack of a specific communicative topography by which the organism can point out an object for reasons other than announcement, or for no reason other than to inspire an emotionless joint awareness of the object's existence.

There has been considerable discussion of the distinction between truly designative acts with referential specificity and acts that are directed to producing an action outcome. Theorists have argued that nonhuman primates communicate primarily as a means of manipulating or influencing other animals rather than as a means of transmitting information about entities (Dawkins & Krebs, 1978; Krebs & Dawkins, 1978). Others have argued specifically that reference is not involved in alarm calls. Within their management view of nonhuman communication systems, the term *"referential specificity* would be modified, to ... *situational specificity.* From the perspective of management, signals do not *refer* to anything. They are pragmatic acts emitted to produce an effect" (Owings & Morton, 1998, p. 201). Further, "from the perspective of management, communication is based upon what it accomplishes, not what it conveys" (p. 231).

Clearly, in true acts of Designation, such as those seen in human infants at the end of the first year of life, management is not all that is at stake. Babies often show an interest in sharing attention independent of management goals.

Vocal Requests and Offers of Objects

At the same time, human infants during the second half of the first year often look at and reach toward an object, indicating their interest by a complex of gesture and vocalization that is often taken as the command "give that to me." In Fig. 12.4 the 6-month-old infant reaches for a toy in the mother's hand while he vocalizes what seems to be a request. In addition, they sometimes reach out to hand an object to another person, looking at the person with clearly directed eye contact and vocalizing in a way that suggests "here, take this." In both cases the vocalization is again nonspecific to the object requested or offered. The communication is about an object to which attention is shared (and about a request or offer of that object), but only the circumstance and gesture designate which object is involved. The vocalization merely serves to draw attention to the object or the proposed action with regard to it. In this sense, such requests or offers provide evidence of the property of vocal Designation.

There is a simple form and a complex form in requests for objects. In the simple form (represented with a 6-month-old infant in Fig. 12.4), the object is in the line of regard between the infant and the listener. When the infant reaches, eye contact with the listener requires little change in gaze direction, and consequently one of the important indicators of shared attention is present only in a weak way, if at all. In the more complex form of requesting (a later-developing capability), the object is not situated between the infant and the listener. To request the object, the infant must reach laterally, turning eye contact toward the object, vocalizing, and turning to gaze back toward the listener. In this more complex form, it is clear that all the key elements of Designation are present (although the hand shape is open), and that in addition the infant indicates a desire that the listener give him or her the object (Butterworth, 1996). The desire is expressed by a conjunction of

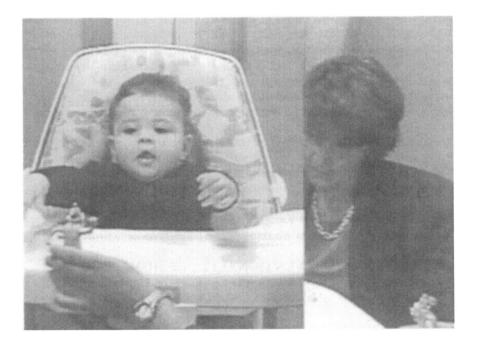

FIG. 12.4.   In this split screen shot, the mother (on instruction from the laboratory assistant) is holding a toy just out of reach to 6-month-old Sebastian, who vocalizes in a way that suggests a request, as he reaches for the object. Printed with permission of the parent.

facial expression, hand shape, and a special vocal pattern that may suggest a sense of urgency.

As indicated earlier, nonhuman primates sometimes do make requests for objects by reaching for them and looking toward a human caretaker (Hopkins & Leavens, 1998; Leavens et al., 1996). Vocalization does not, however, appear to play a key role in such events. Further, if nonhuman primates reach for a desired object, for example, food possessed by a conspecific, they do not typically do so in a way that clearly indicates shared reference. The food, the object of desire, must be in the hands of the conspecific, not off to the side where a request would require some special gestural or vocal indicator of the request (Tomasello, 1996).

Furthermore, offers involving reaching out with an object, vocalizing, and maintaining eye contact are also rare if they occur at all in nonhuman primates. When chimpanzee mothers share food with their infants, they do not do so with the conjunction of actions that includes eye contact, vocalization, and sharing (Tomasello, 1996). Significantly, vocalization is absent and alternating gaze between the object of sharing and the participants in the interaction is also absent.

The topography of food sharing has been studied in several primate groups. I visited the laboratory of Frans de Waal at the Yerkes Institute and had the pleasure of witnessing portions of an experiment on food sharing with new world monkeys. Two animals known to be friends were placed in adjacent cages, and one was given pieces of food that could have been shared by the lucky animal if he would but reach through to the adjacent cage and hand food to the hungry friend. Indeed, sharing did sometimes take place, but the topography of sharing was utterly different from that seen in human infants in the second half-year of life. The common way that the lucky monkey shared food was by eating on the side of the cage that was adjacent to the friend's cage. Occasionally he dropped food segments and the friend reached through to take them. No eye contact, no vocalization to indicate shared reference, and no reaching out to hand food was seen in the videotapes that were shown by the staff at the visit in the laboratory. Food sharing seems to occur in these monkeys, but it would be quite a stretch to call it offering. It appears that vocal Designation is present in nonhuman primates only in very limited forms.

PROPERTY 7: CONVENTIONALITY OF HUMAN SIGNALS AND THE LIMITATION TO FIXED (OR IMMUTABLE) SIGNALS IN NONHUMAN PRIMATES

In differentiating natural signs from arbitrary ones, Condillac (1756) focused on one of the key characteristics of words; namely, that they can be associated with meanings in ways that are unconstrained by the relation between the physical content of the sounds to be spoken and the values to be transmitted. This is the design feature of Arbitrarity, considered later. In fact, there is an additional, more primitive property (implied by Arbitrariness) that allows values of any kind to be assigned to signals by convention (or learning), a property I call Conventionality. The absence of Conventionality in a system of signals results in a condition that might be called *immutability,* a general characteristic of natural (or fixed) signals that obtain their values by processes of evolution rather than of learning.

It may be worth noting that one of the indicators of Free Expressivity, namely conditionability of signals, is required for Conventionality to be present. In practice, Imitability is also required, as learners of new signs typically adapt to models of signs provided within the community of speakers. Conventionality is seen when particular vocalizations are conditioned to particular social uses (values) that are not built into the biologically predetermined repertoire of signals.

Because users of an arbitrary signal must possess the ability to command Conventionality (since they must learn the arbitrary connections), it has been easy to confuse Conventionality with Arbitrariness. Yet conventional signals can obtain in the absence of Arbitrariness. For example, we might decide to designate a reptile that makes a clicking sound with an imitation of the clicking sound. A sign thus formed would not be based on an arbitrary choice of sounds, but it would surely constitute a conventional signal as its existence within any language would depend on some community's acceptance of the pairing. Conventionality is, thus, a logically prior property that can be recruited in the development of communication systems, whether or not the systems possess Arbitrariness.

Nonhuman primates' signals, whether vocal, gestural, facial, or postural are generally immutable and nonconventional in the wild, as far as can be told. For example, from the field studies of Green (1975) we learn that there are perhaps seven distinguishable social situations in which the Japanese macaque vocalizes, and that the seven vocalization types are tied to those circumstances uniquely, each call with its special value. Fossey (1972) claimed that the mountain gorilla has 16 calls, again, each one tied to specific circumstances. The number cited by Fossey may be inflated by the use of liberal criteria for categorization of calls—a more conservative approach might collapse several of the designated calls into broader categories.[9] The key point here is that the functions of each of the vocal categories are relatively fixed; they cannot be exchanged or modified in major ways by learning.

---

[9]The difficulty of arriving at an indisputable number of fixed signals for any species was discussed by Newman (1995), who emphasized that the domain of application of vocalizations is often hard to establish given the nature of observational research. The natural interactive environment always includes many features, and signals may occur in response to any of a number of possibilities or combinations of possibilities within given social contexts. The answer to how many fixed vocal signals humans or nonhuman primates have depends on criteria of categorization utilized by the individual ethologist.

It may also be important to note that although ethologists sometimes use the same term to describe fixed signals of two species, both the values and signal forms may vary across species. Consider the term *laugh*. Its application to a particular chimpanzee vocalization (Provine, 1996) is intended to take note of certain similarities of both form and function in human and chimpanzee. However, chimpanzee laughter is largely voiceless, whereas prototypical human laughter is voiced (including periodic vibrations of the vocal folds). Further, the "vowel-like notes of human laughter are performed by chopping a single expiration, whereas chimpanzee laughter is a breathy panting vocalization" (Provine, 1996, p. 40). The circumstances of laughing may also be notably different in the two species, with chimpanzees being more likely to emit their laughter in response to tickling, and humans in response to many additional social conditions.

Thus, fixed vocal signals vary from species to species, even within the primates. Further, the senses in which signals are fixed may be somewhat variable, with humans showing very high degrees of flexibility. As previously noted, humans have enormous freedom in how they use fixed signals, even though there are some circumstances in which the various human signals seem to be produced involuntarily. We can produce good replicas of any of our fixed signals at will, and we can often suppress them if we have forewarning. There are also variations of usage for fixed signals in other primates in special circumstances, but they seem to be more limited in extent and type as already noted.

The relative fixity of signals in mammals in general may have been prescribed by natural selection. There may be danger to both individuals and communities in allowing variations in the use of vocal signals that may be partly designed to provide quick information regarding threat or danger. In the context of research on display patterns of new world monkeys, Moynihan (1969) noted:

> Alarm patterns ... and threat or other very aggressive patterns ... often are much more conservative during evolution than more ambivalent patterns ... it is usually vital for the individuals perceiving such patterns to react to them instantly ... any sudden evolutionary change in a pattern of this type, no matter how minor, must increase the chances that the signal meaning of the pattern will be misinterpreted. (p. 322)

The relative importance of clear signals about dangers may, then, have helped keep fixed signals fixed in many species, and if so, then humans and their ancestors must have found some special and significant advantages (perhaps not relating to immediate dangers) in variably produced vocal actions, advantages that could justify giving up the security of keeping signals entirely fixed and easily interpreted. Other primates have remained more conservative than humans on this point, and learning appears to have played a much smaller role in vocal actions, even for our closest relatives, the chimpanzees.

Newman (1995) regarded variation in primate vocalizations across individuals or groups as a phenomenon primarily of heritability rather than of learning, and in spite of efforts to demonstrate vocal learning in nonhuman primates, reviewers note that the evidence is often ambiguous whether vocal learning occurs at all in nonhuman primates (Zimmerman, 1995). Locke (1993) emphasized the lack of activity in nonhuman primates to instill vocal patterns in young.

> There is little evidence of explicit vertical teaching among nonhuman primates. Nonhuman primates appear to lack a strong disposition to instruct their young, and their system of contact and alarm calls clearly is better suited to needs that have less to do with culture than survival. (p. 419)

There is, then, a widespread consensus that vocal signals (as well as facial and postural signals; see van Hooff, 1969) in nonhuman primates are relatively fixed. Several qualifications, however, should be made based on modern ethological research. First, although vocalizations in nonhuman primates tend to have fixed form, they are commonly "graded" to allow changes in intensity of expression across a broad range (Marler, 1975). Thus a "threat" call may be produced at low acoustic intensity and yield a low-intensity warning. As the intensity of the vocalization increases, ethologists observe increases in other indicators of degree of hostility as indicated in posture, piloerection, attack gestures, and so on. Clearly the number of signals in a repertoire that includes the design feature of gradation may be, if one wishes, considered indefinitely large. Human fixed signals include gradation possibilities just as nonhuman ones do (see Zeskind, Klein, & Marshall, 1992), and so one might similarly claim that humans possess an infinite number of fixed signals.

This sort of reasoning can be carried to a point of absurdity. It is important not to ignore the abstract functional categories or dimensions that unify graded signals into identifiable groupings, because it is clear that cognitive categorization requires that continua be segmented into functional units (Harnad, 1987). Fixed signals can always be identified as pertaining to a limited number of dimensions. Members of each species must be able to identify and categorize signals along each dimension and across various degrees of gradation for the signals to be of survival value, and ethologists observing species must be able to recognize the signals in their various forms to offer a coherent description of them. The fixity of these signal groupings may be fuzzy (see Gozoules et al., 1995), but both form and function remain describable and gradation does not undermine categorization fundamentally. In the words of Moynihan (1969) describing published attempts to enumerate categories of vocal signals in new world monkeys, "many ... intermediates are listed and given separate names or labels but they obviously are nothing more than variations on a few major themes" (p. 335).

A second qualification regarding fixity or immutability of nonhuman primate signals concerns the assumption that there is no learning at all in the production of primate vocal signals. In fact some learning of sound production does seem to occur. It has been noted that *Macaca nemestrina*, the pig-tailed macaque, develops abnormal vocalizations if deafened early in life (Sutton, 1979). The result does not unambiguously indicate that auditory learning of vocalizations occurs in the pig-tailed macaque (as the effect could depend on auditory feedback from the animal's own voice or the hearing of nonvocal sounds rather than the specific experience of hearing mature conspecific vocalizations), but it is suggestive. Another indication of possible learning is found in differences in vocalization pattern across individuals and groups within a species. As noted earlier, Newman (1995) interpreted such differences as likely reflections of differential heredity. For example, chimpanzees in different groups have been noted to possess calls that differ slightly in a manner that has a dialect-like quality. Mitani, Hasegawa, Gras-Louis, Marler, and Byrne (1992) speculated that the differences may be hereditary rather than acquired, but the conclusion remains in doubt. Green (1975) reported dialect differences in Japanese macaques (*Macaca fuscata*). Hauser (1992a) registered an opinion that there is vocal learning in the genus *Macaca*. He reported that rhesus monkeys show dialect differences across matrilines, and that the differences are modified as individuals change matriline affiliations. Such modifications are clearly relatively minor in the context of possible changes in signal usage and form that are seen in human learning of vocabulary, but they remain a useful addition to our understanding of the flexibility of primate vocal actions. Studies of other primates have not uniformly yielded indications of learned dialects, but it appears to be well verified that the songs of humpback whales (*Megaptera novaeangliae*)

> show regional dialects; within a population, they change progressively over time. … Songs from different oceans or decades share so few sounds, that even the most cursory listening or scanning of spectrograms would reveal significant differences. These observations of obvious geographic dialects in the vocalizations of marine mammals contrast with the more subtle differences described for nonhuman primates. (Tyack & Sayigh, 1997, pp. 226–227)

· This result suggests both the existence of regional dialects in cetaceans and the conventional acquisition of dialects across individual lifetimes. Hauser's (1992a) results on matrilineal variability in vocal patterns suggest that nonhuman primates may have similar abilities to learn dialects although the patterns may be more tenuous and difficult to demonstrate than in the marine mammals.

In addition to apparent vocal dialects across groups of nonhuman primates, there are also recognizable differences that pertain to individuals in every primate species that has been evaluated according to Snowdon et al.

(1986). Members of various species recognize each other by their vocalizations (see Todt, Hammerschmidt, Ansorge, & Fischer, 1995, for barbary macaques; Snowdon, Coe, & Hodun, 1985, and Biben & Bernhards, 1995, for squirrel monkeys; Cheney & Seyfarth, 1980, for vervet monkeys; and Symmes & Biben, 1992, for playback studies showing intraspecies identifiability of individuals). The possibility that such differences are partly instilled or stabilized by experience is hard to rule out. One possibility is that the differences in sounds produced by different individuals are not learned, but that conspecifics do learn to recognize individuals by those differences. Seyfarth and Cheney (1997) drew the distinction among three domains of Conventionality in vocalizations of nonhuman primates. *Vocal production* refers to the ability to articulate vocally, *vocal usage* refers to the ability to transmit communicative values, and *responses* refer to comprehension of vocal calls by others. Based on a review of 34 studies on 14 primate species, the authors concluded:

> Vocal production seems most innate (although it is by no means always fixed at birth) and shows the least modification over time. By contrast, vocal usage is only partially innate and more clearly affected by experience, while infants' responses to the calls of others are almost entirely determined by experience. (Seyfarth & Cheney, 1997, p. 249)

The cited studies suggest that within primate species, groups and individuals under some circumstances learn to command fixed signals in ways that differ significantly across individuals. Cross-fostering studies have also been pursued in the hope of showing learning effects across species boundaries. The studies have yielded mixed results. Seyfarth & Cheney (1997) again reviewed relevant results suggesting that cross-fostering can produce adjustments in the command of fixed signals, especially with regard to comprehension of the fixed signals of fostering parents of a closely related but different species. Masataka and Fujita (1989) found that rhesus and Japanese monkeys not only learned to comprehend but to produce discernibly different vocalizations if raised by mothers of the opposite species. Owren, Dieter, Seyfarth, and Cheney (1993), on the other hand, found little if any change in vocal patterns under similar conditions of cross-fostering.

The most publicized efforts in vocal learning among nonhuman primates may have been those that included fostering of chimpanzees in human families (Gardner & Gardner, 1969; Hayes, 1951; Hayes & Hayes, 1951; Kellogg & Kellogg, 1933). The general conclusion of those studies is that chimpanzees do not learn to produce much if anything in the way of human speech. Charitable listeners credit the learners with less than a handful of ill-pronounced, variably utilized, word-like productions. On the other hand, the comprehension of many spoken words does seem possible (Savage-Rumbaugh, 1988), at least for the less commonly known species of chimpanzees, the bonobos (*Pan paniscus*). Learning of nonvocal signals (hand gestures or pointable visual symbols on communication boards) is undeniable for both chimpanzee species and gorillas (Fouts, 1987; Gardner & Gardner, 1969; Patterson, 1978a, 1978b; Premack, 1971). Even teaching of nonvocal signs by a mother chimpanzee to her infant has been reported (Fouts et al., 1989). That such cross-species learning of communication symbols is possible was quite a surprise when first reported, and its importance should not be minimized. However, it is limited in a variety of ways (in number, specificity, range of application, etc.; see Terrace, 1979) that should also be kept in mind, as human learning of symbols is vastly superior in the same domains.

As emphasized earlier, fixed signals of nonhuman primates are not perfectly fixed in domain of application. Observational research on nonhuman animals is often plagued by uncertainty in the categorization of contexts in which events occur. Investigators are capable of noting many potentially relevant circumstances or eliciting events each time a vocalization occurs, and it falls to the wisdom of investigators to perceive the circumstances that actually elicit the vocalization. Some such observations seem more reliable than others, but it is increasingly clear that some primate vocalizations are produced in circumstances that do not conform to the elicitation criteria that are usually invoked by ethologists. There has been considerable recent discussion of this variability in production of vocalizations, especially by primate infants. Cheney (1984), for example, noted that vervet infants sometimes overgeneralize and use calls in inappropriate circumstances. It is reasoned that vervet infants have to learn the semantic range of calls appropriate in their species. Zimmerman (1995) indicated that even in nocturnal prosimians, very distant primate relatives of humans, infants of the species show variability of usage of vocalizations and even in the type of vocalization that occurs:

> There are vocalizations specific for infants which do not correspond to any vocal pattern in adults. They are found in bushbabies and Malagasy lemurs [though they] ... could not be detected in the less vocal lorisids. Such vocalizations do not seem to have a particular function. They are produced by all infants during affiliative social interactions with social companions and may be intermingled in vocal streams with vocalizations resembling elements of the adult repertoire. (p. 67)

The physical form of these vocalizations, utilized in variable circumstances, appears to be modified with time. In marmosets, it was asserted by Snowdon (1988) that periods of intense vocalizing by infants fit into an adaptive process by which an infant acquires, through practice, the vocal capabilities of the adults of the species. There may be a long-term evolutionary and developmental design to this pattern. Newman (1995) contended:

> There are emerging principles of convergence in the development of macaque and marmoset vocalizations that suggest a conservative general plan transcend-

ing phylogenetic differences. This plan is apparent in the gradual loss of variable sounds originating in the neonatal period. (p. 74)

There is considerable interest in this apparent pattern of infantile vocal lability in nonhuman primates, in part because it hints at a capability that may have been exploited by ancient hominids in evolutionary change. Through *neoteny*, a change where infantile or childhood characteristics of an ancestor species are preserved to later stages of development in descendants, ancient hominids may have exploited the infantile flexibility in vocalization and begun a process of enrichment of vocal repertoire that may have laid a critical foundation for speech. These speculations find support in the vocal responsivity of Kojima's chimpanzee infant discussed earlier.

It is tempting to speculate that the evolutionary potential for vocal development beyond mere fixed signals, development that would have provided a crucial foundation for the development of conventional vocal signals, may have been at least partly present from a very distant time in primates at least during their infancies. Ancestral primate stock (except for the human line) may have failed to exploit the possibilities for vocal growth in part because they appear not to have developed parental face-to-face vocal interactive styles that might have stimulated infants to acquire a free, nonfixed vocalization capability. One might ask, of course, how the ancestral primate parents of ancient hominids could have developed such a style when their own parents had not provided vocal encouragement at a similar point in development. The potential for elaboration of the vocal repertoire of our species may have lain dormant, awaiting biological (mutational) changes that would stimulate interaction on both sides, perhaps making infants even more flexibly vocal, and parents more inclined to engage in vocal interaction for social purposes.

Nonhuman primates do show an ability and inclination to teach each other and their young, under some circumstances, although the documented cases to my knowledge are overwhelmingly nonvocal. Chimpanzee mothers are known to have encouraged nut cracking in their offspring (Boesch, 1991). Several nonhuman primates have been observed to discourage the eating of dangerous plants by their offspring (Caro & Hauser, 1992). New habits (such as opening wrapped packages) are sometimes passed from individual to individual in a troupe (Itani, 1958). There exists documentation of propagation of tool use among 16 chimpanzees that had been liberated to an island—cracking palm nuts with two stones started with one animal, then spread horizontally (Hannah & McGrew, 1987).

I know of no reported cases of positive teaching of vocalizations in nonhuman primates, but Caro and Hauser (1992) reported that when nonhuman primate infants utilize alarm calls inappropriately (as might be expected given the prior cited evidence of flexibility in infant vocalizations), they are sometimes chastised. Studies cited earlier indicating possible dialectal variations or cross-fostering effects on vocalizations in nonhuman primates suggest additional possible ways that learning may occur, but provide no direct indication of vocal teaching by nonhuman primates. Whatever the patterns of learning and teaching by nonhuman primates may be, they are clearly very limited, contrasting starkly with the human norm of ubiquitous social transmission of actions in all modalities at virtually any point in social contact. The human tendency to develop conventional vocal signals appears, thus, to be dramatically advanced with regard to that of any other primate species.

Hockett and Altmann (1968) spoke of a design feature of human languages that they dubbed Specialization. Their use of the term encompasses what is called Conventionality here. For the purposes of this volume, I prefer to limit the term Specialization more severely than Hockett and Altmann did. I view a display as specialized for communication if its primary function, its primary *raison d'etre*, is communicative. Fixed signals, in my usage, show Specialization. Conventionality is more elaborate because it includes the requirement of learning. In this usage, nonhuman primates show specialized vocal systems that lack Conventionality, but there is some indication that important underpinnings for Conventionality (as seen in infant vocal flexibility) may have been available from very distant evolutionary time.

Humans diverge from nonhuman primates on Conventionality, and they do it in an undeniable way by the beginning of the second year of life, when conventional vocabulary begins to be acquired by babies. They do it in a more limited form, often before the onset of fully conventional words, when they begin to use consistent babbling forms in particular contexts (Blake & Fink, 1987), or "phonetically consistent forms" (Dore et al., 1976), word-like sound sequences for which infants and parents apparently negotiate values, as early as the second half-year of life.

The occurrence of Conventionality in a communication system does not impose a requirement of large numbers of communicative signals within a system possessing Conventionality any more than Free Expressivity does. At the same time, the possibility of using vocal units to express oneself freely and of learning communicative units that can be used for further expression opens the door to systems with very large numbers of potential values to transmit. Human languages provide extremely broad vocabularies, numbering in the thousands no matter how one counts and what natural language is considered.

Now and again one encounters cocktail party conversation to the contrary. I recall a physician friend who asserted that his secretary, who was of Amerind heritage, spoke a native American language with only a few hundred words. Leonard Bloomfield, one of the great structural linguists of the midcentury, a serious student of Amerind languages, is said to have recalled a similar incident in which after hearing the bold assertion, he had asked for the name of the impoverished language, but as usual under such circumstances, the assertion then evaporated into "I can't remember the name of the language," and "Oh excuse me while I visit with a friend over there." Bloomfield claimed that no language that had ever been seriously studied had been found to possess fewer than several thousand words. My friend's secretary may have only known a few hundred words of the language her ancestors had spoken, but the limitation was presumably in her knowledge of the language, not in the language itself.

If one takes seriously the numbers of words in dictionaries for languages with long-standing literatures, it would appear that languages can include hundreds of thousands of standard vocabulary items. Individual speakers also can be shown to have receptive knowledge of vast numbers of words, and estimating that number is complicated. Processes of inflectional and derivational morphology allow speakers to construct words that are not typically listed in dictionaries. Languages with so-called agglutinative properties (e.g., Turkish or many of the Amerind languages) sometimes involve more than 1 million inflected options for each root verb form, as well as huge numbers of possibilities for root nouns.

To understand the linguist's notion of inflection, consider a western language like Spanish, which has very few options compared to Turkish, but still has a notable system of verb inflection. The verb *to sing* [*cantar*] is conjugated in the present indicative tense *canto, cantas, canta, cantamos, cantáis, cantan*, meaning *I sing, you* [singular, familiar] *sing, he/she/it sings, we sing, you* [plural, familiar] *sing, they sing*. If we include other conjugations (for past, subjunctive, future, conditional, etc.) Spanish has more than 50 verb forms for each root verb. In much the same sense, highly inflected languages like Turkish have perhaps 2 million forms per verb. Such languages could thus be claimed to include at least hundreds of millions of potential words, if one allows each inflected form (not just each root) to count as a word.

Even in languages like English, where the number of verb forms is limited to a paltry group of four inflectionally different options (kiss, kisses, kissed, kissing), and nouns usually have just two forms (nation, nations), other options for word creation exist. Derivational rules (as opposed to inflectional rules) allow formation of many other words from roots, and these rules often show recursive properties that allow one to build longer and longer words by tacking on the same endings in a specific way, endlessly (consider national, nationalize, nationalization, nationalizational, nationalizationalize, etc.), encouraging the argument that the English vocabulary (and by implication the vocabularies of languages in general) is essentially infinite in size (Pinker, 1994).

The size of human sign systems is indefinitely large from several standpoints. On the one hand, knowledgeable speakers can create new vocabulary items by recruiting the resources of their morphological systems, and on the other hand, they can simply make up new words, either out of thin air, randomly combining syllables and attributing meanings to them at their pleasure (I think, from here on, I may refer to elephants as *akboks*), or by modifying existing words in phonological form or meaning (perhaps I shall refer to any creature with a prominent nose as an *elephantnase*). As other speakers of the language accept the new coinages, new words become a part of the language rather abruptly, and there is essentially nothing that the academies of language can do to stop it.

This ability to form new units of signal and value applies to both sides of the sign in humans—on the one hand, there is an indefinitely large repertoire of possible syllable sequences in natural languages, because there is no fixed limit on the length of words (more about this point later), and on the other hand there is an indefinitely large repertoire of possible values or meanings that can be designated by syllable sequences. We can, as humans, talk about anything we encounter, or anything we can imagine, and we can form vocabulary items from the raw materials of our phonological systems as we go.

Having reminded ourselves of the remarkable vocabulary freedom of human language, it is indeed startling to recognize how little resemblance exists between human and nonhuman systems in this realm. Nonhuman primates possess only small repertoires of signals and these have only small numbers of possible values that pertain to such immediate matters as danger, solicitation, threat, comfort, identification of location, and so on, and each of these is globally defined within the context of either a discrete or graded vocal signal (see Moynihan, 1970). Nonhuman primate systems essentially do not appear to provide latitude for the formation of new vocal signals to represent new ideas or values. Communicative systems of nonhuman primates in the wild are largely fixed on both sides of the sign, essentially limited to less than a dozen signal types that can be graded to create variations on each of the available themes.

The only important provisos to issue here are (a) that gradations of signals occurring in both human and nonhuman primates allow for a range of intensities for some sign types, and (b) that pongids have been shown capable of expanding their repertoires of gestural communicative signals in cases where they are trained to do so by humans (or in exceptional cases when trained to do so by pongids who have been trained by humans). It appears, however, that the numbers of acquirable signs in nonhumans is not very large, probably not more than a few hundred, even in the gestural domain (Terrace, 1979). As for vocal signals, acquisition of any new units appears extremely difficult to demonstrate. The herculean efforts of human investigators living with apes have yielded vocal learning by the pongids that can be deemed ambiguous at best.

From a practical standpoint, having a very large repertoire of signs would appear to require the property of Conventionality because prewiring of a very large number of sign connections might be unworkable. Large repertoires are not, of course, available even to humans at the beginning of life. Human infants begin with a repertoire of fixed signals that is similar in many ways to that of many nonhuman primates, including a small number of signals and a small number of values. Humans begin to diverge from their primate relatives in repertoire size as soon as they begin to acquire words, or as soon as they begin to formulate phonetically consistent forms. At that point Conventionality enters the property repertoire, and enormous lexical possibilities open.

PROPERTY 8: ARBITRARITY OF VALUES

Much has been written over the years about the Arbitrarity of the linguistic sign. Nothing about the sound of the word *rose* connects to the meaning designated except through a linguistic community's historical agreement to maintain the connection. There are several ways that inherent connections can exist between signals and values. Signals can (a) iconically represent their values (as the word *hiss* constitutes a hissing sound), (b) indexically indicate their values (as a track in the snow may index a wildcat, or a cough may index an airway problem), or (c) naturally present values with fixed signals provided by nature and maintained immutably within species. Arbitrary connections bypass all these kinds of connections and establish ties that involve no discernible similarity of signal and meaning, no indexing, and no naturally determined presentation. In keeping with the Arbitrarity principle, words can be formed by random attachments of syllables and values. Any syllables or syllable sequences from the inventory formed in accord with Syllabification principles discussed earlier can be united in signs with any illocutionary force, any concept, or any syntactic function that can be imagined.

Note that Arbitrarity is not the same thing as Conventionality, although the former depends on the latter. One can learn an iconic symbol (note that speakers of foreign languages would not necessarily guess the meaning of the word *hiss*, and it is not the only onomatopoetic word that might be used to represent the notion of hissing) and one can learn to interpret an indexical signal (note that physicians learn to recognize symptoms of disease, some of them in the voice), so it is possible to acquire conventional but nonarbitrary signs. The typical words of natural languages are both conventional and arbitrary.

Human infants begin to use arbitrary vocal signals by about 12 months of age, with the first words of the emergent lexicon. Of course some of the early words are onomatopoetic (e.g., meowing sounds to indicate the kitty), but many of the first lexical items are clearly noniconic. Consider [dada] *daddy*, [gagi] *doggie*, and [ma] *more* among the most common first words in American infants. By contrast, there is no incontrovertible evidence that arbitrary vocal signs have ever been learned by nonhuman primates. The best evidence would seem to be the Hayes' (1951) report of their home-reared chimpanzee having perhaps said *cup*, a contention about which even the proud human foster parents expressed little confidence. Of course visually based signs are far more accessible than vocal ones to nonhuman primates that have been home-reared. The point here is that Arbitrarity is a property that appears to be essentially restricted to humans in the vocal domain, and it is a property that emerges by the beginning of the second year in human infants.

PROPERTY 9: SEMANTICITY: ANALYTICAL REFERENTIALITY AND THE TRANSMISSION OF MEANING

The term *reference* has been utilized in a number of ways, and the differences in usage have been a source of confusion and dispute in the literature on comparative ethology. The key point of contention involves that fact that alarm calls of a variety of mammals, especially of the vervet monkey, have been argued to show vocal reference (Cheney & Seyfarth, 1982; Gozoules et al., 1995; Marler et al., 1992; Struhsaker, 1967). Similarly, food announcement calls are often specific enough to suggest Designation or reference to differing types of food (Hauser, 1996).

The literature on alarm calls was discussed earlier in connection with Designation. It is important to be clear about how (in my usage) Semanticity and Designation are distinct, or more precisely about how Semanticity is a property that presupposes Designation. Vocal Designation requires joint reference, supported by pointing, reaching, eye contact, or some other means of sharing attention,[10] and also supported by vocalization that expresses recognition of, attention to, interest in, or desire for the entity about which attention is shared. Note that in Designation the vocalization need not name the entity or in any way directly refer to it. The vocalization merely supports the act of joint attention. It might, for example, consist of a grunt, an exclamation of surprise, or a cry of frustration.

Semanticity requires an additional component beyond nonspecific vocalization. Again joint reference is implied, but in the case of vocal semantic acts, it is necessary that the speaker make specific vocal reference to the entity or entities about which attention is shared. It is clear that insofar as specific nonhuman primate calls can be elicited by specific classes of food or predators, and insofar as the calls have the effect on their conspecific listeners of drawing attention to specific classes of food or predators, they do indeed have a referential effect.

Vervet monkeys (and a variety of other mammals) are clearly intelligent. There is no reason to doubt, for example, that when the vervet hears the leopard call, the vervet understands that there is danger and that the possible danger owes to the putative sighting of a leopard. Consequently, when the vervet who hears an alarm begins to seek refuge or to look about for the possible predator (see Cheney & Seyfarth, 1980; Weary & Kramer, 1995), it seems reasonable to assume that the vervet has understood through the alarm call that the caller has drawn attention to the possible leopard by making reference to it in the course of sounding the alarm.

There is nothing to gain by quibbling over terminology here. Comparative ethologists have wanted to emphasize the special ways that differentiated

---

[10]In advanced linguistic communication, eye contact is totally unnecessary, of course. Reference can be shared through symbolization alone, and it is the property of Semanticity that makes such disembodied reference possible.

alarm calls demonstrate a foundation for a sort of reference, a function of vocalizations in nonhuman primates that was not known to be present in the
bulk of the vocal repertoires of such animals prior to the discovery of specific
alarm calls. Such an ability to make reference had not been previously documented in nonhumans. Indeed, recent investigations have shown in the specificity of alarm calls that not all aspects of the intentions or the effects of
vocalizations in nonhuman primates are purely emotive. Yes, alarm calls indicate a fearful emotion (as acknowledged in prior characterizations of primate vocal systems), but they also have the effect of designating the object of
fear in the listener, regardless of whether or not that designation is, in and of
itself, intentional on the part of the producer. The demonstration of the existence of specialized alarm calls is, thus, a major achievement in ethology.

Yet it is important to note that in the use of the term reference, in this context, ethologists have tended to talk past one of the intended audiences of the
discussion. Students of human communication and especially of child language tend to use the term in a more restricted way than is implied in the recent
ethological discussion. My goal in this section is both to clarify the fundamental difference in usage and to note that in light of the more restricted usage, humans can be seen to command reference in a more powerful way, and that the
advantage can be seen by the second year of life in the human infant.

The key to the difference in usage resides in the following condition:
When I say a child commands the property of Semanticity (or *referentiality* in
the common usage of the field of child language), I normally intend to indicate that the child is capable of referring to a class of entities analytically, to
designate that class specifically in a way that is free of contextual and illocutionary limitations. A variety of illocutionary forces are possible once
Semanticity is in place.

To illustrate the full power of Semanticity, consider the child who is
prereferential. Suppose a child says [ba] while playing a game involving a ball.
If this is the only circumstance under which the child uses [ba], we cannot be
sure the child is intentionally referring to the class of objects, balls, or
whether the utterance [ba] is merely produced in the context of a particular
game. Therefore we do not know whether the term [ba] analytically designates the class for the child or merely has the effect on mature listeners of invoking their awareness of a class of objects that the mature language
designates by the term *ball*.

One kind of evidence that the child does control Semanticity and its implied analytical referentiality to classes of entities can be seen when the usage
of the term [ba] is extended to new illocutionary conditions. Suppose the
child not only says [ba] while rolling the ball, but also points to the ball, looking up at the parent, then back at the ball while saying [ba], suggesting an illocutionary force we might call labeling. The game is not being played on this
occasion, nothing is requested in such circumstances, and no obvious emotion (only interest) is expressed. Suppose further that when the parent holds

the ball, the same child reaches for it, saying [ba] with a tone suggesting an illocutionary force of solicitation, and then after having been given the ball, the child seems appeased. Finally, suppose the same child points to the ball, and says [ba] with rising intonation, waiting for the adult to confirm that indeed the object is called *ball*. The child's illocutionary force in this last case is that of a question. Such variability of usage within the same child at a single age, pairing a single meaning and sound with multiple forces, provides evidence that the child understands the term [ba] to refer analytically to the class of objects, balls. The word [ba] can be said to have achieved semantic status. When the child uses the term, he or she intends for the listener to understand that in the act of communication, the class of objects is being invoked. By the age of about 18 months, humans use vocalizations in this way, where meaning and illocutionary force are distinguished; the two types of value are independently controlled. Each time the word is used, the class of objects is invoked, but the force and the emotion can be manipulated around the meaning thus transmitted.

It is worthwhile to note that Semanticity is not unambiguously present in the first words of human infants, at about 12 months of age. At this age, individual words usually seem to be tied to particular circumstances and corresponding forces. The ability to use a word in a way that is not bound to a particular illocutionary force, but rather allows the user to choose a force for each utterance, independent of the designated entities, is an achievement of early speech, not necessarily a simple product of associative word use and Conventionality.

The separation of meaning and force appears to occur at about the same point that childhood lexical growth accelerates notably in the so-called vocabulary burst (for discussions see Carey, 1982; Bates et al., 1996). The separation appears to manifest a major new insight that children achieve in the middle of the second year, the recognition that classes of entities can be labeled, and that the labels thus provided can be pure symbols, requiring no association with particular emotions or illocutionary intents.

We are often encouraged to take note of all the associations that can be conjured up in response to a particular word, and it has even been suggested by behavioristic thinkers that the meaning of a word constitutes the conglomerate of all these associations and emotional memories. Again I do not wish to quibble over terminology, but it is important to be clear that this sort of associative conglomerative network is not what I mean (or what linguistic philosophers in general mean) by meaning. Of course there are memories and associations and networks of connection between words and other cognitions, and in the common parlance, they can be said to be a part of meaning. However, in the technical sense of the term, the magic of meanings and the symbols that designate them is that they are founded on a great leap of insight conferring the power to make analytical reference through production or recognition of a vocalization (or some other kind of symbol) in spite of the associative memories (many of which are entirely irrelevant to the meaning) that might be invoked at the same time.

The vocabulary burst may in fact depend on the analytical insight implied by Semanticity. Once children understand that words can be symbols and can be attached to classes without restriction, children are in a position to use that knowledge actively in the development of a lexicon. Indeed, they seem to do so. In the second year of life, during the burst, children are often seen to walk about asking for parents to name objects for them. The rate of vocabulary acquisition during this period is truly astounding, rapidly reaching many words per day by the end of the second year (Carey, 1982).

Note also that the separation of meaning and illocutionary force provides the basis for efficient storage of lexical items. Without Semanticity, in a mind where each word would be required to represent both a meaning and a specific illocutionary force, the lexicon with a certain number of meanings would have to include many different phonological forms for each meaning to express multiple forces associated with that meaning. Real babies do not create lexicons like this, but if they did, here is what we would get: [ba] might mean *ball/solicitation* ("Give me the ball"), [mu] might mean *ball/designation* ("That thing is a ball"), [wo] might mean *ball/question* ("What is that thing [pointing to a ball]?"), and so on. With Semanticity in place, it is not necessary to have different words for each force–meaning pairing. One does not have to use up the available inventory of syllabic units and sequences to cover the multiplicity of forces, and consequently the size of the functional lexicon can be many times smaller. This is the way babies actually develop lexicons: For example, [ba] starts off meaning "ball" with a particular force and then the same syllable is extended to usage in many additional force contexts, with each different force being indicated by intonational or situational information.

The vocabulary burst appears to begin at a point at which some critical vocabulary size is reached (often around 50 words; Bates, 1996). Whether the change is actually burst-like or merely represents a gradual acceleration is of no concern here, because just as the growth of vocabulary may be sudden or gradual, so may the child's command of the insight of Semanticity develop suddenly or gradually. The insight, however fast it develops, may correspond with a period during which the child is feeling the pressure of increasing numbers of lexical items that initially are stored with force and meaning bound up together in each morphemic unit (consisting of a particular syllable or syllabic sequence). If the tie of force and meaning were not released, the pairing of new forces with old meanings would require storage of new lexical items. When the separation occurs, at the moment (or during the period) of referential insight, the child acquires the possibility of structuring storage more efficiently. Now each meaning can be assigned a place in a syllabically coded morphemic system. Each force also can be assigned a place coded in terms of some other kind of information, but the two can be kept separate. As additional individual meanings begin to be assigned a multiplicity of forces, the storage cost does not increase, because one meaning never need be associated with more than one morpheme. Each new meaning merely costs one new space in meaning storage, and the child has access to all the force possibilities for the new meaning automatically, without additional cost in memory. Ultimately the cost of storage for the lexicon is the sum rather than the product of the meanings and the forces. As the size of the lexicon grows, the advantage of the separation of force and meaning in the realm of storage grows accordingly. Even at a small lexicon size, say 20 words, the advantage could be notable. Imagine for the sake of argument that all 20 words are nouns and that there are five possible forces available to the child. That is 100 possible words in a system without Semanticity, but only a quarter as many after restructuring in accord with the analytical insight.

To operate efficiently, this two-layered system of values requires that the insight be applied with great generality. The human system shows this generality by applying the power of Semanticity throughout the lexicon. Absolutely any word that designates a class of entities can be used with a variety of forces, and once the insight is reached by children during the second year of life, this sort of flexibility in the relation of illocutionary force and meaning appears to spread rapidly throughout the lexicon.

Nonhuman primates, in contrast, do not show freedom from illocutionary binding in the use of vocalization. The leopard call in vervets, for example, is essentially restricted to usage as an alarm. Consequently, vocalizations used as alarms do not unequivocally include the analytical characteristic found in human infants. They are not flexibly used to designate, to request, to question, or to sound an alarm, but rather are restricted to one force only.

One proviso is relevant here. The cognitive foundations for Semanticity appear to be present in some nonhuman mammals (especially in apes, given patterns of usage of sign language in laboratory and home-reared pongids), although application of such an ability may be largely restricted to nonvocal domains. In vocal domains, nonhuman animals may restrict the usage of vocalizations to specific functions, in part because the restriction proves advantageous in fostering the kinds of communication that may be most important for the survival of the nonhuman primates that possess, for example, specific alarm and food calls.

It is important not to conclude prematurely that there are never illocutionary variations in usage of calls in nonhuman primates. Some cases of the leopard or eagle call in vervets have been observed in the absence of predators of any kind. Infant vervets sometimes use alarm calls inappropriately and must be instructed, by punishment from mature animals, to restrict the vocalizations to their alarm function (Caro & Hauser, 1992; Cheney, 1984). Thus it might be the case that individual vocalizations could be used more freely in vervets, but that survival needs incline the species to limit the usage. This is a possibility worth considering, but it should also be noted that it is hard to know what the infant vervet intends by these vocalizations produced in presumably inappropriate circumstances. There is no indication that when an infant vervet utilizes an alarm call this way the call has been intended to designate the leopard or some other predator. The call may be merely a sort of babbling, and if so, the act does not represent any kind of Designation or referentiality at all. Therefore, the fact that alarm calls may be used in infancy in the absence of the appropriate predator and in the apparent absence of fear does not provide convincing evidence of the presence of Semanticity in the nonhuman primate.

Perhaps to break up the terminological logjam that seems to separate ethologists from linguists and developmental psychologists, it would be useful to follow the suggestion of Owings and Morton (1998), noted in the earlier section on Designation. The authors advocate a special terminology, referential specificity (for informational meaning) and situational specificity (for illocutionarily bound values). In keeping with the literature in child language, we might modify the proposed terminology slightly and speak of analytical referentiality (Semanticity) in human speech and situationally bound referentiality in nonhuman primate vocal systems. In Hauser's (1996) significant treatise on communication in many species, he took pains to emphasize that the information that is transmitted in nonhuman primate vocal displays is connected, inherently, with context: "Information is a feature *of* an interaction ... not an abstraction that can be discussed in the absence of some specific context" (p. 6). Yet it is precisely this sort of abstraction, an abstraction of information from context, that characterizes the nature of meaning. Humans command information free of context within symbol systems, and the power to do so, founded in Semanticity, begins shortly after infants begin to build their lexicons in the second year of life.

PROPERTY 10: DISPLACEABILITY OF REFERENCE

Semanticity forms a basis for free utilization of words as symbols. On its foundation, children move toward command of a related property that has been termed *displacement* (Hockett & Altmann, 1968) or Displaceability. It is often noted that children begin language learning by talking about the here and now. They limit speaking to the circumstances of the immediate present. However, after Semanticity takes hold, new possibilities arise, and soon children understand and use words in making reference to classes of entities or events that are not currently in the physical setting.

There are three basic ways that children extend reference. First, they make reference to absent objects, as by noting or questioning the location of an object not in view ("Allgone ball" or "Where ball?"). Second, they make reference to objects or events of the past or future, as for example by saying "I hide ball," in response to a question about what the child did with the ball yesterday. In the most remarkable cases of the extension of reference, children learn to make reference to objects that are merely imagined. Mother and child are finger painting with purple, and she asks, "What are you thinking about?" and the child responds, "Purple ball."

The first of the extensions (to objects not present) occurs early in the process of vocabulary acquisition, and was significantly noted among Brown's (1973) summary of early semantic relations. He noted that when children by about 18 months of age begin to talk in multiple-word utterances, much of what they say has to do with existence ("that ball" meaning "that's a ball"), recurrence ("more ball" meaning "there's the ball again") or disappearance ("allgone ball") of objects. The extension of reference to circumstances outside the here and now thus can be said to begin typically at the middle of the second year of life with reference to objects not in view. Reference to past and future and to imaginary objects and events comes later.

The practical power of Displaceability seems fairly obvious. When the child is capable of displacement of reference, the possibility of sharing pure thoughts becomes possible. When our hominid ancestors acquired command of Displaceability, they surely acquired a notable survival advantage, because they had developed one of the key necessities for planning ahead as a group, reflecting on the mistakes of the past, and formulating new approaches for the future. They also acquired the possibility of artistic uses of language based on imagination, uses that may have played an important role in social connections and perhaps in individual mental health. Of course all of these practical functions may have been greatly furthered by subsequent evolution and development of more advanced functions of language that require syntactic structures.

As far as I can tell, nonhuman primates show no species-specific vocal patterns that manifest the Displaceability property. Signs learned by apes in the context of human rearing do show the property, so there is some reason for surprise that it has not been shown to be extended into usage in vocal repertoires of nonhuman primates. There is reason for suspicion that nonhumans may be more adept in this domain than we realize. Consider, for example, the following observation: "In a variety of nonhuman primate species, individuals vocalize before they move off into a new area. Somehow, and this is the mysterious part, such vocalizations appear to serve the function of group coordination and movement" (Hauser, 1996, p. 37).

Research on chimpanzees has shown that individuals that have been informed of the location of a food cache will lead the whole to troop to its location, even when the individuals that are given the privileged information about the location are not high-ranking members of the troop (Menzel, 1988). Even rhesus monkeys appear capable of transmitting such information. In a study by Mason and Hollis (1962) one monkey appeared to have developed undetermined signals to inform a partner monkey of the location of food that was in view of the first monkey; the first monkey who could not reach it, whereas the partner could reach but not see it.

Given such results it cannot be ruled out that planning and coordination of activities is possible through creative communication in nonhuman primates. It is not clear what role vocalization as opposed to postural and gestural actions may play in such communication. To this extent, we are unable to rule out the use of elaborate forms of vocal reference in nonhuman primates. However, it seems unlikely given current observations that any other primate, mature or infant, controls Displaceability to a degree that approximates even the abilities of a 2-year-old human.

PROPERTY 11: PROPOSITIONALITY

The beginnings of syntax are momentous, but still far less elaborate than one might imagine. There need be no function words, no bound morphemes, and no cohesion devices to bind clauses or sentences together in coreference at the point at which syntax begins. There need be no long sentences, no embedding, and no branching of complex phrase structures. In fact the property that begins the process may appear to be nothing more than the stringing together of two lexical items.

The achievement is, however, deceptively significant. There is more than meets the eye in this stringing together, because the resulting utterances have meanings that surpass the sum of the meanings of the words in the resulting string. "Daddy ball" may be interpreted, for example, to mean "Daddy throws the ball" or at least "Daddy does something to the ball." Quite a different meaning from "Daddy plus ball."

By the middle of the second year of life, human infants use two- and three-word sentences expressing a wide variety of semantic relations. Brown (1973) provided a celebrated summary of the commonly occurring semantic relations in early multiple-word utterances of young children all over the world. They include relations that express an awareness of objects and their presence or absence: existence ("there ball"), disappearance ("allgone ball"), and recurrence ("more ball"). They indicate relations among actors and objects in events: agent–object ("Mommy sock"), agent–action ("Daddy throw"), and action–object ("throw ball"). Further, they indicate specialized conditions of objects: possessor–object ("Mommy sock"), location–object ("chair ball"), and attributive–object ("big ball").

The interpretations of semantic relations can be made on the basis of context, or on the basis of intonation. The "Mommy sock" example is taken from Bloom (1970), who explained that her daughter had produced this utterance in two very different circumstances. In one, it was clear that she was indicating a sock belonged to Mommy. In the other she indicated Mommy was doing something to or with a sock. If the child holds the sock and says the utterance with contrastive stress on *Mommy*, it may be taken to mean that the sock belongs to Mommy, whereas if Mommy is putting the sock on, and the utterance is produced with stress on *sock*, it may be taken to mean that Mommy is doing something to the sock.

The number of semantic relations utilized in early child speech tends to be limited to those previously listed and very few additional possibilities. However, the very occurrence of multiple-word utterances represents a dramatic advance over communication in single morphemes.[11] The user of multiple words can be said to form propositions, stating something about something. Both of these somethings are represented by words that possess Semanticity, so the person who commands Propositionality commands the ability to abstract conceptions, to relate them to each other in a new way (remember that the semantic relation is something in and of itself, and is not the sum of the semantic characteristics of the words in a multiword utterance), and then to communicate that relation in a two-term utterance. The child who speaks in multiple words establishes frames of reference (topics) and comments on them. In "allgone ball" the child's topic is the ball, and the comment is that the ball has disappeared.

The only reported cases of multiword Propositionality in nonhuman primates concern apes learning sign language in the context of human rearing. Multisign sequences have been produced by chimpanzees and gorillas, but there remains question about whether the apes use the multiple-term sequences in quite the way humans (even at 18 months of age) do. Rather than producing sequences that are clearly intended to form coherent propositions, it seems possible that chimpanzees and gorillas generally produce successive one-word sequences (Bloom, 1970), where one term at a time is produced and where situational events conspire to create the appearance to the human observer of syntactic structure. If a child says "Mommy" and then a little later "sock," it may be the case that he or she has named both entities in sequence, implying no relation between them. A parent could, of course, impose on such a sequence a richer interpretation than the child intended. Similarly if a chimpanzee signs twice in sequence, it could be that the elements are syntactically unconnected in the chimpanzee mind. There has been quite an argument going on in the literature on ape communication regarding whether or not such sign sequences indicate a command of what I am calling Propositionality (Fouts, 1987; Pinker, 1994; Terrace, 1979; Terrace, Petitto, Sanders, & Bever, 1979).

The argument that has not happened to my knowledge concerns the possibility that vocal utterances of nonhuman primates ever show this sort of Propositionality. It would appear that vocal control of such complex communication is unique to the human species. To my knowledge, Snowdon (1982) described the most elaborate form of combinations of vocal units in nonhuman primates. The quotation refers to the cotton-top tamarin:

---

[11]Of course, utterances consisting of a single word sometimes function as whole sentences. If Bill asks "what's her name?" and Joe responds, "Gertrude," we understand Joe's single word to stand for an implied sentence. The same is true in some utterances of child speech. It is believed by many students of child language that one-word holophrases, especially near the middle of the second year of life, often have a sentential quality, wherein a single word makes a comment on some previously mentioned idea, forming an implied simple sentence.

The meaning of two frequently occurring phrases appeared to be the sum of the individual units. The first phrase consisted of a type E (alarm) chirp and a low arousal alerting call. This combination was always given after initial type E (alarm) chirps had aroused the animals. When this combination phrase occurred, the animals remained stationary and scanned the environment with reduced arousal. A short-time later they began to move about, giving only the low-arousal alerting call. (p. 231)

The description suggests a possible case of primitive Propositionality in a nonhuman primate. However, in the absence of clear Semanticity, it remains possible that the vocal combinations of alerting calls and alarm calls are not intentionally produced, but merely result from the varying awareness of the producer who alternates between thinking that he or she saw the predator or merely thought he or she saw it. The effect on the listener may be intermediate between that of alarm calls alone and alerting calls.

PROPERTY 12: SIGNAL ANALYSIS IN HUMAN VOCALIZATIONS

To this point the discussion of infrastructural properties has been infrasemiotic; it has treated foundations of usage for vocalizations—social usage, context-free usage, and community-based conventional usage. The remaining properties (12–18) to be treated are all concerned with the articulatory and acoustic content of vocalizations themselves. These properties pertain to the infraphonological domain.

Vocal sounds of any creature can by analyzed in terms of just a few physical parameters: fundamental frequency, intensity, duration, and spectrum. When we evaluate the sounds of nonhuman primates, acoustic analysis is often used to provide data on these parameters for each sound type in a species' repertoire. The same approach is used with speech and other human vocalizations.

Let it be clear at the outset that nonhuman primates utilize a wide variety of sound types and that differences among fixed vocal signals in nonhuman primates are based on many physical features. Relatively little study has been devoted to developing a general characterization for the ways that nonhuman primate sounds are differentiated. A recent commentary (Ybarra, 1995) on such work emphasized that there is much more to be done to help overcome the false perception that the anatomy of nonhuman primate vocal tracts severely constrains phonological production. In fact, a wide variety of sounds manipulating spectrum, fundamental frequency, intensity, and duration is physically possible, and as Ybarra (1995) emphasized, "data gathered in my laboratory and ... information from available references ... demonstrates that the vocal tract of non-human primates has morphologically inherent sound output capabilities more diversified than has so far been realized" (p. 186).

Ybarra (1995) was surely correct that there is good reason for interest in evaluating the rich vocal capabilities found in nonhuman primates. However, it is not the physical analysis of sounds that is of primary interest here. In the search for fundamental properties of vocal communication, we seek to characterize capabilities of the organism that uses a communicative system. When we observe the primates, we find a remarkable discontinuity in the deployment of physical parameters to create potential signals or vehicles of communication. Although contrasts among primate vocalizations are specifiable in terms of acoustic parameters, no primate other than the human, as far as we know, actually controls the parameters independently and intentionally in the formation of signals. Evidence of Contextual Freedom in the manipulation of acoustic dimensions has not been reported in nonhuman primates. As in prior cases, we can dispense with providing empirical support for adult human capabilities in these domains, because it is obvious that normal mature persons are able to vary pitch, intensity, duration, and spectrum of speech-like sounds in quite systematic and voluntary ways. Singing represents a systematic implementation of such abilities as art.

Moreover, human infants, by the Expansion stage, already show the ability and the inclination to manipulate the physical parameters of vocalization independently. Expansion stage infants produce both squeals and growls, representing the ends of the pitch continuum. Extremely high fundamental frequencies, presumably the highest ones of which infants are capable, are heard in repetitive, clearly intentional bouts of squealing. Extremely low fundamentals, presumably the lowest possible, are heard in similar bouts of growling. In our longitudinal studies it appears that essentially all human infants do both squealing and growling during the Expansion stage (Oller, 1980a). Why? I have speculated that they do both in an effort to master the acoustic and articulatory dimension of pitch or tonality.

In a similar way, infants appear to practice control of the intensity dimension by producing systematic exemplars from the loudest to the quietest sounds that the vocal tract allows. Infants both yell and whisper, again in systematic bouts of repetitive vocalization, often with no obvious social intent. The vocalizations appear to be produced purely for interest or amusement. Why? I contend that infants seek to control the intensity dimension.

Resonances of the vocal tract are controlled by shaping it, rounding the lips, lowering the jaw, raising the tongue, and so forth. The effect of posturing the tract during vocalization is to produce specific spectral effects associated with the resonant characteristics of the tract in each of its possible shapes. Languages use these various postures to create vowel contrasts. Human infants practice variable posturings and consequent spectral effects during full vowel play. They typically explore the vowel space, producing a wide variety of vowel-like sounds during the Expansion stage (Lieberman, 1980; Pierce, 1974). We have witnessed Expansion stage infants in one period producing long sequences of vowels in one region of the potential space, and then switching to another region of the space, producing a different vowel-like sound repetitively. I submit that this exploration represents a systematic attempt to control the vocal possibilities of resonance.

The last of the four parameters is duration. Again, infants produce sounds with a wide variety of durations. Quasivowels are typically of short duration, often less than 200 msec. Other vocalizations, often full vowels, can be produced with durations many times that long (Robb & Saxman, 1990). Again, infants appear to explore the possibilities of the vocal dimension systematically and thoroughly.

The study of protophone development revealed the tendency of human infants to produce such systematic variability and thus to display control, including Contextual Freedom, over the many acoustic dimensions in terms of which we interpret speech-like sounds. No other mammal has been documented to show such exploration of and systematic control over Signal Analysis. Instead, it might be said that the fixed vocal signals utilized by other mammals show control over Signal Analysis only insofar as gradations in the sounds are used to express different intensities of emotion or intent. The vocal elements of repertoires of nonhuman primates can be said to be holistic in that the internal structure that differentiates one element from another is not independently accessible and analyzable by the organism. Each nonhuman primate utterance type operates as a unified whole, distinct from all other types, yet the complex of acoustic characteristics that yield that distinction from other types remains bound to each utterance, and the parameters of sound are not found to be treated independently in vocal play or in the formation of new potential utterance types. Systematic vocal play or manipulation of Signal Analysis in systematically alternating sequences appears to be essentially absent in nonhuman primates.[12]

PROPERTY 13: CATEGORICAL ADAPTATION

One of the steps in the process of forming a broad and open repertoire of transmission units is founded on Signal Analysis. A powerful communication system requires that new units be formed, and a creature that can systematically control dimensions possesses tools to form units efficiently. I call the formation of new discrete units (new signals) on the basis of systematic manipulation of articulatory and acoustic dimensions Categorical Adaptation.

The adaptation is categorical because distinctions can be created as discrete units along dimensions that are controlled. With this control over quantized dimensions in place, there is the possibility of developing contrastive units as needed for transmission of information, or to put it another way, as needed to form new basic unit types to be used in lexical items.

---

[12]Again, it may be prudent to caution that Elowson and colleagues (1998) found practice-like vocalization in infant marmosets. Whether these activities can be shown to involve analytical manipulation of Signal Analysis remains to be seen.

Signal Analysis provides the raw tools, but quantization is necessary in addition to create workable contrastive units.

The human system of vocal quantization is partly built around a simple but elegant principle that provides contrasting units that are easily categorized and featurally organized in such a way that speakers can generate new signals at will in accord with the language's featural design. Although syllabic signals vary continuously along physical dimensions, they are treated by human speakers and listeners as pertaining to discrete categories. This quantization or discreteness principle (Hockett, 1960a; Hockett & Altmann, 1968) is applied generally to syllabic units and results in signals that are naturally organized into featural groupings. The quantization principle of course applies to categorization of all sorts of stimuli whether visual, tactile, or auditory. Harnad (1987) referred to such categorization as "the groundwork of cognition" in the title of his influential book. Quantization is important to recognize because it forms the basis for discrete transmission units that can be manipulated freely in the formation of phonological vocabulary units, but the uniqueness of human vocal quantization is found not in its mere existence (much of cognition is structured in a quantized fashion throughout the animal kingdom), but rather in its adaptability, to which I return shortly.

To illustrate quantization in speech, consider that [ba] is distinct from [ma] in the same way that [da] is distinct from [na]. In both cases an explosive stop sound [b] or [d] is contrasted with a nasal sound [m] or [n]. Members of each pair are produced through articulation at a particular point in the vocal tract (at the lips for [b] and [m], and at the alveolum for [d] and [n]). Similarly, [ba] is distinct from [da] in the same way that [ma] is distinct from [na] based on a place of articulation feature. Each syllable is analyzable in terms of such features, and speakers are able to vary the features independently. Thus, the syllables are not holistically confined, but are decomposable and reconstructable in terms of features such as place of articulation or nasality. The decomposition and reconstruction allows speakers to make up new syllables. The featural differences are general, applying to other contrasts beyond those presented here as examples, and in each case the differences are treated in accord with the quantization principle.

Quantization can be illustrated experimentally. If one presents syllables repetitively every second or so, gradually changing (through an acoustic manipulation controlled instrumentally) the properties of the syllable from those of [ba] to those of [da] in a dozen steps, there is a region of acoustic change that yields little if any change in perception. The first five or six syllables each gradually modified in the direction of the properties of [da] continue stubbornly to sound like [ba], even though the acoustic properties are changing by a constant amount with each step as measured by the instruments. However, as the change continues, a point is reached where the percept abruptly shifts to [da], and then the remaining syllables in the series sound like [da], even though they also continue to change by the same constant amount that was programmed into the series. This quantization tendency is often called categorical perception (Cooper, Delattre, Liberman, Borst, & Gerstman, 1952; Liberman et al., 1954; Liberman et al., 1956; physical changes within category—[ba] or [da]—tend to be ignored by the ear, whereas physical changes across categories—from [ba] to [da]—are treated as significant).

Two empirical tests are typically made to show categorical perception. The first involves labeling: The syllables on the [ba] side of the boundary are called [ba] and those on the [da] side are called [da], and the shift occurs sharply near the boundary. The second involves discrimination: any pair of syllables that are chosen from within a category are harder to discriminate than any pair that are chosen from between categories.

The advantage of quantization is that the possibility for confusion among signals is constrained (see Harnad, 1987), even in a situation (such as that found in human language) where a large number of signals is utilized. The words *map* and *nap* are perfectly distinct, even though they differ minimally in terms of features. Each word designates a meaning, and small changes in the pronunciation of either word do not disturb that designation. By quantizing features and then applying them generally across pronunciations of many syllables, it becomes possible to develop a large number of signals that are easily recognized based on a small number of vocal manipulations, and each of these signals can be used to designate distinct meanings.

The property emphasized in this section is termed Categorical Adaptation because not only can features be generalized throughout a human linguistic system, but also new features can be acquired in the course of language acquisition. Infants in babbling develop a core set of syllables that they produce in a manner that is judged contrastive by adults. This core set of syllables is relatively universal across infants in a variety of cultures and is based on a small set of features. Universally occurring contrasts include oral versus nasal consonants, stops versus glides, labial versus nonlabial consonants, and high versus low vowels (Jakobson, 1939/1971a). If no further contrasts were added, it would still be possible to create a set of lexical signs far exceeding that of other creatures; however, further contrasts are added. Mature languages typically include many additional features, sometimes requiring remarkable adaptations of articulation in the course of learning. For instance, Bantu languages often include a variety of click consonants (involving velaric suction as in kissing), Indic languages often include a series of retroflex consonants (where the tongue must be curled up and back), and Amerind languages often include numerous ejective stops (requiring a preplosive buildup of high pressure between the glottis and the articulatory closure for stops). Such features must be acquired in pronunciation learning by the child who would speak any of these languages.

Infants begin this process of linguistically specific Categorical Adaptation early, not later than the second year of life, and perhaps even earlier. Some studies suggest that even in the first year of life, infants pronounce syllable-like sounds in a way that shows the special influence of their (soon-to-be) native language (de Boysson-Bardies & Vihman, 1991; Konopczynski, 1985), although others suggest that the adaptation to specific ambient sounds of language may begin later (Olney & Scholnick, 1976; Thevenin, Eilers, Oller, & LaVoie, 1985). The introduction of new syllable types that are based on previously unused features (such as suction-based plosion or retroflexion of the tongue) of sounds would provide undeniable evidence of early linguistically specific Categorical Adaptation.

In addition, however, it should be noted that the generalization of existing features of sound into new syllabic contexts represents another kind of Categorical Adaptation (not requiring new features), and it may occur within the first year of life. By the Canonical stage of vocal development, infants produce syllables that are not only well formed, but in many cases clearly distinct to the adult ear. It is not clear how early in life the ability to generalize features of syllables appears (the question has not been systematically investigated to my knowledge), but it is clear that during the Canonical stage, infants develop a wide variety of syllables that are clearly distinct, and that phonetic properties do seem to be propagated in the system. So, for example, an infant with patterns such as [ba], [da], and [ma] eventually also produces [na], suggesting that the nasality feature found in [ma] has been extended to an alveolar articulation similar to that found in [da]. Such patterns of development, although needing further empirical verification, suggest that during the first year of life, generalization of syllabic patterns is already available to the human infant.

To this point in the discussion of Categorical Adaptation, the entirety of the focus has been on features of well-formed syllables and the infant's ability to acquire new quantal categories of such canonical syllables. It seemed natural to begin the discussion there, because so much research has been done on syllable categorization and quantal characteristics of well-formed speech sounds. However, a persuasive argument can be made that creative Categorical Adaptation begins to occur in the human infant well before canonical syllables have been developed. During the Expansion stage, when infants explore individual dimensions such as pitch or resonance, they create obvious polar contrasts between precanonical syllables of opposite character on the dimensions. The sounds go on to be utilized for a variety of purposes—some social, some nonsocial—tailored to the individual infant's interests. The key observation here is that Categorical Adaptation is built in human infants on the raw foundation of Signal Analysis and does not require well-formed syllables to support it. Categorical Adaptation, then, based on the systematic analysis dimensions of vocalization that are available, begins to develop at least by late in the first half of the first year of life in human infants.

In perception of speech sounds, infants in the very early part of the first year also appear to adapt to the categorical system of their native language. In fact the tendency to perceive quantized vocal signals categorically begins in the newborn period. Infants in the first months of life perceive many syllables in discrete groupings that include the categorical discrimination pattern (Eilers et al., 1981; Eimas et al., 1971; Moffit, 1971; Morse, 1972; Trehub, 1976). The ability to perceive speech-like sounds categorically surely provides a key foundation for infants because they need to be able to recognize distinctions to which they will later be required to adapt in production. During the first year there is additional evidence that infants' perceptual capabilities for sounds relevant to the language of their environment are enhanced (Eilers, Gavin, & Oller, 1982; Eilers, Oller, & Benito-Garcia, 1984; Lasky, Syrdal-Lasky, & Klein, 1975; Streeter, 1976). Further, infants learn specifically to ignore previously perceptible contrasts that prove to be irrelevant in their native languages (Best, 1994; Werker & Tees, 1984).

Nonhuman primates, on the other hand, as far as we know, do not adapt to new featural possibilities in vocalization. Their systems are constrained holistically and are not decomposed or treated analytically by users except insofar as graded signals show systematic variations correlated with intensity of intended communication.

Nonhuman primates appear to be very much more limited in their use of vocal signals and their ability to adapt them to new forms, but it would be far too strong to claim that nonhumans lack discrete vocal categories. Since Marler's (1975, 1976) early work on categorization of vocalizations in primates, a distinction between discrete and graded vocalizations has been well-established. Some species, according to the reasoning, tend to show more graded vocalizations (e.g., macaque), whereas others show more discrete ones (e.g., blue monkey). Vervet alarm calls have been held up as the ideal examples of the discrete pattern. Well-defined acoustic boundaries can be indicated for the different categories of alarm. For example, the call indicating danger from above ("eagle") can easily be distinguished from the call indicating danger from below ("leopard"). Not only does it appear to humans that signals of many nonhuman primate species function discretely, but experimental work with playback of recorded or synthetic calls from conspecifics also indicates that various species recognize the functionally different sounds discretely as such (e.g., Masataka, 1983, for Goeldi's monkeys; Snowdon, 1987b, for pygmy marmosets; or Hopp, Sinnot, Owren, & Petersen, 1992, and May, Moody, & Stebbins, 1989, for Japanese macaques). There is, however, controversy over the extent to which the full pattern of categorical perception of conspecific vocalizations in nonhuman primates has been demonstrated. After reviewing the subject, Hauser (1996) concluded that many studies have explored categorical perception of signals from species-specific repertoires of primates:

> And have provided relatively convincing evidence of categorical labeling functions (classifying stimuli as representative exemplars of one category but not another) but, in general, less convincing evidence of categorical discrimination functions (i.e., enhanced sensitivity at the category boundary). (p. 539)

Nonhuman primates appear thus to show quantization of vocal signals at least to the functional extent implied by the tendency to produce signals that are neatly distinguishable and that are labeled categorically by conspecifics. Nonhuman primates do not necessarily show the tendency to discriminate between-category pairs of stimuli better than within-category pairs.

Surprisingly, there do exist reports of categorical discrimination in nonhumans, but the stimuli in question are human syllables. For example, Kojima & Kitriani (1989) found a tendency toward categorical discrimination of voiced stops at the human category boundary in the chimpanzee. In a more recent example, there is evidence that the /ra/–/la/ distinction of English is treated perceptually in a generally English way by the Japanese macaque (*Macaca fuscata*), even in terms of adjustments of the perceived phonemic boundary under the influence of multiple cues that participate in a trading relation, a feature of categorical perception that had been hypothesized to be human only (Sinnott & Brown, 1997). In fact the initial claim from the early 1970s (Eimas et al., 1971) that human infant perception of speech categories indicated a human specific innate capability has been dismantled systematically. The lowly chinchilla can categorize stop consonants much as adult humans do (Kuhl & Miller, 1978), and a number of birds have been shown to perceive speech syllables categorically as well (Dent, Brittan-Powell, Dooling, & Pierce, 1997; Kluender, Diehl, & Killeen, 1987; Lotto, Kluender, & Holt, 1997). The zeitgeist of research in the current period is amenable to the idea that speech perception is built on an auditory foundation that humans share with other primates, mammals, and even birds (Jusczyk, 1992).

Oddly then, perception of human speech by nonhuman primates and other animals is fairly well-established even though Hauser (1996) questioned the extent of our knowledge of quantization in vocal signals of nonhuman primates themselves. He noted that potential confusion about how nonhuman primates function vocally is attributable to the fact that the distinction between discrete and graded signals

> is problematical on two counts. First, though acoustically bounded signals can be established, vervets often produce heterogeneous call bouts, each bout consisting of different call types (Hauser and Fowler, 1991). Consequently, although the call may represent one unit, a string of calls may represent a higher-order unit and one that makes the discrete-graded distinction more difficult to assess. Second, and more importantly, what we perceive as a discrete call type may not represent the fundamental unit from the vervets' perspective ... [to resolve the matter] we will require more sophisticated observations. (p. 628)

The discussion of quantization and related matters in nonhuman primates has an interest of its own, but it should be made clear that in general the questions are whether fixed signals of various creatures are graded or discrete, and if the latter, whether they are categorically perceived. The same questions could be posed about human fixed vocal signals, with about the same level of intrinsic interest, but as far as I know they have not been raised at all. A comparison between human and nonhuman systems at this level would be appropriate in my opinion. To ask, on the other hand, whether discrete fixed signals of an ape show the properties of human speech in the absence of comparison with human fixed signals is ill-conceived. To a large extent, the concern over categorical perception of vocalizations in nonhuman primates has been confounded by the shoe-horning error considered extensively earlier in this volume. Scholars have been encouraged to evaluate perception and production of sounds in nonhuman primates in a way that is structured according to human unit types that the nonhuman primates simply do not possess. The fact that nonhumans command categorical speech perception is interesting, but it is not balanced to evaluate nonhuman speech perception in the absence of research on fixed signal perception.

Nonhuman primate fixed signals may show vocal quantization at some level, and it seems likely that human fixed signals do as well. Neither human nor nonhuman fixed signals appear to show the flexibility of quantization exhibited by human speech. Vocal features of fixed signals are not generalized to new settings, and consequently, whatever quantization exists cannot be exploited for the purposes of generating novel signals. The lack of reported evidence of the learning of new types of contrasts in vocalization suggests that in nonhuman primates, Categorical Adaptation of vocalizations may be entirely absent. The only cases I know of in which a nonhuman primate has been claimed to produce new sounds are associated with human-reared chimpanzees (see, e.g., Hopkins & Savage-Rumbaugh, 1986; Kellogg & Kellogg, 1933) and the reported results suggested only very limited adaptation.

PROPERTY 14: SYLLABIFICATION

Syllables are the minimal rhythmic units of natural phonological systems. Any temporally based communication system that aims to have broad power requires a rhythmic structure around which to build units of varying complexity. A temporally defined minimal rhythmic unit has the virtue of providing both producer and receiver with a reference point for analysis of the potentially complex stream of units. Without a definition of how these reference units are to be formed, the perceiver of the system would be left to do inefficient searches of communicative events of extremely variable complexities and durations. Therefore syllables (or something resembling syllables) are a natural requirement of any temporally based system of communication.

The human system of Syllabification includes special features that appear to provide the basis for power in vocabulary development or evolution. These key characteristics have been discussed earlier as principles of canonical syllable formation (chaps. 4 and 5). They include potentially differentiable internal structures (segments) bound together by rapid transitions from margin to nucleus. These characteristics of Syllabification are present in the infant by the Canonical stage, which is to say that by 6 months of age or so, the human infant commands a differentiable speech-like structure that is unique among the primates.

Each well-formed syllable includes both a nucleus (or vowel-like element) and a margin (or consonant-like element), and these must be connected through a rapid movement of the vocal articulators, resulting in a rapid formant transition. These characteristics are, of course, key principles of canonical syllable formation for all natural languages. The emphasis here must be on the fact that the internal structure and rapid transition between the elements of that structure provide a critical foundation for a system of manipulable units that can transmit information at high rates (see chap. 5). Formant transitions correspond to rapid and differentiable movements of the vocal articulators, which form the basis for distinctions that yield a potentially huge inventory of syllabic units.

The core method of differentiation among syllables is found in articulation, which can be characterized in terms of the postures and movements of the vocal tract. These differences in posture and movement types yield spectral characteristics changing with time, and these are precisely the kinds of changes that humans use as a primary means to distinguish among vocabulary units. The English word *day* is distinct from *bay* in that the lips articulate the margin of the latter syllable, whereas the tongue articulates the former. The differences in articulators and their movements yield differences in formant transition slopes, and these are easily detected by the auditory system. Changes in how *day* or *bay* are produced in realms of pitch, intensity, duration, or vocal quality (within fairly broad limits) do not change the identity of the syllables or meanings they represent in English. The word *gay* is formed by a different tongue articulation from that used in *day*, and again the resulting formant transition is distinctive. This word can also be pronounced at high or low pitch, high or low intensity, long or short duration, or with any number of vocal qualities without changing its identity as a word. The illocutionary force or emotional content may vary with such changes, but *bay*, *day*, and *gay* remain the same words owing to their articulatory characteristics.

The examples indicate different words of English, but the point here is that the syllables are distinct (independent of meaning) and that the distinctiveness is housed in vocal posture and movement properties that function independently from a variety of other acoustic changes that can be made. Human infants show control over this independent syllabic structure by the Canonical stage. Different syllables, for example [ba] or [dɪ], are produced with well-formed margins, nuclei, and formant transitions, and thus the basis is laid for true vocabulary distinctions.

It appears that no nonhuman primate system of vocalization utilizes articulatory structure of this sort in an extensive, systematic fashion. There are, to be sure, descriptions of the vocalizations of certain monkeys that suggest a minimal margin–nucleus distinction in very small repertoires of units. The terms *mast* (which I interpret as roughly parallel with the notion of margin) and *flag* (roughly, nucleus) have been used to refer to acoustic elements that differentiate at least one pair of vocalizations (one member of the pair is referred to as half-masted) in the squirrel monkey (Smith, Newman, & Symmes, 1982). The differentiation of these monkey calls may depend on articulatory differences, but it is important not to miss the key point that differentiates the monkey usage and human capability. The evidence suggests that the squirrel monkey controls this kind of articulatory distinction within the limited settings and functions that the vocalizations in the repertoire serve. There is no evidence to my knowledge that such articulatory distinctions are a primary basis for the formation of new potential units that appear at first as mere sounds, unconnected to pragmatic functions. Masts and flags appear to constitute fixed patterns of vocalization that cannot be adjusted to create new units of vocalization or to express new functions.

Having developed independent articulatorily based units, human infants possess the groundwork for additional properties (see later) that allow the formation of novel units differentiated by articulatory distinctions not already in the repertoire of species-typical fixed signals. By contrast, the utterance units of nonhuman primate repertoires appear to function holistically, and apparent articulatory characteristics of such vocalizations are not exploited beyond the limited cases of usage in fixed signals. The repertoire of physical distinctions in vocalizations of nonhuman primates is minimal in size, never approaching the syllable inventory possibilities of any natural language, or even of a midcanonical stage human infant.

The limitation of interest here in nonhuman primate vocalization is not of a trivial anatomical sort. I do not claim that nonhuman primates lack the anatomical necessities for producing syllables. On the contrary, the peripheral vocal tracts of all nonhuman primates are (obviously) capable of assuming postures that could yield both formants and formant transitions. To the extent that there is a limitation, it is primarily one of neural control over the vocal tract and the ability to coordinate phonation and articulation in the way humans do. Even these neural limitations are far from absolute. The brains of nonhuman primates make it possible for them, in appropriate social circumstances, to produce quite a range of vocal sounds. Some baboons produce sounds that have formant structure with notable resemblance to human vowels (Andrew, 1976; Owren, Linker, & Rowe, 1993). Perhaps more significantly, although there may be limitations to the types of phonation possible in nonhuman primates, some show the capability to produce sounds that appear to go beyond those that humans control. For example, although it has been claimed that chimpanzees cannot phonate as precisely as humans do

(Keleman, 1948), there are phonatory capabilities in the chimpanzee that are nonetheless notable, including a type called *diplophonia* (implying a coordinated action of lip and nonlip cover layers of the vocal cords) in the work of Keleman. Further, a general conclusion from a recent review (Owren & Linker, 1995) on primate phonation and vowel-like sound capabilities suggested that fields have been reversed since the period of Lieberman's (1968) influential claim that nonhuman primates have severe limitations in vowel-like sound production. Owren and Linker (1995) noted that Lieberman:

> suggested that monkeys and apes are unable to maintain precise control over vocal fold vibration and therefore cannot produce highly regular, tonal sounds analogous to human vowels. While supralaryngeal cavities clearly exert a filtering effect on source energy during non-human primate vocal production, it has also been suggested that significant modification of the vocal tract shape does not occur. ...

> Sufficient data are now available to arguably counter both of these assertions ... highly tonal vocalizations in many different species—calls that indicate a high level of vocal fold control ... pronounced harmonic structure ... F0's ... can be lower ... or many times higher ... than corresponding rates in humans. ...

> ... also ... strong evidence [has been reported] of vocal tract filtering [yielding formant modifications] in a number of nonhuman primates. (pp. 4–5)

Ybarra (1995) concluded that in spite of certain limitations in replicating the human pattern of phonation precisely, the rich glottal control capabilities of many nonhuman primates suggest a "range-expanded capability for phonation, [and] it is conceivable that non-human primates use their consequential F0 diversity to configure a vocal communication repertoire based more on F0 contrasts ... than on formant patterning and transitions" (p. 192).

The ability to produce widely ranging sounds, especially in the domain of F0, has been especially noted in monkey species. *Macaca mulatta*, for example, has been found capable of producing spike-like F0 patterns characterized by a very rapid, steep, and pronounced frequency upsweep that peaks very high and downsweeps just as precipitously (Hauser & Marler, 1993). Human patterns of frequency movement are deemed neither so abrupt nor so wide ranging. According to Hauser and Marler's (1993) review, similar patterns of F0 movement are found in gibbons and squirrel monkeys.

Such rapid frequency changes inevitably inspire comparison with formant transitions of human syllables, and the question of whether these frequency sweeps could have been captured for syllable-like functions through some evolutionary process in nonhuman primates arises. The point of this discussion is that with all the physical potentials of vocalization in nonhuman primates, the human line is the only one that appears to have exploited the potentials of vocalization to command Syllabification. The raw materials (vowel-like spectra, rapid sweeps of sound properties, varying phonatory capabilities) are apparently present to varying degrees in many of our primate relatives, but in spite of these abilities, nonhuman primate utterances appear to have remained functionally holistic. None of the nonhuman animals seems to have reached the point where the internal structuring of syllable-like units became productive and creative, yielding a system of potential contrasts manipulated independently of the ecological and social contexts to which primate fixed signals are bound.

PROPERTY 15: RECOMBINABILITY OF SYLLABLES

Syllabification provides the fundamental units of talk. Categorical Adaptation secures the generalizable quantization of presyllabic and syllabic features and the ability of human speakers and listeners to acquire new features under the influence of their linguistic community. It is another property, however, Recombinability of syllables, that is required to provide the system of Syllabification with the power to produce vocabularies of unbounded size. Through recombination of differing syllables it is possible to create strings of unbounded variety. For example, [ba] and [da], both of which can be words, can be strung together in bisyllabic sequences as [baba], [dada], [bada], or [daba], four new potential words (2^2). Similarly, eight trisyllables can be obtained through recombination of two syllables (2^3). The possibilities increase dramatically as the number of syllables allowed increases, and we have only considered two possible syllable types. As noted, every natural language includes many syllable types. Imagine a natural language with only 10 syllables (an implausibly low number for a natural language to possess); it is clear that 100 (10^2) bisyllabic sequences and 1,000 (10^3) trisyllabic sequences can be formed within the language. Languages with relatively small numbers of distinct syllables tend to have long words. If our imaginary language allows words up to only seven syllables in length (words no longer than *recombinability*), then 10,000,000 (10^7) words could be formed at this length alone.

Languages do not tend to use up every one of the possible ways of recombining individual syllables in creating real vocabulary items, but speakers of languages recognize the possibilities and new words can be formulated as needed. Thus Recombinability is one of the properties that opens the door to the formulation of massive potential vocabularies. Because there is no effective length limitation on words in natural languages, potential phonetic vocabularies of human vocal systems are effectively of indefinite size. The system can be said to be open, by virtue of Recombinability.

The ability to recombine well-formed syllables begins in the Canonical stage, virtually at the point at which sequences of syllables begin to be produced. Early empirical reports on infants in the Canonical stage suggested that reduplicated sequences appeared early in the stage and that variegated (recombinations of distinct) syllables tended to follow (Elbers, 1982; Oller,

1980a) especially in the Integrative stage. Later systematic observation did not confirm this expectation across groups of children (Mitchell & Kent, 1990; Smith et al., 1989), concluding instead that systematic recombination seemed to begin at the very beginning of the production of utterances consisting of multiple well-formed syllables.

No nonhuman primate vocal communication system includes an open system of vocabulary units. The essentially fixed repertoires of vocalization systems in nonhuman primates show no clear indications of Recombinability yielding new vocabulary items. Indeed, the term *vocabulary* does not seem to apply at all, as vocal units in nonhuman primates appear to consist exclusively of fixed signals with fixed values. Vocabulary necessarily implies Conventionality. Reports of vocal sequences in some primate groups suggest that systematic sequences of fixed signals are, however, sometimes manipulated to yield a sort of rudimentary syntax with variable strings, although the potential function of such variations remains obscure (Hauser, 1996).[13] At this time, animals do not appear to use the capability for Recombinability of vocalizations in the creation of new functional units.[14] Still, the systematic use of differing sequences composed of fixed signals is notable and suggests an important parallel with human systems.

PROPERTY 16: RHYTHMIC HIERARCHY

A key aspect of the control of syllabic patterns in speech is associated with hierarchical structuring of rhythmic units. If there were no such structuring, the speaker and listener would be unable to make use of chunking to help manage the processing of long strings. A single syllable, being a minimal rhythmic unit, can constitute a word. At the same time, a single word can consist of many syllables, a phrase can consist of many words, a sentence of several phrases, and a paragraph of several sentences. The ability to manipulate this sort of hierarchical system is critical in human speech, and one of its beginning points is seen remarkably early in life.

The production of multiple well-formed syllables within individual breath groups begins with the Canonical stage. These groupings have all the necessary physical characteristics to serve as words or short, unbroken phrases. Perhaps even more surprisingly, human infants show an ability to produce hierarchical phrasing of primitive syllable-like units even in precanonical protophone production from not later than the third month of life (Lynch, Oller, Steffens, & Buder, 1995; Nathani, 1998; Oller & Lynch, 1992). The precanonical syllables thus produced by infants are of about the same mean

---

[13]In marmoset groups, it has been reported by Elowson et al. (1998) that infants sometimes produce sequences of vocalizations, each of which resembles an adult fixed signal. The sequences, however, appear to be unique, and to have no functional significance, except perhaps as sound play.

[14]Birds also show recombinations of vocal units in song. For an impressive example of apparent recombination see Hailman, Ficken, and Ficken (1987).

durations as syllables in adult citation-form readings (around 300 msec). Higher order rhythmic units of these infant discourses may also match mean durational values of adult speech for phonological feet (roughly, words) and phrases.[15] The same hierarchical ability is reinstated with well-formed syllables during the Canonical stage with the production of reduplicated and variegated babbling, where the nucleus–margin distinction and rapid formant transition requirements are implemented in phrase-like utterances. Infants in the Canonical stage produce word-like groupings of syllables in a single breath group, and by clustering breath groups into larger phrase-like units, they indicate a manipulation that seems designed ultimately to serve the requirements of speech.

This flexible, hierarchical usage of multiple well-formed syllables is unique to humans. At the same time there do exist repetitions of fixed vocal signals in nonhuman primates. For example, the repetitive territorial calls of howler monkeys are a familiar zoo sound. Hauser (1996) commented that "Several primate species (e.g., chimpanzees, mangabeys) produce long-distance calls that consist of multiple units, some of which are repeated. The ordering of the primary units in these calls is consistent" (p. 38).

To say that calls are repeated or that they consist of multiple units is not to indicate that these units operate in a manner that is parallel with well-formed syllabic units. The full human pattern of Rhythmic Hierarchy requires that the minimal rhythmic units be clusterable in consistent higher order units (human infants show at least three levels of hierarchy, and adults show more) that themselves can be manipulated, each syllable type potentially occurring in isolation, or in many utterance positions at the whim of the speaker.

The fact that infants produce at least a three-level scheme of rhythmicity in precanonical vocalizations highlights the logical fact that well-formed syllabicity is not required for infants to produce complex vocal rhythms. Similarly, it is clear that nonhuman animals may be able to produce complex rhythms in the absence of human-like syllables. Owings and Hennessy (1984) contended that rhythmical hierarchies are present in nonhumans. They claimed that animal vocalizations are sometimes

---

[15]The work of Nathani (1998) suggests that higher order rhythmic units may be notably longer in infants than in mature speech. However, methodological differences among the three cited studies in how groupings of infant vocalizations were established for measurement leave this matter unresolved. One possible resolution would depend on the possibility that Nathani's groupings at the phrase level inadvertently encompassed utterances of a higher rhythmic order, the superphrase or line. If so, a reinterpretation of her data would bring them much closer to the outcomes of the other cited studies. The ultimate resolution of this matter will depend on philosophically satisfying and stable procedures for categorizing the phrasing characteristics of unintelligible vocalizations such as those produced by infants. In some sense then the resolution awaits a consensus on definition of canonical higher order rhythmic units, a definition that would help provide a basis for stable procedures of categorization.

structured at multiple levels, loosely analogous to the ways in which human language involves phonemes, words, phrases, sentences, paragraphs and so forth. For example, to make sense of a variety of forms of calling by the many species of ground squirrels, it is necessary to recognize, at a minimum, notes, series of notes, and series of series of notes. (Owings & Hennessy, 1984, cited in Owings & Morton, 1998, p. 77)

The function of these complex rhythms in nonhumans is uncertain. In humans the capability of Rhythmic Hierarchy is implemented in canonical syllables and thus offers a framework within which hierarchical morphological and syntactic structures can be expressed. This rich combination of well-formed Syllabification and Rhythmic Hierarchy is unique to humans and is evident by the second half-year of life.

PROPERTY 17: SEGMENTATION

Categorical Adaptation and Recombinability of syllables are two properties that provide means by which a syllabically based system of vocal transmission can be elaborated to produce an indefinitely large number of potential units. An additional property that affords elaboration of units has been traditionally termed Segmentation, a usage suggesting that syllables are analyzable in terms of chunks or segments corresponding roughly with the level of the alphabet in writing systems of the West.

Having learned to read in the Western world, we are encouraged by the alphabetic tradition to think of speech signals alphabetically. The tendency may also be influenced by a natural phonemic bias in attention, but literacy does seem to play a role as indicated by the fact that illiterate adults often show weak abilities in phonological awareness tasks, and that reading acquisition to some extent seems to support phonological awareness (Ehri, 1989; Tunmer & Rohl, 1991). Whatever the sources of the alphabetic inclination, it is tempting to characterize the sounds of our own language or attempts by children to produce them through phonetic, segmental transcription. This tendency embodies an unspoken assumption that the continuous stream of vocal production is naturally chunked in alphabetic-sized units, and furthermore that not only adults, but also infants and children function in vocal production according to constraints imposed by those units.

In prior chapters of this volume I have made clear that shoe-horning of precanonical infant sounds into segmental chunks is deeply misleading. Infant protophones before the Canonical stage do not fit into segmental-sized bins because they do not include well-formed segmental-sized units. However, once the Canonical stage begins, well-formed syllables are observable, and segmental transcription seems appropriate. From the perspective of mature listeners, the well-formed sounds of canonical infants are of the very same dimensions as the sounds of adults. An infant babble [baba] can count as a perfectly well-formed exemplar of a nursery term that might be pronounced [baba] by adults.

The problem with this segmental portrayal of the infant production is that the perspective of mature listeners is not the only relevant one. The infant may produce well-formed syllables without having a segmental system in mind. What sounds to us like a [b] followed by an [a] may be merely a gestalt syllable to the infant: a single, unanalyzed rapid vocal gesture and consequent formant transition.

In discussing Syllabification and the margin–nucleus distinction that can be discerned in canonical babbling, I have implied that foundations for Segmentation are available at least by the Canonical stage. However, the margin–nucleus distinction is not necessarily coded in the infant mind in terms of contrastable margin and nucleus units (e.g., [b] distinct from [a]), but rather each margin and nucleus in a syllable appears to be treated by infants merely in terms of a beginning point (e.g., [b]) and an ending point (e.g., [a]) for an unanalyzed rapid movement or formant transition.

The contrasts that infants begin to form among syllables during the Canonical stage may, then (from the infant's perspective), be merely contrasts between unanalyzed formant transition types or differing rapid movements. Rather than contrasting margin with margin or nucleus with nucleus, whole syllables may be seen as units. Therefore, [ba] may be distinct from [dɪ] not in terms of four distinctive segments, but merely in terms of two distinctive gestures and transitions.[16]

Segmentation is not, then, a requirement of Syllabification. It is a property of speech organization that infants appear to develop after they have developed well-formed syllables. Similarly, as a separate property of speech systems, Segmentation may have represented an innovation in hominid evolution. What might the advantage of Segmentation be? There are several possible answers. First of all, through Segmentation, the door is opened to recombinations of nuclei and margins of differing character, and such recombinations provide one source of enhancement of the syllabic inventory. For example, [ba] and [dɪ] can be viewed as distinct gestalts, possessing different formant transitions and different corresponding vocal movements. At an early point in development these transitions can be themselves coded featurally (in terms of fast or slow transitions, falling or rising transitions, high slope or low slope transitions, and even presence or absence of transitions). However, if an adjustment is made in the focus of coding, and the beginning points (margins) and endpoints (nuclei) of each syllable are now treated as independent units, the featural focus can also be adjusted to reference the resulting segments directly; with this newly established independence of segments, the possibility of segmental recombination emerges. In our

---

[16]There has been considerable discussion of the nature of Segmentation and its origins, both ontogenetically and phylogenetically, in recent years (Hewes, 1983; Lindblom, 1992). In general, Segmentation is viewed as a solution to a problem. As lexicons get large, syllabically based coding becomes inefficient and Segmentation provides a more efficient approach to coding

example, new syllables [bɪ] and [da] are possible through recombination of margins and nuclei. If an infant's syllabic system includes three different beginning points and three different ending points (e.g., [ba], [dɪ], and [gu]), then the segments can be recombined to form nine new syllables. With six unanalyzed CV syllables having six distinct margin types and nucleus types, it is possible to recombine to form 36 new CV syllables through segmental recombination. The larger the number of syllables in an unanalyzed inventory, the greater the benefit of segmental analysis. To develop large numbers of syllables, it is thus clearly advantageous to analyze syllables segmentally and to recombine the resulting units.

Another way to look at the gains of Segmentation is in terms of storage requirements or memory. Suppose an infant has 12 different syllable types: [ba], [da], [ma], [na], [bɪ], [dɪ], [mɪ], [nɪ], [bu], [du], [mu], and [nu]. These represent all the possible CV combinations of four consonants and three vowels (seven segments). Lexical information for this infant can thus be coded segmentally with five fewer units ($12 - 7$) than the same information can be coded syllabically. In this case the savings are not very impressive. However, suppose the system grows to include 10 consonants and 4 vowels, or 40 CV syllables; now the system includes 14 segments, or 26 fewer units than in the case of unanalyzed syllabic organization of the lexicon. As with recombination in the construction of phonological units, the memory advantages of segmental organization increase as the system grows. If new syllable types (e.g., CVC syllables) are added to the system, then the savings are even more notable. Ten consonants times four vowels times (the same) 10 consonants yields 400 CVC syllables, but still only 14 segments are need to code all the same lexical information. A segmental system pays off both from the standpoint of constructing recombinatorial possibilities and from the standpoint of organization and storage.

When Segmentation of the syllabic system in human infants begins is not clear. It may not begin abruptly, but may instead develop in fits and starts during the second year of life. One of the indications that infants do not have a fully segmental system during late babbling and into the beginning of meaningful speech is that syllables tend to be constrained by coarticulation—margins and nuclei are not entirely independent. Consequently the syllables [ba] and [dɪ] are common, but [bɪ] and [da] are less common. The high vowel [ɪ] tends to be coarticulated with the front and high tongue position of the [d]; in contrast, for the labial articulation of [b], the tongue tends to remain in its more natural, low position, yielding [a] (MacNeilage & Davis, 1990).

Segmentation capability clearly grows during the second year of life as vocabulary size increases. It is speculated that the need to acquire vocabulary presses children into Segmentation. Indeed the development of some kind of segmental analysis may be a natural requirement of any large-scale system of syllabically based communicative units, and it may be true that Segmentation is a predictable development in a wide variety of learning networks at some point of complexity in organizing the storage of syllabic inventories.

Complexity indeed. It is common for languages to include thousands of syllable types based on segmental recombinations. Note, for example, that there are at least 15 vowels and diphthongs in English and that there are at least 23 distinct consonants. If we simply combine these vowels with consonants to form CVC syllables, it is easy to see that there could be as many as $23 \times 15 \times 23 = 7,935$ possible types, assuming that there are no gaps in the distribution. In fact there are a few gaps, but there are other syllable types to take their places; for example, the many types that have other syllabic shapes (e.g., CV, VC, CCV, CCVC, etc.). All these types can be formed because the phonetic features of English can be applied generally to form syllabic types, because human learners are capable of Categorical Adaptation to those features, and because the property of Segmentation frees the system to recombinations of consonants and vowels.

Many other languages do not include syllables of as many forms as English—the CV form is heavily preferred in many languages and this tendency limits the number of distinct syllable types that occur in, for example, Spanish or Japanese. Still, mature speakers of all languages have a remarkably fluid control of all the syllable shapes that fit their particular language's phonotactic plan. Syllable units are formed efficiently according to this plan, and users of any natural language can flexibly manipulate features, generating new syllables (not necessarily used as words in their language) in keeping with the design. Segments can be moved about at will in accord with phonotactic principles of the language. For example, I know of no word /stib/ (*steeb*), but I know that a word could be formed of this syllable, because it meets the featural criteria of English and because each of the segments in this potential word can occur in the phonetic environments of the other segments. If such a word were formed it would follow all the rules of the system, including, for example, the quantization principle. Thus, if *steeb* became a word, it would be discretely different from words such as *steam, steed,* or *steep*. Differences in the pronunciation of *steeb* would be ignored by listeners as long as the boundaries between this and other words with features in common were not crossed.

Not only can I produce such syllables, but I can recognize new syllables that could be part of English, as well as those that could not. Therefore, steeb is recognizable as a part of the potential repertoire, whereas *tleeb* is recognized as not being a part of it. Native speakers of a language intuitively know the rules of phonotactics that govern syllable formation in terms of potential segment sequences. Thus, because I am capable of making up and recognizing acceptable syllables, it can be said that I command the segmental design of the syllabic signals of my language. All normal speakers of natural languages possess this Segmentation capability to produce and recognize new syllables that can be used in forming new words. The Segmentation capability appears to begin by the second year or early in the third year of life.

PROPERTY 18: HOT–COOL SYNTHESIS

Marler (1975) is credited with drawing our attention to the distinction between graded and discrete vocal categories in primates. In his view, some animals show discrete categories and others show graded ones. Some are claimed to show both. Hauser (1996) doubted the distinction has been thoroughly justified, but this potential distinction remains a key topic in the taxonomy of vocal categories of nonhuman primates.

In humans, on the other hand, the graded–discrete distinction exists without question from the first year of life. Graded vocalizations are found from the first days of life in the fixed signal of crying. We recognize very intense cries and differentiate them from moderately or mildly intense cries (Lester & Boukydis, 1992; Zeskind, Klein, & Marshall, 1992). Ultimately, the weakest of cries might be called fusses. Gradations are further heard in later occurring fixed signals, such as laughter or moaning. All the acoustic dimensions can be recruited to the task of expressing these gradations. As cry increases in intensity, the pitch goes up, the loudness increases, the duration of units increases and the resonance patterns expand. In human speech systems, graded vocalization forms the basis for emotional expressivity and nuance. This method of expressing passion has been referred to as the *hot* side of language (Locke, 1993).

With the beginning of Syllabification, an entirely different approach to vocalization takes hold. Syllables are discrete signals, differing sharply, not by degrees. As noted earlier, [ba] is distinct from [da] categorically, and the gradations between the two are systematically ignored. The same is true of the distinction between [ma] and [ba], or any other pairing of contrastive syllables in a natural language.

Syllables form the basis for vocabulary, for meanings, and ultimately for many syntactic devices that are coded syllabically. The meanings and other devices that are designated by syllables are not required to include emotional value. Typically they are merely categories that can be designated, and the syllables that do the designating usually make no emotional comment on the meanings. Locke (1993) called the syllabic aspect of language the *cool* side.

Each syllable can bear a particular meaning, discretely and without gradation toward another meaning. Thus, just as the steps of gradation that we can produce synthetically in a continuum from the syllable *ball* to the syllable *doll* are ignored by English listeners until the boundary is crossed between the two, so is it also true that no gradations of meaning occur along the continuum as it is heard. The most extreme [b]-like syllable for *ball* transmits the very same meaning as does the [b]-like syllable that is closest to the boundary between the contrasting syllables, and with the first syllable on the other side of the boundary, the listener hears the syllable *doll* and interprets the meaning accordingly. Further enhancements of [d]-like quality do not enhance the interpretation.

One of the magical properties of the human system of vocal transmission is found in what I choose to term Hot–Cool Synthesis. Gradations are not lost with the appearance of Syllabification, for the human speaker synthesizes graded nonsyllabic properties into the syllabic frame of utterance, not modifying meaning, but influencing the interpretation of the illocutionary force of utterances and the nuances of emotion that accompany meaning.

I might, on walking through the park, respond to the question "What is that?" by saying, "A maple," flatly and without varying intonation. In this response I transmit the meaning of the word to my interlocutor, along with an illocutionary force appropriate to the question, which is to say, I give an answer or a reply. If I say instead, "A maple," abruptly and sharply, then the utterance may be taken to have the force of a rebuke ("Why in hell are you asking me these stupid questions?"), although the meaning of the word thus pronounced remains unaltered. The degree of my rebuke can be gauged by the degree of sharpness of the intonation, so that there are many possible pronunciations that indicate grades of displeasure. Yet in each case I make reference to a category of trees—maples—and in no way does the degree of intoned rebuke alter the degree to which the category of maples is referred to by the word. The reference is fixed in the lexicon, coded syllabically, and that reference cannot be altered in meaning by intonation or, for that matter, by subtle syllabic changes. The force, on the other hand, is alterable at each pronunciation through the mechanism of Hot–Cool Synthesis.

The ability to synthesize this way begins in the first year of life. As Syllabification is established with the Canonical stage of vocal development, infants quickly elaborate their syllable productions to include a wide variety of intonations and emotional contents. That individual syllable types can be pronounced with squealing high pitch, growling low pitch, or some combination starting with one and ending with the other, indicates the radical ability of human infants to restructure vocalization in the Canonical stage. Even earlier the ability to perform Hot–Cool Synthesis appears in marginal babbling of the Expansion stage. A precanonical syllable-like utterance, already by this age differentiated into consonant-like and vowel-like elements, can be pronounced with varying degrees of intensity or emphasis. Complaints, for example, with varying degrees of intensity may be transmitted this way, with a syllabic frame bearing graded prosodic indicators of distress.

It should be emphasized that the human capability for Hot–Cool Synthesis is entirely flexible and generalizable. Words are not in any way held to a particular degree or type of passion. One can say *detestable* with a sneer and sharp falling contour indicating disgust, or one can say *detestable* lightly, with irony, smiling, and indicating delight. Such a flexible capability is presaged by infant superimposition of varying intonations or other graded properties on individual, distinctive syllables.

No other primate, as far as I can tell, synthesizes graded and discrete calls with such flexibility. In fact the only example of Hot–Cool Synthesis I can muster for nonhuman primates involves fixed signals that can be read as designating fixed referents (predators) with graded intensities. Thus the vervet monkey, for example, has been said to refer to danger from leopards or eagles by differing calls, each of which can be presented in degrees of intensity suggestive of the degree of the danger. To this extent, Hot–Cool Synthesis can be said to be present in the vervet and a variety of other mammals that utilize differentiated alarm calls for more than one predator type (see Hauser, 1996, for a review).

However, *refer* or *referential* in their application here hint at capabilities that have not been indicated in any nonhuman creature. The vervet does not show the human-style flexibility to refer to the leopard, because the vervet cannot refer to the leopard except when announcing danger, and the gradations expressed in different intensities are only able to express varying degrees of perceived danger. In contrast, the human can say leopard to sound the alarm, to name the creature in the cage, to ask the name of the type of pelt that adorns a hat, to criticize the wearer of such a hat, to wonder out loud about the criticism of the wearer of such a hat, to express outrage that one might wonder out loud about the criticism of the wearer of such a hat, and so on. The leopard is not obligatorily referred to with alarm, but can become in the referential system of humans, the object of dispassionate, cool reference, and both the type and degree of emotion or force to be expressed about the leopard can be held apart, manipulated independently, and synthesized at the speaker's pleasure. Thus, I contend, Hot–Cool Synthesis is a property of communication that is, essentially, unique to humans in our experience. This sort of synthesis enters the human repertoire in the first year of life, forming a basis for vast expressivity, and for a means of coding a fundamental distinction between meaning and other communicative values.

It might seem uncertain at first blush that Hot–Cool Synthesis is as necessary to the development of a complex communication system as are many of the other properties we have considered here. Syllabification, for example, is an undeniable requirement of an efficient and broadly applicable signal system. There has to exist a means of structuring transmission units for rapid transmission, and a rhythmic structure based on syllables seems necessary to that end. I strongly suspect that Hot–Cool Synthesis is similarly required by a complex communication system. Illocutionary and emotional information appear to be the natural starting points of communication systems as indicated empirically by the fact that all the mammalian communication systems include emotional expressions, but only the human system richly commands meaning as well as emotional expression. When Semanticity arrives within human infant communication, it arrives in the form of a separation within individual acts of communication between illocutionary and semantic information. Prior to that time, semantics is only weakly present, but the pragmatic functional acts of communication are blatantly apparent. Yet both semantic and illocutionary information are required in any rich system, and I see no way to present such information efficiently within a syllabic system without synthesizing the illocutionary content seamlessly into the syllabic stream. Therefore, as richly complex as Hot–Cool Synthesis may seem as implemented in speech, I suspect it is required by the logical nature of possibilities in the evolution of the capacity to communicate vocally.[17]

THE HIERARCHY OF INFRASTRUCTURAL PROPERTIES
OF POTENTIAL COMMUNICATION SYSTEMS

The 18 properties that have been discussed here are naturally arranged in logical relations forming a hierarchy. The content of the hierarchy may prove to be of substantial importance in the interpretation of ways that communication systems can evolve. The natural logic implied in the hierarchy specifies plausible stages of evolution in communicative systems. When communication proves important to a child or a species, the developmental paths that may be followed are in significant ways specified by the hierarchy.

The hierarchy includes a set of implications whereby it can be stated that the presence in any communicative system of one property implies the presence of another. I refer to properties that are implied as logically *superordinate* and to properties that do the implying as *subordinate*. In some cases these implications appear to be near absolute. For example, it is hard to imagine how a system of semiotics could possess Displaceability in the absence of Semanticity. The former represents the ability to make analytical reference to entities not in the here and now. The latter represents the ability to make analytical reference to entities. The natural logic of development would suggest a path in which Semanticity could be developed before Displaceability, but not the reverse.

In other cases the implicational relations are weaker. Generally Semanticity implies Arbitrarity. Yet it appears possible for there to exist a system that does not possess Arbitrarity but does possess Semanticity. Iconic signals can be fully semantic, and consequently, Arbitrarity could be bypassed (at least temporarily) on the way to Semanticity. However, iconic signaling is inherently cumbersome, because perfect iconicity is not possible—there is no way perfectly to represent concepts with simple symbols since concepts are inherently complex and abstract. As a result, iconic signals do not show perfectly predictable meanings,[18] and they still have to be learned. As a consequence, if a system is to develop rich Semanticity, including a large vocabulary of items that possess the analytical referentiality that Semanticity

---

[17]It is interesting to note that sign languages exploit a similar seamless synthesis of semantic and illocutionary contents. Facial expressions along with intensity and abruptness of movements are used to express illocution, whereas hand configurations, symmetries, and so on are used to transmit semantic content simultaneously with the illocutionary content. Hot–Cool Synthesis appears to be implemented effectively, then, even in a nonvocal mode.

[18]An interesting demonstration of this fact was made by Hoemann (1975), who presented two groups of signs to observers who were naive with regard to American Sign Language (ASL). The signs were selected to constitute iconic and noniconic gestures in the ASL inventory. The observers were to guess the meanings of each sign. The results showed that although the observers were often able to guess the correct meaning of an iconic sign, they were just as likely to be led down a garden path by the iconicity of the sign, guessing incorrectly. Iconic signs turn out to be inherently ambiguous.

requires, it is easiest to proceed if there is no iconicity constraint. Thus I suspect Semanticity weakly implies Arbitrarity. In practice the distinction between weak and strong implications may be of little consequence. If, as I suspect, the properties are the limiting infrastructural frames in self-organization of systems, then practical factors may drive development to accumulate properties according to paths of least resistance that conform strongly to weak implicational constraints.

The hierarchy is complicated by the fact that the properties are not simply binary, but are instead dimensions that can be developed themselves in stages in which individual principles are implemented step by step and by degrees. As a consequence the hierarchical implications that we find among the properties logically allow development to proceed to a limited extent on a superordinate property, then to begin on a subordinate one before development of the superordinate is complete. Development on the subordinate property may then proceed to a point where no further progress is possible until additional growth is seen with respect to the superordinate property.

For instance, Rhythmic Hierarchy is logically subordinate to Syllabification, because rhythm requires a system of minimal rhythmic units. At the same time, well-formed syllables develop in stages, as seen in human infancy. Therefore, Rhythmic Hierarchy can be seen at an early stage implemented with primitive syllables. Long before syllable well-formedness is fully established, phrases composed of multiple precanonical syllables are already produced by infants in the first months of life (Lynch, Oller, Steffens, Buder, 1995; Oller & Lynch, 1992). These phrases, perhaps surprisingly, appear to obey certain key principles of canonical phrase construction in mature language. Both the phrases and the precanonical syllables of which they are composed are produced at durations that conform to mean durations found in mature spoken languages. Therefore, the property of Rhythmic Hierarchy can be present in a vocal system to a degree of elaboration that is permitted by the degree to which Syllabification has developed. As more well-formed syllables enter the inventory, the system has the opportunity to develop the property of Rhythmic Hierarchy further so as to incorporate the more well-formed minimal rhythmic units within its higher order structures. The patterns of logical implication within the hierarchy of properties are thus maintained at various points in time, with progress in steps on each dimension limited by progress in steps on superordinate dimensions.

In the following figures, dotted lines represent weak implications, whereas solid lines represent stronger implications. Free Expressivity implies Contextual Freedom because it is not possible expressively to utilize a vocalization in a manner that is not preset by natural selection unless it is possible to produce the vocalization spontaneously. If one wished to recategorize the properties slightly, it might be said that Free Expressivity is an advanced aspect of a general property of Contextual Freedom, whereas spontaneous vocal production (manifesting a more specific kind of Contextual Freedom) without an expressive component is more simple (see Fig. 12.5).

Directivity implies Free Expressivity weakly, because it is possible to possess the ability to direct fixed vocal signals, bypassing Free Expressivity. However, Directivity gains power as it becomes possible to utilize directed vocalization freely and expressively. Consequently, I presume that significant growth in Directivity is ultimately dependent on significant growth in Free Expressivity, and thus weakly presupposes it.

Interactivity is assumed here to constitute turn-taking with Directivity. It is possible to imagine a very simple system wherein Interactivity could operate without Directivity. Organisms might respond to each other in sequence according to a fixed schedule whereby each event in chains of events is produced reflexively in response to a prior event. This sort of involuntary Interactivity is of little interest in the development of a powerful system of communication. Similarly, the Directivity property of interest here is not accidental and is not part of a reflexive chain of response to specific eliciting

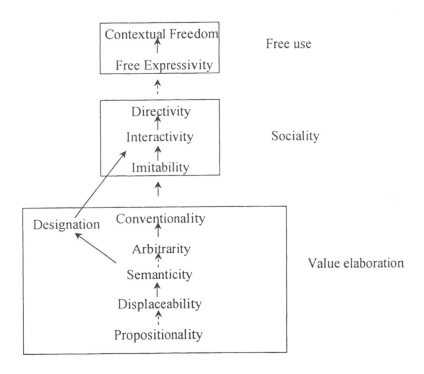

FIG. 12.5.   Hierarchy of potential infrasemiotic properties.

stimuli. Voluntary Directivity is what interests us here, and it requires control of when and how communications are presented.

In the human speech system, the prototypical indicator of Directivity (in simple acts of communication) is eye contact (at least intermittently established) during vocalization. In other systems of vocal communication, Directivity might be controlled most often by a different factor, for example, physical contact. It should be emphasized that Directivity does not require a specific operationalization. What it does require is context sensitivity on the part of the communicator, who must gauge the point of presentation of communication in such a way as to maximize its reception. Because reception can be well monitored during turn-taking, Directivity can be efficiently managed in a situation with Interactivity in progress. One can determine how to direct vocalizations and when to do so by virtue of the schedule of interactive turn-taking. Directivity is logically superordinate to Interactivity in the sense that interactions have beginnings, and there is skill involved in initiation of conversation. There is also skill involved in effective presentation of a single unit of communication that is not followed by conversation. Whether an initial or isolated communication requires gaining eye contact, touching the potential listener, speaking loudly to get attention, or simply waiting for the right moment when someone finishes an activity and appears ready to listen, it is clear that successful Directivity requires that measures be taken to ensure successful reception of the intended message.

Selective Imitability is subordinate to Interactivity because it represents a specialized and delicately structured case of interaction. One might break Imitability down into components of immediate and delayed matching, with the latter being subordinate to the former. Delayed matching, in this usage, would constitute the reconstruction of a perceived event by imitation and would imply memory of the event.

Two-way Conventionality (where both speaker and hearer use the same words) is subordinate to Imitability, because at least one member of any successful conventional conversation has to acquire the vocal usage presented at some point by the other. Children sometimes invent words, but if these are to constitute successful conventional symbols, they must be learned by the caretakers. In general, Conventionality in vocal systems of great power will, I presume, be totally reciprocal, with all members of the community learning the great bulk of the units of communication. This learning involves an inevitable component of imitation, at least at the level of morphemes.

Arbitrariness implies Conventionality because the only way for signals to gain values that are not indexical, not iconic, and not fixed is by learning. Conventional signals can be indexical or iconic, and although they may be learned, these signals are not arbitrary.

Semanticity weakly implies Arbitrariness in theory, but may do so strongly in practice, as noted previously. Semanticity strongly implies Designation, which itself strongly implies Interactivity. One cannot make analytical symbolic reference (Semanticity) without having the ability to make reference (Designation). One cannot make triadic reference (Designation) without interacting with a listener (Interactivity). Displaceability strongly implies Semanticity, because one cannot analytically refer to entities that are not in the here and now (Displaceability) if one cannot make reference to entities in the first place (Semanticity).

Propositionality implies Semanticity because one cannot speak of relations among entities or comment on them in any way until one can make analytical reference to them. Propositionality weakly implies Displaceability in theory but may do so strongly in practice. It is easy to imagine a simple proposition being produced in the immediate context of a simple salient event (e.g., doggie bite). However, it is hard to imagine how Propositionality can function with generality until ideas and their symbolic expressions can be divorced from immediate contexts.

Figure 12.6 presents the infraphonological hierarchy. Categorical Adaptation implies Signal Analysis weakly because adaptation is facilitated by skill and experience in exploration of potential signals. Syllabification exists to some extent in human infants from birth—quasivowels are produced as brief primitive syllables and are clustered in phrases in the first months of life. However, I presume well-formed syllable production depends weakly on control of Signal Analysis and Categorical Adaptation, both of which provide a basis for development of signals meeting the canonical syllable requirements (see chap. 4). Syllabification is implied by Segmentation (segments are parts of well-formed syllables). Recombinability of syllables obviously implies Syllabification, and Rhythmic Hierarchy implies multisyllabic utterances; hence it implies Recombinability. Hot–Cool Synthesis is a feature of utterance according to which prosodic features are systematically imposed on syllables; thus Syllabification is implied by Hot–Cool Synthesis.

The domains of infraphonology and infrasemiotics have been portrayed thus far as independent, when in fact they are themselves interrelated. Signal Analysis sits at the top of our hierarchy of infraphonological properties. However, it is clear that Signal Analysis implies Contextual Freedom of potential signals, a property that has been portrayed as infrasemiotic because it is a characteristic of the usage of sounds rather than an aspect of the nature of the sounds. Yet one cannot explore and command the dimensions of signals unless one has the ability to produce signals freely. In some sense, Contextual Freedom is a property of both infraphonology and infrasemiotics. Consequently, the two diagrams can be portrayed in a unitary fashion with Contextual Freedom at the top.

There is another perhaps more important sense in which the two realms appear to relate as systems of communication develop. Signals function to deliver values, and values require signals to transmit them. Consequently the properties of signals and values tend to be tailored to each other's structural needs and capabilities. Bidirectional lines connecting the two sides of the unified hierarchy diagram (Fig. 12.7) indicate that growth on one side tends to support growth on the other.

Figure 12.7 depicts several logical and practical relations of implication that I presume to occur across the infraphonological and infrasemiotic properties. For example, Imitability supports Categorical Adaptation (some categories can be developed independently through signal exploration, but they cannot be made conventional without some degree of Imitability) and vice versa (the skill to imitate new sounds is surely enhanced by increasing skill in independent Categorical Adaptation). Conventionality implies Categorical Adaptation, the ability to acquire new signal types, whenever a conventional system includes signals that are not innately available to the learner of the communicative system. The reverse is also true; the need for skill in Categorical Adaptation grows with growth in Conventionality, because as the system of value units expands, the need for new categorical units of transmission may grow.

Growth in vocabulary size is fostered by progress on both sides. Creation of a large vocabulary of values and meanings is made possible in part by Conventionality and Arbitrarity, but it would be difficult to store and maintain a large vocabulary in the absence of well-formed Syllabification, supported by Recombinability and Segmentation. Conversely, Syllabification, Recombinability, and Segmentation are all spurred on by growth in vocabulary with Conventionality and Arbitrarity. Semanticity implies Hot–Cool Synthesis because there must be a means by which semantic and illocutionary values can be distinguished within signals. Although Hot–Cool Synthesis can be achieved as a pure signal innovation, merging prosodic and syllabic sound

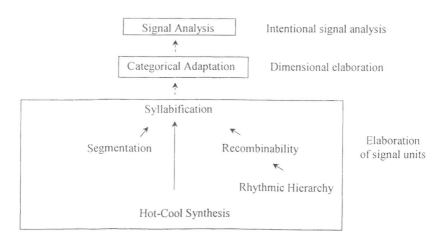

FIG. 12.6.   Hierarchy of potential infraphonological properties.

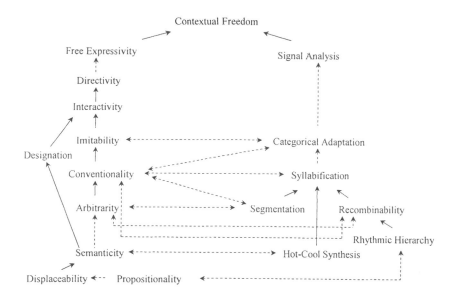

FIG. 12.7. Unified hierarchy of infrastructural properties.

types, the skill to perform it surely grows with the need to use it, which is bolstered by growth in Semanticity. Propositionality implies Rhythmic Hierarchy because propositions naturally structure themselves in phrase-like groupings, especially as they become more elaborate, and the skill to implement Rhythmic Hierarchy may become more elaborate as the need for formulation of propositions grows.

The hierarchy of infrastructural properties suggests natural developmental paths. In preceding chapters I have evaluated the development of infant vocalizations and their utilization and have found stages of development that could be predicted as logical possibilities in the hierarchy. Further, we have seen that nonhuman primates have vocal systems that appear to be simpler than the human one, even in infancy. The properties portrayed in the hierarchy are essentially not present in the nonhuman primates, but if a line of evolution in vocal communication should develop among some other group, it would be sensible to expect development to follow a course consistent with the hierarchy. In chapter 13, I consider a speculative scenario of human evolution, based in large part on the hierarchy and supplemented by the facts of infant vocal development.

ON NATURAL LOGIC

The hierarchical system portrayed here is novel in its details, but it conforms in spirit to the reasoning of a wide variety of thinkers. Perhaps the most influential of these for me is Piaget, whose book *Genetic Epistemology* (1969) argues for the idea that development of the human mind proceeds in accord with necessary constraints on how knowledge can be formed. In some sense this idea posits constraints that are external to the human condition or to the condition of any particular species. These constraints are neither innate characteristics of the mind–body complex nor are they properties of experience. Instead they are the logical requirements that are imposed on any creature that would try to understand the world and command it.

The notion of genetic epistemology, as I understand Piaget to have intended it, suggests, if only indirectly, that there may exist a natural logic of infrastructural properties of communication. These properties, along with their natural hierarchical relations, may constitute an external set of requirements, neither innate nor experience-based, to which all learners of a rich communication system and all species that would develop a rich communication system must conform. If the reasoning is on target, one cannot learn a rich communication system except by going through the steps specified in the hierarchy, not because the mind imposes these limitations nor because experience presents information in a particular order, but because there is no other path available under any circumstances.

This sort of reasoning is familiar in evolutionary speculation. In the sequencing of a set of fossils, the notion of a transformation series is sometimes invoked. The series is specified in terms of a set of logical possibilities of change (Henning, 1979). Henning (1979) argued that the logic could be applied to development just as it can be applied to evolution; my sentiment precisely. If the logic is truly external, it should apply equally to an evolutionary or a developmental series.

In *Ontogeny and Phylogeny*, Gould (1977) summarized the history of the reasoning, noting that from Koffka (1928) to Piaget there have been supporters of the idea that phylogeny resembles ontogeny because

> external constraints impose a similar order on both processes. There are, for example, only so many ways to move from simplicity to complexity, from homogeneity to heterogeneity, from instinct to consciousness. ... Mudcracks, basalt pillars, soap bubbles, bee cells, and echinoid plates are all hexagonal because only a few regular forms can fill space completely. (p. 144)

The reasoning comes right up to date with the writings of Deacon (1997) who argued that the symbolic capabilities of humans are built on a logically necessary foundation:

The competence to interpret something symbolically depends upon already having the competence to interpret many other subordinate relationships indexically,
and so forth. It is one kind of competence that grows out of and depends upon a
very different kind of competence. What constitutes competence in this sense is
the ability to produce an interpretive response that provides the necessary infrastructure of more basic iconic and/or indexical interpretations. (p. 74)

Infrastructural natural logic is the foundation of the theoretical posture
proposed in this book. Given that speculations about external constraints on
development and evolution can be documented throughout the 20th century,
my approach cannot, at a general level, be viewed as novel. What is relatively
new, I think, is the suggestion that natural logic may apply broadly in the evaluation of possible communicative systems, whether they be rich and elaborate as in the case of mature language, or more primitive, as in the case of
human infant vocal communication or the presumable primitive vocal communication systems of our hominid ancestors. This work represents merely a
probe toward development of an infrastructural approach to vocal communication, but I have been encouraged that it may be possible to discover and specifically formulate a wide variety of properties and principles that
communicative systems must possess, along with presuppositional relations
that must obtain among them. The developmental phenomena of human infancy provide a fruitful ground on which to explore the possibilities.

13

Possible Stages of Vocal Evolution in the Human Family

PROTOPHONE STAGES AND NATURAL LOGIC OF LINGUISTIC EVOLUTION

There are those who have suggested that hominids became truly human around the time of the Upper Paleolithic. According to this view we arrived, not gradually, but explosively (Binford, 1981). Language came into the picture along with a variety of additional mental capabilities, such as planful action, in a single leap, perhaps 35,000 to 45,000 years ago. The single leap idea has been fostered by the influential role Chomsky (1967) played in emphasizing the enormous gap between human language and the communication systems of any other species. Most current authors, however, are more amenable to the idea that language may have emerged in our species over a period of millions or at least hundreds of thousands of years in a series of stages, each one offering new properties of language that provided some sort of selectional advantage over prior stages (Bickerton, 1990; Pinker, 1994).

In principle, I am with the latter group. I see no reason to assume that steps roughly parallel to those implied by the study of vocal development in infants may not have taken place in very ancient prehistory. In this chapter, some concrete speculations are laid out consistent with the stages of protophone development and the theory of fundamental properties of communication. In this context it seems perfectly possible that at least as early as *Homo habilis* (perhaps 2 million years ago) our ancestors may have had language-precursor vocal capabilities that surpassed those of any current nonhuman primate. This is a view that seems compatible with that of modern paleontologists (e.g., Leakey, 1994). Not being a paleontologist, I feel a bit sheepish suggesting that even before our ancestors were using stone tools (or leaving evidence of it) they may have already diverged in terms of vocal communication abilities from the ape line. My intent in formulating a speculative scenario of hominid vocal evolution is to begin a process of integrating information from infant vocal development and the natural logic of infrastructural properties into the attempt to specify plausible stages of appearance of speech-like characteristics in our ancestors. The time frames suggested are merely heuristic at this point. The entire sequence could be either compressed by millions of years or expanded by millions without modifying the implied hypotheses regarding plausible sequences in the appearance of vocal communication properties.

It should also be emphasized that to posit that linguistic evolution took millions of years does not in any way rule out the possibility that a rapid advance in both the form and the practical effects of vocal communication may have occurred around the beginning of the Upper Paleolithic era with its cave paintings and other evidences of cultural explosion. This was apparently a period of substantial discontinuity with prior hominid cultural activity, as portrayed by Leakey (1994):

> From about 250,000 years ago, archaic sapiens individuals, including Neanderthals, made tools from prepared flakes, and these assemblages, including the Mousterian, comprised perhaps sixty identifiable tool types. But the types remained unchanged for more than 200,000 years—a technological stasis that seems to deny the workings of the fully human mind.
>
> Only when the Upper Paleolithic cultures burst onto the scene 35,000 years ago did innovation and arbitrary order become pervasive ... we would view language as having had a slow start, slow progress through most of human prehistory, and an explosive enhancement in relatively recent times. (pp. 134–136)

It is the notion of a "slow start" that interests me. The effects of communicative change in very early hominid history may have been extremely significant even if they did not result in massive change in cultural artifacts. They may have been critical to survival of the species, even if they left little physical trace directly implying linguistic capability.

The claim to be evaluated here is not necessarily that our current ontogeny of speech capability recapitulates our prior evolution directly by virtue of genetic programming. The possibility that seems more likely is that to the extent there is similarity of ontogeny and phylogeny in speech, it may be the result of the fact that both modern infants and ancient hominids have been subject to similar constraints of a natural, logical, infrastructural sort. There are inherently natural ways that a vocal communication system might develop. The natural step-by-step possibilities are, I contend, suggested by the properties of communication (and the logical relations among them) outlined in chapter 12, as well as the logic of protophone stages in human infancy as interpreted in light of the principles of canonical syllable formation. The study of infant vocalizations thus provides a natural laboratory indicating some of the ways that the step-by-step process of development or evolution may occur. At each stage of normal vocal development we see new types of vocal action, and these can be interpreted in light of the theory of infrastructural properties and canonical syllable principles that are required for the development of spoken language.

Given this natural logic we may look at the properties and the ways they relate to each other, and we may see possible staging points for evolution just as we see ways of providing interpretation and explication for the facts of infant protophone development and early speech. The idea of a natural logic undergirding the principles of development or the principles of Universal Grammar is hardly new. Piaget (1969) viewed the steps of cognitive development as being guided by what he called *genetic epistemology*, a term that seems generally equivalent to the form I prefer, natural logic. Even Chomsky (1993), long a critic of Piaget and an advocate for the existence of a purely innate language acquisition system in humans, recently speculated about a minimalist program that sounds suspiciously like the sort of natural logic I have in mind:

> Grammatical constructions such as relative clause, passive, verbal phrase, and so on, appear to be taxonomic artifacts, like "terrestrial mammal" or "household pet"; the array of phenomena derive from the interaction of principles of much greater generality. Still more recent work indicates that these principles may themselves be epiphenomenal, their consequences reducing to more general and abstract properties of the computational system, properties that have a kind of "least effort" flavor. This "minimalist" program also seeks to reduce the descriptive technology to the level of virtual conceptual necessity, sharply restricting the devices available for description, which means that the complex phenomena of widely varied languages must be explained in terms of abstract principles of economy of derivation and representation ... computational processes that seem radically different from what was assumed only a few years ago. (p. 51)

Indeed. It would seem to me that in the context of such reasoning, there is no basis for assuming that language is an organ. Rather, language appears to develop in response to communicative pressures and to abide in that development by natural constraints that may have a minimalist flavor. I see no reason that evolution could not resemble development guided by similar minimalist properties of universal import. Both development and evolution may be subject to the same naturally unchangeable constraints on what a powerful vocal communication system might be.

ON THE FIRST STEPS THAT DIFFERENTIATED OUR LINE FROM THAT OF OTHER PRIMATES

This discussion is different from most prior ones in that it starts from the beginning of the potential differentiation of the human and nonhuman lines and aims to show similarities and differences in terms of specific infrastructural properties and principles of unit formation and usage. Other authors who have recently addressed the evolution of language (e.g., Bickerton, 1990; Lieberman,

1968; Pinker, 1994) have started at points of linguistic elaboration that far surpass the ones considered here. The prior works tend to begin with complex syntax, and in so doing they presume that such properties as Semanticity,
Propositionality, Displaceability, Rhythmic Hierarchy, and Segmentation are
all already in place.

The speculative prehistory to be presented in this chapter begins with the
onset of very primitive communicative capabilities. Such capabilities are reflected in the entire hierarchy of properties outlined in the previous chapter.
The first steps that our hominid ancestors took, I propose, along the path toward language involved the evolution of command over these primitive properties. Yet even though they may seem rudimentary in the context of
discussions of full-blown human language, they represent important, even
critical departures from the vocal capabilities of other primates.

NEOTENY AS A DRIVING FORCE
IN HUMAN EVOLUTION OF COMMUNICATION

There are of course many possible scenarios that would be consistent with the
natural logic and the protophone stages. The one presented here suggests a series of stages resembling in important regards the protophone stages of human infancy, and it invokes a possible role for *neoteny* in the development of
hominid vocal capacities.

There are at least two basic ways that evolution occurs—either by mutations in structural genes that introduce new features that may have further effects during development, or by mutations in regulatory genes that produce
changes in the timing of development (heterochrony). Neoteny is one of the
ways that a regulatory change can be manifest. A basic suggestion about
neoteny in the human line is that through a timing change the process of development may have been slowed down so that our hominid ancestors had
longer infancies and longer periods of both physical and intellectual development prior to pubescence than their primate relatives. It has been contended
that "neoteny has been a (probably *the*) major determinant of human evolution" (Gould, 1977, p. 9). In comparing human beings with our genetically
closest living relatives, the reasoning continues:

> Humans and chimps are almost identical in structural genes, yet differ markedly
> in form and behavior. This paradox can be resolved by invoking a small genetic
> difference with profound effects—alterations in the regulatory system that slow
> down the general rate of development in humans. (Gould, 1977, p. 9)

I am fully amenable to the notion that the human line may have changed in
additional ways beyond those attributable to mutations in the regulatory system for timing of development. However, I find the neoteny idea particularly
appealing to help account for a number of evolutionary features in light of two

facts. One is mentioned in the quotation. Neoteny offers the basis for a wide variety of effects based on a minor and local genetic change, one that affects a regulatory system that controls timing of development, without requiring the coordination of a set of simultaneous (and therefore unlikely) mutations. Individual regulatory mutations producing neotenous effects or enhancing prior effects of neoteny may have occurred at various points in human evolution, progressively increasing the degree of difference between humans and other primates in terms of many factors at sexual maturity, including head shape, facial structure, size of brain, hairiness, and many aspects of intellectual and vocal capability. Indeed Leakey (1994) reported calculations that suggest *Homo erectus* was already neotenous, a creature in whom the young were born relatively helpless, even though their mature brain sizes were about 350 cc smaller than those of mature humans. Additional steps of change in the genes regulating developmental timing appear to have taken place even beyond this point, perhaps 2 million years ago.

To the uninitiated, the plausibility of a major role for neoteny in human evolution always seems to be enhanced dramatically by a simple comparison of facial structure and brain case similarities in adult humans and infant chimpanzees. Both show vertical alignment of forehead and face, and relatively similar proportions of brain case to lower face. The comparison of adult humans and adult chimpanzees in contrast shows extraordinary differences, with the adult chimpanzees showing sloping foreheads, prognathous faces, and brain cases much smaller proportionally than humans (see Fig. 13.1).

Much has been written about the importance of brain size differences (usually assessed per unit body weight) between humans and our primate relatives, and it is clear that brain size increased progressively across millions of years in the line that lead to humans (Jerison, 1991; Leakey, 1994; Leigh, 1988; Noble & Davidson, 1996). Humans show a brain weight threefold larger than that of an ape of comparable size. Could it be that the reason language emerged was that the brains of hominids reached some critical threshold of mass that allowed a sudden leap of mental capability?[1] Similar changes may have taken place in many domains of capability that are less easily measured, and it is unclear whether the brain size changes drove the changes in capability or whether the latter were in many cases collateral, simultaneous changes. Pinker (1994) argued that, contrary to the popular brain size reasoning, linguistic growth may have created a survival advantage that may have driven

---

[1]Perhaps the most vigorous defense of the brain size hypothesis was presented by Gibson (1990a), who argued that there is no general pattern of intellectual enhancement attributable to neoteny:

> The state of human brain maturation at birth is by no means unique. In fact, it is totally nondistinctive, being in the middle range among mammals as a whole and only somewhat less mature than that of the neonatal chimpanzee ... if neural altriciality causes intelligence, then altricial mammals in general should have large brains, and opossums, white mice, and laboratory rats should be intellectual giants. In actuality, most altricial mammals have small brains and most large-brained mammals give birth to precocial young. (p. 118)

FIG. 13.1.   Baby and adult chimpanzee from Naef (1926).

brain growth rather than the reverse. Either way, neoteny may have been an important mechanism of change.

A second reason that I find the neoteny hypothesis appealing is based on evidence that a variety of primate species vocalize more and with greater Contextual Freedom in infancy than at other points in life (Biben & Bernhards, 1995; Kojima & Nagumo, 1996, forthcoming; Newman, 1995; Snowdon, 1988; Symmes & Biben, 1992). Kojima's work suggests the possibility that even the chimpanzee, noted for its lack of vocal inclination, appears more able to be stimulated vocally and is more variable vocally in infancy than later in life. Such facts suggest that increasing neoteny could have fostered increasing vocal abilities, ultimately increasing reliance on vocalization as a means of communication.

A SPECULATIVE PREHISTORY
OF HOMINID VOCAL DEVELOPMENT

A possible role for neoteny is prominently considered in the speculative prehistory that follows. The conjectures are organized in seven scenes, each one corresponding to a proposed period of relative stasis that might have occurred in the evolution of the human linguistic capacity during its primitive differentiation from other primate vocal systems. Each scene is also loosely related to (though not identical to) periods of development of linguistic capability (both infraphonological and infrasemiotic) in modern human infants. The similarities between modern infant development and the presumed stages of hominid evolution are attributed to the fact that both are, according to the reasoning, guided at least in part by the requirements of the natural logic of properties of potential communication systems as presented in chapter 12.

The scenes also loosely suggest that the stages of vocal development may have corresponded roughly with various hominid stages that have been posited on the basis of paleoanthropological research. The hominid stages are themselves extremely subject to reinterpretation based on new finds. We can be sure the fossil record is dreadfully incomplete, given, for example, the facts that only 43 of 185 primate species currently in existence can be documented in the available Pliocene/Pleistocene record and that the great majority of the research on early hominids has been largely confined to relatively small regions of Africa (Martin, 1990). Consequently the posited hominid stages can be expected to be reformulated in the future, and in any case, the span of time over which the key events of vocal evolution are proposed to have taken place can only be viewed as an educated guess.

Scene 1: The Neotenous Primates That Vocalized More Than Their Ancestors: Contact Calls Produced With Normal Phonation as a First Step

Imagine a group of ape-like creatures perhaps of the *Australopithecus afarensis* line (or perhaps of a contemporary collateral or a later species), probably already bipedal, not yet using stone tools, but already on the line that would ultimately yield *Homo sapiens*. These human ancestors have a variety of vocalizations fitting into the fixed signal category. One thing that makes them different from their immediately previous ancestors is that the members of this mutated line vocalize more than those of the previous one, perhaps in part because these new ape-like animals are slightly neotenous; they have a somewhat longer infancy than their ancestors. Even in the ancestral group, infants always vocalized more than adults, but in the new group, the vocalization period is prolonged sufficiently that the tendency to vocalize frequently carries over even into adulthood. These new creatures are surviving although the ancestral group is fading out.

An analysis of the vocalization types that occur in these new creatures shows that they have a vocalization that might be called a contact call because it is often used merely to attract the attention of a conspecific, and this call is used much more commonly than in the ancestral group. Importantly, the call is produced quickly at low intensity, within about 300 msec, in a voice with smooth and periodic vibrations of the vocal cords, unlike the fixed signals in the repertoire. Furthermore, the call can be produced with or without a conspecific present, especially in infancy, but also in adulthood. For this reason it begins to appear that this is not a fixed signal. In fact it is not always clear that the function of the call when it is used socially is one of attention attraction. In some cases, the function of the vocalization may be one of maintenance of attention or the seeking of social favors. In yet additional cases, the vocalization appears to be produced for no reason at all, unless one assumes that the producer merely wishes to hear the sound of his or her own voice.

In terms of the infrastructural logic and protophone development models, we might say that the ape-like ancestor has come, to a small degree, to command Contextual Freedom in the production of a vocalization that includes normal phonation, the kind of phonation that we observe in quasivowels of the first month of human life. Further, the new primate has come to command to a minor extent both Free Expressivity and Directivity of vocalizations, because members of this group appear to call for attention with the normally phonated sound.

These are small changes, so why are these mutated creatures surviving as the ancestral type is fading? What might the advantage of the vocal adjustments in the new line be? Perhaps none. Perhaps the changes accompany other modifications associated with neoteny, and these other changes (perhaps intellectual ones, because the brain is slightly larger in this creature than in the ancestral group) are beneficial to survival, in which case the modest changes in vocalization pattern may come at no cost in a broader package. On the other hand, it may be that the new vocalization tendency is directly selected for, because it enhances social contact among members of the group, a factor that has been argued by others to have played a major role in vocal evolution in humans (Dunbar, 1993, 1996; Locke, 1993; Morris, 1967). It might even be true that the little ones who call more to attract attention and use the call further to maintain contact with adults get more effective attention from the parents and other caretakers. The squeaky wheel gets the grease. Further, the adults who also are capable of vocalizing more than their ancestors (although perhaps not as much as their offspring) also vocalize to gain attention and social support. Those who use the call more or perhaps more effectively may have a survival advantage.

It may be important that the call be a relatively quiet one (as quasivowels are), so as not to attract unnecessary attention to the group from potential predators—loud enough to engage the conspecifics nearby, but not too loud. Survival is sometimes fostered by not calling attention to oneself (see review of relevant reasoning in Hauser, 1996). Perhaps even more important is that it may be critical that the vocalization be inhibitable and that it possess the quality of Contextual Freedom to the extent that it can be suppressed in any circumstance in which silence is necessary.

The changeover to a more vocal species may also be fortuitous from the standpoint of a graded change in hairiness and the effects of this change on the role of grooming in the society (Dunbar, 1996; Morris, 1967). Because the new species is neotenous, it may be less hirsute and consequently less inclined to have skin parasites. Perhaps the vocal contact call begins in this species to supplant grooming as a social activity, binding the group together vocally in the current generation and enhancing the ties between family members and friends with vocal sounds that play a portion of the role that touch played exclusively in prior generations.

Scene 2: The Neotenous Primate That Elaborated Vocalization as a Tool of Social Interaction

Imagine now that many generations have passed, and we are in a period of a new species descended from the prior one, perhaps *Australopithecus africanus* or a related group. The band of individuals we see is even more vocally active than the earlier one. All the fixed signals that were available before have been preserved, but the quasivowel-like sound has been elaborated to include articulatory movements of the vocal tract that occur simultaneously with normal phonation. These primitive articulations tend to occur especially often when two intimates (parent and child, mates, siblings, close friends, etc.) are face to face. Even more than in the prior group, these new creatures of the human line use face-to-face vocalization in a way that appears to be taking over the functions that were more commonly served by grooming in prior generations (again see Dunbar, 1996, and Morris, 1967, for speculations on the potential importance of vocal grooming). However, it is notably the case that the new group vocalizes in unison and in alternation using both the old contact call and the new articulatory innovation of the contact call in face-to-face interactions that appear to serve a purpose primarily of social support, in a pattern that resembles Primitive Articulation stage interactions in human infants (Anderson et al., 1977; Beebe, Stern, & Jaffe, 1979; Kaye & Fogel, 1980; Lester, Hoffman, & Brazelton, 1985). Perhaps even more important, these vocalizations occur often in cases of direct eye contact and without the slightest hint of hostility. They appear to function in social bonding and expression of affinity. Of course hostility can be expressed, but when it is, a substantially different display is presented, involving other kinds of sounds that do not show normal phonation or highly variable articulatory patterns.

As with the vocal innovations of the ancestral group, the vocalizations of the new category can be produced either in the social circumstances or in circumstances of pure vocal exercise. The pattern manifests extensive Contextual Freedom, with total inhibitability, along with increasing Free Expressivity, Directivity, and Interactivity. The sounds that are produced show a pattern of exploration that reveals the very beginnings of Signal Analysis.

These primates are even more neotenous than their ancestors and one of the effects of the neoteny is that the elaboration of the vocalizations has been fostered. The primitive articulations utilized by these primates are unlike anything in the rest of the primate world, in part because they are produced sometimes as mere exercise, and in part because their elaborateness of structure and changeability from utterance to utterance is unlike any type of vocalization in the fixed signal repertoire of the species or that of its ancestors. These new primates are able to vocalize and move the articulators at will.

The survival advantages of the vocal innovations in this species may be much the same as the lesser vocal enhancements that occurred in their ancestral species. The social nature of vocalization may provide a fill-in for reduced grooming (hairiness continues to abate), or may even provide an enhanced basis for social connection. The members of this group may be more well-integrated than their neighbors and prior relatives in part because they have a more effective means of nurturing social connections that are increasingly important in the mosaic savannah life, where hunting and gathering have to be conducted cooperatively and where group cooperation in protection from predators is critical. The claim here is not that vocalizations are directly used by these primates as tools of communication during hunting or gathering, but rather that the communicative interactions fostered by the new vocal actions help solidify social connections that are needed in cooperative activities that may be conducted through other sorts of nonvocal communication.

The vocal capabilities of this primate group are compatible with those of human infants in the Primitive Articulation stage. Such infants produce primitively articulated vocalizations with normal phonation in gooing. They use such sounds in face-to-face interaction with caretakers, and appear thereby to establish deep social bonds (Oller, 1980a; Papoušek, 1994). The vocal capabilities of this group also show certain infrasemiotic capabilities that resemble more advanced human infants of the Expansion stage. The Free Expressivity of vocalizations continues to show instrumental uses for vocalizations that are not typically seen in the Primitive Articulation stage. In addition, the current group has begun primitive exploration of sounds, a systematic Signal Analysis. There are relatively few vocal types available, but the new group is just beginning to develop new ones.

Scene 3: The Neotenous Primate That Vocalized Freely and Found Ways to Use New Vocal Types Functionally

The progress of humanization continues in the next era. The new primate in the human line (perhaps a later version of *Australopithecus Africanus*) has a repertoire of vocal signals that is substantially expanded beyond that of the ancestral group. Instead of two vocal types that can be produced freely, there are many. These include the quasivowels and articulated sounds (which already in the immediate ancestral group might have been thought to consist of a number of different sound types given their variety), as well as a number of other signals. Sounds that are often used with specific social values now can be utilized freely in play or vocal exercise. Furthermore, vegetative sounds, such as coughing, can similarly be produced at will. In addition, the newfound freedom of production of sounds has been extended even further. The property of

Signal Analysis has been developed much more fully, and the new hominids produce sounds that are typical of the early Expansion stage in modern human infants. They explore fundamental frequency through very high-pitched and very low-pitched sounds. They produce sounds of high intensity and low intensity and long and short duration, and they explore the space of spectral variations that can be produced through phonation with a variety of vocal tract shapes. These efforts at vocal expansion are pursued in part for the mere interest of it especially among the young of the species.

The brain of these new hominids has expanded further, perhaps entirely as a by-product of continued neotenization, perhaps in part as a result of additional structural mutations that have expanded aspects of the brain to allow richer voluntary control of vocal acts, especially an anterior limbic cortical region and tracts connecting to brain stem sites that are the final stations of motor control of the vocal tract (see Jürgens, 1992, for a review of literature indicating how speech and other vocalizations are controlled). Enhanced neoteny has given the young of these hominids more opportunity to consolidate the ability to vocalize during the early period of special plasticity in vocal development. The mature members of the species maintain, as a result of extended experience, a series of vocal types that can be produced at will. Some of these vocalizations do not have fixed values at all. Others have values that are loosely fixed in that they have typical functions, even though the sounds can be produced with no social intent at all, and the pragmatic intents that are transmitted can be varied dramatically with circumstance. These include vocalizations that modern humans might analogize to squeals, growls, yells, whispers, and raspberries.

In addition, the new hominids produce a wide variety of vowel-like vocalizations (not so wide as in mature humans, but still including at least a half-dozen clearly distinguishable spectral types). These vowel-like sounds actually have two important variable characteristics. One is associated with their intonation and duration. The other is associated with their quality or spectrum. The differentiation plays a significant role in the development of well-formed Syllabification (see chaps. 4 and 5).

In this line of hominids, the newly evolved vocalizations are associated with special pragmatic functions. Growling, for example, is an all-purpose expression of frustration, anger, or threat, depending on the circumstances, and is graded for intensity. To express threat, eye contact (Directivity) is required. Frustration expression through growling, on the other hand, does not include eye contact, and often occurs when the hominids are alone, an indication of further growth in Free Expressivity. Squealing similarly is utilized as an expression of delight, surprise, or even fear, again depending on the circumstances, and again graded for intensity. Even though the squeals and growls have typical values, both these vocal types are explored in infants for no purpose other than to gain control of them (indicating Signal Analysis), and mature members of the species also have the ability to produce them at will.

Of particular interest are the vowel-like sounds that have come to be utilized with varying intonations and durations. These intonations and durational variations are produced in conditions of normal phonation in the new hominids, a fact that differentiates them sharply from squeals and growls. The intonations are produced in differentiable patterns that are used with social and conversational intent. This usage indicates the beginnings of Categorical Adaptation, the ability of the new group to acquire new sounds that can be brought to the service of communication.

One such sound shows a rising contour, and indicates that the speaker wishes the listener to take a vocal turn, to respond to a request (which may be expressed in part gesturally, e.g., by reaching toward a desired object), or to respond to an offer (which can also be expressed gesturally through holding an offered object toward the listener). Another is long, starting with a rapid fall from high pitch and gliding into a slow, long, lower pitch, indicating a desire on the part of the speaker to console or sympathize. A falling contour, not terribly long, but also not abrupt, indicates the end of a vocal turn or a response of assent to a request. An abrupt, short, falling, vowel-like sound expresses refusal, displeasure (although not necessarily threat), or finality (see Fernald et al., 1989, and Papoušek, Papoušek, & Symmes, 1991, for information on intonational patterns and corresponding pragmatic intents that appear to be universal in parent utterances to infants).

The different vowel qualities are of special interest in part because they can be varied independently of the intonational and durational patterns. Primitive vocal Conventionality begins to appear in this group of hominids, and it requires the exploitation of the differing qualities of these vowel-like sounds. Different bands of the new hominids, if they are separated for many generations, come to assign somewhat different functions to the different possible vowels, and also the different bands may use different numbers of the vowels functionally. For example, a wide open sound without lip rounding may be used to indicate assent, and the function can be reinforced by use of the appropriate intonation. A lip-rounded vowel-like sound may be used to express surprise or displeasure, and again the function can be reinforced with an appropriate intonation. With wide lip spreading and teeth nearly clenched, the vowel-like sound may be used to indicate warning. However, none of these sounds has exactly the same value in each band. The vowel qualities are assigned in part conventionally and must be acquired in each generation through imitation. Many combinations of intonation and vowel-like sounds are possible and because they may mix intents, the hominids acquire many gradations along two dimensions simultaneously. If the vowel-like sound used to indicate assent is combined with the intonation that gives the vocal turn to the listener, the result is potentially complex and might be interpreted, for example, to mean something like "You have my permission, but do you really want to go through with this?"

More elaborate Conventionality is seen in the fact that different bands of the new hominids make use of different sounds of the expanding repertoire to subserve different functions and to make primitive reference to different entities. The vocal signals thus used include friction sounds (such as raspberries, produced with either the lips or the tongue) and vowel-like sounds to signal alarm or encourage attack (mobbing). These signals can be specific to specific kinds of dangers or targets of mobbing, and in this way they may partly resemble the alarm calls of modern nonhuman primates (Caro & Hauser, 1992; Macedonia & Evans, 1993; Marler et al., 1992; Struhsaker, 1967). These signals are different, however, in that they incorporate Conventionality. The alarm signals are acquired by the group through processes indicating Imitability and Conventionality. There are differences in how these sounds are used in different, widely separated communities. A friction sound used to indicate snake danger is peculiar to a group that lives in a region where a hissing snake is found. The sound, in fact, resembles the hissing of the snake. A similar sound comes to indicate predator in the grass danger in another group, which finds the hissing sound to resemble the sound of a big cat moving in the grass. These patterns of iconic representation indicate Conventionality without Arbitrarity. They also indicate a primitive kind of Designation, not unlike that found, for example, in modern vervet monkeys (Struhsaker, 1967).

The discovery of interesting or useful things is also accompanied by vocalizations that are tied by convention to particular types of discovery in these new societies. A particular smacking of the lips may be used to indicate discovery of a source of particular types of fruit, for example. Nuts, on the other hand, might be indicated by clicking sounds. Again, the primitive Designation manifest in these vocalizations bears a resemblance to food-specific calls in certain modern monkey groups (Hauser, 1996; Hauser & Marler, 1993).

Facial expression also plays a major role in communication among the new hominids. When vocalizing socially, they often coordinate the sounds with facial expressions, yielding further reinforcement for interpretation of communicative intents (which, it should be noted, show illocutionary forces, but not meanings) and further possibilities for combinations that enrich the total potential repertoire of communications. Gesture is also coordinated with vocalization and facial expression and is utilized alone in many communications. Some gestures have come to be used in roughly the same ways across all members of the species. A request can be indicated by reaching for an object with an open hand while looking at a conspecific that is near the object. At this stage of evolution, the object requested in this way must be located between the requester and the listener, so that little change in line of regard is required between the object and the listener. Offers can be made by reaching out toward another member of the band with an object in hand (see Mundy et al., 1992, for a review of ways that human infants use these kinds of gestures). Other hand signals may also be used, but they tend to be more specific to specific bands.

This new hominid group shows growth in a number of vocal communicative properties over their ancestral group. They use Directivity more extensively, in part because they have many more vocal types through which they can exploit it. The new vocal types have been developed through a growing Contextual Freedom (presumably based on brain changes) that has allowed exploratory Signal Analysis, and both properties are now well established. Vocal Interactivity is more extensive, because the repertoire of vocal communication includes many interactively specific units such as requests, assents, offers, and refusals. Limited vocal Conventionality has entered the system but tends to be based on iconic vocal signals only. Gestural iconic signals may also be involved at this point in the evolution of the hominid line. Categorical Adaptation has just begun to be seen in the fact that new discrete signal types are created through explorations of the dimensionality of signals. The beginnings of Hot–Cool Synthesis can be seen in the utilization of both vowel-like quality and intonational cues simultaneously to transmit complex forces. Syllabification exists, but it is primitive, not yet showing all the characteristics of well-formed syllables in human speech.

The advantages to the new hominid line of the advances in vocal communication may have been various. The vocal system they possess is far more important as a social mechanism, and now plays roles not only in the ways that members of bands connect emotionally, but how they conduct internal and sometimes external affairs. They negotiate primitive deals with gesture and vocalization, by offering, requesting, assenting, and refusing. Their vocal system aids in the process of locating opportunity (food types, objects of interest) and announcing danger of specific types. Perhaps most important, they have opened the communicative system in terms of its potential values. No longer must each vocalization be tied to a fixed function. New values can be sought, although in limited ways.

These new hominids have capabilities that seem predictable on the basis of early Expansion stage infant capabilities. In the early Expansion stage we find exploration of many signal dimensions in vocal play. Signal dimensions are sometimes manipulated simultaneously, synthesizing a wide variety of multifaceted sound types. In this way, new vocal types without any necessary values appear. Early Expansion stage infants also show the capability to control vocalizations of the vegetative repertoire (e.g., coughing playfully). In the same period, human infants use vocalizations of the expanding repertoire intentionally to gain attention, amuse, and express complaints.

Scene 4: The Hominid That Expanded Triadic Reference With Vocal Accompaniment and Elaborated Vocal Articulation

In Scene 4, the hominid line has developed further (to *Homo habilis* perhaps) and now has primitive tools of stone used for cutting and skinning. These hominids have even more elaborate vocalizations than the previous group.

The primary difference in the types of vocalizations is that they include more elaborate articulations than before. The vocal tract moves from wide open to entirely closed during the production of normal phonation. These vocal gestures can involve the lips, the tongue, and the mandible, and voicing can be interrupted during the gestures, whereas on other occasions it is kept constant, indicating that the new line is capable of a substantial degree of voluntary control over movements of the vocal tract.

The new hominids are busy in procurement and preparation of food and in care of the camp space. One of the most notable new features of how they interact is that they point to objects and share attention regarding them with other members of their band.

One member of the band is skinning a rabbit, and he finds his stone to be inadequate. He vocalizes with a particular vowel-like call to get attention from another member, who has other stones within reach. The first hominid waits until the other makes eye contact, then the first points to the stones and looks at them, then back at the listener. The vocalization has a rising intonation, and may be taken, in this circumstance of gesture and physical arrangement of objects and interactants to mean "Do you have a better cutting tool?", although the propositional characteristics of the putative meaning are implied by the circumstances, rather than being expressed linguistically. The pattern reveals Designation, but not yet Semanticity, because the vocalization does not, in and of itself, specify the stones as the objects of Designation.

In another part of the camp, a mother vocalizes a frustration complaint, looking at a rotted piece of fruit she has just opened. An adolescent son within earshot calls to her, then when she gives eye contact, he points to the other side of the camp where a brother is bringing more fruit. This pattern again reveals the communicative property of Designation.

Pointing is a major aspect of this culture. These hominids understand each other's minds more than prior ones did. They use vocalization to support the process of sharing attention to objects. They gain each other's attention often by vocalization, and they often follow eye contact with pointing and gazing toward an object of potential joint interest. The members of the species know a good bit about what their conspecifics think, because they share attention, and they use vocalization to support the development of that sharing. Furthermore, once attention sharing has been established through the sequence of vocalization, eye contact, pointing, and reestablishment of eye contact, the interaction may continue. A new vocalization may be used to indicate some desire, confirmation, or request with regard to the object of reference.

Triadic reference of this sort (I, you, thing) is a fundamental characteristic of linguistic capability (Butterworth, 1996; Mundy et al., 1992; Tomasello & Farrar, 1986), manifesting the property of Designation and laying a critical foundation for Semanticity. The vocalizations that accompany the triadic activities of the new hominids are not, however, fully compatible with Semanticity because the vocalizations do not specifically refer to the objects of attention (or classes of objects) designated in individual interactions. Instead, the vocalizations simply support the establishment and maintenance of joint attention toward whatever object is of interest. It should be recalled that the prior group showed another, more primitive sort of triadic reference embedded within requests and offers. In the case of these limited requests and offers (which continue to be utilized in the new hominid line), the object of joint attention, which the speaker wishes to obtain, is within reach of the listener. One might read the vocalization and gesture complex of the speaker to mean "Give me that thing," or "You may have this thing." In the current case, the object of joint attention need not be involved in any immediate desire and need not be in reach. The reference can be utterly neutral emotionally, involving intellectual interest only. The vocalizations that support such joint reference are similarly unbound to emotional content. They simply call for eye contact, so that the act of shared attention can proceed. Under some, though not all circumstances, one might read the vocalization and gesture complex of the speaker to mean "Look at that thing."

Of course the current group of hominids continues to be capable of making vocal requests or offers in the context of objects, but now those requests or offers can be made either when an object is within reach or when it has been established as a distal joint referent that may be out of the line of regard between speaker and listener, and thus requires that both parties turn their heads to see the object and alternate gaze to confirm the joint referencing: "Go get that thing and bring it to me." The pragmatic information transmitted in these interactions is fairly complex, but the vocalization component of the interaction is simple, involving a single sound that plays merely a supporting role in the comment or request.

The somewhat more elaborate vocalizations of the new hominids are extended into further domains of communication with one important new class of vocal types gaining prominence. These are articulated vocalizations involving wide open vowels. These can be used with the varying intonations described for the ancestral group with regard to unarticulated vowels, with similar pragmatic functions as those used by the ancestral group. These complex sounds can play important roles in negotiations and form important aspects of communications that follow acts of joint attention in ways similar to those of vocalizations evolved in the prior era.

In addition, the vocalization capability of this group of hominids extensively includes the property of Imitability. New signals are created for the community, not just by exploration and gradual assimilation, but by direct modeling. The new humans can imitate sounds that others produce and this ability allows them to begin the process of adaptation toward true lexical abilities.

The major vocal advance of the current species in terms of survivability is found in the support for joint attention and Designation that is provided by vocalization in the group. Joint understanding and reference make it possible for these hominids to work together more effectively with respect to objects. Tool use in these hominids may be greatly buttressed by the growth of joint attention and the vocalizations that help establish and maintain it.

The vocalizations of this species are similar to those of late Expansion stage infants who produce, along with all the earlier sounds, marginal babbling involving varied articulations along with full vowels and normal phonation. Joint reference often begins to be established in late Expansion stage infants as well. No entirely new property of vocal communication is established in this period but foundations are laid for two important ones. By articulating broadly from open to closed vocal tract, the new species establishes an important basis for Syllabification. By developing Imitability, the new species prepares the way for the first vocalizations that in later hominids will show the property of Conventionality. Through the evolution of joint attention and vocal Designation, the species establishes a primary basis for Semanticity.

Scene 5: The Hominid That Discovered Well-Formed Syllabification and Arbitrarity

A major advance is observable in Scene 5. The further neotenized hominids (perhaps early *Homo erectus*) have even larger brains than before, and they have begun both to produce a new class of vocalizations that include enormous possibilities for acoustic differentiation and to use the new vocalizations in a notably new way.

The new vocalization types are produced in brief chunks of 300 msec to 700 msec in most cases, and include normal phonation, with articulation from a closed vocal tract (margin) to an open one (nucleus), and a rapid transition between the two. This Syllabification allows the formation of quite a number of new signals because the rapid spectral transitions produced in these vocalizations are distinguishable in a categorical fashion for contrasting articulations of the lips or tongue (as margins) toward any of several open mouth postures for the syllable nuclei (see chaps. 4 and 5 for a review of the development of well-formed syllables in human infants). The new signals are acquired by members of the group through Imitability and thus show Categorical Adaptation to well-formed syllables.

The evolution of well-formed syllables may have followed the evolution of the capability to use innovated vocal signals (ones not belonging to the fixed signal repertoire) in the emergence of true lexical items. On the other hand, both Syllabification and true lexicalization could have occurred simultaneously. When we see the current group, both syllables and lexical items manifesting Conventionality are already present. A member of the band points to a tree in which a bird has landed. As he points, he produces a crisp syllable that would be well-formed by our own standards, *dih* [dɪ]. The group looks to the tree to see the bird and is satisfied that there is a bird in the tree. There is no necessary action by the group with regard to the bird, because as in many cases with this hominid band, communication can be about an entity without requiring or suggesting any action with regard to the entity. Communication of the triadic sort has been extended in this group to include both joint attention and labeling, and both of these can be utilized in the context of mere intellectual sharing or when desirable in the context of a variety of other interactions—bartering, hunting, criticizing, and so on.

When they label objects, these hominids manifest command of several critical new properties of communication. Not only do they fully show Designation of objects with vocalization, but they also show Semanticity by virtue of their analytical reference to specific entities by means of vocalization. Another property manifest in the new group is Arbitrarity. The syllables that are applied to classes of entities are applied in the absence of any similarity between the sound of the syllable and any obvious property of the class of entities that the syllable represents. The connections between such syllables and their meanings are established through Imitability and Conventionality, and the particular connections can be different for different subgroups of the new hominids. For example, in a faraway band of the same genetic stock, the syllable *dih* may be used to refer to a type of tool rather than to a bird.

The property of Semanticity is manifest by virtue of the fact that multiple illocutionary forces can be transmitted in vocal acts involving the same symbolic reference. The bird can be requested, named, rejected, or its identity as a bird can be questioned by use of the word *dih*, in differing circumstances and with differing intonations. The fact that differing intonations can be utilized with the syllable even as the syllable's reference is maintained indicates that the new hominids command Hot–Cool Synthesis (Locke, 1993).

All the changes noted in this species (Syllabification, Arbitrarity, Semanticity, and increased ability to command Hot–Cool Synthesis) seem to have developed practically simultaneously. This does not indicate that the properties are entirely logically tied together, but rather that practical facts regarding the development of communicative systems within communities press elaboration in each domain, with progress in one laying groundwork for further progress in another. What the new hominids came to need was new ways to express their emerging joint awareness of entities and events in the world. To express that awareness they needed new vehicles of transmission, and plenty of them, so syllables were developed. To express that awareness they also needed the ability to use the new vehicles in correspondence with any new conception, so they came up with Arbitrarity. To express the awareness flexibly, they needed to be able to use newly formed arbitrary vocal signals with a variety of forces, so they came up with Semanticity and Hot–Cool Synthesis. All these things may have happened within a relatively short period of evolution because they were all driven by a need to create a lexicon in the context of an expanding capability for joint attention and joint action with regard to entities.

It is unclear whether the many communicative advances of this group were attributable to neoteny and its many possible epiphenomena or whether they required structural mutations as well. Did the bigger brain create syllables, or did a special mutation or series of mutations create a special ability of the brain and vocal tract to produce syllables? A likely possibility is that precanonical syllables were first recruited to arbitrary lexical formations in a late version of the Scene 4 hominids. However, precanonical (marginal) syllables are slowly articulated. Well-formed, canonical syllables are faster and more efficient. Vowel sounds alone also cannot function as efficiently as well-formed syllables can, in part because the number of potential individual vowels is quite limited. Consequently, natural selection pressure may have soon begun to cull the population so that individuals who produced syllables more quickly, with more canonical transitions, were more likely to survive. Perhaps structural mutations were required or perhaps not, but over some period of evolution, the survivors were members of the group that could produce well-formed syllables.

The survival advantages of Syllabification, Arbitrarity, Semanticity, and Hot–Cool Synthesis are notable. The new hominids can communicate more effectively and more quickly about the things they hunt and gather, the things they use in camp, and the people with whom they interact. Individuals who communicate more effectively are more likely to survive because they are more likely to be able to find food cooperatively and to protect themselves from predators. In a continuation of the deep foundations that began the evolution of the vocal capacity in the hominid line, they are more likely to be fully socially connected with their community. Vocalization is becoming, in this hominid stage, a primary means by which all social transactions, whether emotional, intellectual, or commercial, are conducted.

The hominids of the present scene vocalize in a way that is consistent with the vocal capabilities of Canonical stage human infants. However, Arbitrarity, Semanticity, and Hot–Cool Synthesis represent abilities that correspond to more advanced human infants of the middle of the second year of life. The assumption here is that the evolutionary sequence probably could not be the same as the modern ontogenetic one, as communicative needs may have been required to drive the evolution of Syllabification. It is hard to see why a rich syllable inventory and capability would have appeared and survived if it had no function. On the other hand, once rich communicative functions had begun to be developed, pressure for the development of additional and especially potentially rapidly transmitted vocal categories could create the selectional pressures that may have given rise to Syllabification.

Scene 6: The Early Humans That Discovered Recombinability to Support a Rapidly Growing Need for Vocabulary

In Scene 6 early humans (perhaps of the late *Homo erectus* type) still lack many elaborate linguistic features, but they have made one important new vocal innovation. They recombine syllables in strings, producing an expanded potential lexicon. The appearance of Recombinability owes to the increasing pressure to be able to make communicative reference freely to the many entities, events, emotions, and functions that can be considered jointly in the species. The Scene 5 species developed syllables to expand the repertoire and speed up its utilization, but the numbers of available items in the repertoire of syllables remained limited to perhaps one or two dozen. Through Recombinability, the new group expands that number to 100 or more, where both single syllables and strings of syllables can be used as lexical items.

An additional new property of communication found in the new species is Displaceability. They can talk about entities and events not present in the here and now. For example, in a group with a word meaning *lion*, they can question whether a lion may be nearby, indicate that a lion was seen before (perhaps on returning from a hunt), or note that a lion may have been the author of a kill. The different temporal and spatial references are established by contextual or gestural factors in each case, because linguistic innovations such as past tense or spatially specific phrases have not yet been developed.

The vocal capabilities of these new hominids are consistent with those of late Canonical stage infants or infants in the first months of the second year of life. However, as before, the system of vocal transmission in the new humans is being driven by communicative pressures that are associated with a growing lexical potential. These early humans show much more lexical capability than human infants of the late Canonical stage, and instead resemble modern infants well into the second half of the second year of life, both in terms of Recombinability of syllables and Displaceability of reference.

Scene 7: The Early Humans That Began to Speak in Segmented Syllables and Short Sentences

In this last scene, still well before the beginning of full-fledged human language with its elaborate syntactic systems and indefinitely large classes of potential sentences, we find a group that is very human, but still distinctly limited linguistically (perhaps *Archaic Homo sapiens*). These people talk in ways that resemble the communications of modern humans at the beginning of the third year of life. They produce many words and combine the words in short strings. The size of their potential lexicons has been expanded dramatically through Segmentation of the well-formed syllabic inventory. The new humans produce syllables that represent many recombinations of nuclei and margins drawn from syllables in the species repertoire. A rich base of Categorical Adaptation to new features of segments is also seen having been elaborated beyond abilities of ancestral species. Features in terms of which syllables can be differentiated are now expanded based on elaboration of the featural inventory and Imitability to spread the elaborated forms. Different groups of the new humans show somewhat different segmental features because the elaborations are creative, depending on the community's vocal style. Additions of new featural possibilities within communities are presumably not made by conscious intent, but rather unconsciously (although not uncreatively) in response to the pressure for a broadened lexicon.

The two- and three-word sentences that are produced by these early humans represent powerful tools, manifesting the property of Propositionality, but they lack much of the power that will ultimately appear with the advent of specific syntactic devices, grammatical morphemes, and functions that will allow rich formulations with sequenced and embedded clauses that are coreferenced across sentences and discourses. Still, these early humans seem entirely unlike any other primates. They have huge lexicons, numbering hundreds of items, and they produce creative propositions involving two and three terms chosen from the lexicon. They create new lexical items relatively freely, and they maintain a distinction between illocutionary force and meaning in vocal communication. They can talk about a wide variety of topics and can utilize this capability to plan and critique their own actions or those of others. They can negotiate and dispute, and they have the ability to express many kinds and degrees of social affiliation by talking.

It might be said that the early humans of this stage are speakers of a very limited "pidgin" language, lacking syntactic devices other than those implied by stringing together two or three words. The communications include no grammatical agreement devices, no articles, no particles, no grammatical gender or number, and no cohesion markers. Bickerton's (1981) speculations about "protolanguage" in early humans would appear to begin about at this point or perhaps even a bit later.

The early humans of this stage command Rhythmic Hierarchy in communicative utterances to the limited extent permitted by the short utterances they produce. The utterances are produced with varied intonational contours that are capable of transmitting varied illocutionary forces and emotional messages with each semantically coded sentence. This Hot–Cool Synthesis represents a more complicated mixing of illocution and semantics than seen in the prior stages of vocal development in the human line because now the intonations apply to multiple words, joined together in primitive propositions.

The control of Rhythmic Hierarchy and Hot–Cool Synthesis is also seen in vocalizations that involve more than just a few syllables. The new hominids can produce longer sequences of pure syllabic sound. These sounds are babble play of the variegated or gibberish variety in infants born to these early humans and may include mixtures of real words and babble embedded in sequences of Rhythmic Hierarchy, showing rich intonational variation (see Vihman & Miller, 1988, or Elbers & Ton, 1985, for information on mixed vocal play in late babbling and early speech of infant humans). However, in adults, such babble-like or partially babble-like utterances may acquire an artistic flavor more akin to musical or poetic performance.

The early humans of this, our last scene, are presumably on the threshold of the great explosion of syntactic systems (Bickerton, 1981) and perhaps also of modifications in the mature vocal tract that have been thought to make possible a wider variety of vowel types and formant transitions than those in nonhuman primates or ancient hominids (Laitman & Heimbuch, 1982; Laitman & Reidenberg, 1993; Lieberman & Crelin, 1971). In terms of command of vocal communication properties, these early humans resemble modern human infants 18 to 24 months of age.

LIMITATIONS AND ADVANTAGES
OF THE SPECULATIVE PREHISTORY

I hasten now to reemphasize that the speculative reconstruction is one of many possibilities consistent with the facts of vocal development and infrastructural natural logic of communication. Other orders of events are possible in many cases and much may have depended on the specifics of not only environmental conditions at various stages (e.g., there was intermittently quite a bit of ice to deal with), but also on the accidents of mutations that happened to occur to provide the basis for adaptation.

At the same time the proposed sequence of evolutionary adaptations in vocal communication involves features that appear consistent with other aspects of empirical paleontology. There have been long periods of apparent stasis in human evolution and apparent periods of relatively rapid change (Leakey, 1994). The pattern of paleontological results suggests the existence of capabilities that changed discontinuously at key points, perhaps in keeping with the punctuated equilibrium idea (Eldredge & Gould, 1972) that emphasizes discontinuities in evolution in distinction with the traditional belief in long periods of gradual change through natural selection. This speculative prehistory is concordant with both the possibility of periods of stasis in evolution and with periods of relative stability in development of vocalizations in human infants. At each scene of the evolutionary story, it is possible to formulate plausible selection advantages to the vocal adaptations of the period, some suggested directly by facts of infant development, where socially significant communication and profound cognitive communicative innovations occur within the first year of life. In scaling Mount Improbable, that huge feature of the evolutionary landscape that would seem impossible to conquer in a single leap (Dawkins, 1996), humans may have found ways to move up in stages to plateaus of improved capability.

As we reflect on the tremendous interest that has been found in recent years in the evaluation of complex syntax as a manifestation of the human gift of language, the speculative human prehistory presented here may provide some hints about what the critical underpinnings may have been for the explosion of language posited to have occurred in the Upper Paleolithic era. My guess is that systematic growth in control over a variety of infrastructural properties was required. Each period of growth may have produced a plateau of capability, but formed the groundwork for development toward higher plateaus. Eventually ancient humans may have reached a final plateau from which the scaling of the linguistic peak could proceed.

A large and rapidly growing lexicon appears to be a *sine qua non* of the onset of syntax in children (Bates et al., 1996), and no large lexicon would seem possible in the absence of properties that both elaborate the signal system and allow for arbitrary assignment of meanings though Imitability and Conventionality. Surely, if nothing else is obvious from what we know of child language, the appearance of two-term propositions in the second year of life suggests clearly that it is possible to possess important communicative capability (which may have had critical survival value for ancient humans) without having complex syntax. The proposed stages of development of the human species can be thought, then, to parallel aspects of stages of modern infant language development because both evolution and ontogeny are driven by the same external constraints (Koffka, 1928) of natural logic. Although these constraints do not suggest an absolutely necessary sequence of evolution (any more than they require every infant to go through exactly the same sequence), they do suggest naturally preferable sequences and stages in the possible ways that our ancestors came to be able to talk.

14

Comparing Fixed Vocal Signals Across Humans and Other Modern Primate Species

AN ESPECIALLY USEFUL POINT OF COMPARISON FOR HUMAN AND NONHUMAN VOCAL SYSTEMS

The infrastructural approach offers the opportunity to compare modern vocal systems at the level of properties, a method that lends itself well to illustrating differences between systems that are widely discrepant. The contrasts between human speech and the signaling systems of other species can be clarified and given substance within the properties approach. However, human and nonhuman vocal systems also show notable similarities at the level of certain properties. To focus on the similarities, it may be necessary to leave speech aside and allow comparison of other aspects of the human and nonhuman vocal systems.

Deacon (1997) made a comparable point, noting that human fixed vocalizations and expressions stand in stark contrast to the elements of speech, although bearing important similarities to vocal calls and expressions of other creatures: "We too have a wide range of innately produced and universally understood facial expressions, vocalizations, and gestures. As in other species, they are an irreplaceable component of human social communication. Yet this is not analogous to being bilingual" (p. 33).

In the study of vocal ethology, it is easy to lose sight of the fact that simply comparing speech with another species' vocal system does not make that other vocal system a kind of speech or a kind of language, at least not in the normal senses of the terms. It is easy to recognize that humans are not bilingual by virtue of speaking a native language and using fixed vocal signals. If one grants that fixed vocal signals are not another kind of language for humans, then it makes sense to resist treating the fixed vocal signals of other animals as if they were varieties of language.

Given that speech and fixed signal systems are widely different, why not focus effort on cross-species comparison at a point of greater similarity? Why not compare the human fixed signal system with the fixed signal systems of other animals? This chapter offers an overview of some possibilities suggested by infrastructural modeling for fixed signals, affording comparisons that may show substantial similarities across human and nonhuman systems.

FOUR TYPES OF SIGNALS IN HUMANS

As a background to the proposed approach, consider human vocal signals, categorized under four headings in Fig. 14.1. The four types of vocalization differ in both the flexibility of signal forms within each category and the size of the potential repertoire within each type. Speech is unlimited in repertoire size, but vegetative sounds (cough, sneeze, etc.) and fixed signals (cry, laugh, etc.) are essentially stable at a relatively small number, unchanging across language communities and cultures. Similarly, the forms that vegetative sounds and fixed vocal signals take are stable and recognizable all over the world, whereas the forms of speech are clearly different in different languages, even though they are all governed by a common infrastructure. The protophones (quasivowel, goo, etc.) represent an intermediate class with a larger repertoire than fixed signals or vegetative sounds, but much smaller than speech. Protophones also seem to incorporate some of the flexibility of signal form that is seen in speech, but not all of it.

The values that can be transmitted by the four types of vocalizations (Fig. 14.2) are also notably different. Vegetative sounds acquire interpretation inci-

* *Vegetative*   * Small repertoire, immutable form

* *Fixed signals*   * Small repertoire, immutable form

* *Protophones*   * Larger repertoire, flexible form

* *Speech*   * Unlimited repertoire size, strong flexibility

FIG. 14.1.   Human signal characteristics.

dentally, primarily because listeners make judgments about the bodily condition of the producer of the sounds (Is he choking? Is she allergic? etc.). The social or informational value of vegetative sounds is usually unintentional on the part of the producer. On the other hand, fixed vocal signals have inherent significant social functions (He's threatening me! She's appealing for help! etc.), and they appear to have been shaped through evolution to serve those functions. Their interpretations are not incidental, but are part of a system of communication evolved through natural selection to facilitate social functions (threat, contact, appeasement, etc.) that both producers and receivers command and execute through the signals. Speech is fundamentally different in that its units of transmission have values that can be assigned freely. They can transmit either social functions or any kind of information, concrete or imaginary. Protophones provide an intermediate vocal type with more flexibility of value than fixed signals, but less than speech (see chap. 9).

The ways that connections can be established between signals and values also differ across the types of vocalization (Fig. 14.3). Bodily functions determine the class of interpretations that are normally imposed by listeners on vegetative sounds. Fixed vocal signals have connections with values that can be presumed to have been modified through natural selection, which can be assumed to have favored signals with survival value as communication devices. Consequently, the values of both vegetative sounds and fixed signals are relatively stable across time. Whatever range of values can be transmitted by a vegetative sound or fixed signal today, that range was essentially the same 1,000 years ago and is the same across all human cultures at present. In speech, on the other hand, values can be assigned at the whim of the community of us-

- *Vegetative*   • Indexical bodily functions

- *Fixed signals*   • Fixed social functions

- *Protophones*   • Relatively free social values

- *Speech*   • Entirely free values, social or informational

FIG. 14.2.   Value characteristics in human vocalizations.

• *Vegetative*	• Preset by the nature of bodily functions
• *Fixed signals*	• Predetermined by natural history
• *Protophones*	• Can be set by individuals in play and interaction
• *Speech*	• Flexibly set in social learning

FIG. 14.3. How signals and values are connected in human vocalizations.

ers, and consequently different languages are mutually unintelligible, and ancestral languages are different from modern ones. Protophones have values that in early stages of development seem to resemble those of fixed signals, but clearly migrate in function as infants become increasingly capable of vocalizing in a variety of social contexts where the protophones can be adapted to new purposes and utilized variably from one occasion to another.

The four vocal types present a sort of scale of elaboration of the infrastructural communicative properties that were evaluated in chapter 12. Vegetative sounds show no significant role for any of the 18 properties. Fixed signals indicate some control of the more basic infrasemiotic properties (Contextual Freedom, Free Expressivity, and Directivity), but weak or no control of others. Speech shows control of all the 18 properties, and protophones show development of the properties step by step across the first 18 months of life (see Fig. 14.4).

FIXED SIGNALS AS A POINT OF COMPARISON

Humans and nonhumans share two major types of vocalizations and at a general level, the two types seem to have important features in common across many species. Vegetative sounds (sneezing, coughing, burping, etc.) clearly occur in a wide variety of mammals, including vervets, squirrel monkeys, chimpanzees, gorillas, and my standard poodle. Fixed signals also occur in a wide variety of species. Figure 14.5 provides a summary of general similarities in the apparent design of human fixed vocal signals and those of nonhuman primates.

In signal design, both human fixed signals and those of other primates appear to be relatively immutable and to pertain to a relatively small class (somewhere between four and a few score of vocal types per species, depending on how the counting is done; this is discussed later). In terms of values that can be transmitted, all the systems seem similar. Values represent social functions rather than semantic meanings in the strict sense of the term meaning in both human and nonhuman fixed signals. Further, values are assigned to signals by natural history rather than by convention in both cases. Finally, the same sorts of limitations on the command of infrastructural properties appear to

- *Vegetative*
- **Very weak or none:** no Free Expressivity, no Signal Analysis, no Directivity, no Recombinability

- *Fixed signals*
- **Weak:** some Contextual Freedom, some Free Expressivity, no Signal Analysis, some Directivity, no Recombinability

- *Protophones*
- **Strong:** Consistent growth incorporating properties systematically across the first year-and-a-half of life

- *Speech*
- **Very Strong:** Strong control of all properties of intentional communication

FIG. 14.4. Communicative properties in human vocalizations.

- **Signal characteristics**: Fixed signals in both humans and nonhumans come from a small repertoire, and show relatively immutable form
- **Value characteristics**: Both human and nonhuman systems transmit socially significant functions, not meanings
- **Signal/value connection**: Connections in both cases are predetermined by natural history of the species
- **Incorporation of communicative properties**: Both include involuntary productions, though purposeful control appears to be possible in nonhuman primates, clearly in humans

FIG. 14.5. Both humans and nonhuman primates have fixed vocal signals.

apply roughly equally in human and nonhuman primate systems of fixed vocalizations.

OPERATIONAL-LEVEL COMPARISONS WITH SPEECH IN PRIOR WORK

The notable parallels between human and nonhuman systems across all these domains suggest that it might be fruitful to compare the fixed signal systems more thoroughly, evaluating details of infrastructure in both cases. Such an effort would represent an important shift of attention. The bulk of research in vocal ethology has focused comparison on ways nonhuman animals may or may not use vocalizations in a speech-like manner. Some investigators have made direct comparisons between operational-level alphabetical speech segments and the vocalizations of nonhuman primates. For example, Andrew (1976) provided data suggesting that the gelada baboon produces particular vowel-like sounds. Another study suggested that chimpanzees show vowels and consonant–vowel combinations (Jordan, 1971). In addition, a number of studies have asked whether nonhuman primates and other animals can perceive human speech sounds categorically in patterns similar to those of human listeners (Kojima, Tatsyumi, Kiritani, & Hirose, 1989; Snowdon, 1987). In yet additional work, investigators have asked whether the human pattern of categorical speech sound perception can be found for conspecific fixed signals within nonhuman primates (Kojima & Nagumo, 1996b; Masataka, 1983; May et al., 1989; Snowdon, 1982).

All this work is directed toward evaluation of nonhuman vocal systems in terms of features of speech. Often the efforts focus attention on direct relations between operational-level speech sounds and the operational-level units of the fixed signal system of the nonhuman primates (Fig. 14.6).

PRIOR INFRASTRUCTURAL COMPARISONS

The most instructive comparisons that have been conducted, in my opinion, focus attention on infrastructural issues. For example, in a study of the vocalizations of the cotton-top tamarin, Snowdon (1982) provided an analysis of the monkey system in terms of distinctive features he denominated as upsweep, duration, frequency change, and peak frequency. The physical parameter descriptions were presented in such as way as to illuminate the infrastructural signal dimensions that are manipulated in the distinctive network of sounds used by the monkey. The analysis provided a structure both illuminating synchronic distinctions and suggesting possible routes of differentiation among the categories in evolution.

An effort of this sort lays the groundwork for a comparison between distinctive features of speech systems and distinctive features of another species, comparisons that could be conducted as suggested in Fig. 14.7. The comparison is not directed toward the operational unit types of each system (consequently the diagram shows no arrow of connection at the operational level), but rather toward the infrastructural system of features found in both species. In both cases the same physical parameters provide the raw material for infrastructural description and formulation of infrastructural principles. The comparison focuses on the principles themselves, in terms of both differences and similarities.

In essence, Snowdon's (1982) featural analysis makes clear that the cotton-top tamarin's system of fixed signals is organized in terms of a hierarchy of Signal Dimensionality. Each signal within the system relates to the others physically and is differentiable from them in terms of its placement along specifiable dimensions of acoustics and articulation. Changes in the system, either through natural selection or through learning, would presumably be constrained by the relations defined in the dimensional description.

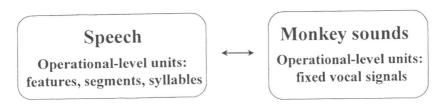

FIG. 14.6.   Comparison of nonhuman vocalizations and speech in the traditional approach.

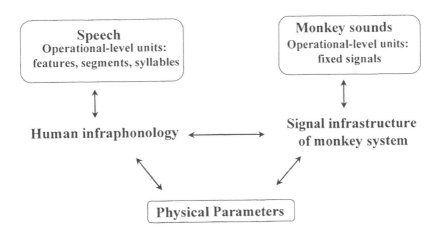

FIG. 14.7.   Comparison of nonhuman sounds and speech is more profitable in the context of infrastructural description.

AN ESPECIALLY PRIMITIVE INFRAPHONOLOGICAL
PROPERTY: SIGNAL DIMENSIONALITY

Signal Dimensionality is, I propose, an especially primitive infraphonological property of potential communicative systems. It is hard to imagine a communicative system (even one confined to only a few fixed signals) without Signal Dimensionality. Logically, it would appear that natural selection must impose Signal Dimensionality on a system as it evolves, because each item within a signaling repertoire must be systematically distinguishable from each other one to provide any survival advantage.[1]

Other infraphonological properties that have been considered in this work are closely related to and dependent on Signal Dimensionality. Signal Analysis, for example, is a more advanced property that can be said to be present in a system if members of the species explore and elaborate dimensions for their own sake, and not merely for communicative purposes. Human infants explore and play with acoustic and articulatory dimensions in the Expansion stage where, for example, squealing and growling present a sort of pitch and voice quality play at extremes along physical dimensions. Signal Dimensionality is a prerequisite to Signal Analysis because it is a part of any system in which signals are systematically differentiable and shaped by natural selection to be so. Once there are a few signals available, differentiated systematically according to dimensions, the groundwork has been laid for possible exploration of the dimensions of differentiation. At this point the property of Signal Analysis can be developed.

Snowdon's (1982) description of the vocalizations of the cotton-top tamarin specifies principles of Signal Dimensionality for the species. Similarly, the fixed vocal system of the squirrel monkey (*Saimiri sciureus*) has been featurally described and given a rich characterization in terms of social values that are transmitted by each signal in work from a group of researchers in Germany (Jürgens, 1982; Ploog, 1992; Winter et al., 1966). For both monkey systems it should prove interesting to compare the featural organization with that of the human fixed signal system, a type of comparison that has usually been bypassed in favor of speech-based evaluation in past research.

INFRASTRUCTURAL COMPARISON OF FIXED SIGNALS

To make the comparison, it is necessary to perform the same kind of featural analysis of the human fixed vocal system that has been performed for the

---

[1]Signal Dimensionality may not be involved, or may be involved less obviously in any system of vegetative sounds precisely because vegetative sounds are a type that are not shaped (or are not strongly shaped) by natural selection to serve communicative purposes. This difference between vegetative sounds and fixed signals is definitional. The former are shaped by bodily needs (respiration, swallowing, etc.), whereas the latter are shaped by communicative needs. Because the vegetative sounds are only incidentally interpreted, they may not be subject to selectional forces that impose acoustic distinctiveness.

nonhumans (see Fig. 14.8). After such analysis, the human and nonhuman systems can be compared at the infrastructural level.

Consider the analysis of the squirrel monkey system provided by the German group as summarized by Ploog (1992). According to the analysis, there are five classes of sounds, each representing a dimension of social function represented in the first column of Fig. 14.9. The names given to the call types in the second column are intended to provide a suggestion about how each of the signals might sound to the human listener.

The interpretation that the German team gives to squirrel monkey vocalizations depends heavily on the idea that each of the five classes of sounds has representatives that span a dimension from low to high intensity. The gradations apply both to the social dimension (e.g., Class II challenge calls range from very mild to extremely aggressive) and to the signal dimension that expresses the social functions. Thus mild challenges are uttered at low acoustic intensity, whereas challenges of greater magnitude are uttered at higher acoustic intensity. Additional physical parameters (other than acoustic intensity) may also contribute to the signal dimension along which challenge calls are varied.

One of the most interesting features of the squirrel monkey system according to the German team's interpretation is that all the classes of sounds appear to lose their distinctiveness at very high intensity. The physical characteristics of the signals tend to merge as intensity increases. The pattern is represented in an intriguing wheel diagram (Fig. 14.10), based on the work of Ploog (1992), and prior work of the German group. Jürgens (1982) pointed out that all the sounds at the hub of the wheel tend to be aversive.

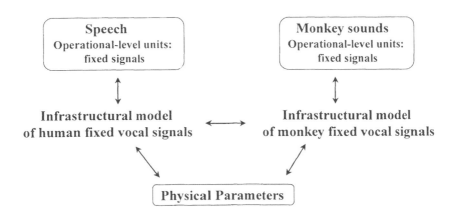

FIG. 14.8.   The most useful comparison of nonhuman sounds and speech may address signals of similar types.

- Class I: Protest
- Class II: Challenge, threat
- Class III: Social contact calls
- Class IV: Group action calls
- Class V: Alarm calls

- Groaning to shrieking
- Purring to harsh growling ('spitting')
- Chirping to squealing (intense isolation calls)
- Twittering to cackling (mobbing calls)
- Clucking to intense alarm calling

FIG. 14.9. Squirrel monkey vocal system (summarized in Ploog, 1992).

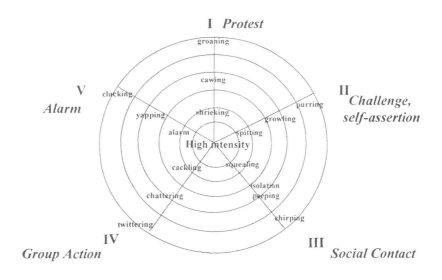

FIG. 14.10. The wheel of squirrel monkey vocalizations (based on Jürgens & Ploog, 1976, and Ploog, 1992).

The wheel diagram provides a stimulating suggestion that systems of fixed vocal communication, in general, may tend to be organized according to simple principles of Signal Dimensionality. For example, systems that have evolved to a point of containing fixed signals might tend to have a few discrete categories of sounds, each of which can be manipulated in gradations that indicate degrees of expression within each category. The gradedness of the signals may constitute a subproperty of Free Expressivity, as each signal within such a system can be presented in accord with the sender's immediate state of emotion or intention. The diagram also hints at mechanisms that may establish or maintain signal distinctiveness; in the course of natural selection, signals that abide by the logical requirements of distinctiveness might tend to fit along dimensions that are easily definable and thus easily perceivable. The system appears to be based on infrastructural parametric manipulation guided by natural selection (see Fig. 14.11).

The insight represented in the wheel diagram may apply with great generality.

The classification system described here, with its general relationships between acoustic structure and functional significance, is valid not only for the squirrel monkey but, in an adapted form, for a much broader group of primates. Its validity even may encompass nonprimate mammals. (Jürgens, 1982, p. 61)

A variety of animals may, then, possess fixed signal systems organized according to a wheel and consequently in accord with infrastructural parametric manipulation. Each spoke of the wheel for each species may represent a dimension representable by a spoke of a wheel along which gradations of pro-

- Nature imposes a scheme upon the sounds
- The pattern should be characterizable as a set of infrastructural principles according to which the sounds of the squirrel monkey are formed and can be systematically modified from one to another
- The system has both gradations and a sort of discreteness (graded within category, discrete across category)
- The system is characterized as unified at high intensity, maximally differentiated at low intensity

FIG. 14.11.   The squirrel monkey pattern suggests parametric manipulation.

duction can be significant. Vocal systems of different species may be profitably compared in terms of the nature of the dimensions represented in their species-specific wheels. It is an intriguing hypothesis that systems will generally show merging of vocal signaling categories at high intensity, at the center of each species-specific wheel. Further, it is notable that the wheel, as presented by the German group, seems to suggest maximal distinctiveness among signals at the ends of the wheel spokes, at lowest intensity.

SIMILARITIES WITH THE HUMAN SYSTEM

It seems possible that many of the same kinds of principles of construction may apply in the case of human fixed signals. Because the human fixed signal system has been studied extremely little,[2] it is necessary to address the possible similarities based on commonsense awareness. Consider the list of characteristics as proposed in Fig. 14.12.

Discrete categories clearly exist in the human system. Crying can often be categorically distinguished from laughter, for example. Graded relationships also clearly exist among various otherwise discrete categories of human vocal signals. It is obvious that there are various degrees of crying and laughter. There are special names that can be applied to these differing degrees, and perhaps they represent side branches from a single spoke. Moaning, whimpering, and fussing (perhaps all representing slight variations on a dimension expressing distress), for example, can all be increased in steps of intensity until they might be called crying. The tendency to merge is seen clearly at very high intensity. Extreme versions of cry-like events, especially brief ones, merge with shrieking, which occurs inherently at high intensity. Furthermore, vocal expressions of passion, which at low intensity might be called sighs, can be similarly scream-like at extremely high intensity. The common parlance asserts that people sometimes "laugh till they cry." Indeed the most intense of laughter often produces tears, and the sounds of laughter can become increasingly similar to crying and eventually to screaming at high intensity. I recall that as a child I would sometimes have to leave the room to regain my composure while watching Danny Kaye. Laughter had merged in this loss of control with other intense emotions both in feeling and expression.

Squealing and growling, which were characterized in chapter 9 as Expansion stage vocal toys, can also be characterized as signals with more or less stable functions in the mature fixed vocal system of humans. Squealing expresses an intense emotion, typically of a sort of uncontrollable delight (as in response to tickling), whereas growling expresses a burst of anger or frustration, often presented as a threat. That these sounds are not required to express the emotions indicated is a tribute to the flexibility of human vocal and expres-

---

[2]Most such research has focused on newborn infant cry, and there is only one significant body of infrastructurally significant research on laughter (see Provine, 1996) as far as I know

- Broad signal types seem relatively discrete with respect to each other (cry is distinct from laughter)
- But each broad type shows modifiability that suggests gradation, much as in the squirrel monkey
- Unity of the system appears to occur at **both** extremes of intensity, whereas the squirrel monkey wheel suggests that distinctions are maximal at the ends of spokes

FIG. 14.12.   Human fixed vocal signals: Is this a wheel?

sive control. To my way of seeing it, squealing and growling represent end-points on a parameter composed of pitch and vocal quality features, but both squealing and growling can be increased in intensity to an extreme that terminates, as with crying or laughter, in the most high-intensity sounds, often referred to as shrieking or perhaps screaming.

Shrieking appears, then, to stand at a central point in a human vocal system involving crying, laughter, and other fixed signal types. However, a two-dimensional characterization of the relations among these categories, as in the German diagram, might prove inadequate to capture all the notable relationships of gradation, because at low intensity also, human signals tend to merge. As crying becomes less intense, it merges with fussing, which after further reductions in intensity merges with grunts and quasivowels. The same merging occurs with laughter, squealing, or growling, all of which can resemble grunts or quasivowels when rendered at very low intensity.

It is as if the wheel diagram bends back on itself in the human system until the ends of each spoke are rejoined in a third dimension. The result might be viewed as a globe (Fig. 14.13) where shrieking is at one pole, where lines of graded relation among categories of vocalization run as lines of longitude to the other pole occupied by quasivowels or grunts. Differentiation among categories of vocalization can be represented by spatial separation on the surface of the globe. Oppositeness could be seen both in the longitudinal dimension and in the latitudinal dimension, where for example squealing and growling might be viewed as latitudinal opposites (or near opposites) that merge through shifts in intensity along longitudinal dimensions.

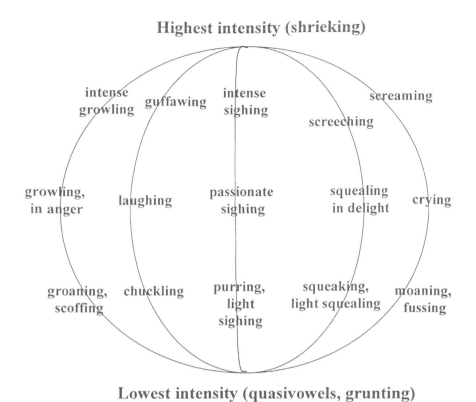

FIG. 14.13.   The globe of human fixed vocal signals.

Three dimensions are probably not enough to characterize fully the essence of human nonspeech vocal signals. I suspect that a similar globe or multidimensional model (with different vocal categories, of course) may characterize some nonhuman primate systems of fixed vocal signals as well. Perhaps even the squirrel monkey's system shows merging of categories at low intensity. If so, the globe diagram may offer a theoretical perspective on how fixed vocal signaling systems are constructed in general in the primates, and perhaps even on how small inventory systems of vocal communication can be efficiently constructed in any species. Characterization of the acoustic and articulatory principles by which gradations are established (longitudinal changes on the globe) as well as the principles that maintain distinctiveness among the discrete categories (latitudinal changes on the globe), might constitute important components of an infrastructural theory of fixed vocal signals (parallel to infraphonological modeling for human syllables).

This work provides only a fragmentary foray into empirical comparisons across species. Laboratory and field research will be needed to address many of the speculations presented here. The goal of the effort has been to suggest comparative approaches that may be fruitful. Figure 14.14 outlines a sequence of steps consistent with the themes developed here.

ON THE SIZE OF FIXED SIGNAL REPERTOIRES

The German group has long emphasized that the size of vocal repertoires may be evaluated in more than one way. The number of spokes on a wheel (or lines of longitude on a globe) of vocal infrastructure represents one important measure, but it is tempting to add categories associated with steps along the dimensions. Certainly in the case of human fixed signals the names of steps (moan, fuss, whimper, etc.) suggest additional categories beyond the five dimensions suggested in the globe diagram. So, we might ask, do humans have five fixed vocal signals as suggested by the dimensions in Fig. 14.13, or 17 as suggested by the names given?

In the various studies of primate vocal call systems, the estimates of numbers of vocal categories have often varied widely. Sutton (1979) provided a table comparing 40 studies evaluating the number of vocal types in 24 species of primates. If we take the numbers in the table at face value, we could assume

- Make comparisons at an infrastructural level
- To the extent possible, formulate infrastructural modeling in the same operational realm for each species (fixed signals compared to fixed signals, vegetative sounds compared to vegetative sounds)
- Evaluate the nature of the physical parameter manipulations that yield gradations within category
- Evaluate the nature of physical parameter manipulations that support differentiation (discreteness) across categories
- Determine whether distinctions neutralize at both extremes of intensity

FIG. 14.14.   First steps in infrastructural modeling to facilitate interspecies comparisons.

that primate fixed signal repertoires range widely, including from 4 to 37 different vocal categories. However, the data in the table suggest that the differences listed may be largely associated with differences in how the counts were made in individual studies. According to Sutton's table, the common chimpanzee (*Pan troglodytes*) was reported to have 6 or 7 vocal types by Andrew, 7 by Marler, 12 by Reynolds and Reynolds, 23 by Goodall, and 32 by Yerkes and Learned. These differences would not seem to be due to different communication systems in the particular animals studied, but rather appear to be due to whether the individual investigative team chose to focus on the number of apparent categorical dimensions in the species or instead to list many of the graded steps along the dimensions.

The squirrel monkey is listed in Sutton's (1979) table as having 26 vocal types based on results from the German team cited (Winter et al., 1966). Yet the same researchers emphasize the conclusion that there are only about five dimensions of discrete vocal signaling in the species. In fact, according to Jürgens (1982), the number of signals can be counted as much higher than 26 if one chooses to focus on small steps along each continuum: "There are hundreds of variants forming gradations and intermediates between a few 'typical' call types" (p. 50).

In one recent comment on the presumed size of the human fixed vocal system with that of other primate species, it was concluded that the human system was surprisingly small:

> Most species of primates have a modest repertoire of innate stereotypic calls; estimates range from fifteen to forty by different researchers. ... Though a small repertoire compared to human vocabularies, it seems large when compared to the few innate human vocalizations. These include laughing, sobbing, screaming with fright, crying with pain, groaning, and sighing. It is difficult to think of others. The list is embarrassingly small compared to call types cited for other primates. (Deacon, 1997, p. 418)

Having never conducted research on nonhuman primates, I am only able to reason from the literature. On that basis I am inclined to draw a different conclusion from that of Deacon. I suspect that the human fixed signal repertoire may be very much like those of many other primate species in terms of both size and structure. The number of dimensions exploited may be small, but the number of steps along the dimensions is much larger, and this pattern appears to hold for many primate species. At least in evaluating the system of the squirrel monkey and a variety of other primate species with graded signals, it seems a worthy hypothesis that they may all be guided in evolution by common infrastructural constraints that tend to yield notable similarities of design. If the hypothesis is on target, the human fixed vocal system may present a typical example of primate communication.

A COMMENT ON THE ORIGINS OF SPEECH

It may be no accident that the pole of low intensity in the human-specific globe pictured in Fig. 14.13 is the pole that appears to provide a particularly important launch point for speech-like vocalizations. Quasivowels represent sounds that are produced with low intensity, and consequently with low emotional content and impact. From here, the human system of protophones takes off in infancy toward utilization of vocalizations in circumstances that require no emotional impetus and transmit no fixed value, but instead lay the groundwork for a system of signals that can be adapted to each user's immediate need. The fact that a wide variety of primitive vocal signals of humans are explored by infants in the Expansion stage suggests that nature's unconscious system of primate Signal Dimensionality (implied by both longitudinal and latitudinal variations in the globe diagram) is exploited by developing children, who seek to control the dimensions, break them apart, and subject them to their growing vocal authority (as seen in Signal Analysis). Ultimately, that effort is exploited in the development of principles from which canonical syllables are formed, and from there, the creation of new units of communication is unlimited.

15

Infrastructural Pursuits
in Vocal Development and Evolution

THE INFRAPHONOLOGICAL INNOVATION

The progress that has been made in infant vocal development research over the past two and a half decades began with the simple decision to abandon description based on operational-level units of mature speech systems and to replace that style of description with a more ethologically straightforward method. In particular the description of infant sounds began to be formulated without alphabetical speech sounds as prime units. Instead, baby sounds were described in terms that attempted to hear the infants' own voices. When we sought to attend to babies on their own terms and to relate to their vocal sounds as parents might, no longer shoe-horning their utterances into preconceived adult segmental speech categories, we found stages of development that had eluded prior generations of scholars (chaps. 1–4).

These protophone stages were mysterious at first, for they consisted of sounds and communications that were not speech, and at the same time did not fit into any of the other categories of sound for which clear functions have been traditionally assigned. They were not vegetative sounds such as burping or coughing, and they were not fixed signals such as crying or laughing. Traditionally protophones had been called babbling, but the term did nothing to explain the stages of development found within them across the first year of life.

The problem with the investigation of babbling is that at each step of proposed interpretation, we are tempted, deeply and powerfully, to impose the categories of adult speech on the infants' sounds. To impose those segmental categories is to commit the error of shoe-horning, and to beg the very question to which we seek an answer. One cannot learn how protophones relate to speech, nor in what sense they constitute precursors to mature speech, if one begins by presuming that they are mature speech. Alphabetical transcription of early infant sounds imposes precisely such an interpretation (chaps. 1–3).

356

A solution to the descriptive quandary was found in backing off from the alphabetical approach. First, protophone description of sounds produced by infants at a variety of ages yielded a model in which protophones were seen to emerge in (at least) four stages. Second, an infrastructural model was formulated to form the basis for interpretation of the progression of protophones across time. The stages of protophone development made eminent good sense in light of the infrastructural model that codified principles by which well-formed minimal rhythmic units are formed in natural human languages. Those infrastructural principles of canonical syllable formation were seen to be accumulated systematically by human infants across the protophone stages (chaps. 4–5).

In the Phonation stage, infants produce short primitive syllables, quasivowels, with the vocal tract at rest in normal phonation, a special kind of vocal cord vibration that constitutes a key requirement of canonical or well-formed syllables. In the Primitive Articulation stage, infants produce, through gooing, articulations of the vocal tract, movements of the tongue or jaw executed during normal phonation. This sort of articulation is a second key requirement of canonical syllables. In the succeeding Expansion stage, infants produce many new sounds, among them full vowel-like sounds that are produced with normal phonation while the vocal tract is open and postured to produce particular spectral effects associated with vowels in natural languages. In addition, full vowel-like sounds are combined with articulated movements of the vocal tract to yield consonant-like sounds in marginal babbling. The infant thus obeys a third key requirement of canonical syllable formation, the requirement that the syllabic nucleus (the vowel-like element) be postured (not at rest). Finally, in the Canonical stage, the infant produces fully well-formed canonical syllables where the articulation from margin (or consonant-like element) to nucleus is rapid, characterized by a quick formant transition. The principles of canonical syllable formation are thus seen to be accumulated systematically across the first half-year of life, and in light of the principles, the protophone stages, previously mysterious, show a pattern of evolution that progressively approximates the aspects of speech (chaps. 4–5).

The principles of canonical syllable formation are encompassed within a general theory of infrastructural properties of natural languages. In its broadest form, the theory represents potential abstract properties of any possible vocal communicative system, human or nonhuman. One of the properties that must be attained by any powerful vocal communicative system is Syllabification, the control of well-formed minimal rhythmic units that can be strung together to form an indefinitely large class of morphemic items (the minimal units of communicative value) or, in the terms of human speech, words.

The principles of canonical syllable formation represent the human implementation of the Syllabification requirement. Other creatures possessing a powerful vocal communication system might define syllables differently. Syllabification is an abstraction that must be put into practice physically by each temporally-based system of communication. The physical nature of syllables as sounds and articulations requires that infraphonological principles specify how physical parameters are manipulated to generate an inventory of well-formed syllabic units. Different creatures with different complex vocal communication systems might develop different principles of Syllabification.

The logic of the human infraphonological definition of the canonical syllable is clear, and it is especially unclouded in light of the systematic manner in which human infants show the accumulation of its principles across the first months of life. The power of the infrastructural interpretation of infant vocal development is illustrated empirically by discoveries and clarifications that could not have been made in the absence of the model. For example, in research guided by infraphonological interpretation (that accords timely onset of canonical babbling a role of primary importance as a sign of normal development), deaf infants prove to be dramatically delayed in the development of speech-like sounds. This fact is of critical importance, yet it was unrecognized in the context of traditional alphabetical description of infant sounds, a style of description that does not recognize the distinction between canonical and noncanonical utterances. In a variety of other cases of potential delay in speech development (prematurity, low SES, or combinations of the two), the onset of canonical babbling proves remarkably robust. The stability of canonical babbling onset under most circumstances, along with the ease with which it is recognized by parents and health professionals, makes it an important candidate for a screening battery. It is now known that infants who begin canonical babbling after 10 months of age are at extreme risk for hearing impairment and a variety of other speech-related disorders (chaps. 5–8).

INFRASTRUCTURAL DESCRIPTION AS A TOOL IN COMPARATIVE ETHOLOGY

The systematic accumulation of principles of canonical syllable formation across the first year of life in human infants is unparalleled, as far as we can tell, in nonhuman primates. The claim should not be surprising, for as far as we can tell, no nonhuman primate possesses a system that includes well-formed Syllabification. Well-formed Syllabification is needed when a system forms a large number of oppositions among minimal units that can be recombined systematically to form an unlimited inventory of morphemic units. Such a system of principles is not required if the inventory of vocal communicative units is small—the system by which a small inventory of fixed signal units can be formed is different (for hints as to how it might be infrastructurally characterized, see the wheel and globe characterizations of fixed signal systems in chap. 14), not needing to provide the kind of potential for productivity that is systematically afforded by a syllabic system. It appears that all nonhuman primates have systems of vocal communication with small numbers of functional category dimensions, and in that context it appears that Syllabification may not be required.

On the other hand, the vocal systems of nonhuman primates resemble greatly the nonspeech fixed vocal system found in humans, the system that includes such categories as crying, laughter, moaning, and shrieking. Here each type of vocalization has its own physical definition, and the nature of differentiation appears to be similar in humans and nonhumans (see chap. 14).

THE GROWTH OF CONTROL OVER BOTH INFRASEMIOTIC AND INFRAPHONOLOGICAL PROPERTIES IN HUMAN DEVELOPMENT

There is much more about the ways the protophone stages unfold that is (as far as can be told at present) unparalleled among the primates. One can examine those stages both in terms of the ways that vocalizations are used and manipulated (an infrasemiotic matter) and in terms of how they sound (an infraphonological matter). Both these examinations reveal remarkable and systematic human infant achievements. The infrastructural approach requires the formulation of abstract properties that constitute construction requirements for communication systems. I have proposed that these properties are enduring aspects of possibility in the evolution of communication. In this view, the properties are presumed to transcend the human condition, and if properly formulated, they may constitute a stable reference point for the interpretation of relations among differing systems of communication, whether the differences are among species or among individuals within species at various points in development (chaps. 11–12).

The formulation of both infrasemiotic properties and infraphonological properties lays the basis for interpretation, then, of important steps in development and important potential similarities and differences between humans and nonhumans in communication. In the Phonation stage, infants produce their primitive quasivowel syllables without obvious social intent, and yet the sounds are not fixed signals. It appears that the quasivowels evidence Contextual Freedom, the ability to produce sounds in the absence of eliciting stimuli, internal or external. Nonhuman primates show fundamental limitations, especially beyond their own infancy, in producing vocalizations in the absence of appropriate stimuli to elicit them. Humans, on the other hand, show total vocal Contextual Freedom in adulthood, and an emergent Contextual Freedom in the first month of life is seen in quasivowels. In the Primitive Articulation stage, human infants engage in rich face-to-face vocal interactions with caretakers, interactions that show an ability on the part of infants to vocalize with clear social intent, manifesting Directivity, and turn-taking or Interactivity. The emotional character of these varied gooing interactions shows that it is possible for babies to produce sounds for the purpose of self-expression, to use sounds that (unlike fixed signals) have no inherent (biologically predefined) signaling value. Such vocal Free Expressivity is essentially not seen to our knowledge in any nonhuman primate.

In the Expansion stage, babies vocalize in ways that include exploration of the possibilities of the vocal system, explorations that pursue individual dimensions of acoustic and articulatory possibility systematically. Exploration of Signal Analysis is unique to humans as far as we know. By developing new contrasting units (potential syllables, phonemic units, or phonological features) along the explored dimensions, infants begin the process of Categorical Adaptation, a process unknown in nonhuman primates. During the Expansion stage, we see early evidence of vocal Imitability, the ability selectively to reproduce vocalizations presented as models. Imitability is a property of powerful communicative systems that is without parallel in nonhumans.

By the Canonical stage, infants produce well-formed syllables that can be adapted categorically to form large inventories of syllables or words. Well-formed Syllabification, along with syllable Recombinability also seen in Canonical stage infants, is unknown in nonhumans, although it is clear that nonhumans are capable of producing complex vocal signals under some circumstances. Human infants at this stage also show Rhythmic Hierarchy in stringing together syllables in phrase-like groupings. Further, they show Hot–Cool Synthesis because the syllable strings are produced with varying intonations that can be used to express a variety of emotional states or illocutionary forces. By the Canonical stage, infants show Designation, the ability to share attention about objects. The vocal Designation capacity is signaled by infants' ability to point to objects, alternating gaze from listeners to objects, and vocalizing to support the joint reference. Nonhumans do not show vocal Designation except in very limited contexts.

By the Integrative stage, human infants show Conventionality, the learning of new word-like units, and early in the stage the learned words can show Arbitrarity in the connection between meaning and sound. By the end of the Integrative stage the properties of Displaceability (referring to objects not in the here and now), Propositionality (formulation of simple sentences in which multiple words express relations among entities), and Segmentation of syllabic units into alphabetical level units are seen. None of these properties is present in any nonhuman primate system of vocal communication as far as we know (see chaps. 9, 11, and 12).

SIMILARITIES AND DIFFERENCES IN HUMAN AND NONHUMAN PRIMATE VOCAL COMMUNICATION

The recognition of these systematic distinctions between human and nonhuman primates requires an infrastructural approach. Even though much of the interpretation presented here is novel, such an approach has origins that date back at least as far as the 17th century (see chap. 11). If we wish to characterize the similarities and differences between human and nonhuman primates in vocal communication, we can begin, then, by considering certain infrastructural properties that have been recognized as important for interspecies comparison for a very long time. Table 15.1 offers a summarial synthesis of comparisons among 21 properties (considered in chaps. 11–14) in humans and in the chimpanzee, our nearest relative. *Yes* and *none* in the table represent relatively clear cases, whereas *little* and *some* represent cases in which empirical data are lacking or ambiguous.

Condillac (see Aarsleff, 1976) discussed a property that is now called Indexicality (Peirce, 1934). Vocalizations that are produced by humans and chimpanzees can be interpreted indexically by mature conspecifics. When the infant of either species cries, for example, the caretaker understands that the cry indexes (or points to) distress. The infant at an early age does not intend to cry, but when cry is elicited, it can be interpreted indexically.

Both humans and chimpanzees have fixed vocal signals and consequently both possess Specialization,[1] the command of signals whose existence is determined by their roles as signals. In this usage, vegetative signals do not show Specialization and their interpretation is purely indexical in the usual case. The property of Specialization was also recognized and discussed by Condillac, although it was not so named.

The property of Arbitrariness was also well recognized in the 17th century by Locke and others (again, see Aarsleff, 1976), and was discussed lucidly by Condillac. This property designates the ability to form symbolic associations between words and meanings for which there are no inherent (either iconic or indexical) associations. Arbitrariness is of course found in most words of human languages but is not found in the vocal system of chimpanzees or other primates.

These three properties—Indexicality, Specialization, and Arbitrarity— were well-recognized as critical bases for interspecies comparison by Condillac in the 18th century. The other properties in Table 15.1 represent adaptations and expansions from more recent work.[2] The table records that among some of the more basic properties, the chimpanzee shows notable development. Not only in Indexicality and Specialization, but in Signal Dimensionality (the use of vocalizations that are organized along acoustic and articulatory dimensions allowing graded production of sounds; see chap. 14), the chimpanzee appears to be no less capable than the human.

However, it should be noted that these three properties (Indexicality, Specialization, and Signal Dimensionality) are the most basic of all the properties that have been discussed in this volume. They are not even included in the hi-

---

[1]I reiterate that although the term comes from Hockett, I intend for it to encompass both fixed signals and conventional ones, whereas he restricted the usage to conventional ones.

[2]Several properties in Table 15.1 were addressed by Hockett and Altmann (1968), and both differences and similarities between the terms and usages here and in Hockett's work are considered in chapter 12. I have adapted terms in a number of cases and added several.

TABLE 15.1
**Summary of Infrastructural Property Command in Humans and
Chimpanzees**

Infrastructural Property of Vocal Communication	Mature Human	Infant Human by 24 months	Mature Chimpanzee	Infant Chimpanzee
Primitive properties				
Indexicality	Yes	Yes	Yes	Yes
Specialization	Yes	Yes	Yes	Yes
Signal Dimensionality	Yes	Yes	Yes	Yes
Infrasemiotic properties				
Contextual Freedom	Yes	Yes	Little	Some
Free Expressivity	Yes	Yes	Little	Little
Directivity	Yes	Yes	Very little	Some
Interactivity	Yes	Yes	Very little	Some
Imitability	Yes	Yes	None	None
Conventionality	Yes	Yes	None	None
Arbitrarity	Yes	Yes	None	None
Designation	Yes	Yes	None	None
Semanticity	Yes	Yes	None	None
Displaceability	Yes	Yes	None	None
Propositionality	Yes	Yes	None	None
Infraphonological properties				
Signal Analysis	Yes	Yes	None	None
Categorical Adaptation	Yes	Yes	None	None
Syllabification	Yes	Yes	None	None
Recombinability	Yes	Yes	None	None
Rhythmic Hierarchy	Yes	Yes	None	None
Segmentation	Yes	Yes	None	None
Hot–Cool Synthesis	Yes	Yes	None	None

erarchical diagrams of properties (see chap. 12). All the 18 properties in the diagrams presuppose the primitive properties.

There are important differences between chimpanzees and humans on all the more advanced properties, each of which represents a domain of intentionality in vocal action. The infant chimpanzee shows somewhat more flexibility than the mature chimpanzee, but the human infant appears to outpace them both by 24 months of age for all the properties of the table, and by much earlier for many of them (chap. 12).

EXPLOSIVE ELABORATIONS OF COMPLEX VOCAL COMMUNICATION

Much pertaining to a rich linguistic capacity is obviously left to develop beyond the point of Hot–Cool Synthesis or simple Propositionality. The properties noted in Table 15.1 are mostly in place by the time typically developing human infants are 18 to 24 months old. The explosive growth of language seen beyond the earliest appearance of Propositionality is the focus of most recent work speculating on vocal evolution. Bickerton (1990) provided an insightful summary of properties of syntax that greatly surpass the system of two-term utterances minimally invoked by the term Propositionality. When Bickerton spoke of grammaticization, the meaningfulness of word-order, the subcategorization of verb arguments, recursion, and deep embedding, he spoke of features that differentiate what he termed *protolanguage* from the full-fledged mature human system. He pointed out that pidgin languages, the schematic languages of trade that have developed in many parts of the world, often show protolanguage-like simplicity. Yet even protolanguage in Bickerton's usage is enormously more complex and powerful than any vocal communicative system found in nonhuman primates or in human infants prior to the second or third year of life.

There are, of course, certain key points that I hope will be preserved from this work. One is that long before the beginnings of grammaticization, human infants have already begun to differentiate themselves from their primate relatives in vocal communication. Another is that both similarities and differences in vocal communication can be seen by comparing humans and nonhumans in the context of infrastructural modeling. Through the magnifying, clarifying lens of a hierarchy of infrastructural properties pertaining to potential communication systems, we see the human infant reaching toward speech through vocal play. Through the same lens we may be able to envision important aspects of the evolution of speech in our hominid ancestors (chap. 13). Although the ontogenetic events of the first year of life do not indicate precisely what course linguistic evolution may have taken, insightful analysis of development helps to reveal both plausible and likely steps.

The historical rejection of Haeckel's maxim that ontogeny recapitulates phylogeny seems in some quarters to have set up a barrier to developmentally based speculations about evolution (see a commentary on this point in Gould, 1977). In my opinion, the key to sensible application of developmental research in evolution is the use of infrastructural modeling. In the approach I have advocated, the ontogeny of language is not thought to recapitulate phylogeny. Instead, both ontogeny and phylogeny are presumed to be governed by a common set of properties and principles of potential infrastructure. Linguistic evolution, by this reasoning, may have gone through steps resembling those of infant vocal development because both are governed by a common set of hierarchically structured possibilities.

The model does not logically preclude a huge leap of evolution in which all the properties I have considered (and even additional ones) might have been incorporated into the human repertoire at once. The popular idea that language must have emerged rather suddenly in evolution, an idea fostered by major technological advances in human artifacts from around the time of the Upper Paleolithic era, suggests that there may have been no step-by-step advancement (Binford, 1981). Still, there are a number of reasons for doubting that human ancestors made a single leap from a vocal system resembling that of our near relatives, the apes, to one of full-fledged speech (see, e.g., Dawkins, 1996; Leakey, 1994; Pinker, 1994). One notion associated with the single-leap idea, that intermediate language-like systems would be irrelevant to survival, seems clearly untenable. Pidgin languages provide an existence proof of the potential importance of intermediate systems in human society (Bickerton, 1981). Also, as argued throughout this volume, the human infant goes through richly structured stages progressively approximating mature language, during each of which elaborate and potentially survival-relevant communication occurs. The infrastructural interpretation of those stages provides clues about the paths ancient hominids may have followed during the original emergence of the speech capacity.

References

Aarsleff, H. (1976). An outline of language origins theory since the Renaissance. In S. Harnad, H. Steklis, & J. Lancaster (Eds.), *The origins and evolution of language* (Vol. 280, pp. 4–13). New York: Annals of the New York Academy of Sciences.

Acebo, C., & Thoman, E. B. (1995). Role of infant crying in the early mother–infant dialogue. *Physiology & Behavior, 57*(3), 541–547.

Albright, R. W., & Albright, J. B. (1956). The phonology of a two-year-old child. *Word, 12,* 382–390.

Anderson, B. J., Vietze, P., & Dokecki, P. R. (1977). Reciprocity in vocal interactions of mothers and infants. *Child Development, 48,* 1676–1681.

Andrew, R. J. (1963). Evolution of facial expression. *Science, 142,* 1034–1041.

Andrew, R. J. (1976). Use of formants in the grunts of baboons and other nonhuman primates. In S. Harnad, H. Steklis, & J. Lancaster (Eds.), *The origins and evolution of language* (Vol. 280, pp. 673–693). New York: Annals of the New York Academy of Sciences.

Ardrey, R. (1961). *African Genesis.* New York: Bantam.

Austin, J. L. (1962). *How to do things with words.* London: Oxford University Press.

Bakeman, R., & Gottman, J. (1986). *Observing interaction: An introduction to sequential analysis.* New York: Cambridge University Press.

Baken, R. J. (1987). *Clinical measurement of speech and voice.* Boston: College-Hill.

Baptista, L. F., & Petrinovich, L. (1986). Song development in the White-crowned sparrow: Social factors and sex differences. *Animal Behavior, 34,* 1359–1371.

Bar-Adon, A., & Leopold, W. F. (1971). *Child language: A book of readings.* Englewood Cliffs, NJ: Prentice-Hall.

Barasch, D. P. (1977). *Sociology and behavior.* Amsterdam: Elsevier.

Barber, L. (1980). *The heyday of natural history.* Garden City, NY: Doubleday.

Bard, K. A. (1990). "Social tool use" by free-ranging orangutans. In S. T. Parker & K. R. Gibson (Eds.), *"Language" and intelligence in monkeys and apes: Comparative developmental perspectives* (pp. 205–218). New York: Cambridge University Press.

Bard, K. A., & Vauclair, J. (1984). The communication context of object manipulation in ape and human adult–infant pairs. *Journal of Human Evolution, 13,* 181–190.

Barlow, G. (1977). Modal action patterns. In T. A. Sebeok (Ed.), *How animals communicate* (pp. 98–134). Bloomington: Indiana University Press.

Barocas, R., Seifer, R., & Sameroff, A. J. (1985). Defining environmental risk: Multiple dimensions of psychological vulnerability. *American Journal of Community Psychology, 13,* 433–447.

Barocas, R., Seifer, R., Sameroff, A. J., Andrews, T. A., Croft, R. T., & Ostrow, E. (1991). Social and interpersonal detriments of developmental risk. *Developmental Psychology, 27,* 479–488.

Barr, R. G., Chen, S., Hopkins, B., & Westra, T. (1996). Crying patterns in preterm infants. *Developmental Medicine & Child Neurology, 38*(4), 345–355.

Bates, E. (1996, September). *From preverbal communication to grammar in children.* Address to the International Symposium on the Emergence of Cognition and Language, Tokyo.

Bates, E., Benigni, L., Bretherton, I., Camaioni, L., & Volterra, V. (1979). *The emergence of symbols: Cognition and communication in infancy.* New York: Academic Press.

Bates, E., Elman, J., Johnson, M., Karmiloff-Smith, A., Parisi, D., & Plunkett, K. (1996). *On innateness* (Tech. Rep. No. 9602). La Jolla: University of California, San Diego.

Bates, E., Elman, J., Johnson, M., Karmiloff-Smith, A., Parisi, D., & Plunkett, K. (1998). On innateness. In W. Bechtel & G. Graham (Eds.), *A companion to cognitive science* (pp. 555–678). Oxford: Basil Blackwell.

Bayley, N. (1969). *Bayley Scales of Infant Development: Birth to two years.* New York: Psychological Corporation.

Beebe, B., Stern, D., & Jaffe, J. (1979). The kinesic rhythms of mother–infant interactions. In A. W. Siegman & S. Feldstein (Eds.), *Of speech and time* (pp. 23–34). Hillsdale, NJ: Lawrence Erlbaum Associates.

Bell, S., & Ainsworth, M. D. S. (1972). Infant crying and maternal responsiveness. *Child Development, 43,* 1171–1190.

Ben-Zeev, S. (1977). Mechanism by which childhood bilingualism affects understanding of language and cognitive structures. In P. A. Hornby (Ed.), *Bilingualism* (pp. 29–56). New York: Academic Press.

Bernhardt, B. (1992). Developmental implications of nonlinear phonological theory. *Clinical Linguistics and Phonetics, 6,* 259–281.

Bess, F. H., & Hall, J. W. (1992). *Screening children for auditory function.* Nashville, TN: Bill Wilkerson Center Press.

Best, C. T. (1994). The emergence of native language phonological influences in infants: A perceptual assimilation model. In J. C. Goodman & H. C. Nussbaum (Eds.), *The development of speech perception: The transition from speech sounds to spoken words* (pp. 167–224). Cambridge, MA: MIT Press.

Biben, M., & Bernhards, D. (1995). Vocal ontogeny of the squirrel monkey, *Saimiri boliviensis peruviensis.* In E. Zimmerman, J. D. Newman, & U. Jürgens (Eds.), *Current topics in primate vocal communication* (pp. 99–120). New York: Plenum.

Biben, M., Symmes, D., & Masataka, N. (1986). Temporal and structural analysis of affiliative vocal exchanges in squirrel monkeys (*Saimiri sciureus*). *Behaviour, 98,* 259–273.

Bickerton, D. (1981). *Roots of language.* Ann Arbor, MI: Karoma.

Bickerton, D. (1990). *Language and species.* Chicago: University of Chicago Press.

Binford, L. (1981). *Bones: Ancient men and modern myth.* San Diego, CA: Academic Press.

Blake, J., & Fink, R. (1987). Sound-meaning correspondences in babbling. *Journal of Child Language, 14,* 229–255.

Bleile, K. M., Stark, R. E., & McGowan, J. S. (1993). Speech development in a child after decannulation: Further evidence that babbling facilitates later speech development. *Clinical Linguistics and Phonetics, 7,* 319–337.

Bloom, K. (1977). Patterning of infant vocal behavior. *Journal of Experimental Child Psychology, 23,* 367–377.

Bloom, K. (1988). Quality of adult vocalizations affects the quality of infant vocalizations. *Journal of Child Language, 15,* 469–480.

Bloom, K., & Esposito, A. (1975). Social conditioning and its proper control procedures. *Journal of Experimental Child Psychology, 19,* 209–222.

Bloom, K., Russell, A., & Wassenberg, K. (1987). Turn taking affects the quality of infant vocalizations. *Journal of Child Language, 15,* 211–227.

Bloom, L. (1970). *Language development.* Cambridge, MA: MIT Press.

Boesch, C. (1991). Teaching among wild chimpanzees. *Animal Behavior, 41,* 530–532.

Bolwig, N. (1963). Facial expression in primates. *Behaviour, 22,* 167–192.

Bonnet, C. (1762). *Considérations sur les corps organisés* [Considerations pertaining to the structure of bodies] (274th ed.). Amsterdam: Marc-Michel Rey.

Bornstein, M. H., & Lamb, M. E. (1992). *Development in infancy: An introduction* (3rd ed.). New York: McGraw-Hill.

Boysen, S., Bernston, G., Hannan, M., & Cacioppo, J. (1996). Quantity-based inference and symbolic representation in chimpanzees (*Pan troglodytes*). *Journal of Experimental Psychology and Animal Behavior Processes, 22,* 76–86.

Brooks, P. L., Frost, B. J., Mason, J. L., & Gibson, D. M. (1986). Continuing evaluation of the Queen's University tactile vocoder. II: Identification of open set sentences and tracking narrative. *Journal of Rehabilitation Research and Development, 23,* 129–138.

Brown, R. (1959). *Words and things.* Glencoe, IL: The Free Press.

Brown, R. (1973). *A first language.* London: Academic Press.

Brown, R., & Bellugi, U. (1964). Three processes in the child's acquisition of syntax. *Harvard Educational Review, 34,* 133–151.

Butterworth, G. (1996, July). *Species typical aspects of manual pointing and the emergence of language in human infancy.* Address to the International Symposium on the Emergence of Cognition and Language, Tokyo.

Byrne, R., & Whiten, A. (1985). Tactical deception of familiar individuals in baboons. *Animal Behavior, 33,* 669–673.

Call, J., & Tomasello, M. (1994). The production and comprehension of referential pointing by orangutans (*Pongo pygmaeus*). *Journal of Comparative Psychology, 108,* 307–314.

Cameron, J., Livson, N., & Bayley, N. (1967). Infant vocalizations and their relationship to mature intelligence. *Science, 157,* 331–333.

Carey, S. (1982). Semantic development: The state of the art. In E. Wanner & L. R. Gleitman (Eds.), *Language acquisition: The state of the art* (pp. 347–389). Cambridge, UK: Cambridge University Press.

Caro, T. M., & Hauser, M. D. (1992). Is there evidence of teaching in nonhuman animals? *Quarterly Review of Biology, 67,* 151–174.

Carroll, J. B. (1971). Language development. In A. Bar-Adon & W. F. Leopold (Eds.), *Child language: A book of readings* (pp. 200–211). Englewood Cliffs, NJ: Prentice-Hall. (Original work published 1960)

Casagrande, C. (1995). *Organisation des interactions sociales dyadiques de nourrissons de 4/5 mois* [The organization of dyadic social interactions in 4–5 month-old infants]. Besançon, France: Université de Franche-Comté.

Catts, H. W. (1986). Speech production/phonological deficits in reading disordered children. *Journal of Learning Disabilities, 19,* 504–508.

Chen, H. P., & Irwin, O. C. (1946). Infant speech, vowel and consonant types. *Journal of Speech and Hearing Disorders, 11,* 27–29.

Cheney, D. L. (1984). Category formation in vervet monkeys. In R. Harre & V. Reynolds (Eds.), *The meaning of primate signals* (pp. 58–72). Cambridge, UK: Cambridge University Press.

Cheney, D. L., & Seyfarth, R. M. (1980). Vocal recognition in free-ranging vervet monkeys. *Animal Behavior, 28,* 362–367.

Cheney, D. L., & Seyfarth, R. M. (1982). How vervet monkeys perceive their grunts: Field playback experiments. *Animal Behavior, 30,* 739–751.

Chevalier-Skolnikoff, S. (1976). The ontogeny of primate intelligence and its implications for communicative potential. In S. Harnad, H. Steklis, & J. Lancaster (Eds.), *The origins and evolution of language* (Vol. 280, pp. 173–211). New York: The New York Academy of Sciences.

Chomsky, N. (1957). *Syntactic structures.* The Hague, Netherlands: Mouton.

Chomsky, N. (1965). *Aspects of the theory of syntax.* Cambridge, MA: MIT Press.

Chomsky, N. (1966). *Cartesian linguistics.* New York: Harper & Row.

Chomsky, N. (1967). The general properties of language. In F. L. Darley (Ed.), *Brain mechanisms underlying speech and language* (pp. 73–80). New York: Grune & Stratton.

Chomsky, N. (1968). *Language and mind.* New York: Harcourt.

Chomsky, N. (1981). *Lectures on government and binding.* Dordrecht, Netherlands: Foris.

Chomsky, N. (1986). *Knowledge of language: Its nature, origin and use.* New York: Praeger.

Chomsky, N. (1993). *Language and thought.* Wakefield, RI: Moyer Bell.

Clark, E. V. (1973). What's in a word? On the child's acquisition of semantics in his first language. In T. Moore (Ed.), *Cognitive development and the acquisition of language* (pp. 65–110). New York: Academic Press.

Clarke-Stewart, A., Perlmutter, M., & Friedman, S. (1988). *Lifelong human development.* New York: Wiley.

Cobo-Lewis, A. B., Oller, D. K., Lynch, M. P., & Levine, S. L. (1996). Relations of motor and vocal milestones in typically developing infants and infants with Down syndrome. *American Journal of Mental Retardation, 100,* 456–467.

Coffey, B. J., & Park, K. S. (1997). Behavioral and emotional aspects of Tourette's syndrome. *Neurologic Clinics, 15*(2), 277–289.

Cole, P. (1975). The synchronic and diachronic status of conversational implicature. In P. Cole & J. L. Morgan (Eds.), *Syntax and semantics: Speech acts* (Vol. 3, pp. 257–288). New York: Academic Press.

Condillac, E. B. de (1756). *An essay on the origin of human knowledge; being a supplement to Mr. Locke's Essay on the human understanding (Translation of Essai sur l'origine des connaissances humaines).* London: J. Nourse.

Cooper, F. S., Delattre, P. C., Liberman, A. M., Borst, J. M., & Gerstman, L. J. (1952). Some experiments on the perception of synthetic speech sounds. *Journal of the Acoustical Society of America, 24,* 597–606.

Cormier, K., Mauk, C., & Repp, A. (1998). Manual babbling in deaf and hearing infants: A longitudinal study. In E. V. Clark (Ed.), *The proceedings of the twenty-ninth annual child language research forum* (pp. 55–61). Stanford, CA: Center for the Study of Language and Information.

Cowan, R. S. C., Blamey, P. J., Galvin, K. L., Sarant, J. Z., Alcantara, J. I., & Clark, G. M. (1990). Perception of sentences, words, and speech features by profoundly hearing-impaired children using a mutichannel electrotactile speech processor. *Journal of the Acoustical Society of America,' 88,* 1374–1384.

Crelin, E. S. (1959). *Anatomy of the newborn: An atlas.* Philadelphia: Lea & Febiger.

Crnic, K. A., Ragozin, A. S., Greenberg, M. T., Robinson, N. M., & Basham, R. B. (1983). Social interaction and developmental competence of preterm and full-term infants during the first year of life. *Child Development, 54,* 1199–1210.

Cruttenden, A. (1970). A phonetic study of babbling. *British Journal of Disorders of Communication, 5,* 110–118.

Darwin, C. (1873). *The expression of emotions.* New York: Hurst.

Darwin, C. (1971). A biographical sketch of an infant. In A. Bar-Adon & W. F. Leopold (Eds.), *Child language: A book of readings* (pp. 26–27). Englewood Cliffs, NJ: Prentice-Hall. (Original work published 1877)

Davis, B. L., & MacNeilage, P. F. (1995). The articulatory basis of babbling. *Journal of Speech and Hearing Research, 38,* 1199–1211.

Dawkins, R. (1996). *Climbing mount improbable.* New York: Norton.

Dawkins, R., & Krebs, J. R. (1978). Animal signals: Information or manipulation? In J. R. Krebs & N. B. Davies (Eds.), *Behavioural ecology: An evolutionary approach* (pp. 282–309). Sunderland, MA: Sinauer Associates.

Deacon, T. W. (1997). *The symbolic species.* New York: Norton.

de Boysson-Bardies, B., Sagart, L., & Bacri, N. (1981). Phonetic analysis of late babbling: A case study of a French child. *Journal of Child Language, 8,* 511–524.

de Boysson-Bardies, B., Sagart, L., & Durand, C. (1984). Discernible differences in the babbling of infants according to target language. *Journal of Child Language, 11,* 1–15.

de Boysson-Bardies, B., & Vihman, M. M. (1991). Adaptation to language: Evidence from babbling and first words in four languages. *Language, 67,* 297–319.

DeCasper, A. J., & Fifer, W. P. (1980). Of human bonding: Newborns prefer their mothers' voices. *Science, 208*(4448), 1174–1176.

Delattre, P. (1966). A comparison of syllable length conditioning among languages. *International Review of Applied Linguistics, 4,* 183–198.

Delattre, P. C., Liberman, A. M., & Cooper, F. S. (1955). Acoustic loci and transitional cues for consonants. *Journal of the Acoustical Society of America, 27,* 769–773.

Dennis, W., & Dennis, M. G. (1940). The effect of cradling practices upon the onset of walking in Hopi children. *Journal of Genetic Psychology, 56,* 77–86.

Dent, M. L., Brittan-Powell, E. R., Dooling, R. J., & Pierce, A. (1997). Perception of synthetic /ba/-/wa/ speech continuum by budgerigars (*Melopsittacus undulatus*). *Journal of the Acoustical Society of America, 102*(3), 1891–1897.

Deputte, B. L. (1982). Duetting in male and female songs of the white-cheeked gibbon (*Hylobates concolor leucogenys*). In C. T. Snowdon, C. H. Brown, & M. R. Petersen (Eds.), *Primate communication* (pp. 67–93). Cambridge, UK: Cambridge University Press.

de Saussure, F. (1968). *Cours de linguistique générale* [General course in linguistics]. Paris: Payot.

Dinnsen, D. A., Chin, S. B., Elbert, M., & Powell, T. W. (1990). Some constraints on functionally disordered phonologies: Phonetic inventories and phonotactics. *Journal of Speech and Hearing Research, 33*, 28–37.

DiPietro, J. A., & Allen, M. C. (1991). Estimation of gestational age: Implications for developmental research. *Child Development, 62*, 1184–1199.

Dodd, B. (1972). Comparison of babbling patterns in normal and Down-syndrome infants. *Journal of Mental Deficiency Research, 16*, 35–40.

D'Odorico, L. (1984). Non-segmental features in prelinguistic communications: An analysis of some types of infant cry and non-cry vocalizations. *Journal of Child Language, 11*, 17–27.

Dore, J., Franklin, M., Miller, R., & Ramer, A. (1976). Transitional phenomena in early language acquisition. *Journal of Child Language, 3*, 13–28.

Dubos, R. (1968). *So human an animal.* New York: Scribner's.

Dunbar, R. (1993). Coevolution of neocortical size, group size, and language in humans. *Behavioral and Brain Sciences, 16*(4), 681–735.

Dunbar, R. (1996). *Gossiping, grooming and the evolution of language.* Cambridge, MA: Harvard University Press.

Dyson, A. (1988). Phonetic inventories of 2- and 3-year-old children. *Journal of Speech and Hearing Disorders, 53*, 89–93.

Eckman, P. (1994). All emotions are basic. In P. Eckman & R. J. Davidson (Eds.), *The nature of emotion* (pp. 15–19). New York: Oxford University Press.

Edwards, M. L. (1971). One child's acquisition of English liquids. *Papers and Reports in Child Language Development, Stanford University, 3*, 101–109.

Edwards, M. L. (1978). *Patterns and processes in fricative acquisition: Longitudinal evidence from six English-learning children.* Unpublished doctoral dissertation, Stanford University, Stanford, CA.

Edwards, M. L. (1995). Developmental phonology. In H. Winitz (Ed.), *Human communication and its disorders: A review* (Vol. IV, pp. 31–79). Timonium, MD: York Press.

Ehri, L. C. (1989). The development of spelling knowledge and its role in reading acquisition and reading disability. *Journal of Learning Disabilities, 22*, 356–365.

Eibl-Eibesfelt, I. (1970). *Ethology: The biology of behavior.* New York: Holt, Rinehart, & Winston.

Eilers, R. E., Gavin, W. J., & Oller, D. K. (1982). Cross-linguistic perception in infancy: The role of linguistic experience. *Journal of Child Language, 9*, 289–302.

Eilers, R. E., Morse, P. A., Gavin, W. J., & Oller, D. K. (1981). The perception of voice-onset-time in infancy. *Journal of the Acoustical Society of America, 70*, 955–965.

Eilers, R. E., Neal, A. R., & Oller, D. K. (1996, April). *Late onset babbling as an early marker of abnormal development.* Poster presented at the International Conference on Infant Studies, Providence, RI.

Eilers, R. E., & Oller, D. K. (1994). Infant vocalizations and the early diagnosis of severe hearing impairment. *Journal of Pediatrics, 124,* 199–203.

Eilers, R. E., Oller, D. K., & Benito-García, C. R. (1984). The acquisition of voicing contrasts in Spanish and English learning infants and children: A longitudinal study. *Journal of Child Language, 11,* 313–336.

Eilers, R. E., Oller, D. K., Levine, S., Basinger, D., Lynch, M. P., & Urbano, R. (1993). The role of prematurity and socioeconomic status in the onset of canonical babbling in infants. *Infant Behavior and Development, 16,* 297–315.

Eilers, R. E., Vergara, K., Oller, D. K., & Balkany, T. J. (1993). Evaluating hearing-impaired children's usage of tactual vocoders. In A. Risberg, S. Felicetti, G. Plant, & K.-E. Spens (Eds.), *Proceedings of the Second International Conference on Tactile Aids, Hearing Aids & Cochlear Implants* (pp. 255–260). Stockholm, Sweden: Akademitryck AB, Edsbruk.

Eimas, P. D., Siqueland, E., Jusczyk, P., & Vigorito, J. (1971). Speech perception in infants. *Science, 171*(303–306).

Ejiri, K. (1998a, July). *Relationship between rhythmic behaviors and canonical babbling in the infant's vocal development.* Berne, Switzerland: International Society for the Study of Behavioral Development.

Ejiri, K. (1998b). Relationship between rhythmic behavior and canoncial babbling in infant vocal development. *Phonetica, 55,* 226–237.

Ejiri, K., & Masataka, N. (1996, September). *Synchronization between preverbal vocal behaviors and motor actions in early infancy.* Paper presented at the 60th Annual Conference of the Japanese Psychological Association, Tokyo.

Elbers, L. (1982). Operating principles in repetitive babbling: A cognitive continuity approach. *Cognition, 12,* 45–63.

Elbers, L., & Ton, J. (1985). Play pen monologues: The interplay of words and babbles in the first words period. *Journal of Child Language, 12,* 551–565.

Elbert, M., & Gierut, J. (1986). *Handbook of clinical phonology: Approaches to assessment and treatment.* San Diego, CA: College Hill Press.

Eldredge, N., & Gould, S. J. (1972). Punctuated equilibrium: An alternative to phyletic gradualism. In T. J. M. Schopf (Ed.), *Models in paleobiology* (pp. 82–115). San Francisco: Freeman, Cooper.

Elman, J. (1993). Learning and development in neural networks: The importance of starting small. *Cognition, 48,* 71–99.

Elowson, A. M., Snowdon, C. T., & Lazaro-Perea, C. (1998). "Babbling" and social context in infant monkeys: Parallels to human infants. *Trends in Cognitive Sciences, 2*(1), 31–37.

Emde, R. N., Gaensbauer, T. J., & Harmon, R. J. (1976). Emotional expression in infancy: A biobehavioral study. *Psychological Issues, 37,* 10.

Feagans, L. V., Kipp, E., & Blood, I. (1994). The effects of otitis media on the language and attention skills of daycare attending toddlers. *Developmental Psychology, 30,* 701–708.

Fenson, L., Dale, P., Reznick, S., Thal, D., Bates, E., Hartung, J., Pethcik, S., & Reilly, J. (1991). *The MacArthur Communicative Development Inventories.* San Diego: San Diego State University.

Ferguson, C. A. (1973). The acquisition of fricatives. *Papers and Reports in Child Language Development, Stanford University, 6,* pp. 61–86.

Ferguson, C. A., & Farwell, C. B. (1975). Words and sounds in early language acquisition: English initial consonants in the first fifty words. *Language, 51,* 419–439.

Fernald, A., Taeschner, T., Dunn, J., Papoušek, M., de Boysson-Bardies, B., & Fukui, I. (1989). A cross-language study of prosodic modifications in mothers' and fathers' speech to preverbal infants. *Journal of Child Language, 16,* 477–501.

Fifer, W. P. (1987). Neonatal preference for mother's voice. In N. A. Krasnegor & E. M. Blass (Eds.), *Perinatal development: A psychobiological perspective* (pp. 111–124).

Firth, J. R. (1957). *Papers in Linguistics 1934–1951.* Toronto: Oxford University Press.

Fischer, K. W., & Lazerson, A. (1984). *Human development: From conception through adolescence.* New York: Freeman.

Foreman, N., & Altaha, M. (1991). The development of exploration and spontaneous alteration in hooded rat pups: Effects of unusually early eyelid opening. *Developmental Psychobiology, 24,* 521–537.

Fossey, D. (1972). Vocalizations of the mountain gorilla (*Gorilla gorilla beringei*). *Animal Behavior, 20,* 36–53.

Fouts, R. S. (1987). Chimpanzee signing and emergent levels. In G. Greenberg & E. Tobach (Eds.), *Cognition, language and consciousness: Integrative levels* (Vol. 2, pp. 57–84). Hillsdale, NJ: Lawrence Erlbaum Associates.

Fouts, R., Fouts, D. H., & Van Cantfort, T. E. (1989). The infant Loulis learns signs from cross-fostered chimpanzees. In R. A. Gardner, B. T. Gardner, & T. E. Van Cantfort (Eds.), *Teaching sign language to chimpanzees* (pp. 280–292). Albany: State University of New York Press.

Fraiberg, S. (1977). *Insights from the blind.* New York: Basic Books.

Fraser, B. (1975). Hedged performatives. In P. Cole & J. L. Morgan (Eds.), *Syntax and semantics: Speech acts* (Vol. 3, pp. 187–210). New York: Academic Press.

Friel-Patti, S., Finitzo-Hieber, T., Conti, G., & Brown, K. C. (1982). Language delay in infants associated with middle ear disease and mild, fluctuating hearing impairment. *Pediatric Infectious Disease, 1,* 104–109.

Frisch, O. R. (1967). Niels Bohr. *Scientific American, 216,* 145–148.

Gardner, R. A., & Gardner, B. T. (1969). Teaching sign language to a chimpanzee. *Science, 165,* 664–672.

Gathercole, V. C. (1982). Decrements in children's responses to big and tall: A reconsideration of the potential cognitive and semantic causes. *Journal of Experimental Child Psychology, 34*(1), 156–173.

Gault, R. H. (1926). Touch as a substitute for hearing in the interpretation and control of speech. *Archives of Otolaryngology, 3,* 121–135.

Gesell, A., & Amatruda, C. S. (1941). *Developmental diagnosis.* New York: Hoeber.

Gibson, K. R. (1990a). New perspectives on instincts and intelligence: Brain size and the emergence of hierarchical mental constructional skills. In S. T. Parker & K. R. Gibson (Eds.), *"Language" and intelligence in monkeys and apes: Comparative developmental perspectives* (pp. 97–128). New York: Cambridge University Press.

Gibson, K. R. (1990b). Tool use, imitation, and deception in cebus. In S. T. Parker & K. R. Gibson (Eds.), *"Language" and intelligence in monkeys and apes: Comparative developmental perspectives* (pp. 205–218). New York: Cambridge University Press.

Gierut, J. (1989). Maximal opposition approach to phonological treatment. *Journal of Speech and Hearing Disorders, 54,* 9–19.

Ginsburg, G. P., & Kilbourne, B. K. (1988). Emergence of vocal alternation in mother–infant interchanges. *Journal of Child Language, 15,* 221–235.

Goldfield, E. C. (1999). Prosody during disyllable production of full-term and preterm infants. *Ecological Psychology, 11*(1), 81–102.

Goldsmith, J. (1976). An overview of autosegmental phonology. *Linguistic Analysis, 2,* 23–68.

Gordon, D., & Lakoff, G. (1975). Conversational postulates. In P. Cole & J. L. Morgan (Eds.), *Syntax and semantics: Speech acts* (Vol. 3, pp. 83–106). New York: Academic Press.

Gould, S. J. (1977). *Ontogeny and phylogeny.* Cambridge, MA: Harvard University Press.

Gould, S. J. (1983). *Hen's teeth and horse's toes: Further reflections on natural history.* New York: Norton.

Gould, S. J. (1989). *Wonderful life: The Burgess Shale and the nature of history.* New York: Norton.

Gozoules, H., Gozoules, S., & Ashley, J. (1995). Representational signaling in non-human primate vocal communication. In E. Zimmerman, J. D. Newman, & U. Jürgens (Eds.), *Current topics in primate vocal communication* (pp. 235–252). New York: Plenum.

Gravel, J. S., & Wallace, I. F. (1992). Listening and language at 4 years of age: Effects of early otitis media. *Journal of Speech & Hearing Research, 35*(3), 588–595.

Green, J. A., Gustafson, G. E., & McGhie, A. C. (1998). Changes in infants' cries as a function of time in a cry bout. *Child Development, 69*(2), 271–279.

Green, J. A., Jones, L. E., & Gustafson, G. E. (1987). Perception of cries by parents and nonparents: Relation to cry acoustics. *Developmental Psychology, 23*(3), 370–382.

Green, S. (1975). Variation of vocal pattern with social situation in the Japanese monkey (*Macaca fuscata*): A field study. In L. Rosenblum (Ed.), *Primate behavior* (Vol. 4, pp. 1–102). New York: Academic Press.

Greenberg, M. T., & Crnic, K. A. (1988). Longitudinal predictors of developmental status and social interaction to premature and full-term infants at age two. *Child Development, 59,* 554–570.

Greenlee, M. (1974). Interacting processes in the child's acquisition of stop-liquid processes. *Papers and Reports in Child Language Development, Stanford University, 7,* 85–100.

Grégoire, A. (1971). L'apprentissage du langage [The learning of language]. In A. Bar-Adon & W. F. Leopold (Eds.), *Child language: A book of readings* (pp. 91–95). Englewood Cliffs, NJ: Prentice-Hall. (Original work publised 1948)

Griffin, D. (1992). *Animal minds.* Chicago: University of Chicago Press.

Grunwell, P. (1982). *Clinical phonology.* London: Croom Helm.

Guralnick, M. J. (1997). *The effectiveness of early intervention.* Baltimore: Brookes.

Gustafson, G. E., & Green, J. A. (1991). Developmental coordination of cry sounds with visual regard and gestures. *Infant Behavior and Development, 14,* 51–57.

Hailman, J. P., Ficken, M. S., & Ficken, R. W. (1987). Constraints on the structure of combinatorial "chick-a-dee" calls. *Ethology, 75,* 62–80.

Hall, K. R. L. (1963). Variations in the ecology of the Chacuna baboon. *Symposia of the Zoological Society of London, 10,* 1–28.

Hallé, P. A., de Boysson-Bardies, B., & Vihman, M. M. (1991). Beginnings of prosodic organization: Intonation and duration patterns of disyllables produced by Japanese and French infants. *Language & Speech, 34*(4), 299–318.

Hannah, A. C., & McGrew, W. C. (1987). Chimpanzees using stones to crack open oil palm nuts in Liberia. *Primates, 28,* 31–46.

Harnad, S. (1987). *Categorical perception: The groundwork of cognition.* Cambridge, UK: Cambridge University Press.

Harper, J., & Williams, S. (1975). Age and type of onset as critical variables in early infantile autism. *Journal of Autism & Childhood Schizophrenia, 5,* 25–136.

Harris, M., Barrett, M., Jones, D., & Brookes, S. (1988). Linguistic input and early word meaning. *Journal of Child Language, 15,* 77–94.

Hart, B. (1991). Input frequency and children's first words. *First Language, 11,* 289–300.

Hart, B., & Risley, T. R. (1981). Grammatical and conceptual growth in the language of psychologically disadvantaged children: Assessment and intervention. In M. J. Begab, H. Garber, & H. C. Hayward (Eds.), *Psycho-social influences in retarded performance: Vol. 2. Strategies for improving competence* (pp. 181–198). Baltimore: University Park Press.

Hart, B., & Risley, T. R. (1992). American parenting of language-learning children: Persisting differences in family–child interactions observed in natural home environments. *Developmental Psychology, 28,* 1096–1105.

Hartelius, L., Buder, E. H., & Strand, E. A. (1997). Long-term phonatory instability in individuals with multiple sclerosis. *Journal of Speech and Hearing Research, 40,* 1056–1072.

Hauser, M. D. (1992a). Articulatory and social factors influence the acoustic structure of rhesus monkey vocalizations: A learned mode of production. *Journal of the Acoustical Society of America, 91,* 2175–2179.

Hauser, M. D. (1992b). A mechanism guiding conversational turn-taking in vervet monkeys and rhesus macaques. *Topics in Primatology: Human Origins, 1,* 235–248.

Hauser, M. D. (1996). *The evolution of communication.* Cambridge, MA: MIT Press.

Hauser, M. D., & Marler, P. (1993). Food associated calls in rhesus monkeys: I. Socioecological factors. *Behavioral Ecology, 4,* 194–205.

Hayes, C. (1951). *The ape in our house.* New York: Harpers.

Hayes, K. J., & Hayes, C. (1951). The intellectual development of a home-raised chimpanzee. *Proceedings of the American Philosophical Society, 95,* 105–109.

Henning, W. (1979). *Phylogenetic systematics.* Urbana: University of Illinois Press.

Hewes, G. W. (1983). The invention of phonemically-based language. In E. D. Grolier (Ed.), *Glossogenetics: The origin and evolution of language* (pp. 143–162). New York: Harwood.

Hinde, R. A. (1970). *Animal behavior* (2nd ed.). New York: McGraw-Hill.

Hjelmslev, L. (1963a). *Le langage* [Language]. Paris: Les Editions de Minuit.

Hjelmslev, L. (1963b). *Prolegomena to a theory of language* (F. J. Whitfield, Trans.). Madison: University of Wisconsin Press.

Hockett, C. (1960a). Logical considerations in the study of animal communication. In W. E. Lanyon & W. N. Tavolga (Eds.), *Animal sounds and communication* (pp. 392–430). Washington, DC: American Institute of Biological Sciences.

Hockett, C. F. (1960b). The origin of speech. *Scientific American, 203,* 89–96.

Hockett, C. (1977). *A view from language: Selected essays.* Athens: University of Georgia Press.

Hockett, C. F., & Altmann, S. A. (1968). A note on design features. In T. A. Sebeok (Ed.), *Animal communication: Techniques of study and results of research* (pp. 61–72). Bloomington: Indiana University Press.

Hodson, B. W. (1980). *Assessment of phonological processes.* Danville, IL: Interstate Press.

Hodson, B. W., & Paden, E. P. (1981). Phonological processes which characterize unintelligible and intelligible speech in early childhood. *Journal of Speech and Hearing Disorders, 46,* 369–373.

Hoemann, H. W. (1975). The transparency of meaning of sign language gestures. *Sign Language Studies, 7,* 151–161.

Hoff-Ginsberg, E. (1991). Mother–child conversation in different social classes and communicative settings. *Child Development, 62,* 782–796.

Hofstadter, A. (1941). Objective teleology. *Journal of Philosophy, 38*(2), 29–39.

Hollien, H. (1974). On vocal registers. *Journal of Phonetics, 2,* 125–143.

Hollingshead, A. B. (1978). *Two Factor Index of Social Status.* Unpublished manuscript, Yale University, New haven, CT.

Holmgren, K., Lindblom, B., Aurelius, G., Jalling, B., & Zetterstrom, R. (1986). On the phonetics of infant vocalization. In B. Lindblom & R. Zetterstrom (Eds.), *Precursors of early speech* (pp. 51-63). New York: Stockton.

Hopkins, W. D., & Leavens, D. A. (1998). Hand use and gestural communication in chimpanzees *(Pan Troglodytes). Journal of Comparative Psychology, 112*(1), 95–99.

Hopkins, W. D., & Savage-Rumbaugh, E. S. (1986). Vocal communication in the pygmy chimpanzee *(Pan paniscus)* as a result of differential rearing experiences. *American Journal of Primatology, 10,* 407–408.

Hopp, S. L., Sinnot, J. M., Owren, M. J., & Petersen, M. R. (1992). Differential sensitivity of Japanese macaques *(Macaca fuscata)* and humans *(Homo sapiens)* to peak position along a synthetic coo call continuum. *Journal of Comparative Psychology, 106,* 128–136.

Ianco-Worrall, A. (1972). Bilingualism and cognitive development. *Child Development, 43,* 1390–1400.

Ingram, D. (1974). Fronting in child phonology. *Journal of Child Language, 1,* 233–241.

Ingram, D., Christensen, L., & Veach, S. (1980). The acquisition of word-initial fricatives and affricates in English by children between two and six. In G. Yeni-Komshian, J. Kavanagh, & C. Ferguson (Eds.), *Child phonology: Vol. 1. Production* (pp. 169–192). New York: Academic Press.

Irwin, O. C. (1947a). Infant speech: Consonant sounds according to manner of articulation. *Journal of Speech and Hearing Disorders, 12,* 402–404.

Irwin, O. C. (1947b). Infant speech: Consonantal sounds according to place of articulation. *Journal of Speech and Hearing Disorders, 12,* 397–401.

Irwin, O. C. (1948). Infant speech: Development of vowel sounds. *Journal of Speech and Hearing Disorders, 13,* 31–34.

Irwin, O. C., & Curry, T. (1941). Vowel elements in the crying vocalization of infants under ten days of age. *Child Development, 12,* 99–109.

Itani, J. (1958). On the acquisition and propagation of a new food habit in the troop of Japanese monkeys at Takasakiyama. *Primates, 1,* 84–98.

Jakobson, R. (1939). *Selected Writings.* The Hague, Netherlands: Mouton.

Jakobson, R. (1941). *Kindersprache, Aphasie, und allgemeine Lautgesetze* [Child language, aphasia, and phonological universals]. Uppsala, Sweden: Almqvist & Wiksell.

Jakobson, R. (1971a). Les Lois phoniques du langage enfantin et leur place dans la phonologie générale [Phonetic rules of infant language and their role in general phonology]. In A. Bar-Adon & W. F. Leopold (Eds.), *Child language: A book of readings* (pp. 75–82). Englewood Cliffs, NJ: Prentice-Hall. (Original work published 1939)

Jakobson, R. (1971b). Why "Mama" and "Papa"? In A. Bar-Adon & W. F. Leopold (Eds.), *Child language: A book of readings* (pp. 212–217). Englewood Cliffs, NJ: Prentice-Hall. (Original work published 1962)

Jasnow, M., & Feldstein, S. (1986). Adult-like temporal characteristics of mother–infant vocal interactions. *Child Development, 57,* 754–761.

Jensen, T. S., Boggild-Andersen, B., Schmidt, J., Ankerhus, J., & Hansen, E. (1988). Perinatal risk factors and first-year vocalizations: Influence on preschool language and motor performance. *Developmental Medicine and Child Neurology, 30,* 153–161.

Jerison, H. (1991). *Brain size and the evolution of mind* [The 59th James Arthur Lecture]. New York: American Museum of Natural History.

Jewett, D. L., Romano, M. N., & Williston, J. S. (1970). Human auditory evoked potentials: Possible brain stem components detected on the scalp. *Science, 167,* 1517–1518.

Johnston, J. R. (1988). Specific language disorders in the child. In N. J. Lass, L. V. McReynolds, J. L. Northern, & D. E. Yoder (Eds.), *Handbook of speech-language pathology and audiology* (pp. 685–715). San Diego, CA: Singular.

Jordan, J. (1971). Studies in the structure of the organ of voice and vocalization in the chimpanzee. *Folia Morphologica, 30,* 323–340.

Jouanjean-L'Antoëne, A. (1994). *Genèse de la communication entre deux jumelles (11–24 mois) et leurs parents: Approche éthologique, différentielle et causale* [The genesis of communication in twins (11–24 months) and their parents: An ethological, differential, and causal approach]. Unpublished doctoral dissertation, Université de Rennes, Rennes, France.

Jürgens, U. (1982). A neuroethological approach to the classification of vocalization in the squirrel monkey. In C. T. Snowdon, C. H. Brown, & M. R. Petersen (Eds.), *Primate communication* (pp. 50–62). Cambridge, UK: Cambridge University Press.

Jürgens, U. (1992). On the neurobiology of vocal communication. In H. Papoušek, U. Jürgens, & M. Papoušek (Eds.), *Nonverbal vocal communication* (pp. 31–42). New York: Cambridge University Press.

Jürgens, U. (1995). Neuronal control of vocal production in non-human and human primates. In E. Zimmerman, J. D. Newman, & U. Jürgens (Eds.), *Current topics in primate vocal communication* (pp. 199–206). New York: Plenum.

Jusczyk, P. W. (1992). Developing phonological categories from the speech signal. In C. Ferguson, L. Menn, & C. Stoel-Gammon (Eds.), *Phonological development: Models, research, implications* (pp. 17–64). Parkton, MD: York.

Kahmi, A. G. (1993). Children with specific language impairment (developmental aphasia): Perceptual and cognitive aspects. In G. Blanken, J. Dittmann, H. Grimm, J. D. Marshall, & C.-W. Wallesch (Eds.), *Linguistic disorders and pathologies: An international handbook* (pp. 625–640). Berlin: Walter de Gruyter.

Karelitz, S., & Fisischelli, V. R. (1969). Infant vocalizations and their significance. *Clinical Proceedings of Children's Hospital, Washington D.C., 25*(11), 345–361.

Kavanagh, J. F. (Ed.). (1986). *Otitis media and child development.* Parkton, MD: York.

Kaye, K., & Fogel, A. (1980). The temporal structure of face-to-face communication between mothers and infants. *Developmental Psychology, 16*(5), 454–464.

Keleman, G. (1948). The anatomical basis of phonation in the chimpanzee. *Journal of Morphology, 82,* 229–256.

Kellogg, W. N., & Kellogg, L. A. (1933). *The ape and the child: A study of environmental influence upon early behavior.* New York: McGraw-Hill.

Kent, R., Osberger, M. J., Netsell, R., & Hustedde, C. (1987). Phonetic development in identical twins differing in auditory function. *Journal of Speech and Hearing Disorders, 52,* 64–75.

Kent, R. D., & Murray, A. D. (1982). Acoustic features of infant vocalic utterances at 3, 6, and 9 months. *Journal of the Acoustical Society of America, 72,* 353–365.

Kessen, W., Levine, J., & Wendrich, K. A. (1979). The imitation of pitch by infants. *Infant Behavior and Development, 2,* 93–100.

Klatt, D. (1976). Linguistic uses of segmental duration in English: Acoustic and perceptual evidence. *Journal of the Acoustical Society of America, 59,* 1208–1221.

Kluender, K. R., Diehl, R. L., & Killeen, P. R. (1987). Japanese quail can learn phonetic categories. *Science, 237,* 1195–1197.

Koenig, W., Dunn, H. K., & Lacy, L. Y. (1946). The sound spectrograph. *Journal of the Acoustical Society of America, 17,* 19–49.

Koffka, K. (1928). *The growth of the mind.* London: Kegan Paul, Trench, Trubner.

Kojima, S., & Nagumo, S. (1996a). *Early vocal development in a chimpanzee infant.* Inuyama, Japan: Primate Institute.

Kojima, S., & Nagumo, S. (1996b). Perception of conspecific calls by Japanese monkeys and Chimpanzees: Harmonic sounds. *The Emergence of Cognition and Language, 3,* 114–118.

Kojima, S., Tatsumi, I. F., Kiritani, S., & Hirose, H. (1989). Vocal-auditory functions of the chimpanzee: Consonant perception. *Human Evolution, 4*(5), 403–416.

Konopczynski, G. (1985). Acquisition du langage: La période charnière et sa structuration mélodique [The acquisition of language: The period of transition and its melodic structure]. *Bulletin d'audiophonologie: Annales scientifiques de l'Université de Franche-Comté, 11,* 63–92.

Koopmans-van Beinum, F. J., Clement, C. J., & van den Dikkenberg-Pot, I. (1998). *Influence of lack of auditory speech perception on sound productions of deaf infants.* Berne, Switzerland: International Society for the Study of Behavioral Development.

Koopmans-van Beinum, F. J., & van der Stelt, J. M. (1986). Early stages in the development of speech movements. In B. Lindblom & R. Zetterstrom (Eds.), *Precursors of early speech* (pp. 37–50). New York: Stockton.

Krantz, M. (1994). *Child development, risk & opportunity.* Belmont, CA: Wadsworth.

Krause, M. A., & Fouts, R. S. (1997). Chimpanzee (*Pan troglodytes*) pointing: Hand shapes, accuracy, and the role of eye gaze. *Journal of Comparative Psychology, 111,* 330–336.

Krebs, J. R., & Dawkins, R. (1978). Animal signals: Mind reading and manipulation. In J. R. Krebs & N. B. Davies (Eds.), *Behavioural Ecology: An Evolutionary Approach* (pp. 380–402). Sunderland, MA: Sinauer Associates.

Kugiumutzakis, G. (1999). Genesis and development of early infant mimesis to facial and vocal models. In J. Nadel & G. Butterworth (Eds.), *Imitation in infancy. Cambridge studies in cognitive perceptual development* (pp. 36–59). New York: Cambridge University Press.

Kuhl, P. K., & Miller, J. D. (1978). Speech perception by the chinchilla: Identification functions for synthetic VOT stimuli. *Journal of the Acoustical Society of America, 63,* 905–917.

Ladefoged, P. (1983). The linguistic use of different phonation types. In D. Bless & J. Abbs (Eds.), *Vocal fold physiology: Contemporary research and clinical issues* (pp. 351–360). San Diego, CA: College Hill.

Lafreniere, P. (1998, August). *Card sharks and poker faces: How developmental research on intentionality and deception can inform evolutionary models.* Paper presented at the Fourteenth Biennial Conference of the International Society for Human Ethology, Vancouver, Canada.

Lafreniere, P. J. (1988). The ontogeny of tactical deception in humans. In R. W. Byrne & A. Whiten (Eds.), *Machiavellian intelligence* (pp. 238–252). Oxford, UK: Clarendon.

Laitman, J. T. (1984). The anatomy of human speech. *Natural History,* pp. 20–27.

Laitman, J. T., & Heimbuch, R. C. (1982). The basicranium of Plio-Pleistocene hominids as an indicator of their upper respiratory systems. *American Journal of Physical Anthropology, 59*(3), 323–43.

Laitman, J. T., & Reidenberg, J. S. (1993). Specializations of the human upper respiratory and upper digestive systems as seen through comparative and developmental anatomy. *Dysphagia, 8*(4), 318–25.

Lambert, W. E. (1981). Bilingualism and language acquisition. In H. Winitz (Ed.), *Native language and foreign language acquisition* (pp. 9–22). New York: New York Academy of Sciences.

Langer, S. (1942). *Philosophy in a new key.* Cambridge, MA: Harvard University Press.

Lashley, K. S. (1951). The problem of serial order in behavior. In L. A. Jeffress (Ed.), *Cerebral mechanisms in behavior: The Hixon symposium* (pp. 112–136). New York: Wiley.

Lasky, R. E., Syrdal-Lasky, A., & Klein, R. E. (1975). VOT discrimination by four to six and a half month old infants from Spanish environments. *Journal of Experimental Child Psychology, 20,* 215–225.

Leakey, R. (1994). *The origin of humankind.* New York: Basic Books.

Leavens, D. A., Hopkins, W. D., & Bard, K. A. (1996). Indexical and referential pointing in chimpanzees *(Pan Troglodytes). Journal of Comparative Psychology, 110*(4), 346–353.

Lee, B. S. (1951). Artificial stutter. *Journal of Speech and Hearing Disorders, 16,* 53–55.

Legerstee, M. (1991). Changes in the quality of infant sounds as a function of social and nonsocial stimulation. *First Language, 11,* 327–343.

Lehiste, I. (1970). *Suprasegmentals.* Cambridge, MA: MIT Press.

Leigh, S. R. (1988). Comparisons of rates of evolutionary change in cranial capacity in *Homo erectus* and early *Homo sapiens. American Journal of Physical Anthropology, 75*(2), 237–238.

Lenneberg, E. (1967). *Biological foundations of language.* New York: Wiley.

Lenneberg, E. (1969). On explaining language. *Science, 164,* 635–643.

Lenneberg, E., Rebelsky, F. G., & Nichols, I. A. (1965). The vocalizations of infants born to deaf and hearing parents. *Vita Humana (Human Development)*, 8, 23–37.

Leonard, L. (1971). A preliminary view of information theory and articulatory omissions. *Journal of Speech and Hearing Disorders*, 36(4), 511–517.

Leonard, L. B., & Schwartz, R. G. (1985). Early linguistic development of children with specific language impairment. In K. E. Nelson (Ed.), *Children's language* (Vol. 5, pp. 291–318). Hillsdale, NJ: Lawrence Erlbaum Associates.

Leopold, W. F. (1939). *Speech development of a bilingual child: Vol. I. Vocabulary growth in the first two years* (Vol. 6). Evanston, IL: Northwestern University.

Leopold, W. F. (1947). *Speech development of a bilingual child: Vol. II. Sound-learning in the first two years* (Vol. 6). Evanston, IL: Northwestern University.

Leopold, W. F. (1971a). Patterning in children's language learning. In A. Bar-Adon & W. F. Leopold (Eds.), *Child language: A book of readings* (pp. 134–141). Englewood Cliffs, NJ: Prentice-Hall. (Original work published 1953)

Leopold, W. F. (1971b). The study of child language and infant bilingualism. In A. Bar-Adon & W. F. Leopold (Eds.), *Child language: A book of readings* (pp. 1–13). Englewood Cliffs, NJ: Prentice-Hall.

Lester, B. M., & Boukydis, C. F. Z. (1992). No language but a cry. In H. Papoušek, U. Jürgens, & M. Papoušek (Eds.), *Nonverbal vocal communication* (pp. 145–173). New York: Cambridge University Press.

Lester, B. M., Boukydis, C. Z., Garcia-Coll, C. T., Peucher, M., McGrath, M. M., Vohr, B. R., Brem, S., & Oh, W. (1994). Developmental outcome as a function of goodness of fit between the infant's cry characteristics and the mother's perception of her infant's cry. *Pediatrics*, 95(4), 516–521.

Lester, B. M., Hoffman, J., & Brazelton, T. B. (1985). The rhythmic structure of mother-infant interaction in term and preterm infants. *Child Development*, 56, 15–27.

Levitt, A. G., & Utman, J. A. (1992). From babbling towards the sound systems of English and French: A longitudinal two-case study. *Journal of Child Language*, 19(1), 19–49.

Levitt, A. G., & Wang, Q. (1991). Evidence for language-specific rhythmic influences in the reduplicative babbling of French- and English-learning infants. *Language & Speech*, 34(3), 235–249.

Lewedag, V. L. (1995). *Patterns of onset of canonical babbling among typically developing infants.* Unpublished doctoral dissertation, University of Miami, Coral Gables, FL.

Lewis, M. M. (1936). *Infant speech.* New York: Harcourt Brace.

Liberman, A. M., Cooper, F. S., Shankweiler, D. P., & Studdert-Kennedy, M. (1967). Perception of the speech code. *Psychological Review*, 74, 431–461.

Liberman, A. M., Delattre, P. C., Cooper, F. S., & Gerstman, L. J. (1954). The role of consonant-vowel transitions in the perception of the stop and nasal consonants. *Psychological Monographs*, 68, 127–137.

Liberman, A. M., Delattre, P. C., Gerstman, L. J., & Cooper, F. S. (1956). Tempo of frequency change as a cue for distinguishing classes of speech sounds. *Journal of Experimental Psychology*, 52, 127–137.

Liberman, I. Y., Shankweiler, D., Fischer, F. W., & Carter, B. (1974). Reading and the awareness of linguistic segments. *Journal of Experimental Child Psychology*, 18, 201–212.

Liberman, M., & Prince, A. (1977). On stress and linguistic rhythm. *Linguistic Inquiry*, *8*, 249–336.

Licklighter, R. (1990a). Premature visual experience accelerates intersensory functioning in bobwhite quail neonates. *Developmental Psychobiology*, *23*, 15–27.

Licklighter, R. (1990b). Premature visual experience facilitates visual responsiveness in bobwhite quail neonates. *Infant Behavior and Development*, *13*, 487–496.

Lieberman, P. (1968). Primate vocalizations and human linguistic ability. *Journal of the Acoustical Society of America*, *44*, 1574–1584.

Lieberman, P. (1975). *On the origins of language*. New York: Macmillan.

Lieberman, P. (1980). On the development of vowel production in young children. In G. Yeni-Komshian, J. Kavanagh, & C. Ferguson (Eds.), *Child phonology* (Vol. 1, pp. 113–142). New York: Academic Press.

Lieberman, P., & Crelin, E. S. (1971). The supralaryngeal vocal tract of the La Chapelle Aux Saints Neanderthal fossil reconstructed by comparative anatomy. *Linguistic Inquiry*, *2*(2), 203–222.

Lieberman, P., Harris, K. S., Wolff, P., & Russell, L. H. (1971). Newborn infant cry and non-human primate vocalizations. *Journal of Speech and Hearing Research*, *14*, 718–727.

Lindblom, B. (1963). Spectrographic study of vowel reduction. *Journal of the Acoustical Society of America*, *35*, 1773–1781.

Lindblom, B. (1992). Phonological units as adaptive emergents of lexical development. In C. Ferguson, L. Menn, & C. Stoel-Gammon (Eds.), *Phonological development: Models, research, implications* (pp. 131–163). Parkton, MD: York.

Lindblom, B. E. F. (1968). Temporal organization of syllable production. *Speech Transmission Laboratory Quarterly Progress and Status Report, Stockholm, Sweden, Royal Institute of Technology*, *2*(3), 1–5.

Lindsay, J. (1970). *The origins of alchemy in graeco-roman Egypt*. New York: Barnes & Noble.

Locke, J. (1965). *An essay concerning human understanding*. London: Dent. (Original work published in the 17th century)

Locke, J. L. (1983). *Phonological acquisition and change*. New York: Academic Press.

Locke, J. L. (1993). *The child's path to spoken language*. Cambridge, MA: Harvard University Press.

Locke, J. L., Bekken, K. E., McMinn-Larson, L., & Wein, D. (1995). Emergent control of manual and vocal-motor activity in relation to the development of speech. *Brain and Language*, *51*, 498–508.

Locke, J. L., & Pearson, D. (1990). Linguistic significance of babbling: Evidence from a tracheostomized infant. *Journal of Child Language*, *17*, 1–16.

Locke, J. L., & Snow, C. (1997). Vocal learning in human and nonhuman primates. In C. T. Snowdon & M. Hausberger (Eds.), *Social influences on vocal development* (pp. 274–292). New York: Cambridge University Press.

Loizos, C. (1969). Play behavior in higher primates: A review. In D. Morris (Ed.), *Primate ethology* (pp. 226–282). Garden City, NY: Anchor Doubleday.

Lorenz, K. (1951). Ausdrucksbewegungen höherer Tiere [Expressive displays in higher animals]. *Naturwissenschaften*, *38*, 113–116.

Lorenz, K. Z. (1963). *Das Sogenannte Bose: Zur Naturgeschicte der Aggression [On aggression]* (M. K. Wilson, Trans.). Vienna, Austria: Dr. G. Borotha-Schoeler Verlag.

Lotto, A. J., Kluender, K. R., & Holt, L. L. (1997). Perceptual compensation for coarticulation by Japanese quail (*Coturnix coturnix japonica*). *Journal of the Acoustical Society of America, 102*(2), 1134–1140.

Loy, J. (1970). Behavioral responses of free-ranging rhesus monkeys to food shortage. *American Journal of Physical Anthropology, 33*, 263–272.

Lynch, M. P., Oller, D. K., & Steffens, M. (1989). Development of speech-like vocalizations in a child with congenital absence of cochleas: The case of total deafness. *Applied Psycholinguistics, 10*, 315–333.

Lynch, M. P., Oller, D. K., Steffens, M. L., & Buder, E. H. (1995). Phrasing in prelinguistic vocalizations. *Developmental Psychobiology, 28*, 3–23.

Lynch, M. P., Oller, D. K., Steffens, M. L., Levine, S. L., Basinger, D. L., & Umbel, V. M. (1995). Development of speech-like vocalizations in infants with Down syndrome. *American Journal of Mental Retardation, 100*(1), 68–86.

Lynip, A. (1951). The use of magnetic devices in the collection and analyses of the preverbal utterances of an infant. *Genetic Psychology Monographs, 44*, 221–262.

Lyons, J. (1991). *Natural language and universal grammar.* Cambridge, UK: Cambridge University Press.

Lyytinen, P., Poikkeus, A.-M., Leiwo, M., & Ahonen, T. (1996). Parents as informants of their child's vocal and early language development. *Early Child Development & Care, 126*, 15–25.

Macedonia, J. M., & Evans, C. S. (1993). Variation among mammalian alarm call systems and the problem of meaning in animal signals. *Ethology, 93*, 177–197.

Macnamara, J. (1967). The bilingual's linguistic performance—A psychological overview. *Journal of Social Issues, 23*, 58–77.

MacNeilage, P. F. (1964). Typing errors as clues to serial ordering mechanisms in language behavior. *Language and Speech, 7*, 144–159.

MacNeilage, P. F. (1970). Motor control of serial ordering of speech. *Psychological Review, 77*(3), 182–196.

MacNeilage, P. F. (1998). The frame/content theory of evolution of speech production. *Behavioral & Brain Sciences, 21*(4), 499–546.

MacNeilage, P. F., & Davis, B. L. (1990). Acquisition of speech production: Frames then content. In M. Jeannerod (Ed.), *Attention and performance XIII: Motor representation and control* (pp. 453–476). Hillsdale, NJ: Lawrence Erlbaum Associates.

MacNeilage, P. F., Davis, B. L., & Matyear, C. L. (1997). Babbling and first words: Phonetic similarities and differences. *Speech Communication, 22*(2–3), 269–277.

MacWhinney, B., & Bates, E. (1989). *The cross-linguistic study of sentence processing.* New York: Cambridge University Press.

Maddieson, I. (1980). UPSID—The UCLA phonological segment duration database. *UCLA Working Papers in Phonetics, 50*, 4–56.

Malatesta, C. Z., Grigoryev, P., Lamb, C., Albin, M., & Culver, C. (1986). Emotion socialization and expressive development in preterm and full-term infants. *Child Development, 57*, 316–330.

Marler, P. (1975). On the origin of speech from animal sounds. In J. F. Kavanagh & J. Cutting (Eds.), *The role of speech in language* (pp. 11–37). Cambridge, MA: MIT Press.

Marler, P. (1976). Social organization, communication and graded signals: The chimpanzee and the gorilla. In P. P. G. Bateson & R. A. Hinde (Eds.), *Growing points in ethology* (pp. 239–280). Cambridge, UK: Cambridge University Press.

Marler, P. (1977). The evolution of communication. In T. A. Sebeok (Ed.), *How animals communicate* (pp. 45–70). Bloomington: Indiana University Press.

Marler, P., Evans, C. S., & Hauser, M. (1992). Animal signals: reference, motivation or both? In H. Papoušek, U. Jürgens, & M. Papoušek (Eds.), *Nonverbal vocal communication* (pp. 66–86). New York: Cambridge University Press.

Marler, P., & Tenaza, R. (1977). Signaling behavior of apes with special reference to vocalization. In T. A. Sebeok (Ed.), *How animals communicate* (pp. 965–1003). Bloomington: Indiana University Press.

Martin, R. D. (1990). *Primate origins and evolution: A phylogenetic reconstruction*. Princeton, NJ: Princeton University Press.

Masataka, N. (1983). Categorical responses to natural and synthesized alarm calls in Goeldi's monkeys (*Callimico goeldi*). *Primates, 24*, 40–51.

Masataka, N. (1992). Pitch characteristics of Japanese maternal speech to infants. *Journal of Child Language, 19*, 213–223.

Masataka, N. (1993). Effects of contingent and noncontingent maternal stimulation on the vocal behaviour of three- and four-months-old Japanese infants. *Journal of Child Language, 20*, 303–312.

Masataka, N. (1996a). Ontogeny of laughter in preverbal infants (in Japanese). *Pediatric Science, 26*(1), 57–61.

Masataka, N. (1996b). *Significance of synchronization between preverbal vocalizations and motor actions in infancy.* Address to the International Symposium on the Emergence of Cognition and Language, Tokyo.

Masataka, N., & Fujita, K. (1989). Vocal learning of Japanese and rhesus monkeys. *Behaviour, 109*, 191–199.

Mason, W. A., & Hollis, J. H. (1962). Communication between young rhesus monkeys. *Animal Behavior, 10*(3–4), 211–221.

Maurus, M., Streit, K. M., Barclay, D., Wiesner, E., & Külmorgen, B. (1988). A new approach to finding components essential for intraspecific communication. In D. Todt, P. Goedeking, & D. Symmes (Eds.), *Primate vocal communication* (pp. 69–87). London: Springer.

Mavilya, M. (1969). *Spontaneous vocalizations and babbling in hearing impaired infants.* Unpublished doctoral dissertation, Columbia University, New York. (University Microfilms No. 70-12879).

May, B. J., Moody, D. B., & Stebbins, W. C. (1989). Categorical perception of conspecific communication sounds by Japanese macaques, *Macaca fuscata. Journal of the Acoustical Society of America, 85*, 837–847.

McCarthy, D. (1971). Language development. In A. Bar-Adon & W. F. Leopold (Eds.), *Child language: A book of readings* (pp. 104–115). Englewood Cliffs, NJ: Prentice-Hall. (Original work published 1950)

McCowan, B., & Reiss, D. (1997). Vocal learning in captive bottlenose dolphins: A comparison with humans and nonhuman animals. In C. T. Snowdon & M. Hausberger (Eds.), *Social influences on vocal development* (pp. 178–207). New York: Cambridge University Press.

McCune, L. (1992). First words: A dynamic systems view. In C. Ferguson, L. Menn, & C. Stoel-Gammon (Eds.), *Phonological development: Models, research, implications* (pp. 313–336). Parkton, MD: York.

McCune, L., Vihman, M. M., Roug-Hellichius, L., Delery, D. B., & Gogate, L. (1996). Grunt communication in human infants (*homo sapiens*). *Journal of Comparative Psychology, 110*(1), 27–37.

Meier, R. P., McGarvin, L., Zakia, R. A. E., & Willerman, R. (1997). Silent mandibular oscillations in vocal babbling. *Phonetica, 54*, 153–171.

Meier, R. P., & Willerman, R. (1995). Prelinguistic gesture in deaf and hearing infants. In K. Emmorey & J. S. Reilly (Eds.), *Language, gesture, and space* (pp. 391–409). Hillsdale, NJ: Lawrence Erlbaum Associates.

Menn, L. (1976). Evidence for an interactionist-discovery theory of child phonology. *Papers and reports in child language development, Stanford University, 12*, 169–177.

Menyuk, P. (1968). The role of distinctive features in children's acquisition of phonology. *Journal of Speech and Hearing Research, 11*, 138–146.

Menyuk, P., Liebergott, J., & Schultz, M. (1986). Predicting phonological development. In B. Lindblom & R. Zetterstrom (Eds.), *Precursors of early speech* (pp. 79–93). New York: Stockton.

Menzel, E. (1988). A group of young chimpanzees in a 1-acre field: Leadership and communication. In R. W. Byrne & A. Whiten (Eds.), *Machiavellian intelligence* (pp. 155–159). Oxford, UK: Clarendon.

Miller, J. F. (1988). The development of asynchrony of language development in children with Down's syndrome. In L. Nadel (Ed.), *The psychobiology of Down syndrome* (pp. 167–198). Cambridge, MA: MIT Press.

Miller, J. L., & Liberman, A. M. (1979). Some effects of later-occurring information in the perception of stop consonant and semivowel. *Perception and Psychophysics, 25*, 457–465.

Miskiel, E., Özdamar, Ö., Oller, D. K., & Eilers, R. (1992). Digital signal processor-based feature extraction vocoder for the deaf. In *Computer-based medical systems: Proceedings of the 5th IEEE Symposium* (pp. 504–509). Durham, NC: IEEE.

Mitani, J. C., Hasegawa, T., Gros-Louis, J., Marler, P., & Byrne, R. (1992). Dialects in wild chimpanzees? *American Journal of Primatology, 27*, 233–243.

Mitchell, G. (1979). *Behavioral sex differences in nonhuman primates.* New York: Van Nostrand Reinhold.

Mitchell, P. R., & Kent, R. D. (1990). Phonetic variation in multisyllabic babbling. *Journal of Child Language, 17*, 247–265.

Moffit, A. R. (1971). Consonant cue perception by twenty- to twenty-four-week-old infants. *Child Development, 42*, 717–731.

Monnier, M., & Willis, H. (1953). Die integrative Tätigkeit des Nervensystems beim meso-rhombo-spinalen Anencephalus (Mittlehirnwesen) [The intergrative function of the nervous system in anencephaly]. *Monastschrift für Psychiatrie und Neurologie, 126*, 239–273.

Monsen, R. B. (1979). Acoustic qualities of phonation in young hearing impaired children. *Journal of Speech and Hearing Research, 22*(2), 270–288.

Moon, C., & Fifer, W. P. (1990). Syllables as signals for 2-day-old infants. *Infant Behavior & Development, 13*(3), 377–390.

Moore, J. M., Thompson, G., & Thompson, M. (1975). Auditory localization of infants as a function of reinforcement conditions. *Journal of Speech and Hearing Disorders, 40*, 29–34.

Morris, C. (1938). *Foundations of the theory of signs.* Chicago: University of Chicago Press.

Morris, D. (1967). *The naked ape.* New York: Dell.

Morse, P. A. (1972). The discrimination of speech and nonspeech stimuli in early infancy. *Journal of Experimental Child Psychology, 14,* 477–492.

Mowrer, O. H. (1952). The autism theory of speech development and some clinical implications. *Journal of Speech and Hearing Disorders, 17,* 263–268.

Moynihan, M. (1969). Comparative aspects of communication in new world primates. In D. Morris (Ed.), *Primate ethology* (pp. 306–342). Garden City, NY: Anchor Doubleday.

Moynihan, M. (1970). The control, suppression, decay, disappearance and replacement of displays. *Journal of Theoretical Biology, 29,* 85–112.

Multhauf, R. P. (1967). *The origins of chemistry.* New York: Franklin Watts.

Mundy, P., Kasari, C., & Sigman, M. (1992). Joint attention, affective sharing, and intersubjectivity. *Infant Behavior and Development, 15,* 377–381.

Murai, J. (1961). Speech development of an infant suffering from a hearing disorder (in Japanese). *Japanese Journal of Child Psychiatry, 2*(1), 75–83.

Murai, J. (1963). The sounds of infants: Their phonemicization and symbolization. *Studia Phonologica, 3,* 17–34.

Myers, R. E. (1976). Comparative neurology of vocalization and speech: Proof of a dichotomy. In S. Harnad, H. Steklis, & J. Lancaster (Eds.), *The origins and evolution of language and speech* (Vol. 280, 745–757).

Mykelbust, H. (1954). *Auditory disorders in children.* New York: Grune & Stratton.

Nakazima, S. (1962). A comparative study of the speech development of Japanese and American English in childhood. *Studia Phonologica, 2,* 27–39.

Nam, C. V., & Powers, N. G. (1983). *Socioeconomic approach to status measurement.* Houston, TX: Cap & Gown.

Nathani, S. (1998). *Phrases, prelinguistic vocalizations, and hearing impairment.* Unpublished doctoral dissertation, Purdue University, West Lafayette, IN.

Nelson, W. L., Perkell, J. S., & Westbury, J. R. (1984). Mandible movements during increasingly rapid articulations of single syllables: Preliminary observations. *Journal of the Acoustical Society of America, 75*(3), 945–951.

Newman, J. D. (1995). Vocal ontogeny in macaques and marmosets: Convergent and divergent lines of development. In E. Zimmerman, J. D. Newman, & U. Jürgens (Eds.), *Current topics in primate vocal communication* (pp. 73–98). New York: Plenum.

Nishimura, B., Watamaki, T., Sato, M., & Wakabayashi, S. (1987). The criteria for early use of nonvocal communication systems with nonspeaking autistic children. *Journal of Autism and Developmental Disorders, 17*(2), 243–253.

Noble, W., & Davidson, I. (1996). *Human evolution, language and mind: A psychological and archaeological inquiry.* Cambridge, UK: Cambridge University Press.

Nwokah, E. E., Hsu, H.-C., Dobrowolska, O., & Fogel, A. (1994). The development of laughter in mother–infant communication: Timing parameters and temporal sequences. *Infant Behavior & Development, 17*(1), 23–35.

Oller, D. K. (1973). The effect of position-in-utterance on speech segment duration in English. *Journal of the Acoustical Society of America, 54,* 1235–1247.

Oller, D. K. (1976, November). *Analysis of infant vocalizations: A linguistic and speech scientific perspective.* Mini-seminar presented at the Convention of the American Speech and Hearing Association, Houston, TX.

Oller, D. K. (1980a). The emergence of the sounds of speech in infancy. In G. Yeni-Komshian, J. Kavanagh, & C. Ferguson (Eds.), *Child phonology: Vol. 1. Production* (pp. 93–112). New York: Academic Press.

Oller, D. K. (1980b, June). *Interpretation of infant vocalizations* [Short course for the Annual convention of the Alexander Graham Bell Association for the Deaf]. Houston, TX.

Oller, D. K. (1986). Metaphonology and infant vocalizations. In B. Lindblom & R. Zetterstrom (Eds.), *Precursors of early speech* (pp. 21–35). New York: Stockton Press.

Oller, D. K. (1989, January). *Comparing development of human and non-human vocal systems.* Paper presented at the Winter Conference on Current Issues in Developmental Psychobiology, Palmas del Mar, Puerto Rico.

Oller, D. K. (1991). Similarities and differences in vocalizations of deaf and hearing infants: Future directions for research. In J. Miller (Ed.), *Research on child language disorders: A decade of progress* (pp. 277–284). Austin, TX: PRO-ED.

Oller, D. K. (1995). Development of vocalizations in infancy. In H. Winitz (Ed.), *Human communication and its disorders: A review* (Vol. IV, pp. 1–30). Timonium, MD: York.

Oller, D. K., Basinger, D., & Eilers, R. E. (1996, April). *Intuitive identification of infant vocalizations by parents.* Paper presented at the International Conference on Infant Studies, Providence, RI.

Oller, D. K., & Eilers, R. E. (1982). Similarity of babbling in Spanish- and English-learning babies. *Journal of Child Language, 9,* 565–578.

Oller, D. K., & Eilers, R. E. (1988). The role of audition in infant babbling. *Child Development, 59,* 441–449.

Oller, D. K., & Eilers, R. E. (1998, July). *Prospective evaluation of language learning in infants with delayed babbling.* Paper presented at the XVth Meeting of the International Society for the Study of Behavioral Development, Berne, Switzerland.

Oller, D. K., Eilers, R. E., & Basinger, D. (in press). Intuitive identification of infant vocal sounds by parents. *Developmental Science.*

Oller, D. K., Eilers, R. E., Basinger, D., Steffens, M. L., & Urbano, R. (1995). Extreme poverty and the development of precursors to the speech capacity. *First Language, 15,* 167–188.

Oller, D. K., Eilers, R. E., Bull, D. H., & Carney, A. E. (1985). Pre-speech vocalizations of a deaf infant: A comparison with normal metaphonological development. *Journal of Speech and Hearing Research, 28,* 47–63.

Oller, D. K., Eilers, R. E., Neal, A. R., & Cobo-Lewis, A. B. (1998). Late onset canonical babbling: A possible early marker of abnormal development. *American Journal on Mental Retardation, 103,* 249–265.

Oller, D. K., Eilers, R. E., Neal, A. R., & Schwartz, H. K. (1999). Precursors to speech in infancy: The prediction of speech and language disorders. *Journal of Communication Disorders, 32,* 4, 223–246.

Oller, D. K., Eilers, R. E., Steffens, M. L., Lynch, M. P., & Urbano, R. (1994). Speech-like vocalizations in infancy: An evaluation of potential risk factors. *Journal of Child Language, 21,* 33–58.

Oller, D. K., Eilers, R. E., Urbano, R., & Cobo-Lewis, A. B. (1997). Development of precursors to speech in infants exposed to two languages. *Journal of Child Language, 27,* 407–425.

Oller, D. K., Levine, S., Eilers, R. E., & Pearson, B. Z. (1998). Vocal precursors to linguistic communication: How babbling is connected to meaningful speech. In R. Paul (Ed.), *The speech/language connection* (pp. 1–23). Baltimore: Brookes.

Oller, D. K., & Lynch, M. P. (1992). Infant vocalizations and innovations in infraphonology: Toward a broader theory of development and disorders. In C. Ferguson, L. Menn, & C. Stoel-Gammon (Eds.), *Phonological development: Models, research, implications* (pp. 509–536). Parkton, MD: York.

Oller, D. K., & Seibert, J. M. (1988). Babbling in prelinguistic mentally retarded children. *American Journal on Mental Retardation, 92,* 369–375.

Oller, D. K., Wieman, L., Doyle, W., & Ross, C. (1975). Infant babbling and speech. *Journal of Child Language, 3,* 1–11.

Olney, R. L., & Scholnick, E. K. (1976). Adult judgments of age and linguistic differences in infant vocalization. *Journal of Child Language, 3,* 145–156.

Osborn, J. (1968). Teaching a language to disadvantaged children. *Monographs of the Society for Research in Child Development, 33.*

Osgood, C. E. (1953). *Method and theory in experimental psychology.* New York: Oxford University Press.

Owings, D. H., & Hennessy, D. F. (1984). The importance of variation in sciurid visual and vocal communication. In J. A. Murie & G. R. Michener (Eds.), *The biology of ground-dwelling squirrels: Annual cycles, behavioral ecology, and sociality* (pp. 169–200). Lincoln: University of Nebraska Press.

Owings, D. H., & Morton, E. S. (1998). *Animal vocal communication.* Cambridge, UK: Cambridge University Press.

Owren, M. J., Dieter, J. A., Seyfarth, R. M., & Cheney, D. L. (1993). Vocalizations of rhesus (*mucaca mulatta*) and Japanese (*M. fuscata*) macaques cross-fostered between species show evidence of only limited modification. *Developmental Psychobiology, 26,* 7, 389–406.

Owren, M. J., & Linker, C. D. (1995). Some analysis methods that may be useful to acoustic primatologists. In E. Zimmerman, J. D. Newman, & U. Jürgens (Eds.), *Current topics in primate vocal communication* (pp. 1–28). New York: Plenum.

Owren, M. J., Linker, C. D., & Rowe, M. P. (1993). Acoustic features of tonal "grunt" calls in baboons. *Journal of the Acoustical Society of America, 94,* 1823.

Oyama, S. (1990). The idea of innateness: Effects on language and communication research. *Developmental Psychobiology, 23*(7), 741–747.

Oyama, S. (1993). How shall I name thee? The construction of natural selves. *Theory and Psychology, 3*(4), 471–496.

Ozdamar, Ö., Oller, D. K., Miskiel, E., & Eilers, R. (1988). Computer system for quantitative evaluation of an electrotactile vocoder for artificial hearing. *Computers and Biomedical Research, 21,* 85–100.

Papoušek, H. (1967). Conditioning during early post-natal development. In Y. Brackbill & G. G. Thompson (Eds.), *Behavior in infancy and early childhood* (pp. 259–274). New York: The Free Press.

Papoušek, H., & Papoušek, M. (1979). The infant's fundamental adaptive response system in social interaction. In E. B. Thoman (Ed.), *Origins of the infant's social responsiveness* (pp. 175–208). Hillsdale, NJ: Lawrence Erlbaum Associates.

Papoušek, H., & Papoušek, M. (1984). Qualitative transitions during the first trimester of human postpartum life. In H. F. R. Prechtl (Ed.), *Continuity of neural functions from prenatal to postnatal life* (pp. 220–244). London: Spastics International Medical.

Papoušek, H., & Papoušek, M. (1987). Intuitive parenting: A dialectic counterpart to the infant's integrative competence. In J. D. Osofsky (Ed.), *Handbook of infant development* (pp. 669–720). New York: Wiley.

Papoušek, M. (1994). *Vom ersten Schrei zum ersten Wort: Anfänge der Sprachentwicklung in der vorsprachlichen Kommunikation* [From the first cry to the first word: The beginning of language development in prespeech communication]. Bern, Switzerland: Verlag Hans Huber.

Papoušek, M., & Papoušek, H. (1989). Forms and functions of vocal matching in interactions between mothers and their precanonical infants. *First Language, 9*, 137–158.

Papoušek, M., Papoušek, H., & Symmes, D. (1991). The meanings of melodies in motherese in tone and stress languages. *Infant Behavior and Development, 14*, 414–440.

Patterson, F. G. (1978a). The gestures of a gorilla: Language acquisition in another pongid. *Brain and Language, 5*, 56–71.

Patterson, F. G. (1978b). Linguistic capabilities of a lowland gorilla. In F. C. C. Peng (Ed.), *Sign language acquisition in man and ape: New dimensions in comparative pedolinguistics* (pp. 161–201). Boulder, CO: Westview.

Peal, E., & Lambert, W. (1962). The relation of bilingualism to intelligence. *Psychological Monographs, 76* (Whole No. 546).

Peirce, C. S. (1934). Pragmatism and pragmaticism. In C. Hartshorne & P. Weiss (Eds.), *The collected papers of Charles Sanders Peirce* (Vol. 5). Cambridge, MA: Harvard University Press.

Pepperberg, I. M. (1990). Conceptual abilities of an African Grey parrot. In S. T. Parker & K. R. Gibson (Eds.), *"Language" and intelligence in monkeys and apes: Comparative developmental perspectives* (pp. 469–507). New York: Cambridge University Press.

Peterson, B. S., & Leckman, J. F. (1998). The temporal dynamics of tics in Gilles de la Tourette syndrome. *Biological Psychiatry, 44*(2), 1337–1348.

Peterson, G. E., & Barney, H. L. (1952). Control methods used in the study of vowels. *Journal of the Acoustical Society of America, 24*(2), 175–184.

Petitto, L. A. (1991). Babbling in the manual mode. *Science, 251*, 1493–1496.

Piaget, J. (1969). *Genetic epistemology.* New York: Columbia Forum.

Pierce, J. E. (1974). A study of 750 Portland, Oregon children during the first year. *Papers and Reports on Child Language Development, 8*, 19–25.

Pinker, S. (1994). *The language instinct.* New York: Harper Perennial.

Ploog, D. W. (1992). The evolution of vocal communication. In H. Papoušek, U. Jürgens, & M. Papoušek (Eds.), *Nonverbal vocal communication* (pp. 6–30). New York: Cambridge University Press.

Pollock, K. E., & Hall, P. K. (1991). An analysis of the vowel misarticulations of five children with developmental apraxia of speech. *Clinical Linguistics and Phonetics, 5*, 207–224.

Potter, R. K. (1945). Visible patterns of sounds. *Science, 102*, 463–470.

Prechtl, H. F. R. (1984). *Continuity of neural functions from prenatal to postnatal life.* London: Spastics International Medical.

Premack, D. (1971). Language in chimpanzee? *Science, 172*, 808–822.

Preyer, W. (1889). *The mind of the child.* New York: Appleton.

Provine, R. R. (1996). Laughter. *American Scientist, 84,* 38–45.

Provine, R. R., & Yong, Y. L. (1993). Laughter: A stereotyped human vocalization. *Ethology, 89,* 115–124.

Quay, S. (1993). *Language choice in early bilingual development.* Unpublished doctoral dissertation, Cambridge University, Cambridge, UK.

Ramey, C., & Campbell, F. A. (1984). Preventive education for high-risk children: Cognitive consequences of the Carolina Abecedarian Project. *American Journal of Mental Deficiency, 88,* 515–523.

Ramsay, D. S. (1984). Onset of duplicated syllable babbling and unimanual handedness in infancy: Evidence for developmental change in hemispheric specialization? *Developmental Psychology, 20*(1), 64–71.

Ramsay, D. S. (1985). Fluctuations in unimanual hand preference in infants following the onset of duplicated syllable babbling. *Developmental Psychology, 21*(2), 318–324.

Resnick, M. B., Armstrong, S., & Carter, R. L. (1988). Developmental intervention program for high-risk premature infants: Effects on development and parent–infant interactions. *Journal of Developmental and Behavioral Pediatrics, 9,* 73–78.

Robb, M. P., & Saxman, J. H. (1990). Syllable durations of preword and early word vocalizations. *Journal of Speech and Hearing Research, 33*(583–593).

Robb, M. P., Saxman, J. H., & Grant, A. A. (1989). Vocal fundamental frequency characteristics during the first two years of life. *Journal of the Acoustical Society of America, 85*(4), 1708–1717.

Robinshaw, H. M. (1995). Early intervention for hearing impairment: Differences in the timing of communicative and linguistic development. *British Journal of Audiology, 29,* 315–334.

Roe, K. V. (1975). Amount of infant vocalization as a function of age: Some cognitive implications. *Child Development, 46,* 936–941.

Roe, K. V., & Drivas, A. (1997). Reciprocity in mothers-infant vocal interactions: Relationship to the quantity of mothers' vocal stimulation. *American Journal of Orthopsychiatry, 67*(4), 645–649.

Rosenblueth, A., Wiener, N., & Bigelow, J. (1943). Behavior, purpose and teleology. *Philosophy of Science, 10,* 18–24.

Ross, G. S. (1983). Language functioning and speech development of six children receiving tracheostomy in infancy. *Journal of Communication Disorders, 15,* 95–111.

Roug, L., Landberg, I., & Lundberg, L.-J. (1989). Phonetic development in early infancy: A study of four Swedish children during the first eighteen months of life. *Journal of Child Language, 16,* 19–40.

Rovee-Collier, C. K., Sullivan, M. W., Enright, M., Lucas, D., & Fagen, J. W. (1980). Reactivation of infant memory. *Science, 208,* 1159–1161.

Rowell, T. E. (1969). Variability in the social organization of primates. In D. Morris (Ed.), *Primate ethology* (pp. 283–305). Garden City, NY: Anchor Doubleday.

Rutter, M. (1978). Diagnosis and definitions of childhood autism. *Journal of Autism & Childhood Schizophrenia, 8*(2), 139–161.

Sachs, Y. (1988). Epigenetic selection: An alternative mechanism of pattern formation. *Journal of Theoretical Biology, 134,* 547–559.

Sameroff, A. J., & Seifer, R. (1983). Familial risk and child competence. *Child Development, 54,* 1254–1268.

Savage-Rumbaugh, E. S. (1988). A new look at ape language: Comprehension of vocal speech and syntax. In D. Leger (Ed.), *Comparative perspectives in modern psychology, Nebraska Symposium on Motivation* (Vol. 35, pp. 201–256). Lincoln: University of Nebraska Press.

Savage-Rumbaugh, E. S., & MacDonald, K. (1988). Deception and social manipulation in symbol-using apes. In R. W. Byrne & A. Whiten (Eds.), *Machiavellian intelligence* (pp. 224–237). Oxford, UK: Clarendon.

Scarr, S. (1983). An evolutionary perspective on infant intelligence. In M. Lewis (Ed.), *Origins of intelligence: Infancy and early childhood* (pp. 191–224). New York: Plenum.

Schwartz, R. G., Leonard, L. B., Messick, C., & Chapman, K. (1987). The acquisition of object names in children with specific language impairment: Action context and word extension. *Applied Psycholinguistics, 8*(3), 233–244.

Schweinhart, L. J., Weikart, D. P., & Larner, M. B. (1986). A report on High/Scope Curriculum Comparison Study: Consequences of three preschool curriculum models through age 15. *Early Childhood Research Quarterly, 1,* 15–45.

Scott, K., & Carran, D. (1987). The epidemiology and prevention of mental retardation. *American Psychologist, 42,* 801–804.

Sebeok, T. A. (1968). Goals and limitations of the study of animal communication. In T. A. Sebeok (Ed.), *Animal communication: Techniques of study and results of research* (pp. 3–14). Bloomington: Indiana University Press.

Seyfarth, R. M., & Cheney, D. L. (1997). Some general features of vocal development in nonhuman primates. In C. T. Snowdon & M. Hausberger (Eds.), *Social influences on vocal development* (pp. 249–273). New York: Cambridge University Press.

Short, A. B., & Schopler, E. (1988). Factors relating to age of onset in autism. *Journal of Autism & Developmental Disorders, 18*(2), 207–216.

Shriberg, L. D., & Kwiatkowski, J. (1980). *Natural process analysis: A procedure for phonological analysis of continuous speech samples.* New York: Macmillan.

Shriberg, L. D., & Kwiatkowski, J. (1994). Developmental phonological disorders: A clinical profile. *Journal of Speech and Hearing Research, 37,* 1100–1126.

Siegel, G. M., Pick, H. L., & Garber, S. R. (1984). Auditory feedback and speech development. *Advances in Child Development and Behavior, 18,* 49–79.

Sigismund, B. (1971). *Kind und Welt* [The child and society]. In A. Bar-Adon & W. F. Leopold (Eds.), *Child language: A book of readings* (pp. 17–18). Englewood Cliffs, NJ: Prentice-Hall. (Original work published 1856)

Simon, B. M., Fowler, S. M., & Handler, S. D. (1983). Communication development in young children with long-term tracheostomies: Preliminary report. *International Journal of Otorhinolaryngology, 6,* 37–50.

Sinnott, J. M., & Brown, C. W. (1997). Perception of the American English liquid /ra-la/ contrast by humans and monkeys. *Journal of the Acoustical Society of America, 102*(1), 588–602.

Siqueland, E. R., & DeLucia, C. A. (1969). Visual reinforcement of nonnutritive sucking in human infants. *Science, 165,* 1144–1146.

Skinner, B. F. (1957). *Verbal behavior.* New York: Appleton-Century-Crofts.

Smith, B., & Oller, D. K. (1981). A comparative study of premeaningful vocalizations produced by normally developing and Down's syndrome infants. *Journal of Speech and Hearing Disorders, 46,* 46–51.

Smith, B. L., Brown-Sweeney, S., & Stoel-Gammon, C. (1989). A quantitative analysis of reduplicated and variegated babbling. *First Language, 9,* 175–190.

Smith, H. J., Newman, J. D., & Symmes, D. (1982). Vocal concomitants of affiliative behavior in squirrel monkeys. In C. T. Snowdon, C. H. Brown, & M. R. Petersen (Eds.), *Primate communication* (pp. 30–49). Cambridge, UK: Cambridge University Press.

Smith, W. J. (1977). *The behavior of communicating.* Cambridge, MA: Harvard University Press.

Snow, C. (1972). Speech to children learning language. *Child Development, 43,* 549–565.

Snow, C. E. (1995). Issues in the study of input: Fine-tuning universality, individual and developmental differences and necessary causes. In B. MacWhinney & P. Fletcher (Eds.), *NETwerken: Bijdragen van het vijfde NET symposium: Antwerp Papers in Linguistics 74* (pp. 5–17). Antwerp, Belgium: University of Antwerp.

Snowdon, C., French, J., & Cleveland, J. (1986). Ontogeny of primate vocalizations: Models from birdsong and human speech. In D. Taub & F. A. King (Eds.), *Current perspectives in primate social dynamics* (pp. 389–402). New York: Van Nostrand Reinhold.

Snowdon, C. T. (1982). Linguistic and psycholinguistic approaches to primate communication. In C. T. Snowdon, C. H. Brown, & M. R. Petersen (Eds.), *Primate communication* (pp. 212–238). Cambridge, UK: Cambridge University Press.

Snowdon, C. T. (1987). A naturalistic view of categorical perception. In S. Harnad (Ed.), *Categorical perception* (pp. 332–354). Cambridge, UK: Cambridge University Press.

Snowdon, C. T. (1988). A comparative approach to vocal communication. In R. A. Dienstbier & D. W. Leger (Eds.), *Comparative perspectives in modern psychology* (pp. 145–199). Lincoln: University of Nebraska Press.

Snowdon, C. T., & Cleveland, J. (1984). "Conversations" among pygmy marmosets? *American Journal of Primatology, 7,* 15–20.

Snowdon, C. T., Coe, C. L., & Hodun, A. (1985). Population recognitions of infant isolation peeps in the squirrel monkey. *Animal Behavior, 33,* 1145–1151.

Snowdon, C. T., Elowson, A. M., & Rousch, R. S. (1997). Social influences on vocal development in New World primates. In C. T. Snowdon & M. Hausberger (Eds.), *Social influences on vocal development* (pp. 234–248). New York: Cambridge University Press.

Sparks, J. (1969). Allogrooming in primates: A review. In D. Morris (Ed.), *Primate ethology* (pp. 190–225). Garden City, NY: Anchor Doubleday.

Sroufe, L., & Waters, E. (1976). The ontogenesis of smiling and laughter: A perspective on the organization of development in infancy. *Psychological Review, 83,* 173–189.

Sroufe, L., & Wunsch, J. (1972). The development of laughter in the first year of life. *Child Development, 43,* 1326–1344.

Stark, R. E. (1980). Stages of speech development in the first year of life. In G. Yeni-Komshian, J. Kavanagh, & C. Ferguson (Eds.), *Child phonology* (Vol. 1, pp. 73–90). New York: Academic Press.

Stark, R. E., Ansel, B. M., & Bond, J. (1988). Are prelinguistic abilities predictive of learning disability? A follow-up study. In R. L. Masland & M. Masland (Eds.), *Preschool prevention of reading failure* (pp. 3–18). Parkton, MD: York.

Stark, R. E., & Nathanson, S. N. (1974). Spontaneous cry in the newborn infant; sounds and facial gestures. In J. F. Bosma (Ed.), *Fourth symposium on oral sensation and perception: Development of the fetus and infant* (pp. 323–352). Bethesda, MD: U.S. Government Printing Office.

Stark, R. E., Rose, S. N., & McLagen, M. (1975). Features of infant sounds: The first eight weeks of life. *Journal of Child Language, 2,* 205–222.

Steffens, M. L., Oller, D. K., Lynch, M. P., & Urbano, R. C. (1992). Vocal development in infants with Down syndrome and infants who are developing normally. *American Journal on Mental Retardation, 97,* 235–246.

Stemberger, J. P. (1988). Between-word processes in child phonology. *Journal of Child Language, 15,* 39–61.

Stern, D. N., Jaffe, J., Beebe, B., & Bennett, S. L. (1975). Vocalizing in unison and in alternation: Two modes of communication within the mother–infant dyad. *Annals of the New York Academy of Sciences, 263,* 89–100.

Stevens, K. N., & House, A. S. (1961). An acoustical theory of vowel production. *Journal of Speech and Hearing Research, 4*(4), 303–320.

Stoel-Gammon, C. (1989). Prespeech and early speech development of two late talkers. *First Language, 9,* 207–224.

Stoel-Gammon, C., & Otomo, K. (1986). Babbling development of hearing impaired and normally hearing subjects. *Journal of Speech and Hearing Disorders, 51,* 33–41.

Stokoe, W. C. (1960). Sign language structure: An outline of the visual communication systems of the American Deaf. *Studies in Linguistics, Department of Anthropology, University of Buffalo, Occasional Papers, 8,* 1–78.

Streeter, L. A. (1976). Language perception of 2–month-old infants shows effects of both innate mechanisms and experience. *Nature, 259,* 39–41.

Struhsaker, T. T. (1967). Auditory communication among vervet monkeys (*Cercopithecus aethiops*). In S. A. Altmann (Ed.), *Social communication among primates* (pp. 281–324). Chicago: Chicago University Press.

Studdert-Kennedy, M. (1980). Speech perception. *Language and Speech, 23,* 45–66.

Surgiura, H., & Masataka, N. (1995). Temporal and acoustic flexibility in vocal exchanges of coo calls in Japanese macaques (*Macaca fuscata*). In E. Zimmerman, J. D. Newman, & U. Jürgens (Eds.), *Current topics in primate vocal communication* (pp. 121–140). New York: Plenum.

Sutton, D. (1979). Mechanisms underlying learned vocal control in primates. In H. D. Steklis & M. J. Raleigh (Eds.), *Neurobiology of social communication in primates: An evolutionary perspective* (pp. 45–67). New York: Academic Press.

Sutton, D., Larson, C., & Lindeman, R. C. (1974). Neocortical and limbic lesion effects on primate phonation. *Brain Research, 71,* 61–75.

Sutton, D., Larson, C., Taylor, E. M., & Lindeman, R. C. (1973). Vocalization in rhesus monkeys: Conditionability. *Brain Research, 52,* 225–231.

Sutton, D., Trachy, R. E., & Lindeman, R. C. (1981). Vocal and nonvocal discriminative performance in monkeys. *Brain and Language, 14,* 93–105.

Symmes, D., & Biben, M. (1992). Vocal development in nonhuman primates. In H. Papoušek, U. Jürgens, & M. Papoušek (Eds.), *Nonverbal vocal communication* (pp. 174–191). New York: Cambridge University Press.

Taine, H. (1971). Acquisition of language by children. In A. Bar-Adon & W. F. Leopold (Eds.), *Child language: A book of readings* (pp. 20–26). Englewood Cliffs, NJ: Prentice-Hall. (Original work published 1877)

Takei, W. (1996, September). *Babbling in the manual mode.* Paper presented at 60th Annual Conference of the Japanese Psychological Association, Tokyo.

Takei, W. (1998). *Babbling in the manual mode.* Berne, Switzerland: International Society for the Study of Behavioral Development.

Tamis-LeMonda, C. S., & Bornstein, M. H. (1991). Individual variation, correspondence, stability and change in mother and toddler play. *Infant Behavior and Development, 14,* 143–162.

Teele, D. W., Klein, J. O., & Rosner, B. (1984). Otitis media with effusion during the first three years of life and development of speech and language. *Pediatrics, 74,* 282–287.

Terrace, H. S. (1979). *Nim: A chimpanzee who learned sign language.* New York: Columbia University Press.

Terrace, H. S., Petitto, L. A., Sanders, R. J., & Bever, T. G. (1979). Can an ape create a sentence? *Science, 206*(4421), 891–902.

Thelen, E. (1981). Rhythmical behavior in infancy: An ethological perspective. *Developmental Psychology, 17,* 237–257.

Thelen, E. (1989). Evolving and dissolving synergies in the development of leg coordination. In S. A. Wallace (Ed.), *Perspectives on the coordination of movement* (pp. 259–281). Amsterdam: North Holland.

Thelen, E. (1994). Three-month-old infants can learn task-specific patterns of interlimb coordination. *Psychological Science, 5*(5), 280–285.

Thevenin, D., Eilers, R. E., Oller, D. K., & LaVoie, L. (1985). Where's the drift in babbling drift? A cross-linguistic study. *Applied Psycholinguistics, 6,* 3–15.

Tiedemann, D. (1971). Über die Entwickelung der Seelenfähigkeiten bei Kindern [On the development of mental faculties in children]. In A. Bar-Adon & W. F. Leopold (Eds.), *Child language: A book of readings* (pp. 13–17). Englewood Cliffs, NJ: Prentice-Hall. (Original work published 1787)

Tinbergen, N. (1951). *The study of instinct.* Oxford, UK: Oxford University Press.

Tinbergen, N. (1952). Derived activities: Their causation, biological significance, origin and emancipation during evolution. *Quarterly Review of Biology, 27,* 1–32.

Titze, I. R. (1994). *Principles of voice production.* Englewood Cliffs, NJ: Prentice-Hall.

Todt, D., Hammerschmidt, K., Ansorge, V., & Fischer, J. (1995). The vocal behavior of barbary macaques (*Macaca sylvanus*): Call features and their performance in infants and adults. In E. Zimmerman, J. D. Newman, & U. Jürgens (Eds.), *Current topics in primate vocal communication* (pp. 141–160). New York: Plenum.

Tomasello, M. (1996, September). *The gestural communication of chimpanzees and human children.* Address to the International Symposium on the Emergence of Cognition and Language, Tokyo.

Tomasello, M., & Farrar, J. (1986). Joint attention and early language. *Child Development, 57,* 1454–1463.

Torrance, E. P., Wu, J., Gowan, J. C., & Aliotti, N. C. (1970). Creative functioning of monolingual and bilingual children in Singapore. *Journal of Educational Psychology, 61,* 72–75.

Tracy, F. (1893). The language of childhood. *American Journal of Psychology, 6,* 107–138.

Tracy, F. (1971). The psychology of childhood. In A. Bar-Adon & W. F. Leopold (Eds.), *Child language: A book of readings* (pp. 32–34). Englewood Cliffs, NJ: Prentice-Hall. (Original work published 1909)

Trehub, S. (1976). The discrimination of foreign speech contrasts by infants and adults. *Child Development, 47,* 466–472.

Trevarthen, C. (1979). Communication and cooperation in early infancy. A description of primary intersubjectivity. In M. Bullowa (Ed.), *Before speech: The beginnings of human communication* (pp. 321–347). London: Cambridge University Press.

Trevarthen, C., & Marwick, H. (1986). Signs of motivation for speech in infants, and the nature of mother's support for development of language. In B. Lindblom & R. Zetterstrom (Eds.), *Precursors of early speech* (pp. 279–308). New York: Stockton Press.

Truby, H. M., & Lind, J. (1965). Cry sounds of the newborn infant. *Newborn infant cry: Acta Paediatrica Scandinavica, 163*, 7–59.

Tunmer, W. E., & Rohl, M. (1991). Phonological awareness and reading acquisition. In D. Sawyer & B. Fox (Eds.), *Phonological awareness in reading: The evolution of current perspectives* (pp. 1–30). New York: Springer-Verlag.

Tyack, P. L., & Sayigh, L. (1997). Vocal learning in cetaceans. In C. T. Snowdon & M. Hausberger (Eds.), *Social influences on vocal development* (pp. 208–233). New York: Cambridge University Press.

van Hooff, J. A. R. A. M. (1969). The facial displays of the catarrhine monkeys and apes. In D. Morris (Ed.), *Primate ethology* (pp. 9–88). Garden City, NY: Anchor Doubleday.

Vanvik, A. (1971). The phonetic–phonemic development of a Norwegian child. *Norsk Tidsskrift for Sprogvidenskap, 24*, 269–325.

Velleman, S. L. (1994). The interaction of phonetics and phonology in developmental verbal dyspraxia: Two case studies. *Clinics in Communication Disorders, 4*, 66–77.

Velten, H. V. (1971). The growth of phonemic and lexical patterns in infant language. In A. Bar-Adon & W. F. Leopold (Eds.), *Child language: A book of readings* (pp. 82–90). Englewood Cliffs, NJ: Prentice-Hall. (Original work published 1943)

Vergara, K. C., Miskiel, L. W., Oller, D. K., & Eilers, R. E. (1995). Training children to use tactual vocoders in a model program. *Seminars in Hearing, 16*(4), 404–415.

Vihman, M. M. (1992). Early syllables and the construction of phonology. In C. Ferguson, L. Menn, & C. Stoel-Gammon (Eds.), *Phonological development: Models, research, implications* (pp. 393–422). Parkton, MD: York.

Vihman, M. M. (1996). *Phonological development: The origins of language in the child.* Cambridge, MA: Blackwell.

Vihman, M. M., & de Boysson-Bardies, B. (1994). The nature and origin of ambient language influence on infant vocal production and early words. *Phonetica, 51*, 159–169.

Vihman, M. M., & Miller, R. (1988). Words and babble at the threshold of language. In M. Smith & J. Locke (Eds.), *The emegent lexicon* (pp. 151–183). New York: Academic Press.

Vinter, S. (1987). Contrôle de premières productions vocales du bébé sourd [Control of the first sounds produced by deaf infants]. *Bulletin d'Audiophonologie, 3*(6), 659–670.

Vinter, S. (1994a). L'analyse du babillage: Une contribution au diagnostic de surdité? [The analysis of babbling: A factor in the diagnosis of deafness?] *Approche Neuropsychologique des Apprentissages chez l'Enfant, 6*(4), 232–238.

Vinter, S. (1994b). *L'émergence du langage de l'enfant déficient auditif: Des premiers sons aux premiers mots* [The emergence of language in the hearing impaired infant: from the first sounds to the first words]. Paris, France: Masson.

von Glaserfeld, E. (1976). The development of language as purposive behavior. In S. Harnad, H. Steklis, & J. Lancaster (Eds.), *The origins and evolution of language* (Vol. 280, pp. 212–226). New York: The New York Academy of Sciences.

Waddington, C. H. (1957). *The strategy of genes: A discussion of some aspects of theoretical biology.* London: Allen & Unwin.

Wallace, I. F., Gravel, J. S., McCarton, C. M., & Ruben, R. J. (1988). Otitis media and language development at 1 year of age. *Journal of Speech and Hearing Disorders, 53,* 245–251.

Wasz-Hockert, O., Lind, J., Vuorenkoski, V., & Valanne, E. (1964). The identification of some specific meanings in the newborn and infant vocalization. *Experientia, 20,* 154.

Waterson, N. (1971). Child phonology: A prosodic view. *Journal of Linguistics, 7,* 179–211.

Waterson, N. (1987). *Prosodic phonology: The theory and its application to language acquisition and speech processing.* Newcastle upon Tyne, England: Grevatt & Grevatt.

Weary, D. W., & Kramer, D. L. (1995). Response of eastern chipmunks to conspecific alarm calls. *Animal Behaviour, 49,* 81–93.

Weber, B. A. (1988). Screening for high-risk infants using auditory brainstem response audiometry. In F. H. Bess (Ed.), *Hearing impairment in children* (pp. 112–132). Parkton, MD: York.

Webster, P., & Plante, E. (1992). Effects of phonological impairments on word, syllable, and phoneme segmentation and reading. *Language, Speech, and Hearing Services in the Schools, 23,* 176–182.

Werker, J. F., & Tees, R. C. (1984). Cross-language speech perception: Evidence for perceptual reorganization during the first year of life. *Infant Behavior and Development, 7,* 49–63.

Wescott, R. W. (1976). Protolinguistics: The study of protolanguages as an aid to glossogonic research. In S. Harnad, H. Steklis, & J. Lancaster (Eds.), *The origins and evolution of language* (Vol. 280, pp. 104–116). New York: New York Academy of Sciences.

West, M. J., King, A. P., & Freeberg, T. M. (1997). Building a social agenda for the study of bird song. In C. T. Snowdon & M. Hausberger (Eds.), *Social influences on vocal development* (pp. 41–56). Cambridge, UK: Cambridge University Press.

West, M. J., Stroud, N., & King, A. P. (1983). Mimicry of the human voice by European Starlings: the role of social interaction. *Wilson Bulletin, 95*(4), 635–640.

White, R. (1989, July). Visual thinking in the Ice Age. *Scientific American,* pp. 92–99.

Whitehurst, G. J., Smith, M., Fischel, J. E., Arnold, D. S., & Lonigan, C. J. (1991). The continuity of babble and speech in children with specific expressive language delay. *Journal of Speech & Hearing Research, 34*(5), 1121–1129.

Wiener, N. (1948). Time, communication and the nervous system. *Annals of the New York Academy of Sciences, 50*(4), 197–219.

Winter, P., Ploog, D. W., & Latta, J. (1966). Vocal repertoire of the squirrel monkey (*Saimiri sciureus*), its analysis and significance. *Experimental Brain Research, 1,* 359–384.

Wishart, J. G., Bower, T. G. R., & Dunkeld, J. (1978). Reaching in the dark. *Perception, 7,* 507–512.

Wolff, P. H. (1969). The natural history of crying and other vocalizations in early infancy. In B. M. Foss (Ed.), *Determinants of infant behavior* (Vol. 4, pp. 81–109). London: Methuen.

Yale, M. E., Messinger, D. S., Cobo-Lewis, A. B., Oller, D. K., & Eilers, R. E. (1999). An event-based analysis of the coordination of early infant vocalizations and facial actions. *Developmental Psychology, 35*(2), 505–513.

Yates, A. J. (1963). Delayed auditory feedback. *Psychological Bulletin, 60*, 213–232.

Ybarra, M. A. S. (1995). A comparative approach to the non-human primate vocal tract: Implications for sound production. In E. Zimmerman, J. D. Newman, & U. Jürgens (Eds.), *Current topics in primate vocal communication* (pp. 185–198). New York: Plenum.

Yoder, P. J., Warren, S. F., & McCathren, R. (1998). Determining spoken language prognosis in children with developmental disabilities. *American Journal of Speech-Language Pathology, 7*, 77–87.

Yoshinaga-Itano, C., Sedey, A. L., Coulter, D. K., & Mehl, A. L. (1998). Language of early- and later-identified children with hearing loss. *Pediatrics, 102*, 1161–1171.

Zarin-Ackerman, J., Lewis, M., & Driscoll, J. M. (1978). Language development in two-year-old normal and risk infants. *Pediatrics, 59*, 982–986.

Zeskind, P. S., & Barr, R. G. (1997). Acoustic characteristics of naturally occurring cries of infants with "colic". *Child Development, 68*(3), 394–403.

Zeskind, P. S., Klein, L., & Marshall, T. R. (1992). Adults' perceptions of experimental modifications of durations of pauses and expiratory sounds in infant crying. *Developmental Psychology, 28*(6), 1153–1162.

Zeskind, P. S., & Lester, B. M. (1978). Acoustic features and auditory perceptions of the cries of newborns with prenatal and perinatal complications. *Child Development, 49*, 580–589.

Zigler, E. F., & Stevenson, M. F. (1993). *Children in a changing world* (2nd ed.). Pacific Grove, CA: Brooks/Cole.

Zimmerman, E. (1995). Loud calls in nocturnal prosimians: Structure evolution and ontogeny. In E. Zimmerman, J. D. Newman, & U. Jürgens (Eds.), *Current topics in primate vocal communication* (pp. 47–72). New York: Plenum.

Zlatin, M. (1975a). *Explorative mapping of the vocal tract and primitive syllabification in infancy: The first six months.* Paper presented at the American Speech and Hearing Association Convention, Washington, DC.

Zlatin, M. (1975b). *Preliminary descriptive model of infant vocalization during the first 24 weeks: Primitive syllabification and phonetic exploratory behavior* (Final Report, Project No 3-4014, NE-G-00-3-0077). Bethesda, MD: National Institutes of Health.

Zlatin-Laufer, M. A., & Horii, Y. (1977). Fundamental frequency characteristics of infant non-distress vocalization during the first 24 weeks. *Journal of Child Language, 4*, 171–184.

Author Index

Subject Index

A

Abstractness, 216–219
Accidental signs, 208, *see also* Signs
Acoustic analysis, 86, 87, 88, 89–90
Acoustic dimension, 287
Acoustic parameters, 12
Adaptation, 270, *see also* Categorical adaptation
Age of amplification, 132–135
Agglutinative properties, 273
Aggression displays, 231–232, 233
Alarm
    calls
        fixed vocal signals, 189
        hominid vocal development, 328
        inappropriate and teaching of
            offspring by nonhuman
            primate mothers, 271,
            280
        referential effect, 276–277
    patterns in New World monkeys, 266
    vocal designation, 261
Allophones, 47
Alphabetical transcription, 3–5
American Sign Language (ASL), 307
Amerind languages, 273, 289
Amplitude, 85, 86–87, 92–93
Anatomy, 212–213
Anger, 155, 169

Anomalies, vocal, 68
Apes, *see also* Nonhuman primates
    communicative deception, 246
    fixed signals and vegetative sounds,
        192
    historical distinctions between
        humans/nonhuman
        communication, 208
    historical roots of language, 205
    imitability, 258
    vocal control compared with
        humans, 229
    vocalization, 2
Apraxia, 144, 145
Arbitrariness, 227, *see also* Hockett communication model
Arbitrarity
    conventionality distinctions, 265
    early speech and vocal development,
        183
    hominid vocal development, 332–334
    infrastructural properties
        communication, 275
        interspecies comparison in
            communicative capacity,
            209
    hierarchy of, 307, 310, 312
    speculation on historical roots of
        language, 206, 207
Articulation, *see also* Back articulation

409

Printed in the USA/Agawam, MA
February 20, 2015

609127.052